THE REAL ESTATE INVESTOR'S TAX GUIDE

FOURTH EDITION

**What Every Investor Needs to Know
to Maximize Profits**

VERNON HOVEN

Dearborn™
Real Estate Education

30 S. Wacker Drive, Ste. 2500, Chicago, IL 60606
www.dearbornRE.com, (312) 836-4400

This publication is designed to provide accurate and authoritative information in regard to the subject matter covered. It is sold with the understanding that the publisher is not engaged in rendering legal, accounting, or other professional service. If legal advice or other expert assistance is required, the services of a competent professional person should be sought.

President: Roy Lipner
Publisher and Director of Distance Learning: Evan Butterfield
Managing Editor, Print Products: Louise Benzer
Development Editor: Anne Huston
Production Coordinator: Daniel Frey
Typesetter: Janet Schroeder
Creative Director: Lucy Jenkins

Library of Congress Cataloging-in-Publication Data

Hoven, Vernon.
   The real estate investors tax guide /Vernon Hoven.—4th ed.
    p.cm.
  ISBN 0-7931-6978-X
    1. Real property and taxation—United States—Popular works.   2. Real estate investment—Taxation—Law and legislation—United States—Popular works.   3. Tax planning—United States Popular works.   I. Title.

KF6540.Z9H68 2003
336.22'0973—dc21   2003010241

Contents

Part I
Taxation At Sales Time

Part II
Like-Kind Exchanges

Part III
Tax Solutions at Purchase and During Ownership

Part IV
The Passive Loss Regulations

Part IV
Real Estate in Troubled Times

Dedication

This book is dedicated to Karen, my wife and my partner. What great patience, love, and support she shows.

Preface

The voluntary tax system, whether it is a consumption tax system (e.g., a national sales tax or VAT tax) or an income tax system, will survive only if we understand and implement or supervise our own tax return preparation, a fact sadly forgotten by many members of the United States Congress! This book attempts to eliminate the aura of mystery surrounding the taxation of real estate. It is specifically written for the real estate investor, that occasional user of real estate tax knowledge, and not for real estate tax specialists.

In my lecturing travels throughout the United States, I discovered that confusion and fear of the Internal Revenue Code are widespread. This bewilderment and trepidation are unwittingly (and in some cases wittingly) promulgated by the two "specialists" in the tax field: Internal Revenue Service employees and their counterparts, independent tax preparers. As contents of most tax libraries demonstrate, numerous books and magazines have been written for the tax professional with advanced knowledge. Also, there are myriad books for taxpayers to help them prepare their tax returns. Very little has been written specifically for the real estate investor. This book meets that need.

You say, "I leave tax law to my tax professional!"

It is ludicrous to think of constructing a building without a strong foundation. Why do we accept the idea that we can invest in real estate without a strong understanding of the basics of real estate taxation?

This book's goal is to present the tax consequences of common types of real estate dealings in a clear and concise manner. The tax alternatives can be dramatic to the taxpayer. This book does not attempt to be a complete digest of every possible tax variation found in the Internal Revenue Code, its rules, regulations, and court cases affecting the taxation of real estate. Instead, it takes the most commonly used areas and explains them fully and simply by use of examples, comments, and tax planning tips.

The material in this book has been presented to thousands of casual sellers and buyers, professional real estate brokers and salespeople, CPAs, and attorneys who are not real estate tax specialists. Mostly, though, it has been used by tax professionals, who are continually surprised at the number of planning tips and easy-to-use forms that make completing tax returns substantially easier. Throughout the book the materials and planning tips are backed up by court cases and tax citations.

After reading this book, share the information with your tax professional—do it as a favor to you! Do not assume that he or she knows all there is to know about real estate taxation. Tax law is too complicated today. This book is written so you will discover new tax planning ideas. Let the tax professional implement those ideas! The tax alternatives will dramatically affect you, the taxpayer.

Acknowledgments

Thanks to:

Jill Hoven, Masters Degree in Communication, University of North Carolina.

Sharon Kreider, CPA, author, national lecturer, and tax practitioner from Santa Clara, whose insightful real estate examples forced me to write realistically, not theoretically, which is easier.

Bill Roos, retired district manager of H&R Block, for all of his practical suggestions and for reading the materials with the taxpayer in mind.

About the Author

VERNON HOVEN's book combines the real-life experience of a practicing CPA and a licensed real estate broker with essential down-to-earth tax materials. He coauthored two national books and has written articles on taxation for numerous national publications.

Vern is a nationally recognized tax lecturer (averaging 100 days a year for CPAs, tax practitioners, and REALTORS® throughout the United States) and has a master's degree in taxation from The University of Denver's School of Law. Vern's dramatic presentation style, humor, and a high-tech teaching style are his trademarks. Numerous state CPA societies have named Vern their "Tax Instructor of the Year" and, during tax season, he is a favorite for interviews on radio (a regular on *Real Estate Today)*, on television, and in newspapers. Additionally, Vern's speaking skills earned him the coveted Certified Speaking Professional (CSP) designation from the National Speakers Association. (One of 350 CSPs out of 3,900 NSA members)

Vern has served on many national boards, including the National Association of REALTORS®, Legislative Committee and the Federal Tax Subcommittee. He also served for two years as National Secretary and three years as National Director-at-Large for the National Real Estate Educators Association.

"Participants will double or triple their new tax planning ideas, Vern promises, "In addition, these concepts will be backed up with citations. . . when available."

Introduction

Many real estate investment strategies used in the 1990s are not nearly as advantageous after the most recent legislative and judicial tax changes. This book dramatically reveals the new tax *do's* and, as importantly, the new tax *don'ts* when investing in real estate . . . which tax strategies are still relevant and which new strategies should be adopted . . . now!

Tax questions by real estate investors can be grouped into five areas of concern, which are listed in order of importance as evidenced by the number of times each area is brought up in previous question-and-answer sessions:

1. Taxation at time of sale
2. Like-kind exchange rules
3. Tax solutions at purchase and during ownership
4. Living with the passive loss regulations
5. Real estate in troubled times

This book is divided into these five parts instead of the typical approach of starting with the acquisition and ending with the sale of real estate. It is designed to go directly to your questions, by topic, without the requirement of reading all the previous pages.

With the new changes relating to

- the sale of a principal residence,
- the new office-in-home rules,
- the new capital gain computation,
- the new judicially created passive loss requirements, and
- the new interest in like-kind exchanges,

this book argues that real estate is a better endeavor now than it has been in the past ten years, but only if the speculator is using the revealed, up-to-date investment tactics coupled with proper application of the enumerated new tax rules. A positive, upbeat book on real estate, it also dispels the negative tax image sometimes mentioned about such investments, helping the real estate industry convince the financing public that ownership of real property is still a marvelous tax venture.

For the first time, an understandable handbook, with appendices, deciphers tax complexity as it applies to real estate investments. *The Real Estate Investors Tax Guide* focuses, in a nuts-and-bolts manner, on the new tax ramifications found in the real estate field and lists the step-by-step, practical tax-planning strategies, with numerous sample forms, applicable to the modern-day real estate industry. For both the first-time buyer and the Certified Financial Planner, it is an ever-handy self-help book, not a shelf edition. It answers hundreds of common tax questions concerning real estate transactions, along with suggesting numerous new tax planning ideas that make real estate investments much more valuable.

Taxation of Profit— How Gains or Losses Are Computed

When an asset is sold, exchanged, or disposed of in any income-taxable manner, the seller must calculate the gain or loss. After performing this calculation, numerous other code sections tell the taxpayer what to do with the gain or loss—that is, how much is taxable or nontaxable, what is deductible or nondeductible, what portion of the gain may be deferred, what portion of the gain may be rolled over, or what portion of the gain may simply be excluded. Additionally, some property transfers need not be reported to the Internal Revenue Service. Why?

A sale or exchange is required before calculating gain or loss. Property *received* by gift or inheritance is *not taxable* because no sale or exchange occurred (but the giver may have to pay some gift or inheritance tax!). Even money received in a refinance is *not taxable* . . . no sale took place.

> ### Tax Tip
>
> When Dad gives Daughter the vacation cabin or Aunt Millie leaves Nephew the family plot, none of the four reports this transfer on his or her income tax return. Only sales or exchanges are reported, and this is a gift and an inheritance.

THE GAIN OR LOSS FORMULA

Once it is determined that the investor must tell the IRS he or she has sold an item, the amount of the gain or loss should seem easy to determine (that is, sales price less original purchase price, or basis). This complex computation should not be underestimated. To calculate gain or loss on *any* sale or exchange, use this basic formula:

Gain or Loss Computation

Sales price		+ $
Less:	Selling expenses	−
Equals:	Net selling price	= $
Less:	Adjusted basis	
	Original cost (or basis)	+ $
	Plus: Improvements	+
	Less: Accumulated depreciation	−
	Equals: Total adjusted basis	− $
Net gain (or loss) on sale		= $

The easiest way to demonstrate each line of this formula is by using a series of examples that become progressively more difficult.

Example:

Roberta purchases ten acres of land for $20,000 in 1994 and sells it to Joe in 2004 for $45,000. Her gain is $25,000, calculated as follows:

Gain or Loss Computation

Net selling price		+ $45,000
Less:	Adjusted basis	
	Original cost (or basis)	+ $20,000
	Equals: Total adjusted basis	− $20,000
Net gain (or loss) on sale		= $25,000

Example:

In the preceding example, assume that Roberta, after purchasing the ten acres of land in 1994, builds a vacation home in 1995 for $150,000 and sells it to Joe in 2004 for $245,000. She pays the following expenses at the time of sale: $17,150 commission (7%); $450 title insurance; $300 attorney's fee; $200 accountant's fee; $4,900 two-point origination fee; and $200 closing costs for a total selling expense of $23,200. Her gain of $51,800 is calculated as follows:

Gain or Loss Computation

Sales price			+ $245,000
Less:	Selling expenses		− 23,200
Equals:	Net selling price		= $221,800
Less:	Adjusted basis		
	Original cost (or basis)	+ $20,000	
	Plus: Improvements	+ $150,000	
	Equals: Total adjusted basis		− $170,000
Net gain (or loss) on sale			= $51,800

Example:

Continuing with the previous example, assume that Roberta rents out the vacation home continuously from January 1, 2001, until the property is sold in January 2004. She claims $16,136 of depreciation (discussed in Chapter 10) on her respective tax returns. Now Roberta's gain is calculated as follows:

Gain or Loss Computation

Sales price			+ $245,000
Less:	Selling expenses		− 23,200
Equals:	Net selling price		= $221,800
Less:	Adjusted basis		
	Original cost (or basis)	+ $20,000	
	Plus: Improvements	+ $150,000	
	Less: Accumulated depreciation	− $16,136	
	Equals: Total adjusted basis		− $153,864
Net gain (or loss) on sale			= $67,936

The above examples leave many other questions unanswered when calculating gain or loss. Therefore, let's start at the beginning and examine each line in the basic formula. Following are the explanations of the terms used in the above calculations.

Tax Tip

Roberta's gain increases by $16,136 ($67,936 – $51,800) over the previous example, which is the exact amount of depreciation she deducted during her period of ownership. If accumulated depreciation increases gain (this portion of the gain is called *depreciation recapture gain*) at the time of sale by the same amount as the prior deductions, why take it? See Chapter 10 on depreciation for the answer.

WHAT IS INCLUDED IN THE SELLING PRICE?

For tax purposes, the amount realized on a sale includes the amount of cash received plus the fair market value of any other property received [§1001(b)[1]]. The amount of the mortgages on the property sold that the purchaser either assumes or takes subject to is also figured into the sales price [§1.1012-1(a)].

When the selling or purchase price is not specifically stated or involves more than cash, the selling/purchase price is arrived at by the following formula:

Sales Price Computation

1. Cash down payment (earnest money deposit) $ _____
2. Cash brought to closing, cash used to pay selling and purchase expenses $ _____
3. Amount received for option to buy $ _____
4. Assumed mortgages or other encumbrances on the property (whether assumed or taken subject to by the buyer) generally at *face* value[*] $ _____
5. *Face* amount of two-party notes (e.g., between buyer and seller) given to seller (mortgage note or trust deeds) or *face* amount of buyer's contracted promise to pay (land contract or contract for deed)[*] $ _____
6. *Fair market value* of third-party obligations (e.g., U.S. Treasury bonds, AT&T debentures) $ _____
7. Face value of liens against property, whether or not buyer is personally liable for the liens (e.g., back taxes, etc.)[†] $ _____
8. *Fair market value* of property (other than cash) received from buyer (e.g., diamonds, free trips, value of services rendered in exchange for the property received, etc.) $ _____

Actual Sales Price[‡] $ _____

---

[*] The principal part of the mortgage cannot include interest because of the imputed interest rules or the original issue discount rules [§483; §§1271-1274].

[†] Includes charges accrued against the property and assumed by the purchaser, such as taxes, mortgage interest and liens.

[‡] Commissions and other selling expenses paid or incurred by the seller do not reduce the selling price even though they do reduce net profit.

---

[1] Throughout this book, the author refers by citation to the Internal Revenue Code, Tax Court decisions, Treasury regulations and rulings, and similar material. Why? It gives the investor a substantive position for taking tax positions suggested in this book, a great tool in a tax audit! As important, these citations save the tax professional research time.

This citation—§1001(b)—refers to Internal Revenue Code section 1001, subsection b. The next citation refers to Department of Treasury regulation §1.1012-1(a), and court cases deciding tax issues are cited as, for example, *FRL Corp. vs. U.S.* (see page 6).

> ### Tax Tip
>
> The selling price for tax purposes is the total assets transferred from the seller to the buyer, whether they are, or are not, mentioned in the sales contract. The contract price contained in the legal documents is normally, but not always, the same as this calculation.

Example:

Ruth purchased an office building from Gary, paying him $10,000 in cash, assuming a $90,000 mortgage, and giving Gary her note (a second mortgage) for $50,000. The sales/purchase price for Ruth and Gary is computed below.

Sales Price Computation

1. Cash down payment (earnest money deposit)	$10,000
4. Assumed mortgages or other encumbrances on the property (whether assumed or taken subject to by the buyer) generally at *face* value	$90,000
5. *Face* amount of two-party notes (e.g., between buyer and seller) given to seller (mortgage note or trust deeds) or *face* amount of buyer's contracted promise to pay (land contract or contract for deed)	$50,000
Actual Sales Price	$150,000

Example:

Mary purchased an apartment building from Don, with a contract price of $150,000 ($10,000 in cash, $90,000 assumed mortgage, and Mary's two-party note for $50,000). When Don started to back out of the transaction at closing, Mary gave Don her $10,000 diamond ring to keep the transaction together. Is the sales/purchase price the $150,000 that the legal documents state or the $160,000 in assets exchanged?

Sales Price Computation

1. Cash down payment (earnest money deposit)	$10,000
4. Assumed mortgages or other encumbrances on the property (whether assumed or taken subject to by the buyer) generally at *face* value	$90,000
5. *Face* amount of two-party notes (e.g., between buyer and seller) given to seller (mortgage note or trust deeds) or *face* amount of buyer's contracted promise to pay (land contract or contract for deed)	$50,000
8. *Fair market value* of property (other than cash) received from buyer (e.g., diamonds, free trips, value of services rendered in exchange for the property received, etc.)	$10,000
Actual Sales Price	$160,000

Tax Tip

The buyer and seller *must* agree on the sales/purchase price. The IRS requires that the seller's sales price be the same as the buyer's purchase price. As silly as this statement sounds, when a buyer acquires more than one property at the same time (i.e., land and building), the purchase price must be allocated among the properties purchased to determine the basis of each [§1060; *FRL Corp. v. U.S.*, 74-2 USTC ¶9560; 33 AFTR2d 74-897 (D Mass 1974)].

There may be a *double* tax penalty if the parties don't agree. The sales/purchase price *of each component* is required to be the same for both parties, and if they are not, the IRS has the power to change the allocation *to the detriment of both parties*. The allocation must be done in a fair and equitable manner, i.e., based on the fair market value of the different assets on the date of purchase [§1.1060-1T(h); §1.61-6(a); see also Chapter 10 for details].

How to compute taxable gain on the sale of property sold on the installment basis.

Example:

Paula purchases business property for $500,000, paying $150,000 in cash over a first mortgage in the amount of $350,000. Years later, she sells the property for $650,000. The terms are $200,000 cash, a purchase-money mortgage of $150,000 and assumption of the first mortgage, which at the time of sale has a balance of $300,000. Expenses of the sale amount to $30,000. During the period of ownership, Paula adds permanent improvements that cost her $50,000, and she is allowed depreciation deductions of $70,000. The gain on the sale is computed as follows:

Gain or Loss Computation

Sales price			
	Cash	$200,000	
	Purchase-money mortgage	$150,000	
	First mortgage assumed	$300,000	
Sales price			+ $650,000
Less:	Selling expenses		– 30,000
Equals:	Net selling price		= $620,000
Less:	Adjusted basis		
	Original cost (or basis)	+ $500,000	
	Plus: Improvements	+$50,000	
	Less: Accumulated depreciation	– $70,000	
	Equals: Total adjusted basis		– $480,000
Net gain (or loss) on sale			= $140,000

WHAT IS INCLUDED IN SELLING EXPENSES?

Example:

Betty Broker instructs Sammy to spend $2,500 sprucing up his property to get it ready for sale. Is this a selling expense? Surprisingly, the answer is NO, even though Sammy would never have spent the money if Betty hadn't told him it was necessary to make the property salable.

Selling expenses.   These are all the expenses incurred to consummate the sales transaction. Selling expenses reduce the selling price. In other words, if a capital gain (defined in Chapter 2) on the sale is realized, the selling expenses reduce that gain; they are not deductible against ordinary income.

Selling expenses **do not** include the following:

1. *Any expenses that physically affect the property (e.g., repairs or improvements)* even if they are to prepare the property for sale
   Answer to above example: Sammy's $2,500 physically affected the home. Therefore, *it is not a selling expense.* (Maybe it is a repair or an improvement, as discussed later in this chapter.)
2. *Prorated items* such as prorated taxes, insurance, interest, and rent
3. *Finance charges* paid by the buyer

Examples of deductible selling expenses include real estate sales commissions, points paid by the seller to the buyer's lending institution, attorney and accountant's fees, settlement charges, closing fees, appraisal fees, advertising, escrow fees, abstract or title search, title examination, title insurance binders, title insurance, title certificate (Torrens) and registration, document preparation, recording fees, transfer tax stamps, survey, pest inspection, and *any other expenses related to the sale other than those physically affecting the property.*

WHAT IS ADJUSTED BASIS?

Definition of adjusted basis when property is purchased for cash or with a mortgage.   Adjusted basis is the *original cost* of property (or basis, if the owner didn't buy the property), *plus* the value of *improvements* made on the property, *minus depreciation* and losses taken while owning it. Original cost is usually the cash transferred and/or mortgage created or assumed at time of purchase. A more extensive formula follows [§1012; §1016].

Adjusted Basis of Property

Original purchase price (or basis) of property sold	+ $
Purchase expenses of property	+ $
Construction and/or reconstruction costs	+ $
Capital improvements subsequent to initial acquisition, construction, and/or reconstruction	+ $
Special assessments, principal only (streets, sewer)	+ $
Less: Depreciation allowed/allowable in prior years	– $
Less: Casualty losses declared in prior years, if any	– $
Less: Demolition losses [§1.165(a)(1)], if any	– $
Adjusted Basis of Property Sold	= $

What is meant by the phrase *or basis* in the above paragraph?   The manner in which the property is acquired affects its basis. For example:

Inherited property.   If property is inherited, the basis to the recipient is usually its fair market value at the time of the decedent's death (a step-up in basis) [§1014].

Gifted property or divorce settlement property.   If property is received as a bona fide gift, the basis to the recipient is usually the donor's basis (called its *carry-over basis*) plus gift tax paid, if any, on the appreciation in value [§1015]. Any property received from a spouse during marriage or incident to a divorce is considered a transfer by gift [§1041].

Exchanged property.   If the property is acquired in a tax-free exchange, the basis of the property received is the basis of the old property surrendered (called the *substituted basis*) decreased by the amount of *boot* received (money, non-like-kind property, etc.) and increased by gain recognized (or decreased by loss recognized) [§1031(d)].

Purchase expenses are added to basis.   Common purchase price expenses include attorney fees [Rev. Rul. 68-528], escrow fees, recording costs, broker's and finder's fees, appraisal costs, surveys, charges for title search and title insurance, costs of acquiring any outstanding leases, inspection fees, and *any expenses related to purchase other than those physically affecting the property.*

Tax Tip

Surprisingly, tax practitioners often find that purchasers overlook the expenses incurred to purchase an asset (usually paid after closing) when calculating their adjusted basis. These acquisition expenses must be added to basis; they cannot be currently deducted. This unnecessarily decreases their depreciation and increases their subsequent gain. The investors commonly pay for these expenses after closing and simply forget.

Construction, reconstruction, and capital improvements are added to basis.   Any money spent to improve existing property or construct new property (or reconstruct if property is damaged) must be added to basis and depreciated. These *capital expenditures* are generally defined as amounts paid (1) to acquire property with a useful life in excess of one year, or (2) to permanently improve property [§263; §1.263(a)-1]. Capital expenditures cannot be currently deducted but must be recovered through annual expenses (called *depreciation deductions*) taken over the useful life of the depreciable property [§167; §168; see Chapter 10]. Tragically, if the tax rules state that a certain capital expense cannot be depreciated (e.g., land), the cost is recovered only at the time of sale.

Repairs and maintenance are not added to basis.   Expenditures for repairs and maintenance are not capital expenditures and thus are generally deductible in the year paid or incurred. Repairs on business or investment property maintain the property in efficient operating condition. These types of repairs may be currently deducted so long as they do not materially add to the property's value or prolong its useful life. Repairs on personal residences are not deductible, nor can they be added to the home's basis.

Tax Tip

Most taxpayers want expenditures on business property to be repairs so that they can currently deduct them. On the other hand, if those same expenditures are made on a personal residence, the taxpayer wants them to be capital improvements. Repairs on a personal residence are never deductible, but capital improvements reduce the gain on a subsequent taxable sale.

The biggest tax question for owners of real estate: *What is the difference between repairs and capital improvements?* When deciding if an expenditure is a repair or an improvement, the following questions must be considered:

- Does the expenditure materially add to the property's value?
- Does it prolong the property's useful life?

If the investor answers yes to either question, the cost is generally a capital expenditure.

Casualty losses reduce basis.   This occurs to the extent of the deductible loss allowable to the owner. Normally, the amount of the loss deduction equals the loss in value less any insurance proceeds recovered, but the loss deduction may not exceed the adjusted basis of the property prior to the occurrence [§1016(a)(1); 1.165-7(b)(1)]. Amounts expended after the casualty are normally added to basis; it is simply another improvement [Rev. Rul. 71-161, 1971-1 CB 76].

TAXATION OF OPTIONS

What is a real estate option?   Sometimes an investor purchases an option to buy real property in the future instead of purchasing the property immediately. This allows the potential buyer to acquire the property within a designated future period of time without fear that the owner will sell it to someone else. Options are often used to allow the buyer enough time to arrange for financing or determine if he or she really wants to purchase the property. The optionee-buyer usually pays only a small fraction of the total purchase price for the right to buy the property in the future.

Example:

Mike, the optionee, pays Bernie, the owner, $5,000 cash for the right (option) to purchase property for an agreed price of $150,000 any time within the next three years.

The potential buyer also retains the right *not* to purchase the property at all; e.g., the receiver of the option may simply let the option "lapse." In this case, the optionee-buyer forfeits the option money as a "penalty" for failure to exercise. This compensates the seller for removing the property from the market.

A tax loophole: Option money is not immediately taxable.   Options create unusual reporting requirements for both the seller of the option and the receiver (buyer) of the option, in that the initial receipt of option money is not a taxable event to either the seller or the buyer. An option is a different asset from the property covered by the option and is treated much the same as a deposit [§1234; *Lucas v. North Texas Lumber Co.*, 281 US 11 (1930)].

Tax ramifications of options.   When real property is anticipated to be sold through the exercise of an option, the option payments do not become income to the potential seller until the option either lapses or is exercised. This creates the unusual situation that allows the seller to receive cash that is not immediately taxable [§1234].

Tax Tip

Therefore, the seller of an option does not immediately report the cash as taxable, and the buyer cannot immediately deduct the payments. How does the buyer report the money? What does the seller do?

First, the tax ramifications to the buyer.

- *When the option is exercised:* When real property is acquired through the exercise of an option, the buyer adds the cost of the option to the purchase price.
- *If the option is allowed to lapse:* If the buyer allows the option to lapse (e.g., the buyer decides not to exercise the option), the buyer is allowed to deduct the option payment as a loss, subject to all the loss restrictions, but only at the end of the option period [§1234(b)(2); §1.1234-1(b)].
- *The character of the loss:* If the option relates to real property, the option is generally considered either a capital asset or a §1231 trade or business property. The character of the loss is determined by the property to which the option applies and therefore would be a capital loss or an ordinary business loss [§1.1234-1(a); §1234(a)(1); defined in Chapter 2].

Investor Hint

Tax practitioners commonly see buyers trying to disguise the option payment as a "lease" payment to accelerate the deduction. This seldom works as the IRS looks to the substance to see if an option actually exists.

Second, the tax ramifications to the seller.

- *Exercise:* If the option is exercised, the option money is included in the sales price of the property sold.
- *Lapse:* If the option is not exercised, the gain is ordinary income. Dealers in options are subject to special rules [§1.1234-1].

The Selling of an Option

> ### Tax Tip
>
> After holding the option for more than 12 months, sometimes investors sell their right to purchase property (i.e., the option) instead of purchasing the property with the option and immediately selling the property. The new owner of the option simply steps into the shoes of the old owner and exercises the option. *Why would a sophisticated investor want to sell the option instead of exercising the option and selling the property?*
>
> The answer is to take advantage of the long-term capital gains tax rates (as discussed in Chapter 2). How long has the investor owned the option? More than 12 months, which is a long-term capital gain. If the investor exercises the option, how long has he or she owned the property? One day, which is a short-term capital gain. By exercising the option, the unsophisticated investor converts a long-term capital gain into a short-term capital gain. Not smart!

Options and related property.   When property is acquired under an option to purchase, the holding period of the property begins on the day after the property is acquired, *not* on the day after the option is acquired. Investors cannot add the time an option is held to the time the property is held after exercising the option in order to satisfy the holding period requirement. However, if the option itself is held for the minimum holding period and then sold, the investor is eligible for capital gain treatment *if the property itself would have been a capital asset in the investor's hands.* Otherwise, the investor has ordinary income [§1.1234-1(a)(1)].

Example:

On January 1, 2002, Tom purchased, for $500, a two-year option to buy a minishopping center having an exercise price of $300,000. Two years later (January 1, 2004) Tom receives an offer of $400,500 for the building. He is willing to claim the whole gain in the year of the sale. On January 1, 2004, Tom exercises the option for $300,000 and the same day sells the building for $400,500. This results in a $100,000 *short-term* capital gain as Tom has owned the property for less than one day, not the required "more than 12 months." By not selling the option, Tom converted a long-term capital gain to a short-term capital gain. He did not know that the option is a different asset from the property it is optioning. Of course, the new buyer does not care what method is used. If Tom sells him the option for $100,500, the option price is added to the exercise price of $300,000, leaving him the same $400,500 basis as if he had purchased it directly from Tom. ■

CONCLUSION

Probably no tax formula is more misunderstood than the gain (or loss) calculation discussed in this chapter. Yet, as discovered in this section, a short methodical procedure makes this amount easy to determine accurately, even when an option to purchase is involved.

Capital Gains Taxation

After computing the gain or loss on the sale of real estate, the seller must decide what to do with that gain or loss. This chapter discusses the many special rules for calculating capital gain treatment at time of disposition and what tax rate to apply to that gain or loss.

In general, there are three different types of tax treatments for gains or losses realized on the sale or exchange of property. They are the

1. *capital gain or loss* method,
2. *ordinary gain or loss* method, and
3. *hybrid* method, capital gain and an ordinary loss.

Capital gain or loss treatment has the tax advantage of not requiring that the gain be taxed at the highest tax rate (e.g., 35%) but has the disadvantage of the loss not being totally deductible. In an attempt to counter the taxation of gain created by inflation (i.e., *real* tax on *phantom* income) and the "bunching" of the entire appreciation into one year, the year of sale, under our progressive tax system (e.g., 10% to 35%) Congress has rejected the simpler pre-1986 60% capital gain deduction method and adopted the alternative "pay-the-lower-of-the-two" tax computation method.

WHAT ASSETS CAN CLAIM CAPITAL GAINS OR LOSSES?

Capital assets can use capital gain rates! Before applying the advantageous capital gains treatment, it has to be ascertained if the property is actually a *capital asset*. Capital gain or loss is only available when a capital asset is sold.

Capital assets include *all* property, regardless of how long held, *with the following exceptions*. It does not include

1. inventory or stock in trade of the taxpayer,
2. property held by the taxpayer primarily for sale to customers in the ordinary course of his or her trade or business (e.g., *dealer's realty*),
3. depreciable property used in a trade or business, and
4. real property used in a trade or business [§1221].

Tax Tip

Most investors are surprised to find that depreciable property (No. 3 above) and business real property (No. 4 above) *are not* capital assets! As will be seen in the "hybrid" method discussed later, most investors prefer *not* having property categorized as a capital asset when the property is to be sold for a loss.

CAPITAL LOSSES

Capital losses may be only partially deductible. A capital loss is a loss on the sale of a capital asset. The additional negative result of an individual's capital loss, if the total capital losses exceed the total capital gains, is that the excess may be deducted from ordinary income only to the extent of $3,000 or the excess of the losses over the gains, whichever is less ($1,500 for married taxpayers filing separately). The excess capital loss may be carried forward for an unlimited period, shielding future capital gain from taxation [§1211(b)].

Capital gains that are absorbed by capital losses, and thereby reduce to zero additional taxable income, can mean "free" money from the sale. However, the investor must utilize capital losses from a taxable account, *not* a pension account. In addition, capital losses offset capital gains, but not ordinary income, generated from a sale.

Investor Hint

Using up large capital loss carryovers. Many investors have such large capital loss carryovers that they'll need to live 100 more years to use up the tax benefit! Reviewing the investor's stock portfolio for capital gains only works *if* there are any gains left in the stock market. Instead, the client can look for capital gains in other places. Potential options to generate capital gains include the following:

- Sell the depreciated (and hopefully appreciated) rental,
- Take taxable boot in an exchange,
- Sell negative basis limited partnership interests to generate phantom income. There are many old tax shelter partnerships with large negative capital accounts. Maybe it's time to abandon the interest to the general partner (or sell the interest to a nonrelative) and recognize the phantom income. Make sure it will be capital gain and not ordinary income before you recommend this move,
- Sell the appreciated vacation home;
- Accelerate installment sale collections,
- Sell the highly appreciated personal residence if gains are in excess of the section 121 exclusion ($250,000/$500,000) and generate a capital gain that can be absorbed by the capital loss carryovers.

ORDINARY GAIN OR LOSS

Ordinary gains or losses are generally entirely taxable or entirely deductible. This includes "income from whatever source derived," including (1) compensation for services, such as fees, commissions, fringe benefits, and similar items; (2) gross income derived from business; and (3) *gains derived from dealer's realty* (e.g., subdivider treating real property as if it were inventory) [§61(a)].

Tax Tip

Real estate investors may find their real estate holdings taxed as ordinary income if the IRS determines they purchased the property to sell it (e.g., dealer's realty). But isn't all property bought with the intention to eventually sell it?

Investors must make the argument that they hold property for other reasons than "for sale," such as for appreciation or for rental income. Careless use of technical tax terms can be very costly—ask Arthur Andersen!

Social Security increased the regular tax rate. Added to the maximum income tax rates (e.g., 35%), ordinary income *may* also have an additional 15.3% self-employment (also known as Social Security) "tax" rate imposed on it if the IRS determines the income is earned in the ordinary course of an active business, such as dealer's realty. This additional tax rate is not imposed if the property is considered a capital asset or a business asset, as discussed next.

HYBRID, CAPITAL GAIN, AND ORDINARY LOSS (§1231 GAIN OR LOSS)

A great tax benefit. *Property used in a trade or business is called §1231 property.* It receives long-term capital gain benefits if there is a net gain; it receives ordinary loss benefits when there is a net loss. Therefore, business property sold for a gain may find only part of that gain taxed (a capital gain), whereas when business property is sold for a loss, it is *entirely* deductible—the best of both worlds!

What items are called §1231 items? Property used in a trade or business, subject to depreciation and held for more than one year, and *business realty* held for more than one year are called §1231 property. Therefore, most property used in a business is §1231 property (e.g., rental property and property used in the taxpayer's business). Real-estate-dealer realty and inventory property held primarily for sale to customers in the ordinary course of business are *not* §1231 property; they are ordinary income property [§1231(b); §61].

§1231 calculation. If the gains exceed the losses on disposition of §1231 assets, then all the gains and all the losses are treated as capital gains and losses. If the net result is a loss, all the gains are taxed as ordinary gains and the losses are deductible in full as ordinary losses.

Example:

Lance sells the following assets that are used in his business and held for more than one year:

	Gain	Loss
Raw land held for future building site	$7,000	$ 0
Automobile		300
Truck		3,700
Computer	$2,000	
	$9,000	$4,000

As the §1231 gains exceed the §1231 losses, each gain and each loss is treated as long-term capital gain or long-term capital loss.

LONG-TERM VS. SHORT-TERM CAPITAL GAIN

12-month long-term holding period. A capital asset is characterized as either a *long-term* or *short-term* capital asset, depending on the length of time the asset is owned *(holding period)* or deemed to have been held under the "tacking" and other rules (§1223). *The period is computed by excluding the day of acquisition and including the day of disposition* (§1222). Long-term capital gain or loss treatment is available only when capital assets are held for *more than 12 months* [§1(h)(5)]. If property is held for a period of one year or less, the asset is characterized as a short-term capital asset and generally is taxed as ordinary gains or losses and not eligible for the 10%/20%/25% capital gain rates. For gains attributable to a passthrough entity, such as a partnership, S corporation, or regulated investment company (RIC), the character of the gain is determined by when the entity received the capital gains.

Tax Tip

Most real estate investors find their real estate sales are eligible for the previously discussed hybrid method, wherein the gain receives the long-term capital gain benefits and the loss receives the ordinary loss treatment. As is fully discussed in the next chapter, most homeowners, though, find their long-term capital gain is not taxable, and their loss is never deductible!

CAPITAL GAIN RATES

Individual Long-Term Capital Gain Rates Reduced to 5% and 15%

5%/15%/25% long-term capital gain rates for sales on or after May 6, 2003.[1] The Jobs and Growth Tax Relief Reconciliation Act of 2003 (JGTRRA-2003) reduced the 10% rate on the adjusted net capital gain to 5% for individuals in the 10% or 15% tax bracket[2] and reduced the 20% rates on the adjusted net capital gain to 15% for individuals in the 25%–35% tax brackets (§1(h)(2)(B) & (C)). This generally has the effect of applying the lower rates to capital assets sold or exchanged (and installment payments received) on or after May 6, 2003, that were held for more than 12 months. In the case of gain and loss taken into account by a pass-through entity, the date taken into account by the entity is the appropriate date for applying this rule. In addition, the 5% tax rate is reduced to 0% (as in "tax free") for taxable years beginning after December 31, 2007, and before January 1, 2009. The 8% and 18% rates are permanently repealed for sales on or after May 6, 2003. Stunningly, the 5%/15% rates revert back to the 10%/20% rates for tax years beginning after December 31, 2008.

---

1. This provision applies to taxable years ending on or after May 6, 2003, and beginning before January 1, 2009. For taxable years that include May 6, 2003, the lower rates apply to amounts properly taken into account for the portion of the year on or after that date.
2. E.g., in 2004, that would be married filing joint taxpayers with taxable income (including capital gains) less than $58,100 and single taxpayers with taxable income less than $29,050.

Tax Tip

The 5% drop in the long-term capital gain rate in 2003 is significant and increases the spread between ordinary income tax and long-term capital gains tax for all taxpayers. The previous spread between the highest income and estate tax brackets was 18.6 percentage points (38.6% less than 20%). As a result of the capital gain rate reduction, the spread increases to 20 percentage points (35% less 15%), making capital gain even more desirable than in the past, creating a new variable to investment decisions. However, the temporary nature of the cuts makes long-term financial planning difficult.

Investor Hint

The personal exemption phaseout and the limit on itemized deductions indirectly increase the taxable income. This can cause the net capital gain to be taxed higher than the advertised 15% rate for a high-income taxpayer. The actual individual "effective tax bracket" experienced by net capital gains may be 17% to 22% or higher because of the 2% personal exemption phaseout and the multiple limits on itemized deductions.

Gifting to lower-income taxpayers, such as children age 14 or older, before sale may result in a maximum 5% rate on the capital gain–a significant tax planning opportunity!

8%/10%/20%/25% long-term capital gain rates for sales before May 6, 2003. For capital assets held more than 12 months which are sold after December 31, 1997,[3] and before May 6, 2003, the maximum tax rate on net capital gains is 20%. For individuals in the 10% or 15% bracket, the long-term capital gain tax rate is 10%, unless the capital asset was owned for at least five years and sold between January 1, 2001, and May 5, 2003, in which a maximum capital gain rate of 8% was applied.[4] There was no requirement that assets eligible for the 8% rate be acquired after 2000. Qualified five-year gain is defined as the aggregate long-term capital gain from property held for more than five years (§1(h)(9)). Depreciation on sales of real estate is recaptured at a 15%/25% rate, even to the gain element of installment-sale payments. Long-term capital gains from the sale of collectibles are taxed at a maximum rate of 28%. Net capital losses are subject to a $3,000 limit per year (§1222(b)).

---

3. For sales (and collections on sales) occurring after May 6, 1997, and before July 29, 1997, the 10%/20% rate applies to assets held more than 12 months. For sales (and collections on sales) occurring after July 28, 1997, and before January 1, 1998, the 10%/20% rate applies to assets held more than 18 months.

4. The 20% long-term capital gain rate was scheduled to drop to 18% for assets *purchased* after December 31, 2000, and subsequently held more than five years [Act Section 311(e) of TRA '97]. Therefore, the 18% rate would not have been available until on or after January 1, 2006! To make matters worse, capital assets purchased before January 1, 2001, would never have been eligible for the 18% rate unless the taxpayer made a special "deemed sale" election (discussed later) prior to filing their 2001 tax return.

Table of Long-Term Capital Gain Rates

Tax Bracket	1/1/01– 5/5/03	5/6/03– 12/31/07	2008	2009
10% and 15%	8%/10%	5%	0%	10%
25% and above	20%	15%	15%	20%

Example:

John's taxable income without capital gains is $10,000. On May 5, 2003, he sells stock with a long-term capital gain of $30,000. The tax due to the capital gains is $1,472 (8% of $18,400)[5] plus $2,320 (20% of the balance of the gain of $11,600), for a total capital gains tax of $3,792 on the $30,000 (i.e., a 12.64% effective tax bracket). After May 5, 2003, the tax due is $920 (5% of $18,400) plus $1,740 (15% of the $11,600 balance), for a total capital gains tax of $2,660 on the $30,000 (i.e., an 8.87% effective tax bracket).

Capital gain and AMT. The same tax rates (e.g., the pre-May 2003 10%/20%/25% rates and post-May 2003 5%/15%/25% rates) apply to capital gains for alternative minimum tax (AMT) purposes. But, this *did not* eliminate the concern that capital gains will aggravate an AMT problem by virtue of being taxed at the generally effective 28% AMT rate instead of the new lower rate.

Tax Tip

AMT is still a major problem for many middle-income and upper-income taxpayers. For example, married taxpayers with $100,000 of W-2 income will pay $5,011 of additional AMT with as little as $200,000 of capital gain. For tax preparers, here are the technical reasons: (1) no 15% tax bracket in AMT; (2) the capital gain reduces the jointly filed married couples AMT $58,000 exemption ($40,250 [Single]/$29,000 [Married Filing Separately]) because of the 25% phaseout over $150,000 AMTI ($112,500 for S and MFS); and (3) much of the itemized deductions, such as state income tax, is not deductible on the AMT return! But married taxpayers with more than $382,000 of ordinary income (end of phaseout) [$273,500 for S and MFS] will normally not experience AMT because of their 35% tax bracket.

Investor Hint

There were no rate reductions for corporations with capital gains. A corporation's top rate stays at 35%. Interestingly, TRA '97 applies the alternative tax rate of 35% to the lesser of the corporation's net capital gain or its taxable income. But this alternative minimum tax rate applies only when the corporation's ordinary income tax rate *exceeds* 35%, resulting in no immediate advantage because of the top corporate tax rate being 35% [§1201(a)(2)].

---

5. The 15% tax rate for a single taxpayer in the year 2003 applied to taxable income up to $28,400.

Types of Gain Not Eligible for the 5% or 15% Rates

Not all gains from the sale of investment property will benefit from the low rates. They are:

1. collectibles (defined below),
2. real estate depreciation recapture (defined below),
3. gain on qualified small business stock (certain original issue stock generally in the manufacturing or retail sector held for more than five years and sold after August 10, 1998), and
4. Net capital gain treated as investment income for purposes of the deduction for investment interest expense.

Exception—Collectibles

The 5%/15% rates apply to most capital assets with the exception of collectibles, such as art, rugs, antiques, any metals, gems, stamps, coins, and alcoholic beverages, which continue to be taxed at the 28% maximum rate. Certain newly minted gold and silver coins issued by the federal government and coins issued under state law are subject to the lower capital gains rates, even though such coins generally qualify as "collectibles" [see §408(m)(2) and (3)].

Exception—Real Estate Depreciation Recapture

Not all gains from the sale of depreciable real property will be able to take advantage of the low rates. The top rate on real property gain attributable to depreciation, but not already "recaptured," i.e., taxed at ordinary income rates, will be taxed at a top rate of 25% rather than the 15% top rate that applies to other capital gain.

Technically (for tax preparers), this is gain on section 1250 property (real property) to the extent the section 1231 (generally business property) gain would have been ordinary income under section 1245 (generally *all* depreciation taken on personal property and all previous accelerated depreciation taken on commercial real property) and was not recaptured under section 1250 (generally, depreciation taken on residential rental property is taken faster than straight-line).

Unrecaptured section 1250 gain is the amount of long-term capital gain that would be treated as ordinary income if the property were section 1245 property. This amount may not exceed the excess of the net section 1231 gain over the gain treated as ordinary income under the rules for nonrecaptured section 1231 losses from the five preceding years.

Example:

On December 31, 2003, Steve sold a residential rental for $800,000 that he had acquired on January 1, 1987 for $500,000. The property's accumulated basis is $175,000. The tax on this sale (ignoring other factors and assuming he is in the top tax bracket) is computed as follows:

		Gain	Tax Rate	Tax
Sales price		$800,000		
Original cost	$500,000			
Less: Accumulated depreciation	− 175,000			
Adjusted basis		− 325,000		
Total gain		475,000		
Less: Gain due to prior depreciation		− 175,000 ×	25% =	$ 43,750
Remaining §1231 capital gain		= 300,000 ×	15% =	45,000
Total tax				$88,750

CAPITAL GAIN RATE CHART

For Sales Creating Long-term Capital Gains in 2004 through 2007:

Your Capital Gain Rate Is:	If Your Regular Tax Bracket Is:	And Your Holding Period Is More Than:	And Your Gain Is From:
5% (after 5/5/03)	10%/15%	12 months	Adjusted net capital gains (excludes prior depreciation, qualified small business stock, and collectibles, but includes Form 1099-R net unrealized appreciation). The gains are eligible for the alternative 10% maximum rate for non-corporate taxpayers.
7½%–14%	10%–35%	60 months	Qualified small business stock issued after 8/10/93 and sold after 8/10/98 (without rollover).
15% (after 5/5/03)	25%–35%	12 months	Adjusted net capital gains (excludes prior depreciation, qualified small business stock, and collectibles, but includes Form 1099-R net unrealized appreciation). The gains are eligible for the alternative 20% maximum rate for noncorporate taxpayers.
15%	15%	12 months	Prior §1250 depreciation and collectibles.
25%	25%–35%	12 months	Prior §1250 depreciation otherwise not subject to recapture.
28%	28%–35%	12 months	Collectibles (such as art, antiques, gems, and stamps).

The $250,000/$500,000 MFJ Exclusion Rule for Gain on Sale of Principal Residence

In 1997, Congress repealed both the (§1034) replacement-of-home rollover statute (i.e., buy equal-or-up to "rollover" the entire gain) and the (§121) one-time over-55 exclusion rule (i.e., exclude up to $125,000 of the gain) and passed a new §121 relief provision applicable to principal residences effective for sales after May 6, 1997 (see the Taxpayers Relief Act of 1997). Why the change? Congress concluded that the reinvestment requirement of the rollover provision was an undesirable burden and the $125,000 exclusion rule was not large enough, as it did not meet the needs of the retiree or empty nester who sells the large family residence and purchases a substantially less expensive home, the divorcee who subsequently rents an apartment, or the homeowner who moves from a high-cost area into a low-cost area (e.g., from Los Angeles to Casper, Wyoming).

The purchase, and later the sale, of a home is generally the most substantial financial transaction encountered by a taxpayer and the home is often a married couple's most significant asset. This chapter describes various tax consequences when selling a personal residence and provides specific examples of the requirements necessary for homeowners to use the new §121 exclusion-of-gain rule. Topics include

- all additional changes based on the new IRS regulations;
- determining if a home is a principal residence;
- applying the exclusion to both married and unmarried joint owners;
- excluding the gain associated with either an office-in-home or vacant land;
- issues when renting out a principal residence;
- fulfilling the three two-year requirements;
- understanding the employment, health, and unforeseen circumstances reduced exclusion rules; and
- problems with unusual dispositions of a home, e.g., bankruptcy, exchange, or sales by trusts.

Investor Hint

The final IRS Regulations §1.121-1, 2, 3 & 4, and proposed IRS regulations §1.121-3T, effective December 24, 2002, cited in this chapter refer to *new* Code §121 and are extensively discussed in this chapter.[1]

Caution

Almost all case citations refer to previous Code §1034 and §121. Always check with your tax practitioner, as new court cases and IRS regulations are constantly being added!

THE EXCLUSION RULE

This exclusion rule provides that up to $250,000 of gain ($500,000 for those married taxpayers filing jointly [MFJ]) realized on the sale or exchange of a principal residence on or after May 7, 1997, is not *taxable* (not just deferred) if certain prerequisites are satisfied. But a taxpayer is eligible for only one maximum exclusion per principal residence [§1.121-2(a)(1)]. This permanent exclusion is allowed repeatedly, each time a homeowner meets the eligibility requirements, but generally no more frequently than once every two years, and permits substantially more homeowners to escape paying capital gains tax when selling their home. This provision is denied to disqualified expatriates [§121(e); §877(a)(1)].

Wealthy homeowners may be forced to report gain!   The amount in excess of the $250,000/$500,000 MFJ exclusion must be included in income even if all of the sales proceeds are reinvested in a new residence.

---

1 A taxpayer elects to retroactively apply these regulations by excluding the gain on the return filed for the year of the sale or exchange. No formal election statement is required. The IRS will not challenge a taxpayer's position that a sale or exchange between May 7, 1997, and December 24, 2002 (the effective date of the final regulations) qualifies for the §121 exclusion if the taxpayer has made a reasonable, good-faith effort to comply with the requirements of §121. Additionally, compliance with the provisions of the proposed regulations that preceded these final regulations generally will be considered a reasonable, good faith effort [§1.121-4(k)].

> **Investor Hint**
> ___
>
> For those homeowners selling principal residences with gains in excess of $250,000/ $500,000 MFJ, the repealed §1034 "roll-over" provision was more beneficial.

Election out of Section 121

It's an option!   The taxpayer can elect *not* to have the gain exclusion apply. The election is made by reporting the principal residence sale, and gain, on Schedule D (Form 1040) Capital Gains and Losses, for the taxable year of the sale or exchange. A taxpayer may make or revoke this election at any time before the expiration of a three-year period beginning on (generally) April 15 following the taxable year in which the sale or exchange occurred [§121(f); §1.121-4(g)].

> **Tax Tip**
> ___
>
> Why would a taxpayer elect to have a gain taxable when it could be tax-free? It took a little imagination, but how about the situation in the next example?

Example:

Dolores marries Alfred on January 1, 2004. On May 15, 2005, Alfred sells his old home for a $10,000 gain. On January 15, 2006, Dolores sells her home for a $500,000 gain. It would be smarter for Alfred to elect to make his $10,000 gain taxable so that Dolores and Alfred can file jointly and use their combined $500,000 MFJ exclusion. If he uses the exclusion against the $10,000 gain, he cannot again use the exclusion until two years after May 15, 2005, and Dolores can only exclude $250,000. Isn't that simple?

IRS Eliminates the Tax Reporting of Most Home Sales

The National Association of REALTORS® estimates that no more than 2.1% of homes sold annually exceed $500,000, and a substantial number of those sales experience gains of less than $500,000. Understanding this, the IRS has concluded that the reporting of excluded gain for all taxpayers is unnecessary and an undue burden. The IRS eliminated Form 2119 in 1998.

Schedule D, Not Form 2119.   In those unusual situations when there is a taxable gain (i.e., the gain exceeds the $250,000/$500,000 MFJ exclusion), report the entire transaction on Form 1040, Schedule D (line 1 or 8, depending on the holding period). Next, insert the allowable exclusion on the line directly below the above-mentioned Schedule D gain by writing "Section 121 exclusion" in column (a) and show the exclusion in the *gain* column (f) as a *loss* (in parentheses). If any depreciation recapture is required, the transaction instead must first be reported on Form 4797, Part III. [See Pub. 523, Ch. 2,

"Reporting the Gain."] Problematically, Schedule D also requires that the homeowner provide the selling price, the selling expenses, and the adjusted basis of the home sold.

How long do we need to keep our receipts?   Generally, three to six years after the sale, but this new exclusion eliminates most record-keeping requirements when home sellers *absolutely know that in the future* they will not experience a home gain of more than $250,000 ($500,000 MFJ for married couples). For homeowners who believe future gain may exceed $250,000, it is very important to retain property records (e.g., proof of the home purchase price and purchase expenses) and receipts of the improvements on the home owned because improvements directly affect the gain of the primary residence sold. If the taxpayer does not retain the receipts on improvements of the home he or she purchases, the IRS may disallow this decrease in gain and, therefore, increase the taxable gain if the exclusion provision is not available to the homeowner.

Investor Hint

If any of the gain was deferred under the previous §1034 "roll-over" rules, the previous adjusted basis records also have to be retained, which may extend the record-keeping back decades! State income tax law differences may also dictate a longer retention period.

No Form 1099-S on most home sales.   The IRS does NOT require IRS notification of any home *sale* (or exchange) of $250,000 or less ($500,000 MFJ for married taxpayers) via Form 1099-S (Proceeds from Real Estate Transactions) by the real estate closing agent (e.g., the title company, real estate broker, or mortgage company), as long as federally subsidized mortgage financing assistance did not exist. But the home seller will have to provide the agent with certain "assurances," as set forth by Revenue Procedure 98-20, at any time before January 31 of the year following the sale or exchange and retained by the agent for four years. The use of the sample certification form contained in Rev. Proc. 98-20 is not required as long as the content and wording of a written certification provide the same information, as required by this revenue procedure. Additionally, the IRS has the authority to increase the dollar amount in the future. The agent may be penalized $50 + $50 for each Form 1099-S violation [§6045(e)(5); (Rev. Proc. 98-20)].

DEFINITION OF PRINCIPAL RESIDENCE

As this large exclusion-of-gain rule only applies to the taxpayer's one "principal" residence, the problems defining principal residence can be placed into four major categories: (1) types of qualified properties, (2) ownership requirements, (3) occupancy requirements, and (4) residences used also for business. This definition of principal residence is the area in which most of the tax problems and IRS controversies arise.

Investor Hint

Essentially, Rev. Proc. 98-20, referred to on page 24, makes the seller inform the real estate closing agent of the following: (1) they have owned and used the residence for two of the last five years; (2) they have not sold or exchanged another home in the two years prior to the sale date; (3) **no portion of the home has been used for business purposes after May 6, 1997;** and (4) the sales price is: (a) $250,000 or less if single, (b) $500,000 or less if married and gain is $250,000 or less, or (c) $500,000 or less, taxpayer is married and joint return is intended, spouse also used (but not necessarily owned) residence for two of the last five years, and spouse also had not sold or exchanged another home in the two years prior to the sale date. Rev. Proc. 98-20 applies to home sales after May 6, 1997.

Where Is Your Principal Residence?

Determined by the facts and circumstances.   No IRS bright-line test identifies the principal residence when the seller has several residences. Whether property is used by the taxpayer as the taxpayer's *residence* and whether the property is used as the taxpayer's *principal* residence depends upon all the facts and circumstances [§1.121-1(b)(2)].

Normally, this is easy to determine. A taxpayer's principal residence is the land and building where the taxpayer *principally domiciles,* based on all the facts and circumstances in each case, including the good faith of the taxpayer. It may be even be located in a foreign country [Rev. Rul. 54-611, 1954-2 CB 159]. As there is no requirement that a principal residence be owned, a motel room or rental apartment may end up being a principal residence [Rev. Rul. 60-189; Rev. Rul. 73-529; *Ziporyn v. Comm.,* TC Memo 1997-151].

Principal residence may be where taxpayer spends *"majority of the time."*   In the case of a taxpayer using more than one property as a residence, if a taxpayer alternates between two properties, the property that the taxpayer uses a majority of the time during the year will ordinarily, but not necessarily, be considered the taxpayer's principal residence. In addition to the taxpayer's use of the property, relevant factors in determining a taxpayer's principal residence include, but are not limited to

- the taxpayer's place of employment;
- the principal place of abode of the taxpayer's family members;
- the address listed on the taxpayer's federal and state tax returns, driver's license, automobile registration, and voter registration card;
- the taxpayer's mailing address for bills and correspondence;
- the location of the taxpayer's banks; and
- the location of religious organizations and recreational clubs with which the taxpayer is affiliated [§1.121-1(b)(2)(i) - (iv); also see Rev. Rul. 71-247].

Only one "principal" residence is possible.   One taxpayer cannot own two principal residences simultaneously because principal is defined as "the most important" [*McDowell v. Comm.*, 40 TCM 301 (1980)].

Example:

Use split between two residences in same year. David owns two residences, one in New York and one in Florida. From 1999 through 2004, he lives in the New York residence for seven months and the Florida residence for five months of each year. In the absence of facts and circumstances indicating otherwise, the New York residence is David's principal residence. He would be eligible for the §121 exclusion of gain from the sale or exchange of the New York residence, but not the Florida residence [§1.121-1(b)(4), Ex. 1].

Properties That Can Qualify

A personal residence may be a single-family house, condominium, cooperative, mobile home, boat, houseboat, house trailer, or motorhome. But property used by the taxpayer as the taxpayer's residence does not include personal property that is not a fixture under local law (e.g., gain on the sale of household furniture) [§1.121-1(b)(1)].

PRIOR TAX PLANNING IDEAS THAT ARE NO LONGER RELEVANT!

Common "rules" under the previous tax provisions are no longer viable, including the following:

- There is no requirement to reinvest the sales proceeds into another home, i.e., taxpayers do not have to buy equal or up within 24 months.
- The requirement that the taxpayer must be at least age 55 has been repealed.
- Fixing-up expenses, including "conditions-of-sale" repairs, are no longer deductible *anywhere*.
- The "moving at least 50 miles" requirement to avoid the once-every-two-year rule has been eliminated.
- The nontaxable gain does not have to be "rolled over" into the new home.
- Renting the home while trying to sell it generally will not cause tax problems.

REQUIREMENTS TO USE THE $250,000/$500,000 MFJ EXCLUSION RULE

The §121 Qualification Requirements

To qualify for this tax break:

1. "Own for two years" rule. The taxpayer, with three notable exceptions discussed later, must *own* the home as his or her principal residence for a total of two years during the five-year period ending on the date of the sale or exchange [§121(a)].

2. "Occupy for two years" rule. The taxpayer, with the same three exceptions, must *use* the home as his or her principal residence for a total of two years during the five-year period ending on the date of the sale or exchange [§121(a)].

3. "No more than once every two years" rule.   The taxpayer cannot report, during the two-year period ending on the date of sale, other sales or exchanges to which §121 applies [§121(b)(3)].

If the taxpayer meets the above qualifications, up to $250,000/$500,000 MFJ of gain from the sale or exchange of the taxpayer's principal residence may be excluded from gross income. But a taxpayer is eligible for only one maximum exclusion per principal residence [§121(b)(1) and (2); §1.121-2(a)(1)]. If a taxpayer does not meet any or all of the three tests for the full exclusion to apply, he or she may still be eligible to exclude a portion of the gain under the *reduced maximum exclusion* rule (discussed later).

Example:

Cindy sells her principal residence for $330,000. She had purchased the home 20 years earlier for $40,000 and had added a $25,000 recreation room to it. She pays commissions and other closing costs of $30,000. Her total gain is forgiven if she uses the $250,000 exclusion rule. ▪

Gain or Loss Computation

Sales price			+ $330,000
Less:	Selling expenses		− 30,000
Equals:	Amount realized		= $300,000
Less:	Adjusted basis		
	Original cost (or basis)	+ $40,000	
	Plus: Improvements	+ $25,000	
	Equals: Total adjusted basis		− $65,000
Gain realized on sale			= $235,000
Less: $250,000 Exclusion			− $250,000
Taxable Gain on Sale			None

Jointly Owning a Home with a "Significant Other"

Dollar limitation.   If two unmarried individuals jointly own and use one principal residence, the $250,000 exclusion provision applies independently to each on a sale of the residence. The home is treated like a duplex owned by a joint venture partnership. Both individuals must report their separate gain on their personal tax returns and therefore may be eligible to exclude from gross income up to $250,000 of gain that is attributable to each taxpayer's interest in the property [§1.121-2(a)(2)].

Exclusion Applies Separately to Each Spouse

What happens if one spouse qualifies and the other doesn't qualify?   For taxpayers filing jointly, if either spouse fails to meet the above requirements, the maximum limitation amount to be claimed by the couple is the sum of each spouse's limitation amount determined on a separate basis as if they had not been married. The $250,000 exclusion applies on a joint return where one or both spouses meet the ownership test, but only one spouse meets the use test or the one-sale-in-two-years test [§121(d)(1) and (2); §1.121-2(a)(1)]. In addition, if a single taxpayer marries someone who has used the exclusion within two years, the taxpayer remains eligible for his or her own $250,000 exclusion on a joint return.

Each spouse may have his or her "principal" residence and each may exclude up to $250,000 of gain. When married couples are not sharing a principal residence, each spouse is able to separately exclude $250,000, as long as each satisfies all the qualification requirements [§121(b)(2)].

If taxpayers jointly own a principal residence but file separate returns, each taxpayer may exclude from gross income up to $250,000 of gain that is attributable to each taxpayer's interest in the property [§1.121-2(a)(2)]. For this purpose, each spouse is treated as owning the property during the period that either spouse owned the property [§1.121-2(a)(3)(ii)].

Example:

Two separate residences, two $250,000 exclusions. During 2003, married taxpayers Hank and Winifred each sell a residence that each had separately owned and used as a principal residence before their marriage. Each spouse meets the ownership and use tests for his or her respective residence. Neither spouse meets the use requirement for the other spouse's residence. Hank and Winifred file a joint return for the year of the sales. The gain realized from the sale of Hank's residence is $200,000. The gain realized from the sale of Winifred's residence is $300,000. Because the ownership and use requirements are met for each residence by each respective spouse, Hank and Winifred are eligible to exclude up to $250,000 of gain from the sale of each of their residences. However, Winifred may not use Hank's unused exclusion to exclude gain in excess of her exclusion amount. Therefore, Hank and Winifred must recognize $50,000 of the gain realized on the sale of Winifred's residence [§1.121-2(a)(4), Ex. 3)].

The $250,000 Exclusion Doubles to $500,000 MFJ If Four Requirements Are Met

1. *Either* spouse *owns* the property for two of the last five years,
2. *Both* spouses *use* the property as their principal residence for two of the last five years,
3. *Neither spouse is ineligible* because more than one sale or exchange has been used during the previous two years, and
4. A husband and wife make *a joint return* for the taxable year of the sale or exchange of the property [§121(b)(2); §1.121-2(a)(3)(i)].

The determination of whether an individual is married shall be determined by the election to make a joint return, not as of the date of the sale or exchange [§1.6013-1(a)].

Example 1:

Unmarried couple jointly own home—each qualifies—two $250,000 exclusions. Doug and Debbie, who are unmarried, own a house as joint owners, each owning a 50% interest in the house. They sell the house after owning and using it as their principal residence for two full years. The gain realized from the sale is $256,000. Doug and Debbie are each eligible to exclude $128,000 of gain because the amount of realized gain allocable to each of them from the sale does not exceed the $250,000 amount available to each [§1.121-2(a)(4), Ex. 1].

Example 2:

Married couple filing jointly—both quality—one $500,000 exclusion. The facts are the same as in Example 1, except that Doug and Debbie are married taxpayers who file a joint return for the taxable year of the sale. Doug and Debbie are eligible to exclude the entire amount of realized gain ($256,000) from gross income because the gain realized from the sale does not exceed the $500,000 amount available to married taxpayers filing a joint return [§1.121-2(a)(4), Ex. 2].

If the three previously mentioned two-year requirements are not met by both, a married couple will, at a minimum, be eligible for the $250,000 exclusion if *either* spouse meets all the requirements. Similarly, if a single taxpayer who is otherwise eligible for an exclusion marries someone who has used the exclusion within the two years prior to the marriage, this provision would still allow the newly married taxpayer a maximum exclusion of $250,000. Once both spouses satisfy the eligibility rules and two years have passed since the last exclusion was allowed to either of them, the taxpayers may exclude $500,000 MFJ of gain on their joint return.

Example 3:

Married couple filing jointly—one qualifies—one $250,000 exclusion. Terry and Carol, who are married, sell their residence and file a joint return for the year of the sale. Carol, but not Terry, satisfies the requirements of §121. They are eligible to exclude up to $250,000 of the gain from the sale of the residence because that is the sum of each spouse's dollar limitation amount determined on a separate basis as if they had not been married ($0 for H, $250,000 for W) [§1.121-2(a)(4), Ex. 4].

Investor Hint

This allows a couple to have two principal residences if they are not living together but are still filing jointly. However, this may also require one jointly owned property to be "bifurcated" if one spouse qualifies and the other spouse does not when only one home is owned.

Tax Tip

Single taxpayers with profits in excess of $250,000 may consider marriage to their over-two-year-live-in to gain an additional $250,000 tax shelter! On the other hand, the marriage better last more than two years for those single taxpayers who don't have live-ins. Tax law is now an incentive to keep the marriage together, but only for those taxpayers who didn't live together before marriage.

Partial Interests

One exclusion per residence!   A taxpayer may apply the §121 exclusion on a sale or exchange of less than the homeowner's entire interest in a principal residence. But when a taxpayer sells a partial interest in the taxpayer's principal residence and more than two years later sells the remaining interest in the same property, only one maximum limitation amount of $250,000 ($500,000 for certain joint returns) applies to the combined sales or exchanges of partial interests. The sale or exchange of a partial interest in the same principal residence is treated as one sale or exchange [§1.121-4(e)].

Example:

In 1991, Toby buys a house that he uses as his principal residence. In 2004 Toby's friend Michael moves into Toby's house and Toby sells Michael a 50% interest in the house, realizing a gain of $136,000. Toby may exclude the $136,000 of gain. In 2005 Toby sells his remaining 50% interest in the home to Edwina, realizing a gain of $138,000. Toby may only exclude $114,000 ($250,000 – $136,000 gain previously excluded) of the $138,000 gain from the sale of the remaining interest [§1.121-4(e)(4)].

In applying the maximum limitation amount to sales or exchanges that occur in different taxable years, a taxpayer may exclude gain from the first sale or exchange of a partial interest up to the taxpayer's full maximum limitation amount and may exclude gain from the sale or exchange of any other partial interest in the same principal residence to the extent of any remaining maximum limitation amount, and each spouse is treated as excluding one-half of the gain from a sale or exchange. For purposes of restricting §121 to only one sale or exchange every two years, each sale or exchange of a partial interest is disregarded with respect to other sales or exchanges of partial interests in the same principal residence, but is taken into account as of the date of the sale or exchange in applying the full $250,000/$500,000 MFJ exclusion to that sale or exchange and the sale or exchange of any other principal residence [§1.121-4(e)(1)(ii)].

What About Those Taxpayers Who Previously Used Their "Once-in-a-Lifetime" Exclusion?

They get it back!   These lucky taxpayers get to use both the old and the new §121 without any penalty! "Pre-May 1, 1997, sales are not taken into account," and, therefore, the once-every-two-year rule is "applied without regard to any sale or exchange before May 7, 1997" [§121(b)(3)(B)].

Specialized Tax Planning Ideas

Tax planning for contractors.   This tax provision has created a new tax shelter for building contractors. A housing contractor who builds and occupies his or her own principal residence and sells it two years after completion seems to be eligible to report up to $250,000/$500,000 MFJ tax-free! If a contractor purchases a "fixer-upper," when sold, is it dealer property or a personal residence? We don't know!

Tax planning for deeply depreciated rentals.   This provision will also create a temptation for landlords to convert single-family rentals to a personal residence for two years and exclude up to $250,000 ($500,000 if MFJ) of a normally taxable capital gain (including the gain created by depreciation taken prior to May 7, 1997)!

Tax planning for highly appreciated vacation homes.   Retired taxpayers with highly appreciated vacation homes (e.g., Palm Springs or Aspen condominiums) will be invited by this provision to move into their second home for two years, thereby earning another $250,000 ($500,000 if MFJ) exclusion. Amazing! They need only to remember that they can't use this rule more than once every two years, with three exceptions delineated later.

THE TWO-YEAR "OWN" AND "USE" RULES

The Seller's Property Must Have Been Owned and Used as Principal Residence for At Least Two of the Last Five Years!

During the five-year period ending on the date of the sale or exchange, the taxpayer must have owned and used the property as a principal residence for periods aggregating two years or more. This two-year ownership and use requirement may be satisfied by establishing ownership and use for either 24 full months or 730 days (365 × 2) during the 60-month time period prior to sale [§121(a); §1.121-1(c)(1)].

Investor Hint

Therefore, the ownership and use requirement can be met in two years; if a homeowner owns and uses the same home for two years, he or she has automatically met the "two-of-the-last-five-years requirement."

Tacking of Time Allowed if Previous Home Destroyed or Condemned

For the ownership and use tests, homeowners may add the time they owned and lived in a previous home that was destroyed or condemned to the time they owned and lived in the home on which they wish to exclude gain. This rule applies if any part of the basis of the home they sold depended on the basis of the destroyed or condemned home [§121(g); §121(d)(5); §1.121-4(d)].

Ownership Requirement

When does a sale occur?   Because the three two-year rules end on the "date of sale," accurate length-of-time determination is imperative. The courts first look to the passage of clear title to recognize transfer of ownership of a residence. In those situations when transfer of title is not clear, the date of sale is generally the earlier of the date "a deed passes (generally the date of the delivery of the deed) *or* (in case of an installment sale such as a contract-for-deed) at the time possession and the burdens and benefits of ownership (from a practical standpoint) are transferred to the buyer" [Rev. Rul. 69-93].

Investor Hint

Therefore, the date of recording or even the signing of the deed may not be the correct date. As most home sales are closed using HUD Form 1, the sale date is commonly the date of the closing statement. On installment home sales, the tax proration date or insurance proration date usually indicates that the burdens and benefits have passed.

The possessions test and burdens-and-benefits test.   The Blantons ended up owing tax on the sale of their personal residence because the final settlement date had to be pushed back on the purchase of the replacement residence. They had bought a residence and later moved in before the seller succeeded in clearing up some problems with his title to the property (a third-party ownership claim in bankruptcy court). Technically, then, the former owner did *not* have legal title and therefore he could not legally transfer it to the couple, even though monies for the purchase had already been paid. When the Blantons sold the home some time later, they excluded the gain using the §121 exclusion. However, the Tax Court decided that even though they satisfied the two-year use test, they failed the two-year ownership test. The Court stated the Blantons did not have title during the period that they lived in the home and were awaiting the clearing of title by the former owner.

Legal vs. Equitable Title

But did the court consider whether the benefits and burdens of ownership had actually passed so as to give the couple *equitable title* to the property during the interim period while they waited for the old owner to clear up title problems? The Tax Court found that the Blantons had the right to possess the property, the duty to maintain it, and a limited right to make improvements. Nevertheless, the court determined that the couple did *not* bear the risk of loss, were *not* responsible for any of the property taxes or insurance, could *not* rent the property to other third parties, and did *not* have the right to "obtain legal title at any time by paying the balance of the purchase price." As a result, the court decided that the "benefits and burdens of ownership" had *not* actually passed until the point in time that they received title to the home. They, therefore, failed to satisfy the test enunciated in *Merrill v. Comm.*, 40 T.C. 66 (1963), where the intent to transfer title is important when the actual transfer is "delayed by circumstances beyond the control of the buyer and seller" and the facts support the conclusion that the buyers had "assumed all the benefits and burdens of ownership" [*Blanton v. Comm.*, TC Memo. 1998-211].

Occasional Absences Permitted

Short temporary absences such as vacations or other seasonal absences are counted as periods of use. Absence from the residence due to a one-year sabbatical is not a temporary absence, but a two-month vacation is temporary. The determination of whether an absence is short and temporary depends on the facts and circumstances [§1.121-1(c)(2)(i); §1.121-1(c)(4), ex. 4 & 5].

Flowcharting the Ownership and Use Test:

The "Ownership" Test

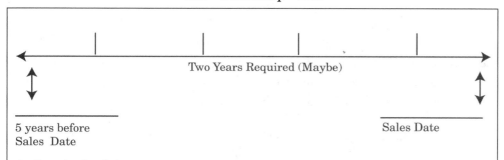

Two Years Required (Maybe)

5 years before
Sales Date

Sales Date

1. Insert sales date.
2. Insert date five years before sales date.
3. During this period, what are the number of days that the home sold was owned: _____days
4. If this number is either 24 full months or 730 days (365 days × 2) during the 60 months prior to sale, the taxpayer has met the required "ownership" test.

The "Use" Test

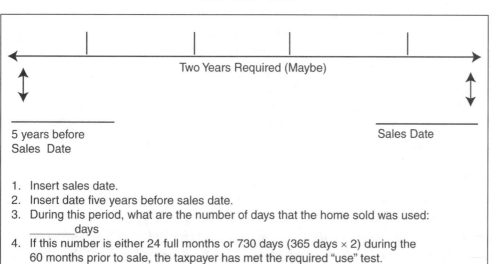

Two Years Required (Maybe)

5 years before
Sales Date

Sales Date

1. Insert sales date.
2. Insert date five years before sales date.
3. During this period, what are the number of days that the home sold was used: _____days
4. If this number is either 24 full months or 730 days (365 days × 2) during the 60 months prior to sale, the taxpayer has met the required "use" test.

The Occupancy Requirement —The Homeowner Must Use the Residence

Use of residence.   As previously stated, for the residence to qualify under the exclusion provision, it must be *purchased and used* by the taxpayer for two years prior to the sale of the old residence. No extension of time is allowed to those taxpayers who are absent from the home for an extended period of time, including members of the uniformed services[1] and the United States Foreign Service, due to employment, but have not purchased a replacement residence.

---

1 For some inexplicable reason, Congress did not include a special relief provision for members of the Armed Forces as contained in prior IRC §1034.

Example:

Two residences qualify within the five-year period. Matilda owns two residences, one in Virginia and one in Maine. During 1999 and 2000, she lives in the Virginia residence. During 2001 and 2002, she lives in the Maine residence. During 2003, she lives in the Virginia residence. Matilda's principal residence during 1999, 2000, and 2003 is the Virginia residence. Her principal residence during 2001 and 2002 is the Maine residence. Matilda would be eligible for the §121 exclusion of gain from the sale or exchange of either residence (but not both) during 2003 [§1.121-1(b)(4), Ex. 2].

"Use" does not necessarily mean "physically occupy"—IRS disagrees. The IRS strictly construes the "use" rule to mean "actually physically occupy," but the Court of Federal Claims rejected this approach for the more liberal "facts and circumstances" test in which both the terms "use" and "principal residence" should be *examined together.* In the *Gummer* case, the taxpayer owned and lived in her home for 22 years before moving into an apartment. Due to declining house values, she didn't sell her home until four years later. On the advice of her REALTOR®, her adult grandchildren lived in the house for 18 months while it was on the market, and she kept furniture in the house to maintain a "lived-in" atmosphere. The Court commented that "depending upon the situation, an individual who does *not* physically occupy the residence for the requisite period may have extenuating circumstances which prevented physical presence but does *not* deny the characterization of 'use' of the property as a 'principal residence' for the requisite time. ... After an absence from the residence is explained under a 'facts and circumstances' test, they may or may not find that the party 'used' the property as their 'principal residence' for the requisite time" [*Gummer v. U.S.*, (FedCl) 98-1 USTC ¶50,401].

The Tax Court has also held that a taxpayer's home did not lose its status as a principal residence while the taxpayer was transitioning to retirement in another state, based on all the facts and circumstances [*Anthony Taylor v. Comm.*, 2001-17].

Example:

IRS disagarees–home used by relative for more than three years not OK. Bobbie owns and uses a house as her principal residence from 1986 to the end of 1999. On January 4, 2000, she moves to another state and ceases to use the house. Bobbie's son moves into the house in March 2001 and uses the residence, rent-free, until it is sold on July 1, 2003. Bobbie may not exclude gain from the sale under §121 because she did not use the property as her principal residence for at least two years out of the five years preceding the sale [§1.121-1(c)(4), Ex. 2].

Only One Year Is Required for the Physically or Mentally Incapacitated

Nursing home exception. A taxpayer who becomes physically or mentally incapable of self-care and who has owned and used a property as a principal residence for at least one year (not two years) during a five-year period is treated as using the property as a residence during any time in which the taxpayer owns the property and resides in a state-licensed facility (including a nursing home) [§121(d)(7); §1.121-1(c)(2)(ii)].

Example:

On January 1, 2003, Edith purchased and moved into her new personal residence. On July 31, 2004, she moved into the Powder River County Memorial Nursing Home but sells her former residence on January 1, 2005. Because Edith owned and occupied the principal residence for at least one year, she is entitled to use the $250,000/$500,000 MFJ exclusion rule. ▪

The Ownership and Use Requirements Do Not Have To Be Met Simultaneously

Satisfaction of both conditions, however, must occur within the five-year period ending on the date of sale or exchange [§1.121-1(c)(1)]. A tenant who purchases the home can count the time as a tenant as part of the *use* requirement. Also, a homeowner can rent out his or her home and still count that time toward the *ownership* requirements [Rev. Rul. 80-172, 1980-2 CB 56].

Example:

Ownership and use at different times OK. Steve rents (as a tenant) a single-family dwelling on January 1, 1999, and vacates the property on January 3, 2001. On December 25, 2001, he purchases the same single-family dwelling and promptly leases it to Donna (a nonrelative). On December 31, 2003, he sells it. Even though he has not used the home as a principal residence for three years, the first $250,000/$500,000 MFJ of gain is non-taxable as long as he has not used the §121 exclusion rule in the last two years (discussed later). But any depreciation taken after May 7, 1997 must be recaptured. Isn't this fun [§1.121-1(c)(4), Ex. 3)]! See Steve's "Ownership and Use" Test on page 36. ▪

$250,000/$500,000 MFJ EXCLUSION AVAILABLE ONLY ONCE EVERY TWO YEARS!

Only One Sale or Exchange Every Two Years

Unless eligible for the reduced maximum exclusion, a taxpayer may not exclude from gross income gain from the sale or exchange of a principal residence if, during the two-year period ending on the date of the sale or exchange, the taxpayer sold or exchanged other property for which gain was excluded under §121 [§121(b)(3)(A)].

Example:

More than one sale in prior two years. Bill sold home No. 1 on December 1, 2003 (which he purchased on May 1, 1995) and excludes $75,000 of gain. He sells home No. 2 on December 30, 2004 (which he purchased on December 15, 2002), and realizes a gain of $100,000. Although Bill meets the two year ownership and use requirements, he cannot exclude any of the gain on home No. 2 as he has sold more than one principal residence within the previous two-year period (between December 30, 2002 and December 30, 2004). ▪

> ### Caution
>
> **The regular exclusion rule is a cliff provision!** The failure to own, or use, a home for the full two years, even by one day, may make the norm-ally tax-free gain become entirely tax-able, i.e., one day the taxpayer doesn't meets the require-ment but the next day he or she would. This type of sudden change in tax results is referred to as a "cliff" provision; or maybe it's called a "cliff" provision be-cause a one-day mistake will drive the homeowner to jump off a cliff!

Steve's "Ownership and Use" Test

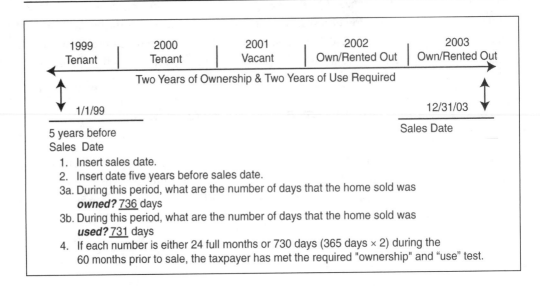

| 1999 Tenant | 2000 Tenant | 2001 Vacant | 2002 Own/Rented Out | 2003 Own/Rented Out |

Two Years of Ownership & Two Years of Use Required

1/1/99

12/31/03

5 years before Sales Date

Sales Date

1. Insert sales date.
2. Insert date five years before sales date.
3a. During this period, what are the number of days that the home sold was *owned?* <u>736</u> days
3b. During this period, what are the number of days that the home sold was *used?* <u>731</u> days
4. If each number is either 24 full months or 730 days (365 days × 2) during the 60 months prior to sale, the taxpayer has met the required "ownership" and "use" test.

SO WHAT HAPPENS IF THE HOMEOWNER CAN'T MEET THE TWO YEAR RULE? NOT TO WORRY—THE REDUCED MAXIMUM EXCLUSION RULE!

Three Exceptions Permit the Homeowner To Still Exclude Some (or All?) of the Gain

If the *primary* reason the homeowner cannot comply with any (or all) of the two-year rules is because of

1. change in place of employment,
2. health, or
3. other unforeseen circumstances, as provided in IRS regulations,

the taxpayer will still be able to exclude a portion of the $250,000/$500,000 MFJ exclusion multiplied by a fraction, the numerator being the shorter of (1) the use period or (2) the period between the two sales dates, and the denominator being two years (730 days). Therefore, taxpayers who have owned or used a principal residence for less than two of the five years preceding the sale or exchange or who have excluded gain from another sale or exchange during the past two years may exclude from gain a reduced maximum amount if the sale or exchange is by reason of a change in place of employment, health, or unforeseen circumstances [§121(c)(2);§1.121-3(a) & (g); TR §1.121-3(b)].

The Formula to Determine the "Reduced Exclusion" Is:

_____	_____	×	_____	=	_____
Own or use days **or** between-sales days	730 days (2 years)		$250,000 or $500,000 MFJ		Maximum excludable gain

Flowcharting That the Exclusion is Only Available Once Every Two Years:

The "Only-Once-Every-Two-Year" Test

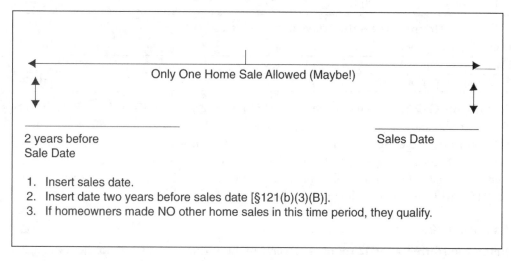

Only One Home Sale Allowed (Maybe!)

2 years before
Sale Date

Sales Date

1. Insert sales date.
2. Insert date two years before sales date [§121(b)(3)(B)].
3. If homeowners made NO other home sales in this time period, they qualify.

Facts and circumstances or various "safe harbors" available.   Taxpayers may establish by the facts and circumstances of their situations that their home sales were for one of the previously mentioned three reasons. In this situation, the taxpayer would deduct the reduced maximum exclusion against the total gain but must be ready to defend his or her position in case of an IRS audit and, if wrong, will be forced to pay back taxes, interest, and penalty. To make things easier for the taxpayer, the IRS has identified various "safe harbors" that will automatically establish that the primary reason for the sale is deemed to be a change in place of employment, health problems, or unforeseen circumstances, thereby eliminating the requirement that the homeowner defend his or her position based on facts and circumstances.

Example 1:

Being transferred more than 50 miles after six months. Jack, a single taxpayer working for AT&T, purchased his Atlanta home on July 1, 1993, and after being transferred to Denver, sold it on August 1, 2003, for a $70,000 gain (nontaxable under §121). He buys a Denver home on July 1, 2003, but after only six months, he is transferred to New York City and sells his Denver home on January 1, 2004, for a $60,000 gain. As he has not owned and used his Denver home for at least two years, his excludable gain is capped by the *shorter period* using the following formulas:

Alternative 1—the "own and use days" rule

Date of current sale:	January 1, 2004
Date five years prior to current sale:	January 1, 1999
Days Denver home owned and used during this period:	
July 1, 2003—Dec. 31, 2003	183 days

Alternative 2—the "days between sales" rule

Date of current sale:	January 1, 2004
Date of previous sale:	August 1, 2003
Total days in period	152 days

Excludable Gain*: 152 days between sales/730 days (2 years) × $250,000 = $52,055*
Result: *The shorter period is 152 days. Therefore. Jack may exclude $51,984 of the $60,000 gain. The entire amount would have been excluded if Jack had been married ($500,000 ÷ 730 days = $685 per day × 152 days = $104,120, but not in excess of the entire gain of $60,000). This excludable amount is capped at $250,000 for single taxpayers and $500,000 MFJ for married filing jointly taxpayers.

Example 2:

Being transferred after 12 months. Twelve months after the purchase of her principal residence, Nancy sells her home due to a change in her place of employment. Even though she has not excluded gain under §121 on a prior sale within the past two years, Nancy is eligible to exclude up to only $125,000 of the gain from the sale of her house (12/24 × $250,000), as she has not owned and used her principal residence for 24 months [§1.121-3(g)(2) Ex. 1].

Example 3:

Use of one spouse's full exclusion and other spouse's reduced exclusion on same home. On January 15, 1999, Bret and Eve marry and Eve begins to use, as her principal residence, Bret's house, which he has owned and used as his principal residence since 1996. On January 15, 2000, Bret sells the house due to a change in Eve's place of employment. Neither Bret nor Eve has excluded gain under §121 on a prior sale or exchange of property within the past two years. Because only Bret has used the house as his principal residence for at least two of the five years prior to its sale, the maximum dollar limitation amount that may be claimed by both will not be $500,000, but instead is the sum of each spouse's limitation amount determined on a separate basis as if they had not been married. Bret is eligible to exclude up to $250,000 of gain because he meets the requirements of §121. Eve is not eligible to exclude the maximum $250,000 exclusion, but because the sale of the house is due to a change in place of employment, she is eligible to claim a reduced maximum exclusion of up to $125,000 of the gain (365/730 × $250,000). Therefore, Bret and Eve are eligible to exclude up to $375,000 of gain ($250,000 + $125,000) from the sale of the house [§1.121-3(g)(2) Ex. 2].

The "Primary Reason for Sale" Requirement

To be eligible to use the reduced exclusion rule, what must first be ascertained is the *primary reason* for the failure to meet any (or all) of the three two-year rules. Once that primary reason is determined, then the taxpayer's *primary reason for the sale or exchange* must be because of

Tax Tip

The advantage to the homeowner of using any safe harbor position is that the IRS agent cannot argue against a safe harbor in an audit.

a change in place of employment, health, or unforeseen circumstances. Whether any of the three requirements are satisfied depends on all the facts and circumstances. In addition, if the taxpayer qualifies for a safe harbor, as described in this section, the taxpayer's primary reason is deemed to be a change in place of employment, health, or unforeseen circumstances. Even if the taxpayer does not qualify for a safe harbor, factors that may be relevant in determining whether the taxpayer's primary reason for the sale or exchange qualifies under the facts and circumstances test include (but are not limited to) the extent to which

- the sale or exchange and the circumstances giving rise to the sale or exchange are proximate in time;
- the suitability of the property as the taxpayer's principal residence materially changes;
- the taxpayer's financial ability to maintain the property materially changes;
- the taxpayer uses the property as the taxpayer's residence during the period of the taxpayer's ownership of the property;
- the circumstances giving rise to the sale or exchange are not reasonably foreseeable when the taxpayer begins using the property as the taxpayer's principal residence; and
- the circumstances giving rise to the sale or exchange occur during the period of the taxpayer's ownership and use of the property as the taxpayer's principal residence.

These factors are suggestive only. No single fact or particular combination of facts is determinative of the taxpayer's entitlement to the reduced maximum exclusion [TR §1.121-3T(b)].

Sale or Exchange by Reason of Change in Place of Employment

Primary reason for home sale must be because of a change in the taxpayer's job location.   If the taxpayer's primary reason for the sale or exchange is a change in the location of the employment of a qualified individual, the reduced exclusion rule is available to the homeowner [TR §1.121-3T(c)(1)].

A **"qualified individual"** includes the taxpayer, the taxpayer's spouse, a co-owner of the residence, or a member of the taxpayer's household [TR §1.121-3T(f)(1-4)].

The following are possible examples:

- A change in the availability in public transportation because of employment location may be considered a primary reason for sale.
- A promotion to an administration position may require a higher level of "entertainment" at home.

Example:

Glen's employer transferred him from the warehouse on 16st Avenue to headquarters on 21th Avenue, five blocks away but on the other side of Interstate 5. Glen can no longer walk to work, so he sells his home after 13 months of ownership and purchases another home on the "right side of the tracks," allowing him to continue walking to work.

Relief available to new employees, transfers, and even the self-employed. Employment means the commencement of employment with a new employer, the continuation of employment with the same employer, or the commencement or continuation of self-employment [TR §1.121-3T(c)(3)].

Example:

Use of "reduced exclusion" by contractors. John Blase, a married contractor who built his personal residence and moved out after six months of occupancy for employment-related purposes, is permitted to exclude up to $125,000 of gain (6/24 × $500,000). Potentially, the "reduced exclusion" provision could be used every six months by simply moving his home office from home to home!

The 50-mile safe harbor rule. A home sale will be considered related to a change in employment (i.e., a safe harbor) if one of the above-mentioned qualified person's new place of work is at least 50 miles farther from the old home than the old workplace was from that home. If the individual was unemployed, the distance between the new place of employment and the residence sold or exchanged must be at least 50 miles. The safe harbor applies only if the change in place of employment occurs during the period of the taxpayer's ownership and use of the property as the taxpayer's principal residence [TR §1.121-3T(c)(2)]. For example:

- An unemployed individual moving more than 50 miles for a new job would qualify [TR §1.121-3T(c)(4), Ex. 1].
- An employed individual being transferred more than 50 miles with the same employer would also qualify [TR §1.121-3T(c)(4), Ex. 2].

Investor Hint

The previous employment requirements of "moving at least 50 miles" and "staying at least 75 percent of the first one- to two-years unless transferred or laid off" requirements have been eliminated and the 50 miles now only becomes a "safe harbor." "Moving at least 50 miles" is still required to deduct employment-related moving expenses [§217(c)(1)].

The facts and circumstances test. If a sale or exchange does not satisfy this 50-mile safe harbor, a taxpayer may still qualify for the reduced maximum exclusion if the facts and circumstances indicate that a change in place of employment is the primary reason for the sale or exchange [TR §1.121-3T(c)(2)].

Example:

Moving only 46 miles but facts confirm change in place of employment. In July 2002, Donna buys a condominium that is five miles from her place of employment and uses it as her principal residence. In February 2003, Donna, who works as an emergency medicine physician, obtains a job that is located 51 miles from her condominium. Donna may be called in to work unscheduled hours and, when called, must be able to arrive at work quickly. Therefore, Donna sells her condominium and buys a townhouse that is four miles from her new place of employment. Because Donna's new place of employment is only 46 miles farther from the condominium than is Donna's former place of employment, the sale is not within the 50-mile safe harbor rule. However, Donna is entitled to claim a reduced maximum exclusion because, under the facts and circumstances, the primary reason for the sale is the change in Donna's place of employment [TR §1.121-3T(c)(4), Ex. 4].

Sale or Exchange by Reason of Health

General rule.   If the *primary reason* a principal residence is required to be sold is related to a disease, illness, or injury[1] of a **"qualified individual,"** who is defined as either

- the taxpayer,
- the taxpayer's spouse,
- a co-owner of the residence,
- a person whose principal place of abode is in the same household as the taxpayer, or
- other close family members of these individuals, such as children, parents, siblings, aunts, uncles, and in-laws [see §152(a)(1) through (8)[2]], even when not living in the same household,

the sale proceeds are eligible for the reduced maximum exclusion rule [TR §1.121-3T(d)(1)].

Qualifying taxpayers include:

- an injured taxpayer who moves in with a daughter [TR §1.121-3T(d)(3), Ex 1];
- a healthy taxpayer who moves closer to an ill parent [TR §1.121-3T(d)(3), Ex. 2];
- taxpayers who move so their child could be closer to a hospital, such as Mayo Clinic [TR §1.121-3T(d)(3), Ex. 3]; and even
- an asthmatic taxpayer who moves from Michigan to Arizona [TR §1.121-3T(d)(3), Ex. 4].

Physician safe harbor rule.   A safe harbor is established if a licensed physician [as defined in §213(d)(4)] recommends a change of residence for the previously described "reasons of health." A sale or exchange that is merely beneficial to the general health or well-being of the individual is not a sale or exchange by reason of health [TR §1.121-3T(d)(1) & (2)].

Example 1:

Taxpayer moving closer to ill parent qualifies. In 2002, Al and Holly purchase a house that they use as their principal residence. In 2003, they sell their house to move into a house closer to Al's father, who has a chronic disease, so that they can provide the care he requires. Because, under the facts and circumstances, the primary reason for the sale of their house is the health of Al's father, Al and Holly are entitled to claim a reduced maximum exclusion [TR §1.121-3T(d)(3), Ex. 2].

---

1 A sale is by reason of health if the primary reason for the sale is to obtain, provide, or facilitate the diagnosis, cure, mitigation, or treatment of disease, illness, or injury of the qualified individual, or obtain or provide medical or personal care for the qualified individual suffering from a disease, illness, or injury [TR §1.121-3T(d)(1)].

2 The definition of qualified individual in the case of health is broader than the definition that applies to the exclusions by reason of change in place of employment and unforeseen circumstances to encompass taxpayers who sell or exchange their residence in order to care for sick family members [TR §1.121-3T(f)(5)].

Example 2:

Taxpayer moving because of physician's recommendation qualifies. Jeff, who has chronic asthma, purchases a house in Minnesota in 2002 that he uses as his principal residence. Jeff's doctor tells him that moving to a warm, dry climate would mitigate his asthma symptoms. In 2003, Jeff sells his house and moves to Arizona to relieve his asthma symptoms. The sale is within the physician's recommendation safe harbor rule and Jeff is entitled to claim a reduced maximum exclusion [TR §1.121-3T(d)(3), Ex. 4]. ■

Example 3:

Taxpayer moving to play golf year-round does not qualify. In 2002, Chuck and Helen purchase a house in Michigan that they use as their principal residence. Chuck's doctor tells him that he should get more exercise, but Chuck is not suffering from any disease that can be treated or mitigated by exercise. In 2003, Chuck and Helen sell their house and move to Florida so that Chuck can increase his general level of exercise by playing golf year-round. Because the sale of the house is merely beneficial to Chuck's general health, the sale of the house is not by reason of his health. Chuck and Helen are not entitled to claim a reduced maximum exclusion [TR §1.121-3T(d)(3), Ex. 5]. ■

Sale or Exchange by Reason of Unforeseen Circumstances

The "primary reason" must be unanticipated. A sale or exchange is by reason of "unforeseen circumstances" if the primary reason for the sale or exchange is the occurrence of an event that the taxpayer did not anticipate before purchasing and occupying the residence [TR §1.121-3T(e)(1)].

Definition of "qualified individual." Sales proceeds or insurance awards are eligible for the reduced maximum exclusion rule if a principal residence is required to be sold because one of the four following individuals—

1. the taxpayer,
2. the taxpayer's spouse,
3. a co-owner of the residence, or
4. a person whose principal place of abode is in the same household as the taxpayer—

experiences an unforeseen circumstance that the homeowner did not anticipate before purchasing and occupying the residence, such as those listed below [TR §1.121-3T(f)].

Safe harbors relating to the physical structure. For example,

- **condemnation or other involuntary conversions:** the home was condemned for public use (e.g., condemned for public highway use) or stolen (e.g., theft of a motor home);
- **damage to home by natural or man-made disaster:** the home was destroyed by a natural disaster (e.g., fire, earthquake, or hurricane) or a man-made disaster (e.g., act-of-war or terrorism) [TR §1.121-3T(e)(3), Ex. 1; also see IRS Notice 2002-60].

Safe harbors relating to a qualified individual. In the case of an above-mentioned qualified individual's

- **death** [TR §1.121-3T(e)(2)],
- **becoming eligible for unemployment compensation:** cessation of employment, making the individual eligible for unemployment compensation [TR §1.121-3T(e)(2)];
- **change in job creates inability to pay mortgage or household expenses:** a change in employment (e.g., a demotion or layoff) or self-employment status that results in the taxpayer's inability to pay housing costs (e.g., homeowner can no longer pay the mortgage payments) and reasonable basic living expenses for the taxpayer's household (including food, clothing, medical expenses, taxes, transportation, court-ordered payments, and reasonable production of income expenses) [TR §1.121-3T(e)(3), Ex. 2];
- **divorce or legal separation:** divorce or legal separation under a decree of divorce or separate maintenance [TR §1.121-3T(e)(2)]; and
- **birth of twins+:** multiple births from the same pregnancy, e.g., the birth of triplets made the recently purchased two-bedroom home too small [TR §1.121-3T(e)(3), Ex. 3; TR §1.121-3T(e)(1)-(3)].

Example:

Inability to make house payments qualifies as an "unforseen circumstance." Douglas, a single taxpayer, is a stockbroker whose place of business in the World Trade Center was destroyed on 9/11. Being unemployed and unable to make his mortgage payments, he sold his home on December 31, 2001, realizing a $50,000 gain. On the date of sale, he had owned the home for 18 months, had used the home as a principal residence for 18 months, and had never used the exclusion rule. The maximum amount of gain excludable under the "reduced exclusion" rule is

18 months	÷	2 years	×	$250,000	=	$187,500
Own or use days **or** between-sales days		730 days (2 years)		$250,000 or $500,000 MFJ		**Maximum excludable gain**

As his total gain was under $187,500, i.e., $50,000, all of it is excludable. ▪

Facts and circumstances.   A taxpayer who does not qualify for one of the above safe harbors may still demonstrate that the primary reason for the sale or exchange is unforeseen circumstances, under a facts and circumstances test, such as

- a radical increase in association dues (e.g., a doubling of condo dues) unanticipated at time of purchase [TR §1.121-3T(e)(3), Ex. 4], or
- engagement breakup [TR §1.121-3T(e)(3), Ex. 6].

Example:

Engagement breakup is an "unforeseen circumstance". In 2003, Dawn and her fiancé Eddie buy a house and live in it as their principal residence. In 2004, Dawn and Eddie cancel their wedding plans, and Eddie moves out of the house. Because Dawn cannot afford to make the monthly mortgage payments alone, Dawn and Eddie sell the house in 2004. Although the safe harbor rules do not apply, under the facts and circumstances, the primary reason for the sale is an "unforeseen circumstance," and Dawn and Eddie are each entitled to claim a reduced maximum exclusion [TR §1.121-3T(e)(3), Ex. 6]. ▪

In addition, the IRS may designate other events or situations as unforeseen circumstances in published guidance of general applicability or in a ruling directed to a specific taxpayer.

Example:

"Heavy traffic" is not sufficient. In 2003, Robert buys a house that he uses as his principal residence. The property is located on a heavily trafficked road. Robert sells the property in 2004 because the traffic is more disturbing than he expected. He is not entitled to claim a reduced maximum exclusion because no safe harbor rules apply and, under the facts and circumstances, the traffic is not an unforeseen circumstance [TR §1.121-3T(e)(3), Ex. 5].

Election to Apply the Maximum Reduced Exclusion Retroactively

Amend return within statutory limitation period permitted! For sales or exchanges between May 7, 1997, and December 24, 2002, taxpayers may elect to apply the provisions of the temporary regulations by filing a return for the taxable year of the sale or exchange, excluding the gain of the principal residence [§1.121-4(j)]. Taxpayers who have already filed a return may generally file an amended return within three years from the original due date [see §6511].

Audit protection. The IRS will not challenge a taxpayer's position that a sale or exchange between May 7, 1997, and December 24, 2002, qualifies for the reduced maximum exclusion if the taxpayer has made a reasonable, good faith effort to comply with the §121 qualification rules and if the sale or exchange otherwise qualifies under §121 [§1.121-4(k)].

Tax Tip

Affected taxpayers who filed 2001 returns and reported gain on the sale of their residence may file an amended return generally within three years.

THE "TACKING OF TIME" RULES

Tacking of a Deceased Spouse's Ownership and Use Allowed

"Tacking" of ownership and use of deceased spouse permitted. If one spouse dies and the home is sold in the year of the deceased spouse's death, the surviving spouse can file as married filing joint, with the $500,000 MFJ exclusion available if *either* spouse had met the three two-year requirements. A taxpayer's period of ownership and use of a residence includes the period during which the taxpayer's deceased spouse owned and used the residence as long as the surviving spouse has not remarried at the time the principal residence is sold [§121(d)(2); §1.121-4(a)(1)]. A surviving spouse is eligible to file a joint return with the decedent spouse only for the year of the decedent spouse's death.

Example:

Deceased spouse's ownership and use passes to surviving spouse. Harry has owned and used a house as his principal residence since 1987. Harry and Anna Nicole marry on July 1, 2003, and from that date they use Harry's house as their principal residence. Harry dies on August 15, 2003, and Anna Nicole inherits the property. She sells the property on September 1, 2003, at which time she has not remarried. Although Anna Nicole has owned and used the house for less than two years, she will be considered to have satisfied the full two-year ownership and use requirements because Anna Nicole's period of ownership and use includes the period that Harry owned and used the property before death [§1.121-4(a)(2), Example].

Caution

The exclusion reduces the next year. When a surviving spouse sells the jointly used principal residence in a year *following* death, the surviving spouse must now file as a single taxpayer, with only the $250,000 exclusion available [§121(d)(2)].

Example:

Home sold after spouse dies. Don and Janice were married on January 1, 2003. At that date, Janice moved into Don's principal residence, which he had owned and used since 1967. Don dies on January 1, 2004, and Janice inherits the property. She continues to use the property as her principal residence until August 31, 2004, at which time she and Don's executor sell it (less than two years after she moved in). She may still make a $500,000 MFJ exclusion because during the five-year period ending on the date of the sale (August 31, 2004), Don had previously satisfied the two-year ownership and use requirements. Janice can "tack" Don's ownership and use to her ownership and use. If she waits until January 1, 2005, she would not need to "tack" Don's time, but she would be able to make only a $250,000 election [§1.121-2(a)(4), Ex. 5 & 6]. ■

Investor Hint

Under current estate taxation, the decedent's share of the principal residence usually experiences a stepped-up basis, eliminating one-half the gain [§1014]. And in a community-property state, the entire basis may be stepped up, depending on how title is held.

TAX PROBLEMS EXPERIENCED AT DIVORCE

Transfer of Residence in Divorce or Legal Separation

When one of the spouses moves out of the residence and starts the divorce or legal separation process, it may take years for the divorce and property settlement to be completed. In dividing up the marital property, the principal residence is usually (a) sold immediately, (b) transferred to one spouse, or (c) delayed and sold in the future as one spouse continues to occupy until some event occurs, such as when the youngest child reaches age 18.

"Tacking" in a Divorce

Tacking of only *ownership* in divorce. When property is transferred between spouses during marriage or transferred incident to a divorce, no gain or loss is recognized and the transfer is treated similar to a gift. No tax form should be filed. This is true even if one of the spouses receives cash for their interest in the home [§1041]. But if a residence is transferred to a taxpayer incident to a divorce or separation agreement, the time during which the taxpayer's spouse or former spouse *owned* the residence can be counted [§121(d)(3)(A); §1.121-4(b)(1)].

Example:

Elizabeth marries and moves into Larry's long-time (more than five years) home on January 1. One month later they divorce, and Elizabeth receives the home as part of her divorce settlement, which she immediately sells for $250,000 cash. Elizabeth's ownership period is deemed five years, not one month. ■

But what about the divorced spouse's *use* period? Tacking of a divorced spouse's previous use was not mentioned in the new exclusion rule. Therefore, it seems not to be permitted.

Example:

As Elizabeth, in the above example, is in possession of the residence at time of sale, she would have to establish her own use period. Therefore, Elizabeth would be able to exclude only 1/24 of any gain because of only one month of use. ▪

Tacking of *use* in divorce allowed in one situation. It is fairly common for divorce courts to order that the family home be sold and the proceeds split between former spouses but that the parent granted custody of the children be given exclusive use of the house rent-free until sale. An individual shall be treated as using property as a principal residence during any period of ownership while such individual's spouse or former spouse is granted use of the property under a divorce or separation instrument [§121(d)(3)(B); §1.121-4(b)(2)]. This law reverses a previous court-created tax provision when the IRS had successfully made the argument that when the use period extended beyond a reasonable time, e.g., two years, the noncustodial parent was not "using" that home as his or her "principal residence" at the time of sale, and taxed the noncustodial parent's gain [*D. D. Bowers v. Comm., T C Memo 1996-333, C. B. Perry v. Comm.,* CA-9, 96-2 USTC ¶50,405].

Example:

Gary and DeAnn's divorce decree requires that they continue to co-own their principal residence after the divorce, with DeAnn granted custody of the children and granted use of the home until the youngest child reaches the age of majority, at which time the home is required to be sold and the proceeds divided evenly. DeAnn can exclude $250,000 of gain once she meets the two-year ownership and use rules, assuming she hasn't used the exclusion rule in the past two years. Additionally, because Gary has owned the property jointly with DeAnn, he can "tack" DeAnn's use to his previous use to meet the two-year use rule. As long as he has not used the exclusion rule within the past two years, he can also exclude $250,000 of gain. ▪

Could this involve property sold 12 years after divorce? Probably, as no time limit was included in the law or regulations.

A Property Settlement in a Divorce May Move the Entire Gain to Just One Spouse

Transfer of property in divorce is a tax-free gift. As previously mentioned, there is generally no gain or loss recognized for transfers of property between spouses. Further, there is no recognition of gain or loss on the transfer of property to a former spouse if the transfer is incident to a divorce [§1041].

Example:

Georgie Ann and Bob own a $490,000 home purchased 20 years before for $60,000 and a $490,000 condo in Aspen with a basis of $490,000. Neither property is encumbered with debt. They get divorced. The divorce court awards the house (and children) to Georgie Ann and the condo to Bob. The following tax shifting occurs:

	Total	Georgie Ann	Bob
Fair market value	$980,000	$490,000	$490,000
Adjusted basis	*550,000*	60,000	$490,000
Total gain	$430,000	$430,000	$ 0

This results in Bob's half of the inherent long-term capital gain being transferred to Georgie Ann. For example, if both parties sell their divided properties the year after the divorce, Bob will pocket $490,000 tax-free and Georgie Ann will find $180,000 ($430,000 – $250,000 exclusion) of long-term capital gain on her single tax return! ▨

The basic policy of §1041 is to treat a husband and wife as one economic unit and to defer, but not eliminate, the recognition of any gain or loss on interspousal property transfers until the property is conveyed to a third party outside the economic unit. To that end, no gain or loss is recognized on the transfer of property from one spouse to another. The property takes a transferred ("carryover") basis in the hands of the recipient spouse; the carryover basis preserves the gain (or loss) until the recipient spouse transfers the property to a third party in a taxable transaction.

Example:

Don and Debbie were recently divorced. Debbie owns raw land with a value of $100,000 and a basis of $10,000. Pursuant to the divorce instrument, Debbie transfers the raw land to Don for $100,000 cash. Because the transfer is incident to a divorce, Debbie does not recognize her realized gain of $90,000. However, Don's basis in the raw land is $10,000, the basis of the transferred property in the hands of the transferor (Debbie) immediately before the transfer [TR §1.1041-1T Q&A 1, 10, & 11]. ▨

PROBLEMS WITH UNUSUAL DISPOSITIONS OF PRINCIPAL RESIDENCES

Unusual Dispositions of Principal Residences

All principal residence dispositions are not cash sales. If they were, life would be simple, but not interesting.

An exchange. Instead of selling a principal residence, homeowners occasionally exchange one personal residence for another personal residence (common in farm exchanges). Exchanges of personal residences are not eligible for tax-free exchanges, and the trading of an old home for another home is treated as a §121 sale. Therefore, the §121 rules apply both to sales *and exchanges* of homes [§1031(a)(1)].

A destroyed or condemned home. When the destruction, theft, seizure, requisition, or condemnation of the principal residence occurs, the taxpayer may use the §1033 two-year rollover of gain provisions *after* applying the $250,000/$500,000 MFJ §121 exclusion rules. The holding and use by the taxpayer of the converted property is tacked to the new property [§121(d)(5); §1.121-4(d)].

The two-year replacement period: The §1033 replacement period begins on the earlier of the date the (a) condemned property was disposed of or (b) condemnation was threatened. The replacement period generally ends two years after the close of the first tax year in which the homeowner realizes any part of the gain on the condemnation [§1033(a)(2)(B)].

Example 1:

Bill and Sandy's home was destroyed by a tornado. Their basis in the residence (but not the land) is $650,000. They receive a $2,000,000 insurance settlement, resulting in a $1,350,000 realized gain. As Bill and Sandy are married, owned and used that home for more than two years, and plan to file jointly, they can exclude $500,000 of the gain [§121]. But they must reinvest $1,500,000 ($2,000,000 – $500,000 exclusion) to avoid recognizing the rest of the gain (under §1033).

Example 2:

On February 18, 2003, fire destroys Sara's house, which has an adjusted basis of $80,000. She had owned and used this property as her principal residence for 20 years prior to its destruction. Sara's insurance company pays her $400,000 for the house and she realizes a gain of $320,000 ($400,000 – $80,000). On August 27, 2004, Sara purchases a new house at a cost of $100,000. Because the destruction of the house is treated as a sale for purposes of §121, Sara will exclude $250,000 of the realized gain from her gross income. For purposes of the §1033 involuntary conversion rules, the amount realized is then treated as being $150,000 ($400,000 – $250,000) and the gain realized is $70,000 ($150,000 amount realized – $80,000 basis). Sara elects under §1033 to recognize only $50,000 of the gain ($150,000 amount realized – $100,000 cost of new house). The remaining $20,000 of gain is deferred, and Sara's basis in the new house is $80,000 ($100,000 cost – $20,000 gain not recognized). Sara will be treated as owning and using the new house as her principal residence during the 20-year period that she owned and used the destroyed house [§1.121-4(d)(4), Ex.].

A foreclosure. The foreclosure or repossession of a principal residence is considered a home "sale" subject to the $250,000/$500,000 MFJ exclusion rules. If the foreclosure "sale" results in a taxable gain (i.e., more than $250,000/$500,000), report this capital gain on Schedule D, Form 1040. Cancellation of any debt (COD) on foreclosure or repossession *may* create *ordinary* income (reported on Form 1040, line 21 as other income), in addition to potential capital gain. This generally occurs when the canceled debt is more than the home's fair market value. Bankruptcy and insolvency relief provisions are available against COD income but not against capital gain [§61(a)(12); §108]. The amount of the gain or loss depends, in part, on whether the taxpayer is personally liable for repaying the debt secured by the home, as shown in the following chart:

If taxpayer is:	Then the selling price includes:
Not personally liable for the debt	The full amount of debt cancelled by the foreclosure or repossession.
Personally liable for the debt	The amount of canceled debt up to the home's fair market value. The taxpayer may also have ordinary income.

Investor Hint

The homeowner is required to inform the IRS what type of income was created, i.e., capital gain or ordinary income. Most homeowners would prefer receiving a capital gain so they can exclude up to $250,000/$500,000. COD income can only be excluded if the homeowner is bankrupt, insolvent, or under certain other technical exceptions.

Investor Hint

Upon foreclosures or repossessions, lenders generally send the homeowner a Form 1099-A (Acquisition or Abandonment of Secured Property). When a debt is canceled, borrowers may receive a Form 1099-C (Cancellation of Debt) instead of Form 1099-A.

Bankruptcy estate may also use the exclusion! Even though the home is owned by a bankruptcy estate of an individual in a Chapter 7 or 11 bankruptcy case, such sales are still eligible for the exclusion of up to $500,000, given the other requirements are met (i.e., the three separate "two-year tests"). Additionally, the IRS will not challenge a position taken prior to December 24, 2002 (the effective date of the final regulations) that a bankruptcy estate may use the §121 exclusion [(§1.1398-3]. [Also see IRS's acquiescence in the case of *Internal Revenue Service v. Waldschmidt (In re Bradley)*, 222 B.R. 313 (M.D. Tenn. 1998), AOD CC-1999-009 (August 30, 1999), and Chief Counsel Notice (35)000-162 (August 10, 1999); *Popa, L.L., In re* (BC-DC) 98-1 USTC ¶50,276; *Kerr, G.T.*, D.C., Wash. 99-1 USTC ¶50,310].

Investor Hint

This is a reversal of both IRS and bankruptcy court positions taken in prior statute §121 cases that held a bankruptcy trustee could *not* use the one-time exclusion for individuals over 55 [*In re Mehr*, 153 B.R. 430 (Bankr. D. N.J. 1993); *In re Barden*, 205 B.R. 451 (E.D. N.Y. 1996), aff'd, 105 F.3d 821 (2d Cir. 1997)].

Ownership by trusts.   If a residence is held by a trust, a taxpayer is treated as the owner and the seller of the residence during the period that the taxpayer is treated as the owner of the trust or the portion of the trust that includes the residence under §§671 - 679 [§1.121-1(c)(3)]. Therefore, the regulations confirm the holdings of Rev. Rul. 66-159 and Rev. Rul. 85-45 regarding treatment of sales of property by certain trusts [also Rev. Rul. 54-583].

Rev. Rul. 66-159 holds that, in cases in which the grantor is treated as the owner of the entire trust under §676 and §671, gain realized from the sale of trust property used by the grantor as the grantor's principal residence qualifies under former §1034 for the roll-over of gain into a replacement residence. Because the grantor is treated as the owner of the entire trust, the sale by the trust will be treated for federal income tax purposes as if made by the grantor.

Tax Tip

Property can be held in a grantor-type trust.

Rev. Rul. 85-45 holds that, in cases in which the beneficiary of a trust is treated as the owner of the entire trust under §678 and §671, gain realized from the sale of trust property used by the beneficiary as the beneficiary's principal residence qualifies for the one-time exclusion of gain from the sale of a residence under former §121. For the period that the beneficiary is treated as the owner of the entire trust, the beneficiary will be treated as owning the property for §121 purposes, and the sale by the trust will be treated for federal income tax purposes as if made by the beneficiary.

Ownership by certain single owner entities, e.g. LLCs.   If a residence is owned by an eligible entity [within the meaning of §301.7701-3(a)] that has a single owner and is disregarded for federal tax purposes as an entity separate from its owner under §301.7701-3, the owner will be treated as owning the residence for purposes of satisfying the two-year ownership requirement of §121, and the sale or exchange by the entity will be treated as if made by the owner.

Tenant-stockholder gets same benefits as homeowner.   The owner of an apartment in a cooperative is called a *tenant-stockholder*. The tenant-stockholder receives a "share of stock" as evidence of ownership, along with a proprietary lease of a specific unit, from the cooperative housing corporation. Sales of the tenant-stockholder's share of stock are eligible for the §121 exclusion. The holding requirements apply to the stock ownership and the use requirements apply to the unit the taxpayer is entitled to occupy [§121(d)(3); §1.121-4(c)].

A sale of a remainder interest is eligible for this exclusion.   Occasionally, homeowners will sell or transfer their principal residence, but retain the right to possess the home until death (an interesting estate planning device). This right of possession is called a *remainder interest* which can be sold, but the purchaser of a remainder interest can maintain possession only as long as the grantor of the remainder interest is alive. At the election of the taxpayer, the gain from the sale or exchange of the remainder interest (but no other type of interest) in a principal residence may use the $250,000/$500,000 MFJ exclusion, unless the sale is to a related party, [as defined both by §267(b) and §707(b), which includes both lineal decedents and over 50% owned corporations and partnerships]. In addition, a taxpayer may make or revoke this election at any time before the expiration of a three-year period beginning on the last date prescribed by law (determined without regard to extensions) for the filing of the return for the taxable year in which the sale or exchange occurred [§121(d)(8); §1.121-4(e)(2)].

PROBLEMS WHEN HOME USED FOR BOTH PERSONAL AND BUSINESS PURPOSES

Can We Rent the House during the Five Year Period?

As long as the home is owned and used as a principal residence two out of the five years prior to sale date, it retains its personal residence character and does not switch to a taxable rental property [§121(a)].

No Residence Exists if the Home Is Converted into a Rental for More than Three Years

Rental less than three years eligible for exclusion.   A homeowner who converts a principal residence into a rental may be faced with a realized and taxable gain in a future sale. Once the personal residence has been rented for more than three of the past five years, the $250,000/$500,000 MFJ exclusion rule is not usable because the property is no longer deemed a principal residence. The taxpayer would be required to reoccupy the property as a principal residence to equal two of the last five years before the sale to reestablish the principal residence status.

Tax Tip

This is one of the most common questions asked of tax practitioners, and the answer is *no exclusion for rentals!* Rentals may use the like-kind exchange rules to defer gain.

Investor Hint

Unanswered is this question: "Does this mean that for a taxpayer to convert a personal residence into a rental eligible for a like-kind exchange, it must be rented for more than three years?" No bright-line time test exists for "holding" a business or investment asset for §1031 purposes. Generally, this proof is demonstrated by the intent of the taxpayer to hold the asset for business or investment purposes, the time period being only one factor. It generally is more important that the taxpayer show a "change-in-mind/change-in-heart" after acquisition of the replacement property.

Example:

Home rented for less than three years OK. Jim has owned and used his house as his principal residence since 1986. On January 31, 2002, he moves to another state. Jim rents his house to tenants from that date until April 18, 2004, when he sells it. Jim is eligible for the §121 exclusion because he has owned and used the house as his principal residence for at least two of the five years preceding the sale [1.121-1(c)(4), Ex. 1]. ■

The prior problem with renting a personal residence. When a personal residence is listed for sale in a "down" or "slow" market, it is common to rent the house until it is sold. Under prior law, care was needed to ensure that the property retained its personal residence character and didn't convert to a rental (which wasn't eligible to use either the prior rollover provision or the prior exclusion rule). The present §121 provides a definitive period of time, three out of five years, during which the home can be rented before it converts into a rental ineligible to use the $250,000/$500,000 MFJ exclusion rule.

Can We Depreciate the Home While it Is Being Rented?

Yes. We can depreciate a personal residence! In *Bolaris v. Comm.,* [81 TC 840 (1983); 776 F2d 1428 (9th Cir 1985)], the Tax Court held as proper the taxpayer's deduction of rental expenses and "residential" depreciation. The court held that a residence that qualifies for the principal residence provisions may also qualify as property held for the production of income and, therefore, allowed *Bolaris* to not only take depreciation but also to defer the ensuing (prior law) gain [see also *Grant v. Comm,* 84 TC 809 (1985)].

> **Caution**
>
> **Depreciation taken after May 6, 1997 must be recaptured!** Any gain attributable to depreciation taken after May 6, 1997 with respect to the prior rental or business use of the principal residence must be recognized in the year of the sale (but, interestingly, not an exchange) [§121(d)(6); §1.121-

> **Tax Tip**
>
> This "tax loophole" allows homeowners to rent the house for up to three years while striving to sell it. Many taxpayers will be tempted to rent their residence and wait for someone to agree to their asking price instead of accepting a lower counter-offer. Additionally, there is no need to keep the property listed during the rental period, as was required under prior law [*Clapham v. Comm.,* 63TC 505 (1975)].

> **Investor Hint**
>
> Therefore, 65.753% of the 1997 depreciation must be recaptured. The period of May 7 through December 31, 1997 is 240 days.

Example:

Post-5/7/97 depreciation must be recaptured. On July 1, 2001, Alfred moves into a house that he owns and had rented to tenants since July 1, 1999. Alfred took depreciation deductions totaling $14,000 for the period that he rented the property. After using the residence as his principal residence for two full years, he sells the property on August 1, 2003. Alfred's gain realized from the sale is $40,000. Only $26,000 ($40,000 gain realized - $14,000 depreciation deductions) may be excluded under §121. Alfred must recognize $14,000 of the gain as unrecaptured depreciation [§1.121-1(d)(2), Example]. ■

What happens if the taxpayer decides not to take the depreciation allowable on a home office? Does the taxpayer still have to recapture the depreciation?   "Depreciation adjustment" is defined as a deduction "allowed or allowable to the taxpayer," which is an adjustment to basis for calculation of gain purposes [§1016; §1250(b)(3)]. Comparing the allowed depreciation (zero when the taxpayer takes no depreciation) or the allowable (presumably greater than zero), the amount to be recaptured is presumably the greater of the two [§1.1016-3(a)(1)]. Therefore, even if the depreciation is not claimed, the adjusted basis of the property must be reduced by the allowable depreciation. ▪

Example:

Gain on office-in-home portion not taxable, but depreciation recaptured. Betty, an attorney, buys a house in 2003. The house constitutes a single dwelling unit but Betty uses a portion of the house as a law office. She claims depreciation deductions of $2,000 during the period that she owns the house. Betty sells the house in 2006, realizing a gain of $13,000. Betty must recognize $2,000 of the gain as depreciation recapture [§1.121-1(e)(4), Ex. 5]. What about the gain other than the depreciation recapture? ▪

Home Used for Both Personal and Business Purposes on Sale Date

Law excludes home gain even on portion used as office-in-home!   No allocation of gain is required if both the residential and nonresidential portions of the property are within the same dwelling unit. The fact that a residence is rented or is used partially for business (i.e., a home office) at the time of sale does not disqualify the gain attributable to the business use, other than depreciation recapture, from the $250,000/$500,000 exclusion. But the §121 exclusion will not apply to the gain allocable to any portion of property sold or exchanged with respect to which a taxpayer does not satisfy the use requirement if the nonresidential portion is separate from the dwelling unit [§1.121-1(e)(1)]. The final regulations provide that the term *dwelling unit* has the same meaning as in §280A(f)(1) but does not include appurtenant structures or other property [§1.121-1(e)(2)].

Example:

Joan sells her personal residence, which contains her deductible office-in-home, for a $100,000 gain. She estimates that the office occupies 10% of her home. She can exclude the entire $100,000 gain other than any depreciation recapture. The $10,000 gain associated with the office-in-home is not taxable. ▪

Investor Hint

This is a reversal of prior IRS pronouncements [see previous §1.1034-1(c)(3)(ii)] and Tax Court cases [*Poague, William W.*, DC-Va 90-2 USTC ¶50,539], which ruled that if the residence was used partially for residential purposes and partially for business purposes (mixed-use property), only that part of the gain allocable to the residential portion was excludable under §121.

Tax Tip

This makes the office-in-home deduction extraordinarily attractive, i.e., a taxpayer is allowed a current tax break with no future taxable gain at time of sale! No longer does the homeowner need to convert the home office back to personal use for two of the last five years to eliminate the gain associated with the prior business use as previously permitted by Rev. Rul. 82-26. Additionally, because taxpayers may elect to adopt these regulations retroactively, this might create a refund for taxpayers who previously reported taxable gain allocable to the business portion of the home in an amount in excess of the depreciation claimed after May 6, 1997.

Tax planning for contractors.   This tax provision has created a new tax shelter for a housing contractor who builds and occupies his or her own principal residence and sells it six months after completion. The contractor seems to be eligible to report up to $125,000 MFJ tax-free—every six months—assuming the contractor moves his or her home office (to use the reduced exclusion rule).

Depreciation recapture still required on office-in-home!   But §121 does not apply to the gain to the extent of any post–May 6, 1997, depreciation adjustments [§1.121-1(e)(1)]. If the depreciation for periods after May 6, 1997 attributable to the nonresidential portion of the property exceeds the gain allocable to the nonresidential portion of the property, the excess will not reduce the §121 exclusion applicable to gain allocable to the residential portion of the property. The taxpayer must use the same method to allocate the basis and the amount realized between the business and residential portions of the property as the taxpayer used to allocate the basis for purposes of depreciation, if applicable [§1.121-1(e)(3)].

Example 1:

Gain on ranch taxable, ranch home not taxable. John owns a property that consists of a house, a stable, and 35 acres. He uses the stable and 28 acres for business (nonresidential) purposes for more than three years during the five-year period preceding the sale. John uses the entire house and the remaining seven acres as his principal residence for at least two years during the five-year period preceding the sale. For periods after May 6, 1997, John claims depreciation deductions of $9,000 for the business use of the stable. He sells the entire property in 2004, realizing a gain of $24,000. Because the stable and the 28 acres used in the business are separate from the dwelling unit, the allocation rules apply and John must allocate the basis and amount realized between the portion of the property that he used as his principal residence and the portion of the property that he used for nonresidential purposes. John determines that $14,000 of the gain is allocable to the nonresidential-use portion of the property and that $10,000 of the gain is allocable to the portion of the property used as his residence. He must recognize the $14,000 of gain allocable to the nonresidential-use portion of the property ($9,000 of which is depreciation recapture and $5,000 of which is adjusted net capital gain). John may exclude $10,000 of the gain from the sale of the property [§1.121-1(e)(4), Ex. 1 & 2].

Example 2:

Basement apartment considered a separate dwelling unit, no exclusion on rental portion. In 2002, Lou buys a three-story townhouse and converts the basement level, which has a separate entrance, into a separate apartment by installing a kitchen and bathroom and removing the interior stairway that leads from the basement to the upper floors. After the conversion, the property constitutes two dwelling units [see §121-1(e)(2)]. Lou uses the first and second floors of the townhouse as his principal residence and rents the basement level to tenants from 2003 to 2007. Lou claims depreciation deductions of $2,000 for that period with respect to the basement apartment. He sells the entire property in 2007, realizing a gain of $18,000. Because the basement apartment and the upper floors of the townhouse are separate dwelling units, Lou must allocate the gain between the portion of the property that he used as his principal residence and the portion of the property that he used for nonresidential purposes. After allocating the basis and the amount realized between the residential and nonresidential portions of the property, Lou determines that $6,000 of the gain is allocable to the nonresidential portion of the property and that $12,000 of the gain is allocable to the portion of the property used as his residence. Lou must recognize the $6,000 of gain allocable to the nonresidential portion of the property ($2,000 of which is depreciation recapture and $4,000 of which is adjusted net capital gain). Lou may exclude $12,000 of the gain from the sale of the property [§1.121-1(e)(4), Ex. 3]. ■

Example 3:

Basement apartment unit converted back to residential use for 2+ years OK. The facts are the same as in Example 2, except that in 2007 Lou incorporates the basement of the townhouse into his principal residence by eliminating the kitchen and building a new interior stairway to the upper floors. Lou uses all three floors of the townhouse as his principal residence for two full years and sells the townhouse in 2010, realizing a gain of $20,000. Lou must recognize $2,000 of the gain as depreciation recapture. Because Lou used the entire three floors of the townhouse as his principal residence for two of the five years preceding the sale of the property, he may exclude the remaining $18,000 of the gain from the sale of the house [§1.121-1(e)(4), Ex. 4]. ■

Example 4:

Gain on office-in-home portion not taxable, but depreciation recaptured. Betty, an attorney, buys a house in 2003. The house constitutes a single dwelling unit, but Betty uses a portion of the house as a law office. She claims depreciation deductions of $2,000 during the period that she owns the house. Betty sells the house in 2006, realizing a gain of $13,000. Betty must recognize $2,000 of the gain as depreciation recapture. She may exclude the remaining $11,000 of the gain from the sale of her house because she is not required to allocate gain to the business use within the dwelling unit [§1.121-1(e)(4), Ex. 5]. ■

Example 5:

No gain or depreciation recapture on nondeductible office-in-home. The facts are the same as in Example 4, except that Betty is not entitled to claim any depreciation deductions with respect to her business use of the house. Betty may exclude all $13,000 of the gain from the sale of her house because she is not required to allocate gain to the business use within the dwelling unit [§1.121-1(e)(4), Ex. 6]. ■

How Much Land Can Be Sold with the Personal Residence?

The vacant land rule—when the home sale exclusion may include gain from the sale of surrounding land. Under what circumstances may vacant land surrounding a residential structure be treated as part of the residence for §121 exclusion purposes? Gain on land considered part of a personal residence can be excluded, but gain on land considered investment property held for appreciation, or business property held for profit, is taxable and may not use the exclusion provisions. A sale of vacant land that does not include a dwelling unit does not qualify as a sale of a taxpayer's residence [§1.121-1(b)(3); Rev. Rul. 56-240; Rev. Rul. 83-50; *O'Barr v. Commissioner*, 44 T.C. 501 (1965); *Roy v. Commissioner*, T.C. Memo. 1995-23; *Hale v. Commissioner*, T.C. Memo. 1982-527]. However, if

- *land is adjacent to home:* the vacant land is adjacent to land containing the principal residence;
- *two-year ownership and use:* the vacant land was owned and used as part of the taxpayer's principal residence;
- *sale of land within two years of sale of home:* the sale or exchange of the dwelling unit occurs within two years before or after the sale or exchange of the vacant land; and
- the sale or exchange of the vacant land satisfies all other §121 requirements, then

the sale of vacant land and the sale of the principal residence is treated as one sale eligible for the §121 exclusion [§1.121-1(b)(3)(i)(A - D; also see *Bogley v. Commissioner*, 263 F.2d 746 (4th Cir. 1959); Rev. Rul. 76-541]. Judicial factors used to determine whether the surrounding land is being used for residential purpose include enjoying unobstructed views of the countryside, living in open spaces, appreciating nature, hiking, and enjoying horseback riding. Only one maximum limitation amount of $250,000 ($500,000 MFJ) applies to the combined sales or exchanges of the vacant land and dwelling unit [§1.121-1(b)(3)(ii)].

Example 1:

Vacant land and home sold to two separate buyers OK. In 1998 Chad buys a house and one acre that he uses as his principal residence. In 1999 he buys 29 acres adjacent to his house and uses the vacant land as part of his principal residence. In 2003 Chad sells the house and one acre and the 29 acres in two separate transactions. He sells the house and one acre at a loss of $25,000. Chad realizes $270,000 of gain from the sale of the 29 acres and may exclude the $245,000 gain from the two sales [§1.121-1(b)(4), Ex. 4].

Example 2:

Vacant land sold, home sold two years later, amended return permitted. In 1991, Sandy buys property consisting of a house and ten acres that she uses as her principal residence. In May 2005, Sandy sells eight acres of the land and realizes a gain of $110,000. She does not sell the dwelling unit before the due date for filing her 2005 return. Therefore Sandy is not eligible to exclude the $110,000 of gain. In March 2007, she sells the house and remaining two acres, realizing a gain of $180,000 from the sale of the house. Sandy may exclude the $180,000 of gain. Additionally, because the sale of the eight acres occurred within two years from the date of the sale of the dwelling unit, the sale of the eight acres is also treated as a sale of the taxpayer's principal residence [see §1.121-1(b)(3)]. Sandy may file an amended return for 2005 to claim an exclusion for $70,000 ($250,000 − $180,000 gain previously excluded) of the $110,000 gain from the sale of the eight acres [§1.121-1(b)(4), Ex. 3].

How Much Acreage Can Be Considered as Part of the Residence When Calculating the §121 Gain Exclusion?

Example:

Farmer McDonald, in contemplating a move to Florida, decides to sell his farm. He receives $1,200,000 for the house, farm buildings, outbuildings, and 500 acres, resulting in a $500,000 MFJ gain. Can he exclude the entire $500,000 MFJ gain? *We know he will try!*

Answer:

No. Only the gain on the personal residence and the land associated with the residence can be excluded.

	Total (500 acres)	Farm (495 acres)	Home (5 acres)
Sales Price	$1,200,000	$1,000,000	$200,000
Adjusted Basis	− 700,000	− 650,000	− 50,000
Total Gain	$ 500,000	$ 350,000	$150,000
		(Taxable)	(Excludable)

Investor Hint

This is an appraiser's relief act! With up to $500,000 MFJ of gain at stake, valuation of multiuse property such as farm property will become one of the largest tax litigation areas in the near future!

It is a "facts and circumstances" test.   An allocation has to be made when "property is used by the taxpayer as his principal residence and part is used for other (investment or business) purposes" [§1.121-1(b)(3)(i)(A - D)].

So how many acres?   Prior IRS rulings and court cases have consistently allowed five to ten acres as part of the residence [*Estate of F. Russell Campbell*, 23 TCM (CCH) 508 (1964); Rev. Rul. 76-541, 1976-2 CB 246; *Bogley v. Comm., 263 F2d 746 (4th Cir 1959)*].

The "one-acre" rule!   Unofficially, the IRS, in farm communities, considers one acre to be associated with the home unless the taxpayer proves that more than one acre is not used for income-producing purposes.

Tax Tip

How much land qualifies when a personal residence is located on a 20-acre "ranchette?" Probably all 20 acres, as the entire acreage is being used for personal purposes.

The following are cases to look at to see arguments that other taxpayers have used to prove to the court that a substantial portion of acreage should be included with the house sale.

Bennett, 8 AFTR2d 5593 (DC Ga., 1961)	All 65 acres considered part of personal residence
Richards, TCM 1993-422	28 of 158 acres considered part of personal residence
OZ Roy, TCM 1995-23	all 100 acres considered part of personal residence
Schlicher, TCM 1997-37	43 of 51 acres considered part of personal residence

Example:

Bob and Janet purchased their home in 1996. In 1997, to protect their view and provide more open space, they purchased the vacant lot next door. They have landscaped the neighboring lot to be part of the usable space for their personal residence. Landscaping includes swings and a sandbox for their grandchildren and they park their RV on the back part of the lot. The facts and circumstances indicate that Bob and Janet intend the lot to be a part of their personal residence. Thus, at the sale of the house and adjoining lot, the gain on the lot would be part of the excludable §121 gain. ▪

Tax Tip

If the taxpayer wants appreciated acreage to be considered part of his or her personal residence for the §121 gain exclusion, he or she should consider the following cautions:

- Do use the property for bona fide residential purposes.
- Do report mortgage interest and taxes on Schedule A.
- Don't use the acreage for business or agricultural use within two years of sale.
- Don't claim farm or business losses on the tax return for at least two years prior to sale.
- Don't show the taxpayer's occupation as farmer or rancher.
- Don't claim a county property tax exemption for farming or agriculture.

HOW TO CALCULATE THE GAIN ON A RESIDENTIAL SALE
The Calculations Required Before Excluding the Gain

Once it has been determined that the sale of the home qualifies for the exclusion-of-gain provision, the homeowner must calculate the realized gain but only reports the taxable gain (if any). This requires a review of the gain (or loss) computation.

Amount of gain on sale of a personal residence.   To calculate the amount of gain on a sale of a personal residence, subtract the selling costs and the adjusted basis from the sales price. The only time depreciation expense is subtracted is when part or all of the house has been used both for business and personal use (e.g., a deductible office-in-home).

Gain or Loss Computation

Sales price		+	$
Less:	Selling expenses	–	
Equals:	Amount realized	=	$
Less:	Adjusted basis		
	Original cost (or basis)	+	
	Plus: Improvements	+	
	Less: Accumulated depreciation	–	
	Equals: Total adjusted basis	–	
Less:	**Deferred gain from prior home sale**	–	
Gain Realized on Sale		=	$

Selling price.   The selling price of the personal residence is calculated using the following formula: the total consideration received, including the amount of cash received, any liabilities the purchaser either assumed or took the property subject to, and the fair market value of *any* other property received [§1001(b)]. If an option to buy was granted and the option was exercised, add the amount the home seller received for the option to the selling price [§1234].

Tax Tip

In most residential sales, the selling price will agree with the Uniform Settlement Statement, HUD Form 1.

Personal property sold is not to be included in the sales price. The selling price of the residence does not include amounts received for personal property (e.g., refrigerator, stove, drapes, furniture, etc.). If personal property is acquired along with the real property, the personal property is assumed to have a zero value [see §1.121-1(b)(1) and previous §1034(c)(2); §1.1034-1(c)(3)(i)].

Selling expenses.   The selling expenses associated with the sale of a personal residence include the expenses incurred to consummate the sales transaction, such as the real estate commission and title insurance. Selling expenses reduce the selling price to arrive at the *amount realized*, sometimes called *net sales price*.

Tax Tip

Selling expenses are usually listed on the Uniform Settlement Statement, HUD Form 1.

Investor Hint

Employees must include in W-2 income (on line 7 of Form 1040) any amount the employer reimburses for expenses of the sale when being transferred to a new location. This amount *cannot* be netted against the selling expenses.

Selling expenses do not include repairs or improvements to prepare the property for sale. Selling expenses do not include any expenses that physically affect the property (e.g., repairs or improvements), even if they are to prepare the property for sale.

Example:

Betty Broker instructs Sammy to spend $2,500 sprucing up his property to get it ready for sale. Is this a selling expense? Surprisingly, the answer is NO, even though Sam would never have spent the money if Betty hadn't told him it was necessary to make the property salable. Sam's $2,500 physically affected the home. Therefore, *it is not a selling expense.* (Maybe it is a repair or an improvement, as discussed below.)

Selling expenses do not include most prorated items, such as fire insurance, real estate taxes, advances on utilities, interest, and the like, even though these items may be "hidden" in the sales price. The buyer and the seller must deduct the real estate taxes for the year of sale according to the number of days in the real property tax year that each owned the home. The seller is treated as paying the taxes up to, but not including, the date of sale. The buyer is treated as paying the taxes beginning with the date of sale.

Investor Hint

If the buyer does pay the seller's share of the taxes (or any delinquent taxes owed by the seller), the payment increases the selling/purchase price of the home. The seller, not the buyer, would be able to deduct the taxes paid by the buyer [§1001(b)]. At first glance, this looks like the seller can net the amounts (by the fact that the sales price increased by the exact amount of the increased tax deduction). This is not true because of the 2% "haircut" experienced by real estate taxes deducted as itemized deductions on Schedule A of Form 1040.

Basis reduced by seller-paid points.   When a seller pays "points" on the sale of a principal residence, the *buyer* may deduct those points as interest, but both *must* subtract these points from the sales/purchase price. If the home was purchased after 1990 but before April 4, 1994, the buyer need reduce basis only if the points were deducted. If the home was purchased after April 3, 1994, the seller-paid points must reduce the buyer's basis, even if not deducted [Rev. Proc. 94-27; Reg. §1.1273-2(g)(5), Example 3].

Amount realized.   The amount realized is the total selling price less the selling expenses.

Construction, reconstruction, and capital improvements.   Because capital expenditures are not depreciable on a personal residence, these costs are only recovered at the time of sale. Examples of qualifying improvements include streets, sidewalks, many special improvement taxes, driveways, garages, basement recreation rooms, appliances, air conditioners, and the like.

Cost means cost: "Sweat equity" is not allowed!   When any part of the new residence is acquired other than by purchase, the value of the part so acquired may *not* be included in the cost of the new residence.

What about improvements that are no longer part of the home?   Adjusted basis does not include the cost of any improvements no longer part of the home.

Example:

Danny puts wall-to-wall carpeting in his home 15 years ago. Last year he replaced that carpeting with new wall-to-wall carpeting. The cost of the old carpeting Danny replaced is no longer part of his adjusted basis. ▉

Repairs and maintenance expenditures.   These *nondeductible* items include painting and papering and other disbursements to keep the home in efficient operation.

Miscellaneous decreases to basis.   These include the following:

1. Insurance payments for casualty losses
2. Deductible casualty losses not covered by insurance
3. Payments received for granting an easement or right-of-way
4. Residential energy credit (generally allowed from 1997 through 1987) claimed for the cost of energy improvements that were added to the basis of the home
5. Adoption credit claimed for improvements that were added to the basis of the home
6. Nontaxable payments from an adoption assistance program of employer that were used as improvements added to the basis of the home
7. First-time homebuyers credit (allowed to certain first-time buyers of a home in the District of Columbia) claimed for 1997
8. Energy conservation subsidy excluded from homeowners' gross income because they received it (directly or indirectly) from a public utility after 1992 to buy or install any energy conservation measure (An energy conservation measure is an installation or modification that is primarily designed either to reduce consumption of electricity or natural gas or to improve the management of energy demand for a home [Pub. 523].)

Recapture of federal subsidy.   If the home sold was financed (in whole or in part) under a federally subsidized program (loans from a tax-exempt qualified mortgage bond or loans with mortgage credit certificates), the seller may owe additional tax and be required to recapture all or part of the benefit the seller received from the program. This recapture is due when the home is sold, exchanged, gifted, involuntarily converted, or any

---

Tax Tip

Most taxpayers want expenditures made on a personal residence to be capital improvements and not repairs. Repairs on a personal residence are never deductible, whereas capital improvements reduce the gain on a subsequent taxable sale. To make use of any "conditions-of-sale" expenditures, (a) characterize the repairs as improvements, when possible; (b) anticipate the required repairs prior to the signing of the contract-to-sell; or (c) have the seller give a price reduction allowance.

---

other disposition. The prior benefits are recaptured by increasing the seller's federal income tax for the year of sale. The involuntary conversion postponement rules [§1033] and the $250,000/$500,000 exclusion of gain provisions [§121] do not apply to this recapture tax. The recapture tax is figured on Form 8828, Recapture of Federal Mortgage Subsidy. This form must be filed even if the seller does not owe a recapture tax.

What Happens if the Residence Is Sold for a Loss?

The loss is nondeductible.   Even though the Internal Revenue Code requires the immediate recognition of all gain on the sale or exchange of property, including the gain on the sale of a personal residence that is not excluded, any loss on the sale of a personal residence is nondeductible, as it is considered a "personal, living, or family" expense. The Internal Revenue Service takes a "heads I win, tails you lose" position on the treatment of a gain or loss on the sale of a personal residence [§1001(c); §262; §1.262-1(b)(4); §1.165-9(a)].

Investor Hint

Employees must include in W-2 income (on line 7 of Form 1040) any amount the employer reimburses for a loss on the sale of a home. This amount *cannot* be included as part of the selling price.

Converting a home into a rental makes the loss deductible.   Can a personal residence be converted to a business use prior to sale date and thereby convert the nondeductible personal loss to a deductible one? Theoretically, it is possible but difficult [§165(c)(1) and (2)]. It is not known what the length of time is before a personal residence becomes a rental, although the antithesis is known: If the home is rented for less than three of the last five years before sale, §121 considers it a personal residence.

One argument for the taxpayer: How a residence is being used *at the date of sale* is of major importance in determining whether property is business or personal [*U.S. v. Winthrop*, 5 Cir. 1969, 417 F.2d 905]. Therefore, the taxpayer must prove that the property is a rental when sold, and the conversion is not done for tax purposes only [*William C. Horrmann*, 17 TC 903 (1951)].

What would be the basis in a conversion? The adjusted basis for determining loss for property converted from personal use is the *smaller* of (1) the fair market value of the property at the time of conversion or (2) the adjusted basis of the property at the time of conversion. Therefore, the loss created prior to conversion is still not deductible, either at the time of conversion or at the time of sale [§1.165-9(b)(2)].

CONCLUSION
Under the New Rules, the Gain Is Free, if You Can Prove:

1. the sales price of the home was $250,000 or under ($500,000 if married filing a joint return [MFJ]), or
2. the costs and improvements eliminate any *taxable* gain (i.e., above $250,000/$500,000 MFJ), and
3. the original cost of the home sold (generally done by making available HUD Form 1 to the IRS auditor), and
4. that no more than one home has been reported in the previous two years from sale date, and
5. that no prior depreciation has been taken on the home after May 7, 1997.

For some taxpayers, reporting home gain has become substantially simpler. For married taxpayers who sell their principal residence for less than $500,000, none of the capital gain is taxable as long as they have not excluded another home gain within two years and no depreciation has been tsaken (e.g., because they deducted an office-in-home) after May 7, 1997. But if homes are sold with gains in excess of $500,000, married taxpayers will, for the first time, *have* to pay taxes upon the sale of their principal residence, even if they purchase a more expensive home within two years. This chapter has guided you through the labyrinth created by the new sale-of-home tax rules.

Installment Sales

A seller selling on the installment plan may report gain on the installment method. When a taxpayer sells property and some or all of the payments for sale are to be paid in the future (commonly by a purchase-money mortgage, a trust deed, or a contract-for-deed), the transaction generally is called an *installment sale*. When installment reporting of the gain is available, it is an important financing and tax planning option for both the seller and the buyer.

Example:

Jeanette sells investment property for $80,000. She had purchased this property four years ago for $50,000. She agrees to receive a 5% down payment ($4,000) in the year of the sale and a note for the other 95% to be received over ten years commencing the year after the sale.

Why use the installment method? To spread the taxable gain over multiple years. A taxpayer who sells real property on the installment plan is allowed to have a pro-rata portion of the total gain taxed *as each installment is actually received. Thus, the seller, instead of paying the whole tax in the year of the sale, may spread the tax on the gain over the period during which the installments are received* [§453].

Without the installment method of reporting gain, a taxpayer would be required to report the entire capital gain in the year of the sale, a severe tax hardship that in most cases would make owner financing economically unfeasible. If the tax cannot be deferred, the sale has created a cash liability against a paper profit.

Example (continued):

In Jeanette's situation, she would owe the following:

Total gain:	$30,000	
Times: 20% tax bracket	× 20%	(assuming maximum capital gains rate)
Equals: Estimated tax due	$ 6,000	

As can be easily seen, Jeanette must come up with an additional $2,000 just to cover her estimated tax bill! Congress realized that this was an undue tax burden and therefore permitted the installment method of accounting for tax due, allowing Jeanette to spread the estimated $6,000 tax due over the ten-year contract period.

WHAT ARE SOME OTHER IMPORTANT REASONS FOR USING, OR NOT USING, AN INSTALLMENT SALE?

1. Taking payments over a period of time may facilitate the sale and improve the price.
2. Deferment of a long-term capital gain may provide the opportunity to offset it with a loss realized in the future.
3. If a profitable sale takes place in the year of a business-operating loss, the investor may want to push the gain ahead and have it taxed at the taxpayer's regular tax rate rather than use it to reduce the amount of current loss that can be carried back against a previous year's ordinary income.
4. Taxpayers can save tax by deferring gain to years when their tax bracket may be lower.
5. Postponing the taxability of gain offers a speculation on the possible reduction in the rate of tax on capital gain. If the rate seems likely to be increased, the gain can be accelerated by sale of the installment obligation.

WHAT IS AN INSTALLMENT SALE?

One Payment in Year after Sale Occurs

An installment sale is the disposition of property when the seller receives at least one payment *after* the close of the taxable year in which the sale or exchange occurs [§453(b)]. Generally, when the seller finances the buyer's purchase, the transaction is an installment sale.

Installment reporting is mandatory (unless a proper "election out," discussed later in this chapter, is made). Installment reporting requires that the taxpayer report the gain from the sale over the period of time the proceeds will be received. Installment reporting is permitted regardless of the amount of payments received in the year, even if the entire purchase price is received in a lump sum in a year subsequent to the sale year [§15A.4453-1(b)]. The IRS rule that two or more installments payable in two or more taxable years were required to qualify any sale for installment reporting has been eliminated.

There is no limitation on initial payment. There is no minimum or maximum amount of payment required to be received in the year of the sale. Taxpayers may receive more than 30% down and still use the installment method of reporting. The requirement that "no more than 30% of the gross selling price may be received in the tax year of the sale" was eliminated in 1980.

May losses be reported on the installment basis? No, the entire loss must be reported in the year of the sale [Rev. Rul. 70-430, 1970-2 CB 51].

Is there an IRS tax form that is used when reporting installment gains? Yes, Form 6252 is used.

HOW MUCH OF EACH INSTALLMENT PAYMENT IS RECOGNIZED FOR TAX PURPOSES?

Gain Is Proportioned to Each Future Installment Payment

The following four formulas, in combination, explain how to calculate the gain to be reported on the taxpayer's tax return for each year the taxpayer receives principal payments on an installment obligation.

1. Formula To Calculate Realized Gain

Selling price	+	$
Less: Adjusted basis*	−	
Selling expenses	−	
Equals: Gross profit to be realized [§15A.453-1(b)(2)(v)]	=	$

2. Formula To Calculate Contract Price

Selling price	+	$
Less: Assumed mortgage†	−	
Equals: Contract price	=	$

*Ordinary income depreciation recapture is added to basis.

†This cannot exceed the adjusted basis.

3. Formula To Calculate Gross Profit Percentage

Realized gain ($_____) ÷ Contract price ($_____) = %_____ Gross profit percentage
    (Formula 1)   (Formula 2)

4. Formula To Calculate Recognized Gain Each Year

Gross profit percentage (_____%) × Payments ($_____) = $_____
                    (Formula 3)   (Principal only)   (Recognized gain)

Basis recovery. Under the installment method, generally only a portion of the amount received each year is taxable; the remainder is a tax-free recovery of basis. How is this done?

Gross profit percentage determines the amount that is annually taxable.   The amount of each installment payment treated as income is determined by multiplying the payment received by a fraction called the *gross profit percentage*. The gross profit percentage is the ratio of the gross profit realized to the total contract price [§453(c); §15A.453-1(b)(2)(i)].

Example (continued):

Jeanette will receive a total of $80,000 over a ten-year period. Of this $80,000, $50,000 is a return of her capital investment and $30,000 is the gain she experiences on the sale. Therefore, every dollar that she receives involves ⅝ return of capital ($50,000 ÷ $80,000) and ⅜ gain ($30,000 ÷ $80,000).

Sales price	$80,000	(Contract price)
Less: Basis	− 50,000	(⅝ of total contract price)
Equals: Total gain	$30,000	(⅜ of total contract price)

Therefore, Jeanette's pro-rata portion of the gain in the year of the sale and the subsequent tax are calculated as follows:

Principal payment received	$4,000	(Part of contract price)
Less: Basis	− 2,500	(⅝ of $4,000 principal)
Gain reported in year of sale	1,500	(⅜ of $4,000 principal)
Times: 20% tax bracket	× .20	
Equals: Estimated tax due	$ 300	

Tax savings: The installment method of reporting gain results in reducing Jeanette's tax due from $6,000 to $300 in the year of the sale. Theoretically, the $6,000 tax bill is paid over the period of the contract (ten years). However, because we have a progressive tax system, and with proper tax planning, the estimated tax bill can be substantially decreased.

Five Basic Installment Sale Definitions

Before the gain to be recognized under the installment method of reporting can be calculated, the taxpayer must understand: (1) selling price, (2) selling expenses, (3) adjusted basis, (4) contract price, and (5) payments made by the buyer in the year of sale.

Investor Hint

Luckily, some of these have been fully discussed previously in the book, so only a recapitulation is done here.

Selling price. Chapter 1 illustrates the formula for calculating the sales price when the selling or purchase price is not specifically stated or involves more than cash and/or the assumption of mortgages. The amount realized on an installment sale includes the amount of cash received plus the fair market value of any other property received and to be received. The amount of the mortgages on the property sold that the purchaser either assumes or takes subject to is also figured into the sales price. Commissions and other selling expenses paid or incurred by the seller do not reduce the selling price even though they do reduce net profit.

What happens if the note is reduced in the future? If the parties to an installment sale afterward agree to reduce the selling price, the gross profit percentage changes. The seller simply recalculates the gross profit ratio for the remaining payments and reports the now-correct remaining profit. The seller cannot amend any prior tax returns and file for a refund [§108(e)(5)].

How imputed interest affects selling price. Buyers and sellers may manipulate the tax consequences of an installment sale by varying the interest rate in seller-financed transactions. Previously this was done to convert ordinary interest income to long-term capital gain, but with the repeal of the capital gain deduction, this is no longer as large a tax issue. Nonetheless, it still is important as illustrated in the next planning tip.

Tax Tip

By decreasing the interest rate and increasing the sales price of depreciable property, the seller decreases the interest income and increases capital gain; the buyer normally will not care because all this does is decrease the interest expense and increase the depreciation expense. On the other hand, by increasing the interest rate and decreasing the sales price of property, the buyer increases the currently deductible interest expense; sellers won't care if they can offset this current interest income (e.g., with carryover net operating losses).

The IRS has, to a large extent, limited this tax plan with the imputed interest rules [§483] and the original issue discount rules [§1271-1274], by "imputing" an interest rate in the sales contract unless a statutorily set minimum rate of interest is expressed in the agreement. The rate at which interest is imputed is generally 100% or more of the applicable federal rate (AFR) determined under a "three-month rule" [§1.483-3(a);§1.1274-4].

Example:

On May 21, 2003, D. J. Roberts sells a lot on Flathead Lake for $12,600. The contract provides for a down payment of $3,600 at the time of sale with the balance of $9,000 to be paid in three equal installments due yearly from the date of sale. The contract makes no provision for interest payments. Under §483, the total "unstated interest" under the contract is equal to the excess of the total payments over the total of the present values discounted at a 2.78% rate compounded semiannually [see Rev. Rul. 2002-40]. The present value of $9,000 discounted at 2.78% is $8,522. Therefore, the selling price is actually $12,122 ($3,600 + 8,522) and the unstated interest is $478. The interest ($478) will be taxed as ordinary income, not as a long-term gain. ■

Tax Tip

Care should be exercised by sellers to ensure that they do not generate excessive amounts of ordinary income because of unstated or imputed interest. Unstated interest is used to reduce the stated original sales price and, as noted before, the "selling price" is the amount used to determine the long-term gain.

What are selling expenses? Selling expenses are the expenses incurred to sell the property such as real estate brokerage fees, title insurance, transfer tax, recording fees, and survey fees. Chapter 1 illustrates the selling expense computation.

What is "adjusted basis"? As explained in Chapter 1, the adjusted basis is the original cost (or basis) of the property plus the value of any improvements made on the property by the seller and minus accumulated depreciation and losses taken.

A new definition—what is total contract price? In most cases, the *total contract price* is equivalent to the amount that the seller will physically receive—cash and other property. The *total contract price* (not the *total selling price*) is important, as it is used to determine the part of each installment payment to be included in income.

Example:

Willy sells some land for $100,000 that he had purchased for $60,000 several years ago as an investment. There is a $20,000 mortgage on the property that the buyer assumes. Willy's gross profit percentage is calculated as follows:

Formula 2: Contract Price		Formula 1: Realized Gain	
Selling price	$100,000	Selling price	$100,000
Mortgage assumed	– 20,000	Basis of property	– 60,000
Equals: Contract price	$ 80,000	Equals: Gross profit	$ 40,000

Formula 3: Calculation of Gross Profit Percentage

Realized gain ($40,000)	÷	Contract price $80,000	=	50%
(Formula 1)	÷	(Formula 2)	=	Gross profit percentage

In other words, Willy receives $80,000 (not $100,000) over the term of the contract. As $40,000 of the $80,000 to be received is gross profit, Willy's gross profit percentage is 50%; that is, 50% of each dollar received each year must be reported as capital gain. In this example, Willy receives a $20,000 down payment in 1998 and collects the balance at $20,000 each year over the following three years. He will report taxable income (long-term gain) as follows:

1998	$20,000	×	50%	=	$10,000	
1999	$20,000	×	50%	=	$10,000	
2000	$20,000	×	50%	=	$10,000	
2001	$20,000	×	50%	=	$10,000	
Contract price =	$80,000				$40,000	= Gross profit

WHAT IS INCLUDED IN THE "TOTAL PAYMENTS MADE BY BUYER IN YEAR OF SALE"?

Payments made by the buyer in the year of sale include both cash and the fair market value of *any other property* received by the seller. All payments received by the seller on account of the sale during the year of sale are also included [§15A.453-1(b)(3)].

Investor Hint

Strangely, it is more logical to first examine one item that is *not* to be included in the total payments made by the buyer before analyzing what is included.

What is not included in the total payments made by the buyer in the year of sale?
Any notes between buyer and seller and any assumed mortgages are excluded from the buyer's total payments.

Mortgage liens are not considered a payment. The buyer's evidence of indebtedness and the buyer's "assumptions of" mortgages and "taking property subject to" mortgages do not constitute payments made by the buyer in the year of the sale unless the evidence of indebtedness is payable on demand or readily tradeable or is secured by cash or cash equivalent (e.g., Treasury notes) [§453(f)(3); §453(f)(4); §15A.453-1(d)(3)(i)].

What happens when there is an excess of mortgage over basis?   As previously mentioned, mortgage liens are not included in the total contract price *unless they exceed the seller's adjusted basis.* When the assumed mortgage exceeds the seller's basis, the *excess* is considered an initial payment [§15A.453-1(b)(2)(iii)].

Example:
On August 1, 2003, Lynn sells a lot in Phoenix for $100,000 that has an adjusted basis of $30,000 and on which she owes a mortgage balance of $40,000 (she refinanced it). Robin takes the property subject to the existing mortgage, paying $30,000 cash down, and agreeing to pay the remaining $30,000 in six equal annual installments, plus interest, starting December 31, 2003. The initial payments are calculated as follows:

Payments Made by Buyer in Year of Sale

Cash down payment	$30,000
Plus: Payment of any installment due during year of sale ($30,000 ÷ 6 years)	+ 5,000
Plus: Excess of mortgage assumed ($40,000) over seller's basis ($30,000)	+10,000
Equals: Total initial payments	$ 45,000

Note: Here the excess of the old mortgage over basis ($40,000 – $30,000 = $10,000) is treated the same as cash. The seller is treated as having received $45,000 in the year of sale ($35,000 cash plus $10,000 excess mortgage over basis) and is taxed more gain than the physical cash on hand in the year of sale. ■

Tax Tip

Make sure that the excess of the existing mortgage over basis is added to the cash received when estimating the maximum amount of gain the seller is willing to include in taxable income. Use of a *wraparound mortgage* (to be discussed later) is one alternative to avoid this problem.

What happens to the gross profit percentage when the mortgage exceeds basis?

If the mortgage does exceed the seller's basis, only the basis is included in the total contract price, and the gross profit will always be the same as the total contract price. The gross profit percentage will always be 100% and all payments received are to be included as income.

Example:

Willy sells some land for $100,000 that he had purchased for $60,000 several years ago as an investment. There is a $70,000 mortgage on the property, which the buyer assumes. Willy's gross profit percentage is

Formula 2: Contract Price		**Formula 1: Realized Gain**	
Selling price	$100,000	Selling price	$100,000
Mortgage assumed* —	60,000*	Basis of property —	60,000
Equals: Contract price	$ 40,000	Equals: Gross profit	$ 40,000

* Not in excess of basis

In this case, Willy will receive $40,000 ($30,000 cash plus $10,000 excess of mortgage assumed over the seller's basis), which is the entire contract price.

Formula 3: Calculation of Gross Profit Percentage

Realized gain ($40,000)	÷	Contract price $40,000	=	100%
(Formula 1)	÷	(Formula 2)	=	Gross profit percentage

Using a wraparound mortgage to avoid including in income the excess amount of mortgage over the seller's basis. As pointed out earlier, when mortgaged property is sold and the buyer either assumes or takes subject to the mortgage, the amount of the mortgage, to the extent it exceeds the seller's basis, is considered payment received by the seller in the year of sale.

Tax Tip

There is a way to arrange the sale that allows the seller to avoid reporting large amounts of the gain in the year of sale. With a *wraparound mortgage,* the buyer neither assumes nor takes subject to the mortgage, so the whole problem is neatly avoided. Following is a description of how this type of arrangement works.

The wraparound mortgage plan. Along with the down payment, the buyer gives the seller a mortgage *for the difference between the down payment and the selling price*—the total amount remaining to be paid. The wraparound mortgage payments should, of course, cover the seller's payments on the existing mortgage. The seller remains liable on any existing mortgages on the property, and no liability is transferred to the buyer. The wraparound mortgage can be deposited with an escrow agent, who collects the buyer's payments on the wraparound mortgage, makes the payments on the seller's mortgage, and forwards the balance to the seller.

IRS regulations try to restrict "wraps." Even though the IRS has repeatedly lost its challenges to the use of wraparound mortgages in court, this does not discourage the IRS. In February 1981, the IRS issued regulations that treat the excess of mortgage over basis as a payment to the seller even when using the wraparound technique. In other words, whether the buyer legally assumes the mortgage or not, the IRS's position is that the buyer has assumed the mortgage (and therefore no wraparound mortgage exists) [§15A.453-1(b)(3)(ii)]. These proposed regulations have subsequently been overruled by the Tax Court, and the IRS has acquiesced to the decision [*Professional Equities, Inc.,* 89 TC 165, (1987); Acq. 1988-37 IRS 4].

Tax Tip

Even though the IRS agreed to the court decision without protest, it is also without enthusiasm, as the regulations dealing with wraparound mortgages have not been withdrawn or modified. In addition, it warns in the acquiescence that caution should be exercised in extending the application of the *Professional Equities, Inc.,* decision to any similar case unless the facts and circumstances are substantially the same (which is always a difficult standard). To avoid potential IRS penalties, conservative tax-planning advisors recommend that investors should disclose, by a Form 8275-R, that they are not abiding by the current regulations. This advice, of course, will also subject the tax return to an IRS audit!

Caution

The Internal Revenue Service has often attacked the wraparound method when it is used to "defer" the paying of taxes (as in the example on page 71). Their philosophy is that since the tax-payer has the money (because of the previous refinance) the taxpayer should have to pay the tax associated with the refinance at the time of sale. In all but the most blatant abuse cases the courts have overruled the IRS and have allowed the postponing of gain when the wraparound method is used [*Stonecrest Corp. v. Comm.,* 24 TC 659].

PAYMENTS THAT MUST BE INCLUDED IN THE YEAR OF THE SALE

Most taxpayers, and tax preparers, are stunned by the IRS's broad definition of the *first year total payments*. The importance of this calculation cannot be overemphasized as it determines the proper amount of income reported in the first and each subsequent tax year. Many tax practitioners simply subtract the assumed mortgage from the sales price to back into the amount of the total payments that must have been made in the year of the sale. This simplistic, though often accurate, calculation may leave out some rare "deemed" payments (e.g., some assumed mortgages do not qualify for this exclusion, such as no. 13 in the following list).

Payments made by the buyer in the year of sale [§15A.453-1(b)(3)]. This list is followed by extensive examples.

1. Cash down payment or cash deposit, even if made in a year before the year of sale [Rev. Rul. 73-360]
2. Other cash, such as cash at closing
3. Option paid, even if received in a prior year, which is considered part of the down payment
4. Payment of any installment(s) due during year of sale (interest payments received on the installment note *are not reportable* here but are reportable as interest income)
5. Premature payments of a later year's installment
6. Fair market value of property (other than like-kind property) received from the buyer (e.g., boats, cars, etc.)
7. Notes or other evidence of indebtedness of *third* parties that are assigned to the seller as part of the consideration for the sale [§15A.453-1(b)(3)(i)]
8. Any obligation payable on demand [§453(f)(4)(A)].
9. Corporate or government bonds or other evidence of indebtedness issued by a corporation or government body either (a) with coupons attached or (b) in registered form unless taxpayer establishes that they are not readily marketable or (c) in any other form designed to render them readily tradeable in an established securities market [§15A.453-1(e)(1)]
10. Excess of mortgage assumed over seller's basis [§15A.453-1(b)(2)(ii)]
11. Cancellation of indebtedness owed by the seller to the purchaser
12. Selling expenses of seller paid by the purchaser in the year of sale, such as legal expenses
13. Charges accrued against the property and assumed by the purchaser (i.e., taxes, mortgage interest, and liens), which are paid by the purchaser in the year of sale and are directed to be paid out of the proceeds of the sale
14. When the taxpayer sells property to a creditor and the seller's indebtedness is canceled in consideration of the sale [§15A.453-1(b)(3)(I)]
15. Amounts paid by the buyer in discharging the mortgage if the buyer pays the seller's full mortgage in the year of sale instead of assuming it [*Ralph Sterling v. Ham*, (DC) 3 USTC 3 F. Supp. 386]

Commissions and other selling expenses paid or incurred by the seller do not reduce the payments made by the buyer in the year of the sale, even though they do reduce the net profit.

What happens when the taxpayer sells an installment obligation? Instead of waiting to collect all or some of the buyer's obligations, the seller may choose to dispose of the debt instrument before maturity. When this is done, the gain or loss from disposing of the obligations must be reported in the year of the disposition. The gain or loss will be the difference between the seller's basis in the debt instruments and what is received for them. The seller's basis in the obligation is the unrecovered cost. If the seller disposes of the obligation other than by sale or exchange, the gain or loss is found by comparing the basis (unrecovered cost) with the fair market value at that time. The gain or loss retains its identity, that is, long-term, short-term, or ordinary income.

What happens when the buyer makes an earnest-money deposit and a subsequent down payment in different years?

Example:

A contract for sale for $80,000 is signed in 2003 at which time Bob, the buyer, pays $10,000. The title is closed in 2004 at which time Bob pays another $15,000. Dennis, the seller, takes back a mortgage for $55,000.

Under these circumstances, the 2003 payment is treated as part of the payment in the year of sale (2004). It is not 2003 income. The seller has received $25,000 as the initial payment to be reported in 2004. ■

What happens when the buyer pays part of the purchase price in cash and the rest in securities and a promissory note?

Example:

Bill pays $15,000 cash at closing and gives Sue securities (Microsoft stock) worth $10,000 and a note for $55,000. Sales price is $80,000 with no mortgage assumed.

Under these circumstances, the seller is treated as having received an initial payment of $25,000. This may cause a larger amount of the gain to be taxed in the first year than the seller has the cash to pay. ■

Tax Tip

Sue could take Bill's note for $65,000 secured in part by the pledge of the securities. This reduces the initial payment to $15,000.

What happens when the buyer makes a prepayment in the year of the sale?

Example:

An $80,000 sale occurs in 2003, and Cynthia, the buyer, pays $24,000 at the closing. Ken, the seller, takes back a mortgage for the balance, with the first $10,000 payment due on

January 1, 2004. In December 2003, Cynthia prepays the first installment, which includes $1,000 principal amortization (she is trying to deduct $9,000 of interest!).

Note: Unhappily, Ken must add the $1,000 to his other payment ($24,000) received in 2003, the year of the sale. In addition, the $9,000 interest also becomes taxable in 2003. This, of course, increases the tax he must pay. ▨

Tax Tip

Make sure that the contract for sale and mortgage bond or note have a provision barring prepayment of installments. If the buyer tries to prepay, return the money.

May the seller have the buyer pay the full sales price in cash into an escrow and still use the installment method of reporting?   No. With this type of escrow arrangement, the seller is no longer counting on the buyer for the remaining payments but on the escrow itself [§15A.453-1(b)(5)(Example 8); §15A.453-1(b)(3)(I); Rev. Rul. 73-451, 1973-2 CB 158].

Tax Tip

In one rare case the sellers were given the option not to accept the buyer's offer to pay the full purchase price in cash and instead insist on installment payments using an escrow arrangement, solely to reduce the tax consequences of the sale. Evidently, the court decided that a substantial restriction of the seller's right to receive the sale proceeds existed [*E. Grannemann,* DC Mo. 87-1 USTC ¶9287, 649 F. Supp. 949].

Substitution of an escrow arrangement as security following an installment sale also ends the seller's ability to report the sale on the installment plan [Rev. Rul. 77-294, 1977-2 CB 173].

The cancellation of an installment obligation.   If the installment obligation is canceled or becomes unenforceable, the cancellation or lapse will be treated as a disposition of the obligation resulting in taxation of the gain at cancellation.

The bequest of an installment obligation to the obligor.   The decedent seller's estate is deemed to have made a taxable disposition of an installment obligation in any case where the obligation is transferred by bequest to the obligor or in which the estate allows the obligation to become unenforceable.

Example:

Derrick purchases investment property from his father for $100,000 on July 1, 2003, agreeing to pay $10,000 (plus interest) on each anniversary date for ten years. Three years later Derrick's father dies and in his will forgives Derrick's $70,000 installment obligation.

The father's estate must include this cancellation of installment obligation as income, the same as if Derrick paid the estate the $70,000 in cash. ▪

WHAT OTHER ITEM IS NOT TO BE INCLUDED IN THE INITIAL PAYMENTS?

Like-Kind Exchange Property Received Is Not Considered a Payment, Is Not Considered in the Total Contract Price, and Reduces the Gross Profit

As mentioned previously, another item not to be included in the total payments made by the buyer in the year of the sale is any like-kind property. An investor in real estate can take simultaneous advantage of both the tax-free exchange provisions (discussed in Chapters 5 through 8) and the installment gain provisions. Like-kind property is not treated as a payment when it is received in an installment transaction if the exchange of property qualifies under the like-kind exchange rules. In addition, the contract price computation disregards the value of the like-kind property; the contract price consists solely of the sum of the money received, in the year of sale, the fair market value of other property received and the face amount of the installment obligations. It also requires that the gross profit be reduced by the amount not recognized by reason of the tax-free exchange [§453(f)(6); Reg. §1.1031(k)-1(j)(2)].

Example:

In 2003, Sylvia sells an apartment house with an adjusted basis of $400,000 for an investment condominium in Martha's Vineyard worth $200,000 and an installment obligation for $800,000, with $100,000 payable in the year of the sale and the balance payable in 2004.

Selling price:		
Fair market value of like-kind property received		$ 200,000
Installment obligation	+	800,000
Equals: Sales price	=	$1,000,000

Formula 2: Contract Price		**Formula 1: Realized Gain**	
Selling price	$1,000,000	Selling price	$1,000,000
Less: Fair market value		Less: Basis of	
of LKE property	– 200,000	property	– 400,000
		Less: LKE property	– 200,000
Equals: Contract price	$ 800,000	Equals: Gross profit	$ 400,000

Formula 3: Calculation of Gross Profit Percentage

Realized gain ($40,000) ÷ Contract price $100,000 =   40%
(Formula 1)   ÷   (Formula 2)   =   Gross profit

Formula 4: Calculation of Recognized Gain Each Year

Gross profit percentage (40%)	×	Payments $20,000	=	$8,000
(Formula 3)		(Principal only)	=	(Recognized gain)

Formula 3: Calculation of Gross Profit Percentage

Realized gain ($400,000)	÷	Contract price $800,000	=	50%
(Formula 1)	÷	(Formula 2)	=	Gross profit percentage

Formula 4: Calculation of Recognized Gain Each Year

2003 gain to be reported	
Initial payment	$100,000
Times: Gross profit percentage	× 50%
Equals: 2003 gain	= $ 50,000
2004 gain to be reported	
Subsequent payments	$700,000
Times: Gross profit percentage	× 50%
Equals: 2004 gain	= 350,000
Total Gain Reported on Installment Basis	$400,000

The *basis* of the like-kind property received is determined as if the obligation had been satisfied at its face amount. Thus, the taxpayer's basis in the property transferred is first allocated to the like-kind property received (but not in excess of its fair market value) and any remaining basis will be used to determine the gross profit ratio [Rev. Rul. 65-155, 1965-1 CB 356].

Example (continued):

In the previous example, Sylvia's basis in the like-kind property received, the condominium, is zero.

ALLOCATING CAPITAL GAIN ON INSTALLMENT SALE OF REAL PROPERTY

"Front-loaded" method to be used. The regulations provide that when the capital gain from an installment sale consists of both 25%-rate gain and 20%-rate gain, then as payments are received, the 25%-rate gain is taken into account before any 20%-rate gain is included. If part of the capital gain from an installment sale is from unrecaptured §1250 depreciation (25% rate), the taxable portion of the payments received is considered first to be from the unrecaptured §1250 depreciation. Once all unrecaptured §1250 depreciation is taxed, the balance of the installment sale payments is considered to be adjusted net capital gain (20% rate)[Reg. §1.453-12(a)].

> ### Investor Hint
>
> This means that if the total gain recognized from the sale is less than the 25%-rate gain, then none of the gain will be taxed as 20%-rate gain.

Prior year installment sale collections. Payments received from a prior year installment sale are taxed assuming that all payments received prior to the law change were first taxed as unrecaputred §1250 depreciation. Thus, if the taxable gains reported in prior years exceed the amount of unrecaputred §1250 depreciation on the property, subsequent gains are taxed first at the 25% rate until the total taxable amount equals the unrecaptured §1250 amount.

Assumptions for the following example. In the following IRS example, the sale took place in December, with annual payments in December. The taxpayer, an individual whose taxable year is the calendar year, does not elect out of the installment method. The installment obligation bears adequate stated interest, and the property sold is real property held in a trade or business that qualifies as both §1231 property and §1250 property. In all taxable years, the taxpayer's marginal tax rate on ordinary income is 28%. The following example illustrates the rules of this section [see §1.453-12(d) Ex.1].

	1998	1999	2000	2001	2002	2003-2007	Total Gain
Sales Price: 12/1998	10,000						
Adjusted Basis (20%)	2,000						
Total Gain (80%)	8,000						
Prior Depreciation @ 25%	3,000						
Appreciation @ 20%	5,000						
Payment (10)	1,000	1,000	1,000	1,000	1,000	5,000	10,000
Installment Gain: 80%	800	800	800	800	800	4,000	8,000
Taxed at 25%	800	800	800	600	---	---	3,000
Taxed at 20%	---	---	---	200	800	4,000	5,000
Remaining to be taxed at 25%	2,200	1,400	600	---	---	---	---

DEPRECIATION RECAPTURE: PROBLEMS WITH INSTALLMENT SALES

Ordinary income depreciation recapture. When the property sold is a depreciable asset, part or all of the gain *may* be required to be "recaptured" as ordinary income (called *Section 1231/1245 depreciation recapture*) that is totally taxable in the year of the sale. The ordinary income depreciation recapture is fully recognized in the year of the sale even if no payments are received in that year [§453(i)].

Capital gain depreciation recapture. Additionally, any prior "straight-line depreciation" taken must be "recaptured" at a 25% capital gain rate. As was covered in Chapter 2, this type of prior depreciation taken (called *Section 1231/1250 depreciation recapture*) is subject to the higher 25% capital gain rate, not eligible for the 20% capital gain rate.

Amount of the "ordinary income" depreciation recapture. Luckily, §1245 "ordinary income" depreciation recapture is generally defined as *excess* depreciation, or that depreciation taken over what normally is calculated on the straight-line basis for the same period of time. Because most real property placed in service before 1981 and after 1986 may *only* be depreciated using the straight-line method, there generally is only capital gains depreciation recapture [§1250(b)(1)].

Tax Tip

If the depreciation recapture amount is burdensome, the seller should demand a cash payment at closing substantial enough to pay the projected tax liability on the increased gain created by the recapture. Ordinary income depreciation recapture must be included in current income, whether or not enough cash payments are received by the seller.

Any "ordinary income" depreciation deductions that are recaptured are added to the basis of the obligation, regardless of the amount of principal payment received in that year [§453(i)].

Example:

This illustrates the dangers of "ordinary income" depreciation recapture. Mark sells property for $20,000 cash and a note of $80,000, payable in four equal annual installments of $20,000, each bearing an adequate interest rate. Mark's adjusted basis is $30,000, with another $30,000 of ordinary income depreciation recapture (that must be fully recognized in the year of the sale).

Caution

If commercial real property was purchased between 1981 and 1987 *and* the property was depreciated using the accelerated depreciation method, a disaster occurs, as the *entire* accumulated depreciation must be recaptured [§1245(a)(3)(A); §1250(c)]!

Formula 2: Contract Price		**Formula 1: Realized Gain**	
Selling price:	$100,000	Selling price:	$100,000
Mortgage assumed:	– 0	Basis of property	– 60,000*
Equals: Contract price:	$100,000	Equals: Gross profit:	$ 40,000

*Ordinary income depreciation recapture of $30,000 is added to $30,000 basis.

Formula 3: Calculation of Gross Profit Percentage

Realized gain ($40,000)	÷	Contract price $100,000	=	40%
(Formula 1)	÷	(Formula 2)	=	Gross profit

Formula 4: Calculation of Recognized Gain Each Year

Gross profit percentage (40%)	×	Payments $20,000	=	$8,000
(Formula 3)		(Principal only)	=	(Recognized gain)

Total Gain To Be Reported in Year of Sale:

Depreciation recapture (ordinary income)		$30,000
Installment gain (capital or §1231/§1250 depreciation		
recapture gain)	+	$ 8,000
Total gain to be reported in year of sale*	=	$38,000

*Therefore, even though Mark received only $20,000 cash in the year of the sale, Mark is required to report a total gain of $38,000, of which $30,000 is ordinary income. The character of the other $8,000 of gain depends on whether the property is a capital asset or business (§1231) property.

Any depreciation deductions that are recaptured are added to the basis of the obligation. This happens regardless of the amount of principal payment received in that year [§453(i)].

ELECTING OUT OF THE INSTALLMENT METHOD IS OPTIONAL

The taxpayer may elect to report the entire gain in the tax year the sale occurs. When electing to report the entire gain in the year of the sale, the taxpayer should state on the appropriate tax form (Schedule D or Form 4797) "I elect out of the installment method" in addition to reporting *all* the gain. But a taxpayer who reports an amount realized that equals the selling price and includes the full face amount of any installment obligations received in connection with the sale is considered to have made an effective election that the installment sales provisions of §453 are not applicable [§15A.453-1T(d)(3)(i)]. This election generally must be made on or before the due date (including extensions) for filing the taxpayer's return for the year of sale [§453(d)(1); §15A.453-1(d)(3)].

Tax Tip

Why accelerate reporting gain by electing out of the installment reporting method?
1. The seller may have another capital loss that can absorb this capital gain.
2. The seller may have an expiring net operating loss.
3. This election is also recommended if the seller's tax rates are anticipated to increase, either by congressional action or if the seller anticipates escalating into a higher tax bracket. Electing out of the installment reporting makes instant use of the loss and may reduce the current year's tax to zero.

Caution

This election often "flags" a return for a future IRS audit!

A late election is normally not permitted. Unless the IRS determines that the taxpayer has a good cause for failing to make the election on time, late elections are not allowed [§15A.453-1(d)(3)].

A change of mind after election is also normally not permitted. A valid election out of the installment method cannot be revoked without IRS permission [§15A.453-1(d)(4)].

> **Tax Tip**
>
> An election out can be especially damaging when, in a subsequent audit, the IRS disallows expenses or increases income that the taxpayer originally did not take into account when reporting all the gain instead of using the installment method! The IRS says, "Tough bounce"—you should have done it correctly in the first place (as if they knew)!

WHO CANNOT USE THE INSTALLMENT METHOD?
Dealers, Certain Related Party Sales, and Stock Sales

Sales of property by a real estate dealer [§453(b)(2)], certain sales of depreciable property to a controlled entity [§453(g)(1)(A)], sales or exchanges of marketable stock and securities [§453(k)(2)], and sales or exchanges between spouses [§1041] do not qualify for the installment method.

Tax planning for real estate dealers. A *dealer* is a taxpayer who buys real estate to sell it. An *investor* is a taxpayer who purchases real property for appreciation or income. Therefore, a real estate agent who treats his or her own property as an investment will normally not be a dealer to property he or she personally holds and may use the installment method on that property. Terminology is very important for this determination.

Sales of time-shares and residential lots may be entitled to use the installment method. The installment method is permitted for certain dealer-type sales to individuals of (1) time-share rights to use, or time-share ownership interest in, residential real property for not more than six weeks; (2) rights to use specified campgrounds for recreational purposes; and (3) residential lots, but only if the taxpayer (or related person) is not making any improvements to the lots [§453(i)(2)(B)].

> **Caution**
>
> This prevents one individual from selling property to a family member on the installment plan (and deferring the tax liability) and the family member then reselling the same property for cash. In essence, the related party is treated as the initial seller's agent when making a second disposition.

   The price to pay is interest on the deferred tax. In the case of sales of time-shares and residential lots, installment reporting is permitted only if the dealer elects to pay interest on the tax deferred by the use of the installment method. The interest rate is approximately the current federal rate; the interest amount is based on the tax that would have been paid in the year of sale without the installment method and is calculated from the date of sale to the date the payments are received. Even though it is added to the tax due, it is deductible by the dealer as an interest deduction [§453(i)(3)].

RESALE BY A RELATED BUYER—INSTALLMENT SALES
The Two-Year Rule

   When the initial seller sells property to a related person on the installment method and the related person disposes of the property (for example, a sale for cash or by gift or exchange), generally within two years of the original sale, the initial seller will have to recognize the gain that would otherwise be deferred rather than continuing the installment reporting [§453(e)].

Investor Hint

This does not prohibit installment sales between related parties. It only becomes applicable when the related party purchaser subsequently sells the property.

Who are related parties? Related parties include spouses, children, grandchildren, parents, grantor-fiduciary relationships and fiduciary-beneficiary relationships for trusts, corporations (if 50% or more of the value of the stock is owned directly or indirectly by such person), and partners in proportion to their share in the partnership interest [§453(f)(1)].

Example:

Ty owns a condominium that has a fair market value of $300,000 and a tax basis of $100,000. On July 1, 2003, Ty sells the condominium to his son, Laird, for $300,000. Laird pays his father a cash down payment of $5,000 and gives him a note to pay the balance in ten annual installments of $29,500 each (plus interest), beginning September 1, 2004. On July 2, 2003, Laird sells the condominium for $300,000 cash.

Under the above resale rule, Ty is treated as receiving $300,000 from the installment sale in 2003. Ty must report all $200,000 gain from the sale on his 2003 income tax return even though he only received $5,000 in cash!

If Laird waits more than two years (July 2, 2005) after the initial installment sale, the resale rule will not apply to Ty.

Exceptions to the resale rule. These include a second disposition resulting after the death of the seller or related purchaser, certain involuntary conversions, or establishing to IRS satisfaction that one of the resale's principal purposes was not to avoid paying federal income tax [§453(e)(6), (7)].

RELATED PARTY SALES—SALES OF DEPRECIABLE PROPERTY

Penalty Is Conversion to Ordinary Income

When a sale of depreciable property is between specified related persons, the entire gain may be recharacterized as ordinary income [§1239], and when that happens the installment reporting is not permitted [§453(g)(1)(A)]. The seller must treat all payments to be received as received in the year of the sale. This prevents a sale to a related person who starts depreciating the stepped-up full "fair-market-value" basis without a simultaneous reporting of income by the related seller [§453(g)(l)(B)(i)].

Who is a related party? In this case, the definition of related parties is generally (1) a taxpayer and a partnership or corporation in which the taxpayer has 50% ownership, (2) two or more partnerships in which the same persons own more than 50% of the capital or profits, and (3) a taxpayer and any trust in which such taxpayer (or spouse) is a beneficiary [§1239(b)].

Exception. A sale of depreciable property to a related person *may* use the installment method *if* the seller can establish to the satisfaction of the IRS that tax avoidance was not one of the principal purposes of the sale or that the seller did not derive any significant tax deferral benefits from the sale [§453(g)(2)].

SUMMARY

As the foregoing discussion illustrates, the installment method of reporting gains on real property sales provides an excellent mechanism for minimizing the tax costs. Figure 4.1 is a worksheet for calculating the gain of an installment sale. Again, a word of caution. The taxpayer must be careful to meet all the requirements for reporting under this method.

FIGURE 4.1 Installment Sale Worksheet

INSTALLMENT SALE WORKSHEET

PART I - GROSS PROFIT

1. Sales Price	$
2. Adjusted basis of property sold	-
3. Selling expenses	-
4. Gross profit	$

PART II - CONTRACT PRICE

5. Cash downpayment	$
6. Fair market value of other property received	+
7. Face value of purchaser's note	+
8. Excess of assumed mortgage over adjusted basis	+
9. Contract price	$

PART III - GROSS PROFIT PERCENTAGE

10. Divide item 4 by item 9	%

PART IV - PAYMENTS RECEIVED IN YEAR OF SALE

11. Cash downpayment	$
12. Fair market value of other property received	+
13. Principal payments on purchaser's note	+
14. Excess of assumed mortgage over adjusted basis	+
15. Other payments	+
16. Payments in year of sale	$

PART V - RECOGNIZED GAIN (YEAR OF SALE)

17. Payments received in year of sale (item 16)	$
18. Gross profit percentage (item 10)	x
19. Recognized gain	$

PART VI - RECOGNIZED GAIN (IN YEARS AFTER SALE)

20. Principal payments received in year	$
21. Gross profit percentage (item 10)	x
22. Recognized gain	$

Tax-Free Exchanges

HISTORY OF INTERNAL REVENUE CODE SECTION 1031

The advice "Don't put off until tomorrow what can be done today" was not written by a taxpayer. Advance tax planning often properly postpones until tomorrow what normally is considered today's tax liability. Better yet, with proper tax planning, taxpayers can take it (i.e., the tax due) with them when they die. Internal Revenue Code Section 1031 (commonly known as the *like-kind exchange* or *LKE section*) contains one method a taxpayer may use to defer today's tax bill. Although taxes on an exchange are actually deferred, not eliminated, the popular expression of "tax-free exchanges" is used in this chapter.

A gain occurring (i.e., realized) on a tax-free exchange will not be taxable (i.e., recognized) in the year of the sale. This is an exception to the taxing theory that all gains are taxable at the time of sale or receipt of money. As far back as 1921, the United States Congress felt, when it passed the like-kind exchange rules, it was inappropriate to recognize "theoretical" gains and losses. It concluded that evaluating all the different "horse trades" would not justify the potential revenues to be derived from them.

As a matter of fact, Congress stated in a later report that if taxpayers would be required to report all their theoretical gains and theoretical losses each year, the taxpayers' claims for theoretical losses "would probably exceed any profits" [H.R. Dept., No. 704, Revenue Act of 1934, 73rd Congress, 2d Sess.]. It is comforting to note that the taxpayers of the 1930s and the taxpayers of the 1990s are, in all probability, remarkably similar.

Investor Hint

Throughout Chapters 5 through 8, which discuss the subject of like-kind exchanges, the materials and planning tips are backed up by court cases and tax citations. Why?

After reading the LKE chapters, share the information with your tax professional—do it as a favor to you! Do not assume he or she knows all there is to know about like-kind exchanges. Tax law is too complicated today. These chapters are written so you will discover new tax-planning ideas. Let the tax professional implement those ideas, some of which you will suggest after reading these chapters. These tax alternatives will be dramatic to you, the taxpayer.

What is an exchange? §1031 states: "No gain or loss shall be recognized on the exchange of property held for productive use in a trade or business or for investment if such property is exchanged solely for property of like kind which is to be held either for productive use in a trade or business or for investment" [§1031(a)(1)].

The tax difference between a sale and an exchange. Before discussing the ramifications of a tax-free exchange, let us examine the taxation of a taxable sale.

Example:

Debbie owns an apartment house (on leased land) in Atlanta, which she purchased for $100,000. The property has a fair market value of $225,000 on December 1, 2003. She has taken $75,000 of straight-line depreciation since her purchase. She wants to sell it and buy an apartment house in Depoe Bay, Oregon, that has a fair market value of $225,000. Her taxable gain when she sells the Atlanta property would be $200,000, calculated as follows:

Sales price		$225,000
Less: Adjusted basis		
Original cost	$100,000	
Minus: Depreciation	− 75,000	
Adjusted basis		− 25,000
Equals: Long-term capital gain		$200,000

Tax due on sale: Debbie's tax, assuming she is in the 28% tax bracket, would be $43,750:

	Gain		Gain Rate		Tax Due
Depreciation recapture	$ 75,000	×	25%	=	$18,750
Long-term capital gain	$125,000	×	20%	=	$25,000
Total gain	$200,000				
Estimated tax					$43,750

A sale and subsequent reinvestment of proceeds, instead of an exchange, will result in Debbie's paying $43,750 of unnecessary taxes.

Investor Hint

To be more dramatic, add your state tax rate to the federal rates and then calculate the tax savings!

Example (continued):

No tax due on exchange. Instead of selling, Debbie trades her $225,000 Atlanta apartment house for the $225,000 Depoe Bay apartment. None of the $200,000 gain is recognized on Debbie's tax return; she would file a Form 8824 and report a §1031 tax-free exchange, thereby currently saving $43,750 in federal taxes. (This like-kind calculation is easy, as is demonstrated later in this chapter.)

Is the only benefit saving taxes? No! By exchanging, an investor not only saves taxes but can use this increase of their net worth, or "equity," to acquire additional real estate. Coupled with the magic of leverage, this creates dramatic results.

Example:

Using an 80% loan-to-value ratio, Debbie can use the $43,750 tax savings as a 20% down payment to acquire $218,750 of additional real estate ($43,750 ÷ .20)! Of course, she would have to structure the acquisition as part of the above exchange. ■

May part of the gain be taxable in an exchange? Yes. Part of the total gain may be tax-free and part may be taxable. The allocation of the gain occurs when the investor receives unlike property (called boot, which is defined more precisely later). As is discussed more thoroughly in Chapter 8, the like-kind exchange gain calculation may be summarized as follows;

Boot received	_____
Less: Exchange expense	− _____
Plus: Net mortgage relief	+ _____
Equals: Gain recognized	= _____ *

* But not greater than the realized gain

Tax Tip

This means the exchange is taxable to the lower of the gain or the boot! Don't worry—all the above terms are clearly explained in Chapter 8.

May a loss be recognized in an exchange? No. Loss from an exchange will not be recognized even though money or nonqualifying property is received [§1031(a)(1)]. Most investors generally try to avoid using an exchange when they are involved in a transaction that would create a tax loss if the property were sold (how to avoid an exchange is discussed later in this chapter).

What happens to the loss? The loss not recognized increases the basis of the property acquired. Hence, the loss is not eliminated, but instead is carried forward to the new property received in the exchange.

Example:

Helen exchanges her office building, which has an adjusted basis of $85,000, for an apartment building, which has a fair market value of $80,000. The $5,000 loss is a non-recognizable loss affecting only the basis of the property received. Helen's new basis will be $85,000; that is, the fair market value of the new building plus the unrecognized loss ($80,000 + $5,000). ■

When a loss is recognized on a partially tax-free exchange because unlike property is transferred, the recognized loss decreases the basis of the property received. The sales price of the unlike property given is the fair market value of the property received.

CALCULATION AND REPORTING REQUIREMENTS

It is easy to calculate the gain that is tax-free! Most investors and tax preparers consider the like-kind exchange computation to be very difficult. After looking at the IRS's Like-Kind Exchanges Form 8824 (found as Figure 5.7 at the end of this chapter) and our worksheet (Figure 5.1), you may be inclined to confirm this misconception. Don't let the forms scare you. Nothing could be farther from the truth.

This beginning like-kind exchange chapter allows the first-time exchanger to quickly hand-calculate the gain on *any* proposed exchange *without understanding the LKE requirements.*

The calculation is the easy part. The hard part is answering the question, "Do we have a qualified like-kind exchange?" The subsequent chapters answer that question.

The examples in this chapter relate to the worksheet in Figure 5.1 and are labeled with line numbers from the worksheet where appropriate. So how easy is this calculation? Let's start from the beginning.

How exchanges are really put together.
Step 1: Negotiate the equity. Exchanges start with negotiating the financial economics, not the tax ramifications, of the transaction; that is, "Is the net equity in your property the same as the net equity in my property? If not, how much are you (or I) willing to add to the pot?"

Step 2: Determine the basis and expenses. Once the above equity figures are determined, only two other pieces of information are needed for the exchange calculation:

1. The exchange expenses
2. The adjusted basis of the property given

Step 3: Calculate. We use an uncomplicated one-page worksheet to "number-crunch" the data accumulated, shown in Figure 5.1. This worksheet is divided into five parts:

1. Equity Calculation
2. Part I—Basis of Property Conveyed
3. Part II—Total Realized Gain (or Loss)
4. Part III—Recognized (Taxable) Gain
5. Part IV—Basis of New Property

It is easy. We need only to accumulate financial data for the equity calculation and Part I. Once we have these figures, the calculation (Parts II, III, and IV) is a simple arithmetic exercise. This sum determines the nontaxable portion of the gain. So let's see the worksheet in action.

1. Equity calculation: As mentioned previously, the first step in preparing a transaction as an exchange is to ascertain the equities of each party and calculate which party, if any, must contribute additional assets. This is done by what has become known in the exchange field as the "napkin test" (FMV means fair market value).

		Gives	**Receives**
E1. FMV of property exchanged	E1	_____	_____
E2. Less: Existing mortgages	E2	_____	_____
Equity (1–2)		_____	_____
E3. Net boot added (Plug figure**)		_____ *	_____ #
(**Difference between equities)		_____	_____
Do equities balance? (1–2 + 3)[G = R]		_____ =	_____
Detail of boot added		_____ *	_____ #
E4. Cash	E4	_____	_____
E5. Other financing	E5	_____	_____
E6. Other unlike property (B1)	E6	_____	_____

A "sweetener" or "evener" may be required to balance the exchange economically (line E3).

FIGURE 5.1 Sample Section 1031 Tax-Free Exchange Worksheet

Copyright - Hoven - 2003

**SECTION 1031
TAX-FREE
EXCHANGE
OF PROPERTY**
———
WORKSHEET

exchangez.pm5

EQUITY CALCULATION	Form 5.1		Gives	Receives
E1. FMV of property exchanged	E1		+$	+$
E2. Less: Existing mortgages	E2		−	−
Equity (1 - 2).			=	=
E3. Net boot added (plug figure**).	E3		+ *	+ #
(**Difference between equities)				
Do equities balance? (1-2+3) [G = R]			=	=
Detail of boot added				
Cash	E4		*	#
Other financing.	E5		*	#
Other unlike property	E6		*	#

PART I - BASIS OF PROPERTY GIVEN
EXCHANGE DATE:

Description:
1. Cost (or other basis) of property given - [date purchased:_____] 1   +$
2. Depreciation allowed or allowable 2   −
3. Adjusted basis of property given up (line 1 less line 2). . . . . 3 $

PART II - REALIZED GAIN (LOSS)

4. FMV of qualifying property received (line E1-R)   (Form 8824, Line 16) . . . . . .4 $
5. Cash received (line E4-R) 5   +$
6. Less: Cash given (line E4-G) 6   −
7. Fair market value of other (boot) received (line E6-R) 7   +
8. Less: FMV of boot (other than cash) given up (line E6-G) 8   −
9. Net liabilities assumed by other party (line E2-G less E2-R but not < zero) 9   +
10. Exchange expenses. 10   −
11. Total consideration received (add lines 5 thru 10)   (Form 8824, Line 15) . . . . . . 11 $
    LESS:
12. Adjusted basis of qualified property given up (line 3) 12   +$
13. Net liabilities assumed by taxpayer (line E2-R less E2-G but not < zero) 13   +
14. Total consideration given (add lines 12 and 13). . . . . . (Form 8824, Line 18) . . . 14 $
15. GAIN REALIZED ON EXCHANGE (line 4 plus line 11 less line 14) (Form 8824, Line 19) . . . . . . 15 $

Proof: A Simple Check
FMV of Prop Exch:_____
Less: Adj. Basis: _____
Gain (if sold): _____

PART III - RECOGNIZED TAXABLE GAIN

CASH AND BOOT
16. Cash and boot (other than cash) received (add lines 5 and 7) . . 16   +$
17. Cash and boot (other than cash) given (add lines 6 and 8) 17   −
18. Exchange expenses (line 10). 18   −
19. Net cash and boot (other than cash) received (line 16 less lines 17 and 18) . . . 19   +/−$
MORTGAGE RELIEF
20. Mortgage on property given (line E2-G) 20   +$
21. Mortgage assumed on property received (line E2-R) 21   −
22. Net mortgage relief (line 20 less line 21; if less than zero, enter zero). 22   +$
23 GAIN RECOGNIZED (line 22 +/- line 19; line 23 cannot exceed) . . . . (Form 8824, Line 20). . . 23 $
               line 15; if less than zero, enter zero

PART IV - BASIS OF NEW PROPERTY
Description:

24. Adjusted basis of LKE property given (line 3). 24   +$
25. Adjusted basis of boot property given (Form 8824, Line 13). . . . 25   +
26. Cash given (line 6). 26   +
27. Mortgage assumed on property received (line E2-R) 27   +
28.   Subtotal (Plus) 28   +$
29. Cash received (line 5) 29   +$
30 Mortgage on property given (line E2-G). 30   +
31.   Subtotal (Minus) 31   −$
32. Plus: Gain recognized on exchange (line 23) 32   +
33. Plus: Gain recognized on boot given (line 8 less line 25 but not < zero) (Form 8824, Line 14) 33   +
34. Less: Loss recognized on boot given (line 25 less line 8 but not < zero) (Form 8824, Line 14) 34   −
35. Exchange expenses (line 10) 35   +
36. BASIS OF ALL NEW PROPERTY RECEIVED (28,31,32,33,34,35) 36
37. BASIS OF BOOT PROPERTY RECEIVED (FMV) (LINE 7) 37
38. BASIS OF LIKE-KIND PROPERTY RECEIVED (LINE 36 LESS LINE 37) (Form 8824, Line 25) . 38 $

Proof: A Simple Check
FMV of Prop Rec'd: _____
Less: Gain *not* taxed:_____
New Basis: _____

Example:

Remember Debbie with her $225,000 apartment in Atlanta in the previous example? Let's prove that her exchange is fully tax-free.

Equity Calculation

		Debbie Gives Atlanta	and Receives Depoe Bay
E1. FMV of property exchanged	E1	$225,000	$225,000
E2. Less: Existing mortgages	E2	0	0
Equity (1–2)		$225,000	$225,000

Investor Hint

Our "napkin test" determines that both equities are equal.

E3. Net boot added (Plug figure**)	E3	0*	0#
(**Difference between equities)			
Do equities balance? (1 – 2 + 3) [G = R]		$225,000 =	$225,000
Detail of boot added		*	#
E4. Cash	E4	0	0
E5. Other financing	E5	0	0
E6. Other unlike property (B1)	E6	0	0

2. Part I—Compute the adjusted basis of the property being given: The formula for calculating the adjusted basis of the property to be conveyed for an exchange is the same calculation as used in a sale. Each line in this formula is thoroughly discussed in Chapter 1.

Exchange Adjusted Basis Computation

Adjusted basis:

Original cost (or basis)	+	
Plus: Purchase expenses	+	
Plus: Improvements	+	
Equals: Cost (or other basis) of property given	=	1
Less: Accumulated depreciation	–	2
Total Adjusted Basis (1 – 2):	=	3

Investor Hint

The numbers in front of the dollar amounts refer to the Like-Kind Exchanges worksheet.

Exchange Adjusted Basis Computation

Adjusted basis:

Original cost (or basis)	+			$100,000
Equals: Cost (or other basis) of property given	=	1		$100,000
Less: Accumulated depreciation	−	2	$	75,000
Total Adjusted Basis (1 − 2):	=	3	$	25,000

Tax Tip

This is all the information needed to calculate the tax ramifications of a tax-free exchange! To see all these numbers together, see the worksheet in Figure 5.2 and the IRS Form 8824 in Figure 5.3.

Investor Hint

Debbie participates in a like-kind exchange and finds that the entire $200,000 gain is nontaxable, thereby saving her $43,750 of current taxes.

Tax Tip

The basic rule in exchanges: Be the party who trades equal or up—both in fair market value and in debt—and don't receive any boot [§1031(a)(1)]! This is what Debbie did in the previous example. This basic rule will be fully explained in the following chapter on requirements of like-kind exchanges, but next we will demonstrate what happens if the parties *do not* trade equal or up.

LET'S TRY A MUCH MORE COMPLICATED EXAMPLE

This is an actual example from the IRS's regulations [§1.1031(d)-2 (Example 2)]. Even though you may not understand the "why," you will be able to calculate the tax-free and taxable portion of the gain with the same ease as in the previous example.

Example:

Donna owns an apartment with an adjusted basis of $100,000 and a fair market value of $220,000, but subject to a mortgage of $80,000. Edward wants to trade his apartment to Donna. Edward's apartment has an adjusted basis of $175,000 and a fair market value of $250,000, but is subject to a mortgage of $150,000. To even equity, Edward agrees to pay Donna $40,000 in cash [§1.1031(d)-2 (Example 2)]. Closing is January 1, 2004. ∎

FIGURE 5.2   **Sample Section 1031 Tax-Free Exchange Worksheet Completed**

Copyright - Hoven - 2003

SECTION 1031 TAX-FREE EXCHANGE OF PROPERTY
───
WORKSHEET
exchange2.pm5

		DEBBIE	DEPOE BAY
EQUITY CALCULATION Form 5.2		Gives	Receives
E1. FMV of property exchanged E1		+$225,000	+$ 225,000
E2. Less: Existing mortgages E2		−	−
Equity (1 - 2).		= 225,000	= 225,000
E3. Net boot added (plug figure**). E3		+ *	+ #
(**Difference between equities)			
Do equities balance? (1-2+3) [G = R]		= 225,000	= 225,000
Detail of boot added			
Cash E4		*	#
Other financing. E5		*	#
Other unlike property E6		*	#

PART I - BASIS OF PROPERTY GIVEN
EXCHANGE DATE:12/1/98

Description: DEBBIE'S ATLANTA APARTMENT

1. Cost (or other basis) of property given - [date purchased: 11/1/85] 1	+$100,000	
2. Depreciation allowed or allowable 2	− 75,000	
3. Adjusted basis of property given up (line 1 less line 2). 3	$ 25,000	

PART II - REALIZED GAIN (LOSS)

4. FMV of qualifying property received (line E1-R) (Form 8824, Line 16) 4	$ 225,000	
5. Cash received (line E4-R) 5	+$	
6. Less: Cash given (line E4-G) 6	−	**Proof: A Simple Check**
7. Fair market value of other (boot) received (line E6-R) 7	+	FMV of Prop Exch:225,000
8. Less: FMV of boot (other than cash) given up (line E6-G) 8	−	Less: Adj. Basis: 25,000
9. Net liabilities assumed by other party (line E2-G less E2-R but not < zero)9	+	Gain (if sold): 200,000
10. Exchange expenses 10	−	
11.Total consideration received (add lines 5 thru 10) (Form 8824, Line 15) 11	$	
LESS:		
12. Adjusted basis of qualified property given up (line 3) 12	+$ 25,000	
13. Net liabilities assumed by taxpayer (line E2-R less E2-G but not < zero) 13	+	
14. Total consideration given (add lines 12 and 13). . . . . . (Form 8824, Line 18) . . . 14	$ 25,000	
15. GAIN REALIZED ON EXCHANGE (line 4 plus line 11 less line 14) (Form 8824, Line 19) 15		$ 200,000

PART III - RECOGNIZED TAXABLE GAIN

CASH AND BOOT

16. Cash and boot (other than cash) received (add lines 5 and 7) . . 16	+$	
17. Cash and boot (other than cash) given (add lines 6 and 8) 17	−	
18. Exchange expenses (line 10). 18	−	
19. Net cash and boot (other than cash) received (line 16 less lines 17 and 18) . . . 19	+/−$ -0-	

MORTGAGE RELIEF

20. Mortgage on property given (line E2-G) 20	+$	
21. Mortgage assumed on property received (line E2-R) 21	−	
22. Net mortgage relief (line 20 less line 21; if less than zero, enter zero). 22	+$ -0-	
23 GAIN RECOGNIZED (line 22 +/- line 19; line 23 cannot exceed line 15; if less than zero, enter zero) . . . . (Form 8824, Line 20). . . 23	$ -0-	

PART IV - BASIS OF NEW PROPERTY
Description: DEPOT BAY PROPERTY

24. Adjusted basis of LKE property given (line 3). 24	+$ 25,000	**Proof: A Simple Check**
25. Adjusted basis of boot property given (Form 8824, Line 13). . . . 25	+	FMV of Prop Rec'd: 225,000
26. Cash given (line 6). 26	+	Less: Gain *not* taxed:200,000
27. Mortgage assumed on property received (line E2-R) 27	+	New Basis: 25,000
28. Subtotal (Plus) 28	+$ 25,000	
29. Cash received (line 5) 29	+$	
30 Mortgage on property given (line E2-G) 30	+	
31. Subtotal (Minus) 31	−$	
32. Plus: Gain recognized on exchange (line 23) 32	+	
33. Plus: Gain recognized on boot given (line 8 less line 25 but not < zero) (Form 8824, Line 14) 33	+	
34. Less: Loss recognized on boot given (line 25 less line 8 but not < zero) (Form 8824, Line 14) 34	−	
35. Exchange expenses (line 10) 35	+	
36. BASIS OF ALL NEW PROPERTY RECEIVED (28,31,32,33,34,35) 36		25,000
37. BASIS OF BOOT PROPERTY RECEIVED (FMV) (LINE 7) 37		
38. BASIS OF LIKE-KIND PROPERTY RECEIVED (LINE 36 LESS LINE 37) (Form 8824, Line 25) . 38		$ 25,000

FIGURE 5.3 Sample IRS Form 8824

Form **8824**	**Like-Kind Exchanges**	OMB No. 1545-1190
Department of the Treasury Internal Revenue Service	(and section 1043 conflict-of-interest sales) ► Attach to your tax return.	**200** 109

Name(s) shown on tax return	Identifying number
	517–

Part I — Information on the Like-Kind Exchange

Note: *If the property described on line 1 or line 2 is real or personal property located outside the United States, indicate the country.*

1 Description of like-kind property given up ► DEBBIE'S ATLANTA APARTMENT

2 Description of like-kind property received ► DEPOT BAY PROPERTY

3	Date like-kind property given up was originally acquired (month, day, year)	**3** 11/01/86
4	Date you actually transferred your property to other party (month, day, year)	**4** 12/01/02
5	Date like-kind property you received was identified (month, day, year) (see instructions)	**5** 12/01/02
6	Date you actually received the like-kind property from other party (month, day, year)	**6** 12/01/02

7 Was the exchange made with a related party (see instructions)? If 'Yes', complete Part II. If 'No', go to Part III.
a ☐ Yes, in this tax year   b ☐ Yes, in a prior tax year   c ☒ No

Part II — Related Party Exchange Information

8 Name of related party	Related party's identifying number
Address (number, street, and apartment, room, or suite number)	

City or town	State	ZIP code	Relationship to you

9 During this tax year (and before the date that is 2 years after the last transfer of property that was part of the exchange), did the related party sell or dispose of the like-kind property received from you in the exchange? ☐ Yes ☐ No

10 During this tax year (and before the date that is 2 years after the last transfer of property that was part of the exchange), did you sell or dispose of the like-kind property you received? ☐ Yes ☐ No

If both lines 9 and 10 are 'No' and this is the year of the exchange, go to Part III. If both lines 9 and 10 are 'No' and this is not the year of the exchange, stop here. If either line 9 or line 10 is 'Yes,' complete Part III and report on this year's tax return the deferred gain or (loss) from line 24 unless one of the exceptions on line 11 applies. See Related party exchanges in the instructions.

11 If one of the exceptions below applies to the disposition, check the applicable box:
a ☐ The disposition was after the death of either of the related parties.
b ☐ The disposition was an involuntary conversion, and the threat of conversion occurred after the exchange.
c ☐ You can establish to the satisfaction of the IRS that neither the exchange nor the disposition had tax avoidance as its principal purpose. If this box is checked, attach an explanation (see instructions).

Part III — Realized Gain or (Loss), Recognized Gain, and Basis of Like-Kind Property Received

Caution: *If you transferred and received (a) more than one group of like-kind properties or (b) cash or other (not like-kind) property, see Reporting of multi-asset exchanges in the instructions.*

Note: *Complete lines 12 through 14 only if you gave up property that was not like-kind. Otherwise, go to line 15.*

12	Fair market value (FMV) of other property given up	**12**	
13	Adjusted basis of other property given up	**13**	
14	Gain or (loss) recognized on other property given up. Subtract line 13 from line 12. Report the gain or (loss) in the same manner as if the exchange had been a sale	**14**	
15	Cash received, FMV of other property received, plus net liabilities assumed by other party, reduced (but not below zero) by any exchange expenses you incurred (see instructions)	**15**	0.
16	FMV of like-kind property you received	**16**	225,000.
17	Add lines 15 and 16	**17**	225,000.
18	Adjusted basis of like-kind property you gave up, net amounts paid to other party, plus any exchange expenses not used on line 15 (see instructions)	**18**	25,000.
19	**Realized gain or (loss).** Subtract line 18 from line 17	**19**	200,000.
20	Enter the smaller of line 15 or line 19, but not less than zero	**20**	0.
21	Ordinary income under recapture rules. Enter here and on Form 4797, line 16 (see instructions)	**21**	0.
22	Subtract line 21 from line 20. If zero or less, enter -0-. If more than zero, enter here and on Schedule D or Form 4797, unless the installment method applies (see instructions)	**22**	0.
23	**Recognized gain.** Add lines 21 and 22	**23**	0.
24	Deferred gain or (loss). Subtract line 23 from line 19. If a related party exchange, see instructions	**24**	200,000.
25	**Basis of like-kind property received.** Subtract line 15 from the sum of lines 18 and 23	**25**	25,000.

BAA **For Paperwork Reduction Act Notice, see separate instructions.**   FDIZ2112L 12/05/02   Form **8824** (2002)

Equity Calculation

		Donna Gives Donna's Apt.	and Receives Edward's Apt.
E1. FMV of property exchanged	E1	$220,000	$250,000
E2. Less: Existing mortgages	E2	− 80,000	−150,000
Equity (1 − 2)		$140,000	$100,000

Tax Tip

Our "napkin test" determines that Donna has $40,000 more equity, and Edward needs to "sweeten the deal" by the difference between the two equities.

		Donna Gives	and Receives
E3. Net boot added (Plug figure**)	E3	0*	$ 40,000#
(**Difference between equities)			
Do equities balance? (1 − 2 + 3) [G = R]		$140,000 =	$140,000
Detail of boot added		*	#
E4. Cash	E4	0	$ 40,000
E5. Other financing	E5	0	0
E6. Other unlike property (B1)	E6	0	0

Example (continued):

Continuing with the example above, Donna's tax preparer informs us that she originally purchased the property for $228,583, with $25,000 allocated to land and has accumulated $128,583 ($203,583 × 63.16%; see Chapter 10 for details) of depreciation during her twelve-year ownership. The exchange expenses are $5,000.

Exchange Adjusted Basis Computation

Adjusted basis:

	Original cost (or basis)	+		$220,000
	Plus: Purchase expenses	+		8,853
Equals:	Cost (or other basis) of property given	=	1	$228,583
	Less: Accumulated depreciation	−	2	$128,583
Total Adjusted Basis (1 − 2):		=	3	$100,000

Tax Tip

This is all the information needed to calculate the tax ramifications of a tax-free exchange! To see all these numbers together, see the worksheet in Figure 5.4 and the IRS Form 8824 in Figure 5.5.

FIGURE 5.4   Sample Section 1031 Tax-Free Exchange Worksheet

Copyright - Hoven - 2003

SECTION 1031 TAX-FREE EXCHANGE OF PROPERTY ───── WORKSHEET

exchange4.pm5

EQUITY CALCULATION Form 5.4	DONNA Gives	EDWARD Receives
E1. FMV of property exchanged E1	+$ 220,000	+$ 250,000
E2. Less: Existing mortgages E2	− 80,000	− 150,000
Equity (1 - 2).	= 140,000	= 100,000
E3. Net boot added (plug figure**). E3	+ *	+ 40,000#
(**Difference between equities)		
Do equities balance? (1-2+3) [G = R]	= 140,000	= 140,000
Detail of boot added		
Cash E4	*	# 40,000
Other financing. E5	*	#
Other unlike property E6	*	#

PART I - BASIS OF PROPERTY GIVEN   EXCHANGE DATE: 1/1/98

Description: DONNA'S APARTMENT

1. Cost (or other basis) of property given - [date purchased: 11/1/86] 1	+$ 228,583
2. Depreciation allowed or allowable 2	− 128,583
3. Adjusted basis of property given up (line 1 less line 2). 3	$ 100,000

PART II - REALIZED GAIN (LOSS)

4. FMV of qualifying property received (line E1-R) (Form 8824, Line 16) 4	$ 250,000	
5. Cash received (line E4-R) 5	+$ 40,000	**Proof: A Simple Check**
6. Less: Cash given (line E4-G) 6	−	FMV of Prop Exch: 220,000
7. Fair market value of other (boot) received (line E6-R) 7	+	Less: Adj. Basis: 105,000
8. Less: FMV of boot (other than cash) given up (line E6-G) 8	−	Gain (if sold): 115,000
9. Net liabilities assumed by other party (line E2-G less E2-R but not < zero) 9	+	
10. Exchange expenses. 10	− 5,000	
11.Total consideration received (add lines 5 thru 10) (Form 8824, Line 15) 11	$ 35,000	
LESS:		
12. Adjusted basis of qualified property given up (line 3) 12	+$100,000	
13. Net liabilities assumed by taxpayer (line E2-R less E2-G but not < zero) 13	+ 70,000	
14. Total consideration given (add lines 12 and 13). . . . . . (Form 8824, Line 18) . . . 14	$ 170,000	
15. GAIN REALIZED ON EXCHANGE (line 4 plus line 11 less line 14) (Form 8824, Line 19) 15	$ 115,000	

PART III - RECOGNIZED TAXABLE GAIN

CASH AND BOOT

16. Cash and boot (other than cash) received (add lines 5 and 7) . . 16	+$ 40,000	
17. Cash and boot (other than cash) given (add lines 6 and 8) 17	−	
18. Exchange expenses (line 10). 18	− 5,000	
19. Net cash and boot (other than cash) received (line 16 less lines 17 and 18) . . . 19	⊕ −$ 35,000	

MORTGAGE RELIEF

20. Mortgage on property given (line E2-G) 20	+$ 80,000	
21. Mortgage assumed on property received (line E2-R) 21	− 150,000	
22. Net mortgage relief (line 20 less line 21; if less than zero, enter zero). 22	+$ -0-	
23 GAIN RECOGNIZED (line 22 +/- line 19; line 23 cannot exceed) . . . .(Form 8824, Line 20). . . 23	$ 35,000	
line 15; if less than zero, enter zero		

PART IV - BASIS OF NEW PROPERTY   Description: EDWARD'S APARTMENT

24. Adjusted basis of LKE property given (line 3). 24	+$ 100,000	**Proof: A Simple Check**
25. Adjusted basis of boot property given (Form 8824, Line 13). . . 25	+	FMV of Prop Rec'd: 250,000
26. Cash given (line 6). 26	+	Less: Gain *not* taxed: 80,000
27. Mortgage assumed on property received (line E2-R) 27	+ 150,000	New Basis: 170,000
28. Subtotal (Plus) 28	+$ 250,000	
29. Cash received (line 5) 29	+$ 40,000	
30 Mortgage on property given (line E2-G). 30	+ 80,000	
31. Subtotal (Minus) 31	−$ 120,000	
32. Plus: Gain recognized on exchange (line 23) 32	+ 35,000	
33. Plus: Gain recognized on boot given (line 8 less line 25 but not < zero) (Form 8824, Line 14) 33	+	
34. Less: Loss recognized on boot given (line 25 less line 8 but not < zero) (Form 8824, Line 14) 34	−	
35. Exchange expenses (line 10) 35	+ 5,000	
36. BASIS OF ALL NEW PROPERTY RECEIVED (28,31,32,33,34,35) 36		170,000
37. BASIS OF BOOT PROPERTY RECEIVED (FMV) (LINE 7) 37		
38. BASIS OF LIKE-KIND PROPERTY RECEIVED (LINE 36 LESS LINE 37) (Form 8824, Line 25) . 38		$ 170,000

FIGURE 5.5   **Sample IRS Form 8824**

Form **8824**

Department of the Treasury
Internal Revenue Service

Like-Kind Exchanges
(and section 1043 conflict-of-interest sales)
► **Attach to your tax return.**

OMB No. 1545-1190

200
109

Name(s) shown on tax return

Identifying number
517-

Part I   Information on the Like-Kind Exchange

Note: If the property described on line 1 or line 2 is real or personal property located outside the United States, indicate the country.

1   Description of like-kind property given up ►   DONNA'S APARTMENT

2   Description of like-kind property received ►   EDWARD'S APARTMENT

3 Date like-kind property given up was originally acquired (month, day, year)	**3**	11/01/87
4 Date you actually transferred your property to other party (month, day, year)	**4**	1/01/02
5 Date like-kind property you received was identified (month, day, year) (see instructions)	**5**	1/01/02
6 Date you actually received the like-kind property from other party (month, day, year)	**6**	1/01/02

7   Was the exchange made with a related party (see instructions)? If 'Yes', complete Part II. If 'No', go to Part III.
  a ☐ Yes, in this tax year   b ☐ Yes, in a prior tax year   c ☒ No

Part II   Related Party Exchange Information

8   Name of related party | Related party's identifying number

Address (number, street, and apartment, room, or suite number)

City or town | State | ZIP code | Relationship to you

9   During this tax year (and before the date that is 2 years after the last transfer of property that was part of the exchange), did the related party sell or dispose of the like-kind property received from you in the exchange? ☐ Yes ☐ No

10 During this tax year (and before the date that is 2 years after the last transfer of property that was part of the exchange), did you sell or dispose of the like-kind property you received? ☐ Yes ☐ No

If both lines 9 and 10 are 'No' and this is the year of the exchange, go to Part III. If both lines 9 and 10 are 'No' and this is **not** the year of the exchange, stop here. If either line 9 or line 10 is 'Yes,' complete Part III and report on this year's tax return the deferred gain or (loss) from line 24 **unless** one of the exceptions on line 11 applies. See **Related party exchanges** in the instructions.

11 If one of the exceptions below applies to the disposition, check the applicable box:
  a ☐ The disposition was after the death of either of the related parties.
  b ☐ The disposition was an involuntary conversion, and the threat of conversion occurred after the exchange.
  c ☐ You can establish to the satisfaction of the IRS that neither the exchange nor the disposition had tax avoidance as its principal purpose. If this box is checked, attach an explanation (see instructions).

Part III   Realized Gain or (Loss), Recognized Gain, and Basis of Like-Kind Property Received

Caution: If you transferred **and** received (**a**) more than one group of like-kind properties or (**b**) cash or other (not like-kind) property, see **Reporting of multi-asset exchanges** in the instructions.

Note: Complete lines 12 through 14 **only** if you gave up property that was not like-kind. Otherwise, go to line 15.

12 Fair market value (FMV) of other property given up	**12**	
13 Adjusted basis of other property given up	**13**	
14 Gain or (loss) recognized on other property given up. Subtract line 13 from line 12. Report the gain or (loss) in the same manner as if the exchange had been a sale	**14**	
15 Cash received, FMV of other property received, plus net liabilities assumed by other party, reduced (but not below zero) by any exchange expenses you incurred (see instructions)	**15**	35,000.
16 FMV of like-kind property you received	**16**	250,000.
17 Add lines 15 and 16	**17**	285,000.
18 Adjusted basis of like-kind property you gave up, net amounts paid to other party, plus any exchange expenses **not** used on line 15 (see instructions)	**18**	170,000.
19 **Realized gain or (loss).** Subtract line 18 from line 17	**19**	115,000.
20 Enter the smaller of line 15 or line 19, but not less than zero	**20**	35,000.
21 Ordinary income under recapture rules. Enter here and on Form 4797, line 16 (see instructions)	**21**	35,000.
22 Subtract line 21 from line 20. If zero or less, enter -0-. If more than zero, enter here and on Schedule D or Form 4797, unless the installment method applies (see instructions)	**22**	0.
23 **Recognized gain.** Add lines 21 and 22	**23**	35,000.
24 Deferred gain or (loss). Subtract line 23 from line 19. If a related party exchange, see instructions	**24**	80,000.
25 **Basis of like-kind property received.** Subtract line 15 from the sum of lines 18 and 23	**25**	170,000.

BAA **For Paperwork Reduction Act Notice, see separate instructions.**   FDIZ2112L 12/05/02   Form **8824** (2002)

Note: Donna participates in a like-kind exchange and finds that $35,000 of her $115,000 gain is taxable. Can she avoid this gain? The answer to that question requires you to read the remaining like-kind exchange chapters!

Investor Hint

Donna did not (1) "go equal or up" and (2) receive any boot, as the LKE rules require for a fully tax-free exchange.

Figuring fair market value in an exchange is easy! Adding together the equity and assumed mortgages of each party equals the fair market value of the properties!

Example:

	Donna	Edward
Existing mortgage:	$ 80,000	$150,000
Plus: Equity	+140,000	+100,000
Equals: Fair market value	$220,000	$250,000

Let's try one more problem:

Example:

What about the other party to the exchange—Edward? His tax preparer informs us that he originally purchased the property for $216,117, with $30,000 allocated to land, and has accumulated $41,117 ($186,117 × 22.092%) of depreciation during his ownership. His exchange expenses were $4,500 [§1.1031(d)-2 (Example 2)]. Closing was January 1, 2004.

Equity Calculation

		Edward Gives Edward's Apt.	and Receives Donna's Apt.
E1. FMV of property exchanged	E1	$220,000	$220,000
E2. Less: Existing mortgages	E2	−150,000	− 80,000
Equity (1 − 2)		$100,000	$140,000
E3. Net boot added (Plug figure**)	E3	$ 40,000*	$ 0#
(**Difference between equities)			
Do equities balance? (1 − 2 + 3) [G = R]		$140,000 =	$140,000
Detail of boot added		*	#
E4. Cash	E4	$40,000	0
E5. Other financing	E5	0	0
E6. Other unlike property (B1)	E6	0	0

Exchange Adjusted Basis Computation

Adjusted basis:

	Original cost (or basis)	+		$200,000
	Plus: Purchase expenses	+		16,117
	Plus: Improvements	+		
Equals:	Cost (or other basis) of property given	=	1	$216,117
	Less: Accumulated depreciation	−	2	$ 41,117
Total Adjusted Basis (1 − 2):		=	3	$175,000

> **Tax Tip**
>
> To see all these numbers together, see the worksheet in Figure 5.6 and the IRS Form 8824 in Figure 5.7.

Note: Edward participates in a like-kind exchange and finds that $25,500 of his $70,500 gain is taxable. Can he avoid this gain? Read on!

> **Tax Tip**
>
> *Isn't it easier than you first thought?* As can be seen, to calculate the taxable and nontaxable gain on an exchange, it is not necessary to know or understand any other terms or concepts, such as "What is *boot?*" "What do we do with *mortgage relief?*" and "What is the basis of the new property received?" To eliminate the gains for Donna or Edward, though, it is necessary to understand the minimum requirements for a tax-free exchange, *as are fully discussed in Chapter 8!*

§1031 IS MANDATORY

An exchange must be reported as an exchange. Section 1031 is not subject to election or waiver, and if all the exchange elements are present, the taxpayer must report the transaction as an exchange.

> **Tax Tip**
>
> However, §1031 and its associated nonrecognition of gain or loss can be intentionally avoided by evading one of the six exchange elements listed in Chapter 8 [Rev. Rul. 75-292, 1975-2 CB 333].

One-party exchanges common. An exchange may be taxable to one party and tax-free to the other; it need not be tax-free to both parties for §1031 to apply [Rev. Rul. 75-292, 1975-2 CB 333].

FIGURE 5.6   **Sample Section 1031 Tax-Free Exchange of Property Worksheet**

Copyright - Hoven - 2003

SECTION 1031 TAX-FREE EXCHANGE OF PROPERTY
————
WORKSHEET

exchanged.pm5

EQUITY CALCULATION Form 5.6		EDWARD Gives	DONNA Receives
E1. FMV of property exchanged E1		+$ 250,000	+$ 220,000
E2. Less: Existing mortgages E2		− 150,000	− 80,000
Equity (1 - 2) .		= 100,000	= 140,000
E3. Net boot added (plug figure**) E3		+ 40,000 *	+ #
(**Difference between equities)			
Do equities balance? (1-2+3) [G = R]		= 140,000	= 140,000
Detail of boot added			
Cash E4	*	40,000	#
Other financing. E5	*		#
Other unlike property E6	*		#

PART I - BASIS OF PROPERTY GIVEN   EXCHANGE DATE: 1/1/98

Description: EDWARD'S APARTMENT		
1. Cost (or other basis) of property given - [date purchased: 1/1/91] 1	+$ 216,117	
2. Depreciation allowed or allowable 2	− 41,117	
3. Adjusted basis of property given up (line 1 less line 2) 3	$ 175,000	

PART II - REALIZED GAIN (LOSS)

4. FMV of qualifying property received (line E1-R) (Form 8824, Line 16) 4	$ 220,000	
5. Cash received (line E4-R) 5	+$	*Proof: A Simple Check*
6. Less: Cash given (line E4-G) 6	− 40,000	FMV of Prop Exch: 250,000
7. Fair market value of other (boot) received (line E6-R) 7	+	Less: Adj. Basis: 179,500
8. Less: FMV of boot (other than cash) given up (line E6-G) 8	−	Gain (if sold): 70,500
9. Net liabilities assumed by other party (line E2-G less E2-R but not < zero) 9	+ 70,000	
10. Exchange expenses. 10	− 4,500	
11.Total consideration received (add lines 5 thru 10) (Form 8824, Line 15) 11	$ 25,500	
LESS:		
12. Adjusted basis of qualified property given up (line 3) 12	+$ 175,000	
13. Net liabilities assumed by taxpayer (line E2-R less E2-G but not < zero) 13	+	
14. Total consideration given (add lines 12 and 13). . . . . . (Form 8824, Line 18) . . . 14	$ 175,000	
15. GAIN REALIZED ON EXCHANGE (line 4 plus line 11 less line 14) (Form 8824, Line 19) 15	$ 70,500	

PART III - RECOGNIZED TAXABLE GAIN

CASH AND BOOT

16. Cash and boot (other than cash) received (add lines 5 and 7) . . 16	+$	
17. Cash and boot (other than cash) given (add lines 6 and 8) 17	− 40,000	
18. Exchange expenses (line 10). 18	− 4,500	
19. Net cash and boot (other than cash) received (line 16 less lines 17 and 18) . . . 19	+/−$ 44,500	

MORTGAGE RELIEF

20. Mortgage on property given (line E2-G) 20	+$ 150,000	
21. Mortgage assumed on property received (line E2-R) 21	− 80,000	
22. Net mortgage relief (line 20 less line 21; if less than zero, enter zero) 22	+$ 70,000	
23 GAIN RECOGNIZED (line 22 +/- line 19; line 23 cannot exceed) . . . . (Form 8824, Line 20) . . . 23	$ 25,500	
line 15; if less than zero, enter zero		

PART IV - BASIS OF NEW PROPERTY   Description: DONNA'S APARTMENT

24. Adjusted basis of LKE property given (line 3). 24	+$ 175,000	*Proof: A Simple Check*
25. Adjusted basis of boot property given (Form 8824, Line 13). . . . 25	+	FMV of Prop Rec'd: 220,000
26. Cash given (line 6). 26	+ 40,000	Less: Gain *not* taxed: 45,000
27. Mortgage assumed on property received (line E2-R) 27	+ 80,000	New Basis: 175,000
28. Subtotal (Plus) 28	+$ 295,000	
29. Cash received (line 5) 29	+$	
30 Mortgage on property given (line E2-G). 30	+ 150,000	
31. Subtotal (Minus) 31	−$ 150,000	
32. Plus: Gain recognized on exchange (line 23) 32	+ 25,500	
33. Plus: Gain recognized on boot given (line 8 less line 25 but not < zero) (Form 8824, Line 14) 33	+	
34. Less: Loss recognized on boot given (line 25 less line 8 but not < zero) (Form 8824, Line 14) 34	−	
35. Exchange expenses (line 10) 35	+ 4,500	
36. BASIS OF ALL NEW PROPERTY RECEIVED (28,31,32,33,34,35) 36		175,000
37. BASIS OF BOOT PROPERTY RECEIVED (FMV) (LINE 7) 37		
38. BASIS OF LIKE-KIND PROPERTY RECEIVED (LINE 36 LESS LINE 37) (Form 8824, Line 25) . 38		$ 175,000

FIGURE 5.7   **Sample IRS Form 8824**

Form **8824**	**Like-Kind Exchanges**	OMB No. 1545-1190
	(and section 1043 conflict-of-interest sales) ► **Attach to your tax return.**	**200**
Department of the Treasury Internal Revenue Service		**109**

Name(s) shown on tax return	Identifying number
	517-

Part I	**Information on the Like-Kind Exchange**

Note: *If the property described on line 1 or line 2 is real or personal property located outside the United States, indicate the country.*

1 Description of like-kind property given up ►   EDWARD'S APARTMENT

2 Description of like-kind property received ►   DONNA'S APARTMENT

3	Date like-kind property given up was originally acquired (month, day, year)	**3**	1/01/92
4	Date you actually transferred your property to other party (month, day, year)	**4**	1/01/02
5	Date like-kind property you received was identified (month, day, year) (see instructions)	**5**	1/01/02
6	Date you actually received the like-kind property from other party (month, day, year)	**6**	1/01/02

7 Was the exchange made with a related party (see instructions)? If 'Yes', complete Part II. If 'No', go to Part III.
a [ ] Yes, in this tax year   b [ ] Yes, in a prior tax year   c [X] No

Part II	**Related Party Exchange Information**

8 Name of related party	Related party's identifying number
Address (number, street, and apartment, room, or suite number)	
City or town State ZIP code	Relationship to you

9 During this tax year (and before the date that is 2 years after the last transfer of property that was part of the exchange), did the related party sell or dispose of the like-kind property received from you in the exchange?....... [ ] **Yes**   [ ] **No**

10 During this tax year (and before the date that is 2 years after the last transfer of property that was part of the exchange), did you sell or dispose of the like-kind property you received?.................................... [ ] **Yes**   [ ] **No**

*If both lines 9 and 10 are 'No' and this is the year of the exchange, go to Part III. If both lines 9 and 10 are 'No' and this is **not** the year of the exchange, stop here. If either line 9 or line 10 is 'Yes,' complete Part III and report on this year's tax return the deferred gain or (loss) from line 24 unless one of the exceptions on line 11 applies. See **Related party exchanges** in the instructions.*

11 If one of the exceptions below applies to the disposition, check the applicable box:
a [ ] The disposition was after the death of either of the related parties.
b [ ] The disposition was an involuntary conversion, and the threat of conversion occurred after the exchange.
c [ ] You can establish to the satisfaction of the IRS that neither the exchange nor the disposition had tax avoidance as its principal purpose. If this box is checked, attach an explanation (see instructions).

Part III	**Realized Gain or (Loss), Recognized Gain, and Basis of Like-Kind Property Received**

Caution: *If you transferred **and** received **(a)** more than one group of like-kind properties or **(b)** cash or other (not like-kind) property, see **Reporting of multi-asset exchanges** in the instructions.*

Note: *Complete lines 12 through 14 **only** if you gave up property that was not like-kind. Otherwise, go to line 15.*

12	Fair market value (FMV) of other property given up	**12**		
13	Adjusted basis of other property given up	**13**		
14	Gain or (loss) recognized on other property given up. Subtract line 13 from line 12. Report the gain or (loss) in the same manner as if the exchange had been a sale		**14**	
15	Cash received, FMV of other property received, plus net liabilities assumed by other party, reduced (but not below zero) by any exchange expenses you incurred (see instructions)		**15**	25,500.
16	FMV of like-kind property you received		**16**	220,000.
17	Add lines 15 and 16		**17**	245,500.
18	Adjusted basis of like-kind property you gave up, net amounts paid to other party, plus any exchange expenses **not** used on line 15 (see instructions)		**18**	175,000.
19	**Realized gain or (loss).** Subtract line 18 from line 17		**19**	70,500.
20	Enter the smaller of line 15 or line 19, but not less than zero		**20**	25,500.
21	Ordinary income under recapture rules. Enter here and on Form 4797, line 16 (see instructions)		**21**	25,500.
22	Subtract line 21 from line 20. If zero or less, enter -0-. If more than zero, enter here and on Schedule D or Form 4797, unless the installment method applies (see instructions)		**22**	0.
23	**Recognized gain.** Add lines 21 and 22		**23**	25,500.
24	Deferred gain or (loss). Subtract line 23 from line 19. If a related party exchange, see instructions		**24**	45,000.
25	**Basis of like-kind property received.** Subtract line 15 from the sum of lines 18 and 23		**25**	175,000.

BAA For Paperwork Reduction Act Notice, see separate instructions.   FDIZ2112L 12/05/02   Form **8824** (2002)

WHEN IS AN EXCHANGE NOT ADVISABLE?

Generally, real estate investors wish to avoid an exchange transaction in the following situations:

1. **When property could be sold for a loss.** This is because the loss on an exchange is not currently deductible, and the loss on a sale may be fully currently deductible as a §1231 ordinary business loss.

2. **When a taxable gain can be offset with other currently deductible losses that result in minimal tax due.** Exchanges generally cost more money to complete than sales transactions and, thus, current losses are normally more valuable than deferred losses.

3. **When liquidity is required.** This usually occurs at the time of retirement or for medical or other emergencies.

4. **When investors do not want any other property.** An example is when the individual wishes to discontinue managing the real estate and is tired of being a landlord.

Chapter

Types of Simultaneous Exchanges

TWO-PARTY EXCHANGES—A SWAP!

The two-party exchange (Figure 6.1) is the simplest to understand, but also the most difficult exchange to accomplish, because not only must both parties be willing to trade properties but the properties and equities must be of approximately the same value. In reality, this seldom happens.

MULTIPARTY OR THREE-LEGGED EXCHANGES

May a three-party exchange be arranged? What happens if one party in an exchange does not want any property owned by the other party but rather wants a third party's property? Exchanges involving three parties are about as common as two-party exchanges are rare, and a three-party exchange may turn a taxable sale into a nontaxable exchange.

Only one party need desire a tax-free exchange! Strange as it may sound, a multiparty exchange often involves only *one* party interested in an exchange, coupled with one buyer and one seller. Properly structured, the objectives of all parties can be accomplished in a multiparty or a three-legged exchange. The taxpayer, of course, is seeking to avoid recognition of gain in the disposition of the appreciated property.

Is a three-legged exchange a sham transaction? May the Internal Revenue Service pierce a multiparty or three-legged exchange on the grounds that it is being done for tax purposes only and therefore is a sham? *No,* according to *Alderson v. Comm.,* 317 F2d 790 (9th Cir. 1963) and many other subsequent cases; it is form over substance. The IRS also recognizes multiparty exchanges [Rev. Rul. 77-297, 1977-2 CB 304].

The *Starker III* case [*T. J. Starker v. U.S.,* 602 F2d 1341 (CA-9, 79-2 USTC ¶9451)] was considered an exchange for three reasons:

1. *Exchange, not sale, planned.* The taxpayer claimed that he intended from the outset of the transaction to receive nothing but like-kind property.
2. *Integrated plan exists.* All the recorded evidence indicated an exchange occurred.
3. *No actual or constructive receipt of cash.* The taxpayer never handled any cash in the course of the transaction.

THREE COMMON VARIATIONS OF A MULTIPARTY EXCHANGE

There are generally three varieties of multiparty exchanges. They are

1. the three-party "Alderson" exchange,
2. the three-party "Baird Publishing" exchange, and
3. the four-party "Accommodator" exchange.

All other types of exchanges are mere variations of these familiar types of exchanges.

Three-Party Alderson Exchange—Purchase First, Then Exchange

Why putting together an exchange is so difficult. What normally is found in exchange transactions is one seller who needs cash, one buyer with cash, and our client, who wants an exchange, with none of the parties directly wanting what the other is offering.

FIGURE 6.1 **Two-Party Exchange**

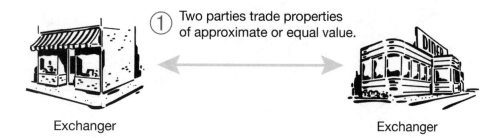

Two parties trade properties of approximate or equal value.

Exchanger   Exchanger

The solution. In the Alderson exchange, the buyer assists, as a middleman (and normally with the services of a facilitator), to effect an exchange by first purchasing the property the exchanger wishes to receive by trade [*Alderson v. Comm.*, 317 F2d 790 (9th Cir. 1963)].

Example:

Moe owns a retail building that he purchased five years ago for $150,000. Curley offers to buy the property for $250,000 cash but Moe turns him down because he does not want to recognize $100,000 of capital gain. Moe would rather exchange his building for Joe's $250,000 diner. Joe wants to sell his diner for cash, not trade it for another building. The solution is simple. With the help of a facilitator, which is the usual practice, Curley buys Joe's diner for $250,000 cash. Now Curley exchanges his newly acquired diner for Moe's retail building. Everyone is happy! Curley owns Moe's retail building; Moe owns Joe's diner and because of the arranged exchange does not owe *any* taxes; and Joe has his $250,000 cash (less the taxes he must pay on his gain). ◼

The mechanics. The Alderson exchange, illustrated in Figure 6.2, is consummated in two separate transactions, each of which should be accomplished by separate but dependent escrows, generally closed simultaneously with the help of the facilitator. First, in escrow 1 (the purchase/sale escrow), the buyer purchases the diner from the seller for cash. Second, in escrow 2 (the exchange escrow), the buyer transfers the diner to the exchanger in exchange for the store. In this case, the buyer is acting as a middleman or accommodator with the diner being transferred twice. Escrow 1 and escrow 2 normally close concurrently (resulting in the purchase of only one title insurance policy).

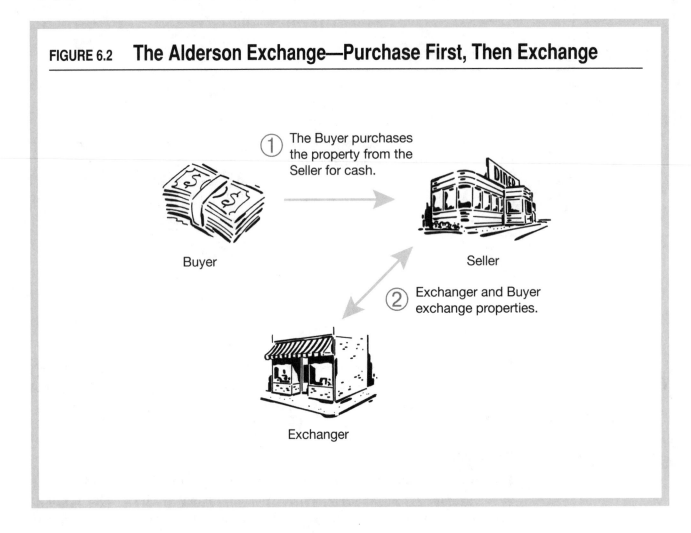

FIGURE 6.2   The Alderson Exchange—Purchase First, Then Exchange

① The Buyer purchases the property from the Seller for cash.

Buyer

Seller

② Exchanger and Buyer exchange properties.

Exchanger

Buyer must report exchange portion of the transaction as a sale. The buyer of the diner has a taxable sale, not a tax-free exchange (even though the exchanger has a tax-free exchange) as the property is being acquired by the buyer for an exchange, not for business or investment purposes. However, normally the buyer does not care, as the purchase price and the sales price (fair market value) are identical [§1001; Rev. Rul. 77-297; Rev. Rul. 75-291].

Three-Party Baird Publishing Exchange—Exchange First, Then Purchase

The Baird Publishing exchange is a simple variation of the Alderson exchange, with the exchange step of the transaction occurring before the sale, the middleman being the seller instead of the buyer and again generally assisted by a facilitator. The transaction is illustrated in Figure 6.3 [*J. H. Baird Publishing Co. v. Comm.*, 39 TC 608 (1962)].

The mechanics. As with the Alderson exchange, the Baird Publishing exchange is consummated in two separate transactions, each of which should be accomplished by a separate but dependent escrow, and again generally closed simultaneously with the help of the facilitator. First, in escrow 1 (the exchange escrow), the seller transfers the diner to

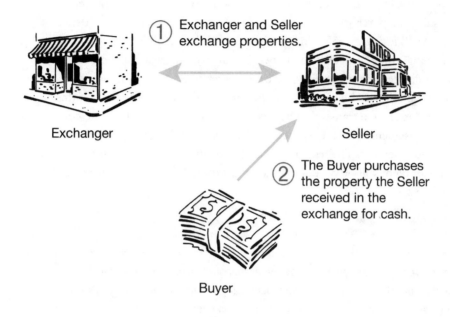

FIGURE 6.3   Three-Party Baird Exchange—Exchange First, Then Purchase

① Exchanger and Seller exchange properties.

Exchanger

Seller

② The Buyer purchases the property the Seller received in the exchange for cash.

Buyer

the exchanger in exchange for the store. Second, in escrow 2 (the sales/purchase escrow), the seller sells the store to the buyer for cash. In this case, the seller is acting as a middleman or accommodator with the store being transferred twice. Escrow 1 and escrow 2 normally close concurrently. In this case the seller must report the sales transaction, reportable on Form 1040, Schedule D, Sale in the year of the exchange [§1001].

Other Essential Ingredients in an Exchange

Exchanger may direct what property he or she wants. In most cases, the exchanger may directly locate, negotiate, and assist in the acquisition of the property for which he or she wishes to exchange [*Rutland v. Comm.*, 36 TCM 40 (1977); Rev. Rul. 77-297, 1977-2 CB 304; PLR 8110028].

Exchange property, not cash. Exchangers will recognize gain when the courts determine they actually "sold" property and then reinvested the money by purchasing like-kind property, even when there existed an intent for a tax-free exchange [*Carlton v. U.S.*, 385 F2d 238, (5th Cir. 1967)]. The opposite is also true.

THE "REVERSE-STARKER" EXCHANGE

Warning about seller receiving property before giving up property in a simultaneous exchange. Sometimes an outside party also is trying to buy the seller's property before the exchanger can secure it. It is often asked: "Can the exchanger purchase the seller's property *before* the buyer transfers his or her property to the exchanger?" Generally, no, as this results in a purchase with a a subsequent taxable sale, and the evidence is the title transfer [*Smith v. Comm.,* 537 F2d 972 (8th Cir. 1976); §1.1031(k)-1(a)]. Yet, in two private letter rulings, the IRS allowed a utility company to acquire a utility easement before the original utility easement was disposed of (i.e., a reverse exhange of utility easements) without commenting on the previous citation or even the loss." The facts of this case present a reverse exchange transaction between the two parties, in which the conveyance of the new easement to the Taxpayer is to be followed by relinquishment to Company F of the old easement. The real property interests involved are similar to each other and the new easement will serve functions identical to those of the old easement" (PLR 9814019 and 9823045).

Tax Tip

Some other alternatives exist, though, that allow the exchanger to control disposition of the property prior to the time of the exchange without technically purchasing the property, such as the use of a lease or a purchase option. Another option is described below.

The Reverse Starker exchange—accommodators may purchase before exchange.

An accomodator (which is discussed later) may acquire the seller's property in contemplation of the exchange, and subsequent to the closing time the accommodator can negotiate a transfer to the buyer, if desired. This is then followed by the buyer, accommodator, and exchanger effecting the exchange. Both the Tax Court and the Fifth Circuit conclude that a §1031 exchange is being properly completed in this situation. *And the exchanger can loan the accommodator the money to acquire the seller's property.* The loan is repaid from the buyer's cash purchase [*Biggs v. Comm.,* 69 TC 905 (1978), *aff'd,* 632 F2d 1171 (5th Cir. 1981); *124 Front Street, Inc.,* 65 TC 6 (1975)].

Investor Hint

It makes sense to use accommodators and facilitators, allowing flexibility that a normal exchanger doesn't have. These professionals are generally familiar with the unique requirements to maintain exchange status, such as those described in the following text.

Reverse-Starker Exchanges—IRS Provides Safe Harbor

The IRS has finally fulfilled its promise to provide guidance on reverse-Starker exchanges, a promise made in 1991 in the preamble to the final regulations for deferred like-kind exchanges. Rev. Proc. 2000-37 provides guidance on how to structure a transaction that will qualify under §1031 as tax deferred when the replacement property must be acquired before the disposition of the old.

Reverse-Starker exchanges since 1991. To facilitate reverse like-kind exchanges, taxpayers have engaged in a wide variety of transactions, including so-called parking transactions; i.e., one of the properties is "parked" with an accomodation party. In the parking arrangements, taxpayers attempt to arrange the transaction in such a way that the accommodation party has enough of the benefits and burdens relating to the property to be treated as the owner for federal income tax purposes. Rev. Proc. 2000-37 provides a safe harbor that allows a taxpayer to *treat the accomodation party as the owner of the property* for federal income tax purposes, thereby enabling the taxpayer to accomplish a qualifying like-kind exchange.

Replacement property is owned by accommodator. In some situations the desired replacement property is "parked" with an accommodation party until such time as the taxpayer arranges for the transfer of the relinquished property to the ultimate transferee in a simultaneous or deferred exchange. Once such a transfer is arranged, the taxpayer transfers the relinquished property to the accommodation party in exchange for the replacement property, and the accomodation party then transfers the relinquished property to the ultimate transferee.

Relinquished property is owned by accommodator. In other situations, an accommodation party may acquire the desired replacement property on behalf of the taxpayer and immediately exchange such property with the taxpayer for the relinquished property, thereafter holding the relinquished property until the taxpayer arranges for a transfer of such property to the ultimate transferee.

Safe harbor for qualified exchange accommodation arrangements. Specifically, Rev. Proc. 2000-37 provides that the IRS will not challenge the qualification of property as either "replacement property" or "relinquished property" [as defined in §1.1031(k)-1(a)], nor will it challenge the treatment of the exchange accomodation titleholder as the beneficial owner of such property for federal income tax purposes, if the property is held in a Qualified Exchange Accommodation Arrangement (QEAA). For purposes of this revenue procedure, property is held in a QEAA if all of the following six requirements are used.

1. **Ownership not vested in taxpayer or disqualified person:** Qualified indicia of ownership of the property are held by a person (the "exchange accomodation titleholder") who is not the taxpayer or a disqualified person (as discussed after these six requirements), and such person is subject to federal income tax. If the exchange accomodation titleholder is treated as a partnership or S corporation for federal income tax purposes, more than 90% of its interests or stock must be owned by partners or shareholders who are subject to federal income tax. Such qualified indicia of ownership must be held by the exchange accomodation titleholder until the property is transferred. (See "Definition of a Disqualified Person" in Chapter 7.)

What are qualified indicia of ownership? For this purpose, "qualified indicia of ownership" means legal title to the property, other indicia of ownership of the property that are treated as beneficial ownership of the property under applicable principles of commercial law (e.g., a contract for deed), or interests in an entity that is disregarded as an entity separate from its owner for federal income tax purposes (e.g., a single member limited liability company) and that holds either legal title to the property or such other indicia of ownership.

2. **Intent to qualify under §1031:** At the time the qualified indicia of ownership of the property are transferred to the exchange accommodation titleholder, it is the taxpayer's bona fide intent that the property held by the exchange accommodation titleholder represent either replacement property or relinquished property in an exchange that is intended to qualify for nonrecognition of gain (in whole or in part) or loss under §1031.

3. **Written agreement within five days:** No later than five business days after the transfer of qualified indicia of ownership of the property to the exchange accommodation titleholder, the taxpayer and the exchange accommodation titleholder enter into a written agreement (the "qualified exchange accommodation agreement") that provides that the exchange accommodation titleholder is holding the property for the benefit of the taxpayer to facilitate an exchange under §1031 and Rev. Proc. 2000-37 and that the taxpayer and the exchange accommodation titleholder agree to report the acquisition, holding, and disposition of the property as provided in Rev. Proc. 2000-37. The agreement must specify that the exchange accommodation titleholder will be treated as the beneficial owner of the property for all federal income tax purposes. Both parties must report the federal income tax attributes of the property on their federal income tax returns in a manner consistent with this agreement.

4. **Identification of relinquished property within 45 days:** No later than 45 days after the transfer of qualified indicia of ownership of the replacement property to the exchange accommodation titleholder, the relinquished property is properly identified. Identification must be made in a manner consistent with the principles described in §1.1031(k)-1(c). For purposes of this section, the taxpayer may properly identify alternative and multiple properties, as described in §1.1031(k)-1(c)(4).

5. **Transfer within 180 days:** No later than 180 days after the transfer of qualified indicia of ownership of the property to the exchange accommodation titleholder, (a) the property is transferred {either directly or indirectly through a qualified intermediary [as defined in §1.1031(k)-1(g)(4)]} to the taxpayer as replacement property; or (b) the property is transferred to a person who is not the taxpayer or a disqualified person as relinquished property.

6. **Maximum time in QEAA is 180 days:** The combined time period that the relinquished property and the replacement property are held in a QEAA does not exceed 180 days.

Example:

Arnold wants to exchange his fourplex for an upscale duplex. Unfortunately, he finds the duplex of his dreams before he finds a buyer for the fourplex. A qualified exchange accommodation titleholder may acquire ownership of the duplex and hold it for Arnold until he finds a buyer for his property. Once Arnold finds a buyer (must be within 180 days), he will exchange the fourplex for the duplex. Providing the requirements of Rev. Proc. 2000-37 are met, Arnold's reverse Starker exchange qualifies under §1031. ■

Permissible agreements. Property will not fail to be treated as being held in a QEAA as a result of any one or more of the following legal or contractual arrangements, whether or not such arrangements contain terms that typically would result from arm's-length bargaining between unrelated parties with respect to such arrangements.

1. **Exchange accommodation titleholder may be qualified intermediary:** An exchange accommodation titleholder that satisfies the general requirements of the qualified intermediary (accommodator) safe harbor [as set forth in §1.1031(k)-1(g)(4)] may enter into an exchange agreement with the taxpayer to serve as the qualified intermediary in a simultaneous or deferred exchange of the property under §1031.

2. **Taxpayer may guarantee debt to buy property:** The taxpayer or a disqualified person guarantees some or all of the obligations of the exchange accommodation titleholder, including secured or unsecured debt incurred to acquire the property, or indemnifies the exchange accommodation titleholder against costs and expenses.

3. **Taxpayer may loan funds to buy property:** The taxpayer or a disqualified person loans or advances funds to the exchange accommodation titleholder or guarantees a loan or advance to the exchange accommodation titleholder.

4. **Taxpayer may use property:** The property is leased by the exchange accommodation titleholder to the taxpayer or a disqualified person.

5. **Taxpayer may improve or service property:** The taxpayer or a disqualified person manages the property, supervises improvement of the property, acts as a contractor, or otherwise provides services to the exchange accommodation titleholder with respect to the property.

6. **Predetermined price OK:** The taxpayer and the exchange accommodation titleholder enter into agreements or arrangements relating to the purchase or sale of the property, including puts and calls at fixed or formula prices, effective for a period not in excess of 185 days from the date the property is acquired by the exchange accommodation titleholder.

7. **Taxpayer may or must cover fluctuations in value:** The taxpayer and the exchange accommodation titleholder enter into agreements or arrangements providing that any variation in the value of a relinquished property from the estimated value on the date of the exchange accommodation titleholder's receipt of the property be taken into account on the exchange accommodation titleholder's disposition of the relinquished property through the taxpayer's advance of funds to, or receipt of funds from, the exchange accommodation titleholder.

A qualified accommodator is a person (as referred to in the safe harbors above)

1. who is not the taxpayer or a disqualified person (discussed in the next section) *and*
2. who acts to facilitate a deferred exchange by entering into a written agreement (called the *exchange agreement*), and, as required by the exchange agreement, *acquires* the relinquished property from the taxpayer, transfers the relinquished property, acquires the replacement property, and transfers the replacement property to the taxpayer [§1.1031(k)-1(g)(4)(iii)].

> ### Tax Tip
>
> The word *acquire* means either actual acquisition or assignment of the right to purchase.

How Not To Do a Reverse-Starker Exchange

Taxpayer's agent receives replacement property prior to the date on which the taxpayer transfers the relinquished property. The original plan was for Bill to assign the contract of sale of his office building, the relinquished property, to Albert, the accommodator, who would complete the sale of the office building and use the proceeds to acquire Sharon's shopping center, the replacement property. Bill would then have the accommodator transfer the shopping center to him to complete the exchange. This would have resulted in a tax-free exchange, whether a simultaneous or deferred like-kind exchange.

However, at closing, the attempted sale of Bill's office building fell through. To make things worse, Sharon demanded that closing on the acquisition of the shopping center be completed immediately. Therefore, prior to contracting the sale of the office building, Bill closed on the purchase of the shopping center on *Date 1, but had the property titled to A, an accommodator.* (Remember, Bill could not have directly purchased the property as, under the like-kind exchange regulations, Bill *must* give up his property before receiving the replacement property.) Bill negotiated the purchase; Bill provided the funds; Bill was personally liable on the purchase money mortgage, while Albert was not. Bill ordered that the shopping center be titled to Albert. There was no evidence that Albert would have been involved in the transaction but for Bill. The IRS therefore concluded that Albert was not a qualified like-kind exchange accommodator, but was actually acting as Bill, i.e., an agent of Bill.

On Date 2, Bill contracted to sell the office building to Bonnie. Bill then entered into an exchange agreement with Albert and assigned the contract of sale to Albert. On Date 3, Albert closed on the sale of the office building to Bonnie, and on Date 4, Albert transferred part of the shopping center to Bill. On Date 5, Albert transferred the remainder of the shopping center to Bill. As Bill had actually purchased the shopping center on *Date 1* before disposing of the office building, the transfer on Date 5 was irrelevant (LTR 200039005).

> ### Caution
>
> A legal document, generally called an *exchange agreement,* must exist evidencing the relationship between the exchanger and the accommodator.

> ### Caution
>
> This letter ruling was released prior to the issuance of Rev. Proc. 2000-37. It has been included in this manual to illustrate how not to perform the so-called reverse Starker exchange.

> ### Investor Hint
>
> Of course, this result could have been avoided, and the like-kind exchange rules applied, by simply following the Rev. Proc. 2000-37, the new reverse exchange rules.

Other Essential Ingredients in an Exchange

Contractual interdependence. The closing of each escrow (leg of the exchange) *should* be contingent on the closing of all escrows. However, contractual or mutual interdependence of the separate transactions in a multiparty exchange is not necessarily a critical factor so long as the exchanger never has actual or effective control of the cash [compare *Barker v. Comm.,* 74 TC 555 (1980), with *Brauer v. Comm.,* 74 TC 1134 (1980) and *Biggs v. Comm.,* 69 TC 905 (1978), *aff'd* 632 F2d 1171 (5th Cir. 1981)].

Exchange, not sale, must be planned. The escrows should be part of an *integrated plan* showing that the exchanger wishes to effect a §1031 exchange. This is evidenced by showing that an integrated plan for a like-kind exchange is conceived and implemented; the exchanger's actions are consistent with exchanging; the conditions required to effect that intent are met; the contracts providing for the necessary series of transfers are interdependent; and *no cash proceeds from the sale of the original property are actually or constructively received by the exchanger* [*Garcia v. Comm.,* 80 TC 491 (1983), *acq.* 1984-1 CB 1].

Exchanger must not actually or constructively receive cash. As a general rule, the problem with not using an accommodator is that a transaction will constitute a taxable sale and not an exchange if the exchanger *actually or constructively* receives money or other property (boot) for the relinquished property before he or she actually receives the like-kind replacement property. The result is that the exchange becomes a taxable sale and subsequent repurchase, not an exchange, even though the taxpayer desired an exchange from the inception.

Actual receipt. The taxpayer is in *actual receipt* of money or property *at the time* the taxpayer actually receives such money or property or receives the economic benefit of such money or property (e.g., pledging the property as security for a loan) [§1.1031(k)-1(f)(2)].

Constructive receipt. The taxpayer is in *constructive receipt* of money or property at the time such money or property is credited to the taxpayer's account, set apart for the taxpayer, or otherwise made available so that the taxpayer *may* draw upon it at any time or so that the taxpayer can draw upon it if notice of intention to withdraw is given [§1.1031(k)-1(f)(2)].

Example:

Barb transfers a $100,000 fair market value (FMV) rental property to Carol in a deferred exchange on May 17, 2003. On or before November 13, 2003 (the end of the exchange period), Carol is required to purchase and transfer the property identified by Barb. At any time after May 17, 2003, and before Carol has purchased the replacement property, Barb has the right, upon notice, to demand that Carol pay $100,000 cash in lieu of acquiring the property. ■

Result:

No §1031(a) exchange available. It is a taxable sale followed by a subsequent repurchase because Barb has the unrestricted right to demand cash as of May 17, 1998. This is constructive receipt as of that date [§1.1031(k)-1(f)(3)].

Can we change to an exchange after we sign an offer-to-sell, i.e., in midstream?

Yes. The IRS allows the taxpayer to change a sale to an exchange *at any time prior to closing* [see the deferred exchange regulations, §1.1031(k)-1(a)]. The Tax Court looks at the form of the transaction over its substance [*Leslie Q. Coupe,* 52 TC 394 (1969)]. As long as an exchange is "intended," most court decisions find the details of the transaction are insignificant [*Rutland v. Comm.,* 36 TCM 40 (1977); *Biggs v. Comm.,* 632 F 2d 1171 (5th Cir. 1981), *aff'g* 69 TC 905 (1978); *Garcia v. Comm.,* 80 TC 491 (1983), *acq.* 1984-1 CB 1].

The qualified exchange may even contain the contingency that the transaction may, at the option of the exchanger, convert back to a cash sale [*Antone Borchard,* TCM 1965-297], or, alternatively, if the buyer cannot find a suitable property, the exchanger may demand cash [*Barker v. Comm.,* 74 TC 555 (1980)].

Four-Party (Neutral Accommodator) Exchange

Sometimes buyers of real estate want only to pay their money and be done with the deal. They have little interest in, or are unable to fund, the purchase of "replacement property" for the exchanger. The seller may also be uncomfortable in being the middleman. What happens if a buyer or a seller simply doesn't want to be bothered with this complication and starts looking for other property? How can the exchanger or real estate agent keep the deal together?

When either the buyer or the seller is unwilling to act as the accommodator, a fourth-party escrow agent may act as a go-between to help facilitate the exchange [*Earlene T. Parker,* 74 TC 555 (1980)]. In such cases, "intermediaries" and "accommodators" have sprung up to facilitate regular exchanges—and now deferred exchanges. This is the same as a three-party exchange, except that a fourth-party accommodator assists all parties to effect the exchange (see Figure 6.4).

The mechanics. With the IRS blessing of direct deeding, the exchanger may deed the property directly to the buyer. The buyer then transfers the money to the accommodator (not to the exchanger). Finally, the accommodator pays for the seller's property, and the seller is permitted to deed the property directly to the exchanger. Before these IRS pronouncements, three or more separate escrows were required, with the exchanger receiving each deed and subsequently granting each deed [Rev. Rul. 90-34, I.R.B. 1990-16; §1.1031(k)-1(g)(4)(iv)].

Tax Tip

Again, the agreements between all the parties are encouraged to be mutually interdependent parts of one integrated plan with each contingent upon the successful completion of the other transactions.

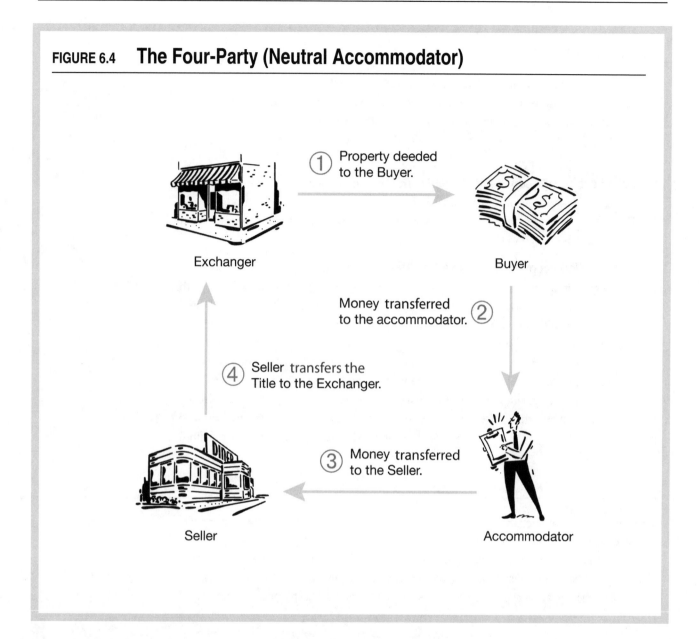

FIGURE 6.4   The Four-Party (Neutral Accommodator)

Does the use of a fourth-party accommodator create constructive receipt via the principal-agent relationship? No. The use of a third-party or fourth-party accommodator may actually prevent actual or constructive receipt. According to the Tax Court, followed belatedly by the IRS, in the case of simultaneous transfers of like-kind properties involving a qualified accommodator, the qualified accommodator is not considered the agent of the taxpayer for purposes of the like-kind exchange rules. In such cases, the transfer and receipt of property by the taxpayer is treated as an exchange. This IRS position applies to transfers of property made by taxpayers on or after June 10, 1991 [*Brauer v. Comm.*, 74 TC 1134 (1980); §1.1031(b)-(2)].

Investor Hint

This rule does *not* imply that fourth-party accommodators *must* be used in simultaneous exchanges, i.e., buyers and sellers may still act as the middleman. This was confirmed by a telephone conversation with the authors of the deferred exchange regulations.

Who can be a fourth-party escrow agent? In numerous court cases, title companies, real estate agents, and attorneys have all qualified as independent accommodators. In addition, the IRS has created a "safe harbor" qualified accommodator, discussed next and more fully described in Chapter 7.

Using a qualified accommodator's participation. This practice prevents the taxpayer from constructively receiving the purchase money. The IRS has announced that both simultaneous and deferred exchanges are permitted (but not required) to be facilitated by the use of a *qualified intermediary* (clearly a new growth industry in the exchange field) *if* the exchanger's rights to receive the money or other property held by the accommodator are *substantially limited or restricted.* In this case the qualified accommodator is not considered the agent of the taxpayer (an agent is normally a disqualified person). The accommodator may actually purchase the property (even from money advanced directly by the exchanger) and then effect an exchange or simply assign the contractual right to purchase the property desired (see subsequent discussion on direct deeding) [§1.1031(k)-1(g)(4)(i),(vi)].

Investor Hint

This does not mean that other parties (e.g., the taxpayer's present attorney or accountant) cannot be accommodators for simultaneous exchanges even though they are disqualified for deferred exchanges (as discussed in the next paragraph). It simply means that the IRS will look more closely at simultaneous exchanges when "safe harbor" accommodators are not used.

Who may be a "qualified" accommodator in an exchange? A qualified accommodator is one

1. who is not the taxpayer, related to the taxpayer, or an agent of the taxpayer in the past two years (as discussed below) *and*
2. who acts to facilitate a deferred exchange by *entering into a written agreement* (called the *exchange agreement*) and, as required by the exchange agreement, *acquires* the relinquished property from the taxpayer, transfers the relinquished property, acquires the replacement property, and transfers the replacement property to the taxpayer [§1.1031(k)-1(g)(4)(iii)].

No agent of the taxpayer—within the past two years. Anyone who is the agent of the taxpayer at the time of the transaction is disqualified. For this purpose, *a person who has acted as the taxpayer's employee, attorney, accountant, investment banker or broker, or real estate agent or broker within the two-year period* ending on the date of the transfer of the first of the relinquished properties *is treated as an agent of the taxpayer* at the time of the transaction.

Real estate agents, escrow agents, and title companies qualify. The performance of the following services will *not* be taken into account in determining who is an agent:

1. *Putting together an exchange.* Services for the taxpayer with respect to exchanges of property intended to qualify for nonrecognition of gain or loss under §1031

2. *Routine financial, title insurance, escrow, or trust services* for the taxpayer by a financial institution, title insurance company, or escrow company [§1.1031(k)-1(k)(2)]

Investor Hint

The above means that normally the exchanger can safely use the real estate agent who is putting together the exchange but not his or her present lawyer or accountant. Evidently, the IRS writer of these regulations trusts real estate agents more than attorneys and accountants!

A further discussion on four-party accommodators and their required qualifications is found in Chapter 7, on deferred exchanges.

Direct deeding. Does "acquire" mean that the accommodator (e.g., buyer/seller/facilitator) actually has to momentarily take physical title to both properties? No. Some accommodators take momentary or "sequential" title for administrative purposes, but it is not necessary.

To answer the above concern, the IRS came up with its own definition of the word *acquire,* probably to comply with previous judicial decisions [Rev. Rul. 90-34, I.R.B. 1990-16; §1.1031(k)-1(g)(4)(iv), *Biggs v. Comm.,* 69 TC 905 (1978); *Brauer v. Comm.,* 74 TC 1134 (1980)].

Investor Hint

This "blink-of-the-eye" ownership can be potentially catastrophic for the buyer/seller/accommodator in light of the *hazardous waste liability* (i.e., Superfund or toxic waste liability). The liability to pay for cleanup costs in removing hazardous, toxic, or dangerous waste found on a property reaches *any* owner of a property, even if that owner did not create such waste or cause its release into the environment.

Acquiring. *Acquiring,* in the deferred exchange regulations, rejects the general tax principle definition of acquisition for deferred exchange purposes and treats accommodators *as if they acquired* and transferred title, if they

1. *actually acquire and transfer legal title* to that property (the least desirable option); *or*
2. *enter into an "agreement" (e.g., an assignment) with a person other than the taxpayer* (either on its own behalf or as the agent of any party to the transaction) *for the transfer of the relinquished property* to that person and, pursuant to that agreement, the relinquished property is transferred to that person; *or*
3. *enter into an agreement with the owner of the replacement property* (either on its own behalf or as the agent of any party to the transaction) *for the transfer of that property* and, pursuant to that agreement, the replacement property is transferred to the taxpayer [§1.1031(k)-1(g)(4)(iv)].

Assignment of contract permitted. Solely for these purposes, an accommodator is treated as entering into an agreement if the rights of a party to the agreement are assigned to the accommodator *and if all parties to that agreement are notified* in writing of the assignment on or before the date of the relevant transfer of property [§1.1031(k)-1(g)(4)(v)].

Example 1:

Direct deeding to accommodator. The facts:

May 1:   Barb receives $100,000 cash offer-to-purchase from Danny on her office building. Danny hates exchanges and Barb hates paying taxes.

May 2:   Barb signs a qualified exchange agreement with qualified Acme Accommodators.

May 3:   Acme and Danny sign $100,000 offer-to-purchase/sell.

May 17:   Barb deeds office building to Acme.

May 17:   Acme deeds office building to Danny, and Danny delivers $100,000 cash to Acme; funds are placed in a qualified escrow.

June 3:   Barb identifies Eldon's $80,000 apartment house.

August 9: Eldon deeds apartments to Acme, and Acme delivers $80,000 cash out of escrow to Eldon.

August 9: Acme deeds apartments to Barb along with $20,000 cash.

Tax results:

Barb is not in actual or constructive receipt of the $100,000, and Acme properly *acquired and transferred* both the office building and the apartments. Barb's transfer of the office building and acquisition of the apartments qualifies as a §1031 exchange. The $20,000 is taxable boot [§1031(b); §1.1031(k)-1(g)(8)(Example 3)]. ▪

The accommodator never has to take technical title! The transfer of property in a deferred exchange that is facilitated by the use of a qualified accommodator may actually occur via a *direct deed* of legal title by the current owner of the property to its ultimate owner [§1.1031(k)-1(g)(4)(iv)].

Example 2:

Assignment of purchase agreement to accommodator. The facts:

May 1:   Barb *signs* $100,000 cash offer-to-purchase/sell her office building to Danny. Danny hates exchanges and Barb hates paying taxes.

May 2:   Barb signs a qualified exchange agreement with qualified Acme Accommodators.

May 2:   Barb *assigns* her interest in Danny's offer to Acme.

May 17: Barb notifies Danny of assignment.

May 17: Barb deeds office building *directly* to Danny.

May 17: Danny delivers $10,000 cash to Barb and $90,000 cash to Acme's qualified escrow.

June 1:   Barb identifies Eldon's $90,000 ranch.

July 5:   Barb *signs* $90,000 offer-to-purchase/sell on ranch.

July 5:   Barb *assigns* her interest in Eldon's ranch to Acme.

July 5:   Barb notifies Eldon of assignment.

August 9: Acme delivers $90,000 cash out of escrow to Eldon.

August 9: Eldon deeds ranch *directly* to Barb.

Tax results:

Barb is not in actual or constructive receipt of the $100,000, and again Acme properly *acquired and transferred* both the office building and the ranch. Barb's transfer of the office building and acquisition of the ranch qualify as a §1031 exchange. Both state law on agency and general tax principles are disregarded. The $10,000 is boot, taxable under §1031(b) [§1.1031(k)-1(g)(8) (Example 4)]. ▪

Example:

How to do it wrong. The facts:

May 1:   Barb *signs* $100,000 cash offer-to-purchase/sell with Danny on her office building. Danny hates exchanges and Barb hates paying taxes.

May 2:   Barb signs a qualified exchange agreement with qualified Acme Accommodators.

_____: Barb *doesn't assign* her interest in Danny's offer to Acme.

_____: Barb *doesn't notify* Danny of assignment.

May 17: Barb deeds office building *directly* to Danny.

May 17: Danny delivers $100,000 cash to Acme; funds are placed into qualified escrow.

June 1:   Barb identifies Milton's $100,000 trailer park.

August 9: Acme purchases Milton's $100,000 trailer park.

August 9: Milton deeds trailer park to Acme.

August 9: Acme deeds trailer park to Barb.

> **Caution**
>
> The pot theory is also questionable in deferred exchanges as indicated by the previous example on assignments, and, therefore, the use of a qualified accommodator is a more conservative option [§1.1031(k)-1(g)(8)(Example 5)].

Tax results:

Because Barb transferred her office building directly to Danny under Barb's purchase/sell agreement with Danny, Acme did not acquire the office building from Barb and transfer the office building to Danny. Moreover, because Acme did not acquire legal title to the office building, did not enter into an agreement with Danny to transfer the office building to Danny and was not assigned Barb's rights in her agreement to sell the office building to Danny, Acme is not treated as acquiring and transferring the office building. Thus, Acme was not a qualified accommodator. Barb did not exchange the office building for the trailer park. Rather, Barb sold the office building to Danny and purchased, through Acme, the trailer park. Therefore, the transfer of the office building does not qualify for nonrecognition of gain or loss under §1031 [§1.1031(k)-1(g)(8) (Example 5)]. ▪

The pot exchange. Sometimes it is easier to have all the parties throw the assets brought to the exchange (i.e., cash or property) into one big escrow "pot" and have that escrow directly deed the property or cash to the ultimate recipient.

Problems with the pot exchange. The use of one escrow, instead of multiple escrows, may cloud the sale portion of the Alderson or Baird multiparty exchange. This exchange method is not specifically approved for simultaneous exchanges, even though Rev. Rul. 57-244 (1957-1 CB 247) does approve a three-party contract where there is a three-way exchange of property without the sale of any of the properties; it was successfully used in *W. D. Haden Co. v. Comm.,* 165 F2d 588 (5th Cir. 1948). For purposes of safety when using a pot exchange, there should exist contractual interdependence and a restriction of the receipt of cash by the exchanger.

7

Deferred Exchanges

DOES THE EXCHANGE OF PROPERTY HAVE TO BE SIMULTANEOUS?

Have you ever wanted to sell some of your, or your client's, property for cash with the plan to reinvest it in the future and during the interim deposit the money in an interest-bearing account *but* not pay the capital gains tax associated with the sale (i.e., defer the gain)? Until December 1979, most tax practitioners said "impossible"! We assumed that the trading of property had to be done concurrently. Then along came the *Starker* cases, commonly known as *Starker I, Starker II,* and *Starker III,* from Corvallis, Oregon, which has made the impossible a reality [*Bruce Starker v. U.S.* DC-Ore 75-1 USTC ¶9443; *T. J. Starker v. U.S.,* 432 F. Supp 864 (DC-Ore. 1977), 602 F2d 1341 (CA-9, 79-2 USTC ¶9451)].

The *Starker* facts. T. J. Starker (T. J.) owned $1,502,500 of timbered property that Crown Zellerbach Corporation (Crown) wanted to buy. T. J. wished to effect a like-kind exchange but, after viewing Crown's present land assets, found none to his liking. The two parties entered into an exchange agreement wherein T. J. would *immediately* transfer title to Crown. In return, Crown would record an unsecured $1,502,500 "exchange value credit" on its financial records. In addition, Crown would purchase property over the next five years that T. J. found acceptable and that he instructed Crown to purchase. After Crown's purchase, the corporation would transfer title to T. J. and reduce the "exchange value credit" by the purchase price of the property. If any cash was left at the end of the fifth year, the remaining cash would be transferred to T. J., as T. J. did not have the right under the contract to demand cash in lieu of property.

In addition, the account was credited with an annual 6% "growth factor" (some, including the courts, called it *disguised interest*), theoretically to reflect timber growth on the parcels conveyed by the taxpayer.

Although the taxpayer selected nine like-kind parcels to be conveyed, none of which was owned by T. J. at the time the exchange agreement was executed, the Ninth Circuit Court of Appeals found that the taxpayer did not have control over the cash used by Crown to purchase these parcels. The transaction was held by the Ninth Circuit to constitute a §1031 exchange and T. J.'s additional $301,000 tax assessment was refunded to him as the gain was declared not to be recognized.

Problem with *Starker* exchanges. How long? How long could Starker defer identifying and locating the property? Theoretically, if it was more than six years, the statute of limitations would have made any cash remaining exempt from taxes. This problem was solved by Congress in 1984 by the "deferred exchange" rules, followed by IRS interpretative regulations finalized on May 1, 1991.

Effective date. The effective date for the final regulations dealing with "Treatment of Deferred Exchanges" is for transactions on or after June 10, 1991. Transactions between May 16, 1990, and June 10, 1991, may rely on the proposed regulations [§1.1031(k)-1(o)].

WHAT DOES NOT QUALIFY AS A DEFERRED EXCHANGE?

As discussed previously concerning simultaneous exchanges, (1) a sale and subsequent purchase does not qualify as a deferred exchange; (2) a deferred exchange must be structured as an exchange, not a purchase; and (3) the taxpayer cannot receive the replacement property *prior to* the date on which the taxpayer transfers the relinquished property (e.g., no "receiving before giving up" exchanges) [§1.1031(k)-1(a)].

TIME LIMITS IMPOSED ON NONSIMULTANEOUS LIKE-KIND EXCHANGES

For any deferred exchanges, the following limits apply:

1. *Identified:* All properties to be received *must be identified within 45 days* after the taxpayer transfers the relinquished property.

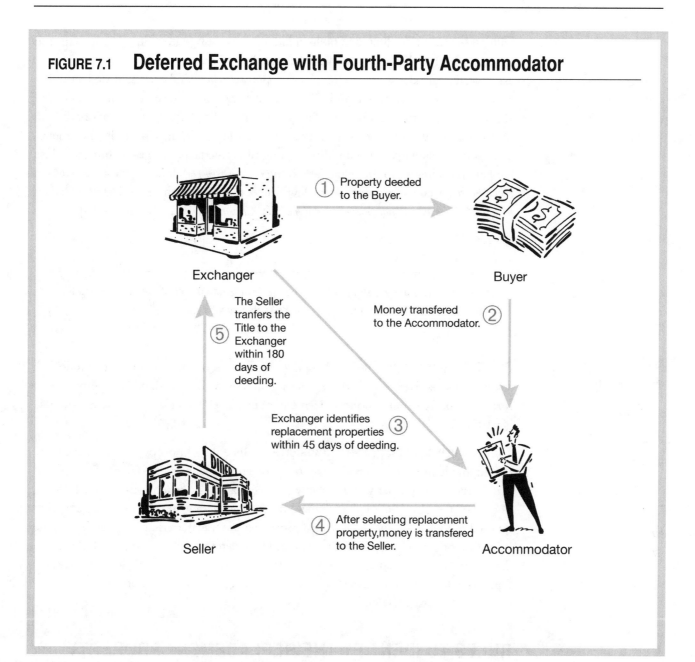

FIGURE 7.1 **Deferred Exchange with Fourth-Party Accommodator**

① Property deeded to the Buyer.

Exchanger

Buyer

⑤ The Seller tranfers the Title to the Exchanger within 180 days of deeding.

② Money transfered to the Accommodator.

③ Exchanger identifies replacement properties within 45 days of deeding.

④ After selecting replacement property, money is transfered to the Seller.

Seller

Accommodator

2. *Received:* The exchange of titles must be *completed, or properties received, within strict time limits,* not more than 180 days (or, if earlier, the due date, including extensions, of the taxpayer's tax return for the tax year the relinquished property was transferred) after the transfer of the exchanged property [§1031(a)(3); §1.1031(k)-1(b)(1)].

The entire deferred exchange 45/180-day process is easily illustrated in Figure 7.1.

Filing a tax return on time can make a like-kind exchange taxable! A tax trap can occur by the 180 days "or, if earlier, the due date of the tax return" requirement. For example, if a calendar-year taxpayer gives property in a like-kind exchange, on December 31, the 180 days would end on June 27 of the next year. But if the individual files on April 15, this shortens the allowable exchange period to 105 days. As corporations file on March 15, they would only have 74 days to complete an exchange! Luckily, the requirement adds "including extensions." In other words, if the taxpayer files on time, they lose the period of time from the filing date to the end of the 180 days. Investor Christensen received replacement property after filing his tax return but before the 180 days . . . *and no §1031 like-kind exchange was allowed* [*Orville E. Christensen,* TC Memo 1996-254]!

Tax Tip

Prudent investors participating in an exchange in the last quarter of the year extend the filing date of their tax return to maximize the replacement period to 180 days.

Penalty for noncompliance. If these dates (i.e., 45/180 days) are not strictly followed, any property received outside these dates is considered "not-like-kind" property. Therefore the tax-free transaction is deemed a taxable sale and a subsequent purchase [§1.1031(k)-1(a)].

Time starts when first property transferred. Once the old property is conveyed, the period for identifying the replacement property ends exactly 45 days later and the period for, receiving the property ends exactly 180 days later—no extensions are available. If, as part of the same deferred exchange, the exchanger transfers more than one relinquished property and the relinquished properties are transferred on different dates, the identification period and the exchange period are determined by reference to the *earliest* date on which any of such properties are transferred and ends exactly 45/180 days (or filing date) later, even if the beginning or ending date is a Saturday, Sunday, or legal holiday [§1.1031(k)-1(b)(1)(iii)].

RULES TO IDENTIFY THE REPLACEMENT PROPERTY WITHIN 45 DAYS

The IRS promulgated strict rules on how to properly identify the property in the 45-day period, but it does not require the filing of separate identification forms.

The identification time period. The identification period begins on the date the taxpayer transfers the relinquished property and ends at midnight 45 days thereafter [§1.1031(k)-1(b)(2)(i)].

Example:

Barb transfers a $100,000 fair market value rental property to Carol in a deferred exchange on May 17, 2003. On July 2, 2003, Barb hand-delivers to Carol written, signed instructions to purchase a $100,000 office building.

(45 Days after Transfer Date)

5 /17/03 ◄━━━━━━━━━━━━━━━━► 7/1/03

"Identification Period"

Tax result:

No §1031 exchange as the replacement property was identified outside the 45-day identification period [§1.1031(k)-1(c)(7)(Example 1)].

Not Timely Identifying Replacement Property Kills Tax-Free Swap

In this instance, an accountant sold two properties, intending to do a tax-free swap pursuant to the like-kind rules under Code §1031. Sales proceeds were held in an escrow account, and two weeks later, he found a building that needed renovation but otherwise suited his needs. However, he was too busy to carry on the necessary negotiations for acquisition of the building and never formally identified it as the replacement before eventually buying it more than 45 days later. Worse yet, on the IRS Form 8824, he "mistakenly" (or so he said), inserted an identification date more than 45 days after the date the property was transferred. The Tax Court ruled that the exchange did not qualify under the like-kind rules. Even though he bought the building within the overall 180-day limitation period, he did not otherwise satisfy the 45-day identification rule, thus making the transaction taxable [*Terry D. Smith;* TC Memo. 1997-109].

How to Properly Identify Property within the 45 Days

The identification must be in a written document, signed and delivered. Property must be designated as replacement property in writing, signed and delivered (either by hand or mailed, faxed, or otherwise sent) to the person obligated to transfer the replacement property *or* to any other person involved in the exchange (other than the taxpayer or a "disqualified person," which is defined later), such as any of the other parties to the exchange, an accommodator, an escrow agent, or a title company. A document signed by all parties prior to the end of the 45 days is also sufficient [§1.1031(k)-1(c)(2)].

Investor Hint

There is no requirement that this identification be evidenced by a listing agreement or an option, but it probably is imprudent to identify three different properties without the permission of the present owner. Why? As is discussed later in this chapter, some or all of the identified properties *must* be received within the 180 days!

The property description must be unambiguous.

- *Describing real property.* Exchanger may use legal description, street address, or distinguishable name (e.g., Trump Tower).
- *Describing personal property.* Description must be specific (e.g., truck must designate make, model, and year) [§1.1031(k)-1(c)(3)].

Example:

Barb transfers a $100,000 fair market value rental property to Carol in a deferred exchange on May 17, 2003. On July 1, 2003, Barb hand-delivers to Carol written, signed instructions to purchase "unimproved land located in Powder River County with a fair market value not to exceed $100,000."

Tax result:

No §1031 exchange, as the property description is not specific enough [§1.1031(k)-1(c)(7)(Example 3)]. ■

Property that is to be produced or constructed in the future also qualifies but must follow special rules, which are discussed later in this material.

Limitations on how many replacement properties may be designated (the alternate and multiple property rules).

Regardless of the number of relinquished properties in the same deferred exchange, the maximum number of replacement properties the taxpayer may designate is three; if more than three properties are identified, then property value may not exceed twice the aggregate fair market value of the property given up; and if both more than three properties *and* twice fair market value are identified, then the exchanger must purchase 95% of *all* the properties identified.

Investor Hint

All property identified *must* be used in these calculations unless the property has been properly revoked [§1.1031(k)-1(c)(4)(iii)].

Test 1—The "three-property rule."

The taxpayer may designate three properties of any fair market value [§1.1031(k)-1(c)(4)].

Example:

Barb transfers a $100,000 fair market value rental property to Carol in a deferred exchange on May 17, 2003. On June 28, 2003 Barb hand-delivers to Carol written, signed instructions identifying real properties J, K, and L as potential replacement properties (fair market values of $75,000, $100,000, and $125,000, respectively). On August 1, 2003, Barb informs Carol which of the three properties she wishes.

Tax result:

§1031 exchange available, as no more than three properties are identified within the proper time frame [§1.1031(k)-1(c)(7)(Example 4)].

Investor Hint

The dollar amount that must be designated is *not* the "net-equity" value, even though the transaction may have been brought together as a "net-equity" exchange. The dollar amount is the fair market value without regard to liabilities secured by the property. So what is *fair market value* to the IRS? Uncertainty reigns as two appraisers seldom agree, and that includes IRS appraisers.

What is a property? For example, Diana owns a ranch comprising of three separately purchased properties that are exchanged (one deed) with Charles for 20 commercial lots (again via one deed). Admittedly there are 23 separate parcels, but are there two or 23 properties?

Tax result:

There is no specific answer in the §1.1031(k)-1 deferred exchange regulations. The "multiple-property" exchange regulations (discussed in Chapter 8) conclude that the three ranch properties are one "exchange group" and the 20 lots are one "exchange group" [§1.1031(j)-1(a)(2)(i)]. ▨

Investor Hint

The author is certain this is not the answer the regulation writers wanted, with all the potential abuse provided by this conclusion! The use of a different street address for each commercial property may allow the IRS to dubiously argue that there are 20 properties, not one property [§1.1031(k)-1(c)(3)]. When appropriate, therefore, the taxpayer will want to avoid this type of "unambiguous" description. The *incidental property rule* probably is not applicable, as it does not directly address the issue when similar properties are in the same group [§1.1031(k)-1(c)(5)(ii)]. Conclusion: no clear answer exists.

Test 2—The "200% rule." If the taxpayer designates more than three properties, the total fair market value of all the identified properties may not exceed 200% of the fair market value (on the transfer date) of the property given up [§1.1031(k)-1(c)(4)].

Example:

Barb transfers a $100,000 fair market value rental property to Carol in a deferred exchange on May 17, 2003. Also on May 17, Barb hand-delivers to Carol written, signed instructions identifying real properties M, N, P, and Q as potential replacement properties (with fair market values of $30,000, $40,000, $50,000, and $60,000, respectively). The written document provides that by July 2, 2003, Barb will orally inform Carol which of the identified properties Carol is to transfer to her.

Tax result:

§1031 exchange available. Even though more than three properties were identified within the proper time frame, the aggregate fair market value ($180,000) does not exceed 200% of the property given up ($100,000 × 200%) [§1.1031(k)-1(c)(7)(Example 5)]. ■

Test 3—Purchase 95% of all identified property. If the taxpayer purchases 95% of the aggregate fair market values of all properties originally identified, the three-property and the 200% limitation rules do not apply. For this purpose, the fair market value of each identified replacement property is determined as of the earlier of the date the property is received by the taxpayer or the last day of the exchange period [§1.1031(k)-1(c)(4)(ii)].

Blanket 45-day exception. If all the property to be acquired is *received* within 45 days, the identification rule is waived [§1.1031(k)-1(c)(1)].

Segregating incidental property disregarded. For both the three-property rule and the 200% rule, property need not be separated if

1. in a standard commercial transaction, the property is typically transferred together with the larger item of property and
2. the aggregate fair market value of all such property does not exceed 15% of the aggregate total [§1.1031(k)-1(c)(5)(i)].

Example:

Furniture, laundry machines, and other miscellaneous items of personal property will not be treated as separate property from an apartment building with a fair market value of $1,000,000 if the aggregate fair market value of the furniture, laundry machines, and other personal property does not exceed $150,000. In such case, for purposes of the three-property rule, the apartment building, furniture, laundry machines, and other personal property are treated as one property. Moreover, when describing replacement property, the apartment building, furniture, laundry machines, and other personal property are all considered to be unambiguously described if the legal description or street address of the apartment building is specified, even if no reference is made to the furniture, laundry machines, and other personal property [§1.1031(k)-1(c)(5)(ii) (Example 2)]. ■

Previously identified property may be revoked before the end of the 45 days. Taxpayers may change their minds and substitute other property they wish to identify at any time before the end of the 45-day identification period so long as the revocation is done in substantially the same manner as the original identification (i.e., written, signed, and delivered revocation to the person originally notified) [§1.1031(k)-1(c)(6)].

Example:

Barb transfers a $100,000 fair market value rental property to Carol in a deferred exchange on May 17, 2003. On May 20, 2003, Barb identifies real properties R and S as potential replacement properties by hand-delivering to Carol written, signed instructions. On June 4, 2003, Barb identifies real properties T and U as replacement property.

Caution

Violation of all three tests makes the exchange fully taxable [§1.1031(k)-1(c)(4)(ii)].

On June 5, 2003, Barb telephones Carol and orally revokes R and S (fair market values of R, S, T, and U are $50,000, $70,000, $90,000, and $100,000 respectively).

Tax result:

No §1031 exchange available. Because the property was identified in writing, it must be revoked in writing—oral revocation is invalid. Thus, there are now four properties involved that exceed 200% of the fair market value of the property transferred. Barb is treated as if she did not identify any replacement property [§1.1031(k)-1(c)(7)(Example 7)]. ■

Investor Hint

Even though Barb identified four properties *during* the 45-day identification period, if she had revoked R and S in writing, we only test for more than three properties on the 45th day [§1.1031(k)-1(c)(4)(iii)]. Before that date, it is "flex" time. Therefore, Barb would have identified only two properties for this rule.

HOW TO PROPERLY RECEIVE PROPERTY WITHIN THE REQUIRED TIME FRAME

The regulations provide that replacement property is received before the end of the exchange period (i.e., the filing date or 180 days after transfer) if the replacement property received is "substantially the same" property as was identified [§1.1031(k)-1 (d)(1)].

Investor Hint

An example in the regulations demonstrates that receiving at least 75% of the indicated property is substantial but does not indicate a lower limit [§1.1031(k)-1(d)(2)(Example 4)].

If the taxpayer identifies more than one replacement property, the receipt rules apply separately to each.

The exchange period. The exchange period begins on the date the taxpayer transfers the relinquished property and ends on the earlier of the 180 days thereafter or the due date (including extensions) for the taxpayer's tax return for the taxable year in which the transfer of the relinquished property occurs [§1.1031(k)-1(b)(2)(ii)].

Example 1:

Microsoft, Inc., files its federal income tax return on a calendar-year basis. Microsoft and Chrysler enter into an agreement for an exchange of property that requires that Microsoft transfer Warehouse X to Chrysler. Under the agreement, Microsoft is to identify like-kind replacement property, which Chrysler is required to purchase and to transfer to Microsoft. Microsoft transfers Warehouse X to Chrysler on November 16, 2003.

The identification period ends at midnight on December 31, 2003, 45 days after the date of transfer of Warehouse X. The exchange period ends at midnight on March 15, 2004, the due date for Microsoft's federal income tax return for the taxable year in which the corporation transferred Warehouse X. However, if Microsoft, Inc., is allowed the automatic six-month extension for filing its tax return, the exchange period ends at midnight on May 15, 2004, 180 days after the date of transfer of Warehouse X [§1.1031(k)-1(b)(3)]. ▪

Example 2:

Barb transfers a $100,000 fair market value rental property to Carol in a deferred exchange on May 17, 2003. On or before November 13, 2004 (the end of the exchange period), Carol is required to purchase and transfer the property identified by Barb. If the fair market value of the replacement property(ies) is greater or less than the rental property transferred in May, they both agree to pay the difference in cash the day after Barb receives the replacement property.

(45 Days after Transfer Date)

5 /17/03 ◄————————————►7/1/03

"Identification Period"

(180 Days after Transfer Date)

5 /17/03◄————————————►11/13/03

"Identification Period"

Barb identifies real properties J, K, and L as potential replacement properties in the exchange agreement (fair market values of $75,000, $100,000 and $125,000, respectively). On July 26, 2003, Barb instructs Carol to acquire K for $100,000. On October 31, 2003, Carol purchases K and transfers it to Barb.

Tax result:

§1031 exchange available. Property K was identified before the end of the identification period and received before the end of the exchange period [§1.1031(k)-1(d)(2)(Example 1)]. ▪

Example 3:

With the same basic facts as those described in example 2 above, Barb identifies real property P as replacement property in the exchange agreement (P is two acres of unimproved land with a fair market value of $250,000). On October 3, 2003, Barb tells Carol to purchase only 1.5 acres for $187,500 and transfer it to her, with Barb paying the $87,500 back to Carol.

Tax result:

§1031 exchange available. The fair market value of the property *received* ($187,500) is 75% of the fair market value of P as of the date of receipt. Therefore, Barb is considered to have received substantially the same property she identified [§1.1031(k)-1(d)(2)(Example 4)]. ▪

THE CONSTRUCTION EXCHANGE—SPECIAL RULES FOR IDENTIFYING AND RECEIVING PROPERTY BEING PRODUCED OR CONSTRUCTED

In general. One of the strangest provisions in the final regulations permits, with limitations, the taxpayer to participate in an exchange even if the replacement property is not in existence, or is being produced, at the time the property is identified [§1.1031(k)-1(e)(1); PLR 9413006]. The tricky part is that the replacement property must still be properly identified (within the 45 days) and *received* within the proper time frame (i.e., 180 days). To produce includes to construct, build, install, manufacture, develop, or *improve* [§263A(g)(1)].

Investor Hint

Exchangers smack their lips over this one. Imagine—the taxpayer can sell a business property for cash, have the money delivered to an accommodator, build another business property, and call it a tax-free exchange!

Replacement property being produced must be properly "identified." Identification must be as accurate as possible (e.g., for buildings to be constructed, use the legal description of the land and as much detail as practical) [§1.1031(k)-1(e)(2)(i)]. For the 200% rule and the incidental rule, the taxpayer must use the fair market value of the property as of the date it is expected to be received by the taxpayer [§1.1031(k)-1(e)(2)(ii)].

The constructed property must be *substantially the same* as identified. If substantial changes are made after identification, the replacement property will *not* be considered substantially the same as identified and the exchange will be deemed a taxable sale and subsequent repurchase. Variations due to usual or typical production changes are not taken into account [§1.1031(k)-1(e)(3)(i)].

> **Caution**
>
> Transfer of property for construction services is not an exchange [§1.1031(k)-1(e)(4); see also discussion on "services to be rendered" in Chapter 8].

Receiving personal property. There is *no* extension of time (i.e., for the 180-day rule), and the property *must be finished* within the exchange period [§1.1031(k)-1(e)(3)(ii)].

Receiving real property—it doesn't have to be finished! There is *no* extension of time (i.e., for the 180-day rule), *and* if the real property is in the construction phase (but not completed at time of receipt), the end product must be substantially the same as originally identified. However, real property does not have to be completed within the exchange period [§1.1031(k)-1(e)(3)(iii)].

Can we extend the 180 days through the back door? Probably. As the 180 days do not start to toll until after the *taxpayer transfers the relinquished property*, simply stalling the closing date results in extending the time [§1.1031(k)-1(b)(2)(ii)]. This should not be too risky if the legal contracts contain a "specific performance" clause and a large down payment.

> ### *Investor Hint*
>
> A four-month postponement added to the 180 days equals almost ten months to complete the building!

THE SAFE HARBOR RULE TO AVOID CONSTRUCTIVELY RECEIVING MONEY

The problem—receiving too much security. After the exchanger has given the property, the exchanger typically is unwilling to rely on the buyer's *unsecured* promise to transfer the like-kind replacement property. Thus, exchangers often structure deferred exchanges where the buyer's obligation to transfer the like-kind replacement property to the exchanger is guaranteed or secured, typically using an escrow arrangement. But the exchanger *must* avoid actual or constructive receipt of the money (or other property). How?

The solution—restrictions on receiving the cash. If the right to demand the cash is subject to a "substantial limitation or restriction" [discussed below and at §1.1031(k)-1(g)(6)], there will not be actual or constructive receipt unless (or until) the limitations or restrictions lapse, expire, or are waived. In addition to these "escrow instructions" (discussed in the next paragraph), the regulations provide three liberal safe harbors (discussed thereafter) wherein the taxpayer can be given security and still use the §1031 deferral of tax rules.

> ### *Caution*
>
> Possession, in lieu of deed transfer, by a new owner cannot take place as that is also considered to start the 180 days. Therefore, a rental agreement is recommended for this "extension" period.

> ### *Investor Hint*
>
> It is recommended that the next paragraph be included in the exchange agreement or escrow instructions required between the exchanger and the accommodator [see subsequent discussion on qualified accommodators and at §1.1031(k)-1(g)(4)(iii)].

Substantial limitations or restrictions exist if the taxpayer does not have the right to receive, pledge, borrow, or obtain the benefits of the money or other property until

1. *after 45 days if no identification is made.* After the end of the (45-day) identification period, if the taxpayer has not identified replacement property before the end of the identification period, *or*
2. *after property is received.* After the taxpayer has received all of the identified replacement property to which the taxpayer is entitled (this will be the most common situation), *or*
3. *after 45 days and contingencies exist.* After the later of the end of the identification period and the occurrence of a material and substantial contingency that relates to the deferred exchange, is provided for in writing, and is beyond the control of the taxpayer or a "disqualified person" if the taxpayer identifies replacement property, *or*

4. *after the exchange period (e.g., 180 days)*. Otherwise, after the end of the exchange period [§1.1031(k)-1(g)(6)].

The above paragraph satisfies the requirement that the exchange agreement expressly limit the exchanger's rights to receive, pledge, borrow, or otherwise obtain the benefits of the money or other property before the end of the exchange period until the exchange is completed or the exchange requirements can no longer be met.

Investor Hint

Investors who don't specifically include the above wording in the exchange document run the risk of losing the advantages of the §1031 exchange rules. Investor Hillyer didn't use the above safe harbor rule and was *deemed* to have constructively received the money. The exchange was taxable because he was *deemed* to have touched the money. (*Michael Hillyer*, TC Memo 1996-214)!

What is this saying? Generally, the exchanger cannot touch the money until after he or she receives the property or the 180 days lapse. But the exchanger may pay closing costs and pay or receive prorated items out of these funds in advance without the funds being deemed constructively received (e.g., commissions, prorated taxes and rent, recording or transfer taxes, and title company fees) [§1.1031(k)-1(g)(7)].

State law irrelevant. The regulations clarify that the terms of the agreement, rather than state law, determine whether the limitations imposed by a safe harbor with respect to a taxpayer's rights to receive, pledge, borrow, or otherwise obtain the benefit of money or other property are satisfied [§1.1031(k)-1(g)(4)(vi)].

HOW TO PROPERLY STRUCTURE THE DEFERRED EXCHANGE

Because the above escrow instruction rules give little assurances as to how an exchanger can, or cannot, structure a successful transaction, the IRS suggests three safe-harbor entities to be used to close exchanges [§1.1031(k)-1(g)].

Follow These Rules and You Have a Tax-Deferred Exchange

Use of these safe-harbor rules results in a determination that the taxpayer is not, either directly or through an accommodator that may be an agent, in actual or constructive receipt of money or other property.

Red flag for audit if safe-harbor rules not used. If taxpayers go outside these safe-harbor rules, they may still argue against actual or constructive receipt of the cash based on all of the facts and circumstances. The IRS, however, states that transactions not structured to come within the safe harbors will be carefully scrutinized—a red flag for audit! Therefore, the biggest task for taxpayers is making sure that the transaction fits within the confines of the safe-harbor regulations.

Caution

If the exchanger has a "right" to the money, even if he or she doesn't actually "use" the money, this "right" ruins these safe-harbor rules. Even if a transaction is within the three safe-harbor rules, to the extent that the taxpayer has (or later receives) the ability or unrestricted right to receive money or other property before the taxpayer actually receives like-kind replacement property, the transfer of the property will not qualify for a tax-free exchange [§1.1031(k)-1 (g)(1)].

Safe harbor 1—The buyer (not the seller!) continues to hold the money but with a security or guarantee arrangement. Once the exchanger has transferred the property (and now the buyer has both the property and the money!), he or she may secure the buyer's promise to pay with like-kind replacement property, or cash, by *one or more* of the following collateral arrangements:

1. A mortgage, deed of trust, or other security interest in property (other than cash or a cash equivalent), usually from the buyer
2. A standby letter of credit that satisfies all of the requirements of §15A.453-1 (b)(3)(iii) and that does not allow the taxpayer to draw on the standby letter of credit except upon a default of the transferee's obligation to transfer like-kind replacement property to the taxpayer
3. A guarantee of a third party [§1.1031(k)-1(g)(2)]

Tax Tip

Even though this is exactly the financial arrangement in *Starker*, this safe harbor is rarely used. Most exchangers shy away from this option as the buyer ends up with both the like-kind property *and* the money for a period of time.

Example:

Barb transfers a $100,000 fair market value rental property to Carol in a deferred exchange on May 17, 2003, and the same day Carol secures her promise to purchase and transfer an office building suitable to Barb with a mortgage on the rental property.

Tax result:

§1031 exchange available. There is no constructive receipt of cash. A mortgage used as collateral qualifies under the safe-harbor rules, and Barb does not have the unrestricted right to the money before she actually receives the replacement property.

Safe harbor 2—Cash put into qualified escrow accounts and qualified trusts. More commonly, the exchanger may require that the buyer deposit the cash (or its equivalent) into a qualified escrow account or a qualified trust, without the exchanger being considered in actual or constructive receipt of the cash. Rights conferred upon the exchanger under state law to terminate or dismiss the escrow holder of a qualified escrow account or the trustee of a qualified trust are disregarded for this purpose [§1.1031(k)-1(g)(3)].

A *qualified escrow account* is an escrow account in which the escrow holder is not the taxpayer or a disqualified person (defined later in this section) and the substantial-limitations-or-restrictions-must-exist rules apply against the cash deposited [§1.1031(k)-1(g)(3)(ii)].

A *qualified trust* basically follows the above escrow account rules [§1.1031(k)-1(g)(3)(iii)].

Investor Hint

The escrow agreement *must* preclude the taxpayer from taking the cash unless and until he or she fails to designate the replacement property by a certain date. Therefore, if he or she designates property, the escrow agent (bound by the escrow instructions) is required to use the escrow funds to acquire the replacement property and transfer it to the taxpayer.

Investor Hint

Be careful that the taxpayer does not *pledge* his or her promise to receive the property (e.g., the exchanger receives a cash loan from a lending institution and pledges the right in the escrow as security for the loan)! This can be a trap for the unaware!

Example 1:

Cash placed in escrow: Barb transfers a $100,000 fair market value rental property to Carol in a deferred exchange on May 17, 2003, and Carol deposits $100,000 cash in escrow as security for Carol's obligation to perform under this contract. On or before November 13, 2003 (the end of the exchange period), the escrow is required to purchase and transfer the property identified by Barb. If the designated property's fair market value is above, or below, the $100,000, either Barb or Carol, as applicable, will make up the difference in cash one day after the replacement property is received by Barb.

Additional facts:

The escrow agreement also provides as follows: The funds in escrow are to be used to purchase the replacement property. If Barb fails to identify replacement property on or before July 1, 2003, Barb may demand the funds in escrow at any time after July 1, 2003. If Barb identifies and receives replacement property, then Barb may demand the balance of the remaining funds in escrow at any time after she has received the replacement property. Otherwise, Barb is entitled to all funds in escrow after November 13, 2003. The escrow holder is not a related party. Pursuant to the terms of the agreement, Barb identifies replacement property, and Carol purchases the replacement property, using the funds in escrow, and transfers the replacement property to Barb.

Tax result:

§1031 exchange available. There is no constructive receipt of cash as the escrow qualifies under the safe-harbor rules and as Barb does not have the unrestricted right to the money before she actually receives the replacement property [§1.1031(a)-3(g)(7)(Example 1)]. ■

Example 2:

Contingency released before property transferred: Barb transfers a $100,000 fair market value rental property to Carol in a deferred exchange on May 17, 2003, and Carol deposits $100,000 cash in escrow as security for Carol's obligation to perform under this contract. Also on May 17, Barb identifies an office building as replacement property.

Additional facts:

The escrow agreement provides the following stipulations: The funds in escrow are to be used to purchase the replacement property. Barb may demand the funds in escrow at any time after the later of July 1, 2003, and the occurrence of any of the following events: (1) the office building is destroyed, stolen, seized, requisitioned, or condemned, or (2) a determination is made that the regulatory approval necessary for the transfer of the office building cannot be obtained in time for it to be transferred to Barb before the end of the exchange period.

In addition, Barb may demand the funds in escrow at any time after August 14, 2003, if the office building has not been rezoned from residential to commercial use by that date. Otherwise, Barb is entitled to all funds in escrow after the earlier of November 13, 2003, and the time at which Barb has received all of the identified replacement property to which she is entitled. The escrow holder is not a disqualified person. The office building is *not* rezoned from residential to commercial use on or before August 14, 2003.

Tax result:

No §1031 exchange after August 14, 2003. From May 17, 2003, until August 15, 2003, Carol's obligation to transfer the replacement property to Barb is secured by cash held in a qualified escrow account, and Barb does not have the immediate ability or unrestricted right to receive money or other property before she actually receives the like-kind replacement property. Therefore, Barb is determined not to be in actual or constructive receipt of the $100,000 in escrow from May 17, 2003, until August 15, 2003.

Because she had the unrestricted right to the money after that date, however, on August 15, 2003, Barb has the unrestricted right, upon notice, to draw upon the $100,000 held in escrow. Because Barb constructively receives the full amount of the consideration ($100,000) before she actually receives the like-kind replacement property, the transaction is treated as a sale and not as a deferred exchange. The result does not change merely because Barb chooses not to demand the funds in escrow and continues to attempt to have the office building rezoned and to receive the property on or before November 13, 2003 [§1.1031(k)-1(g)(7) (Example 2)].

Example 3:

Contingency not released: If the office building had been rezoned on or before August 14, 2003, and Carol had purchased the building and transferred it to Barb on or before November 13, 2003, the transaction would have been a qualified exchange [§1.1031(k)-1(g)(7)(Example 2)(iii)].

A taxpayer may receive money or other property directly from a party to the transaction (other than the qualified escrow holder, trustee, or accommodator) and not violate the *substantial limitations or restrictions rules.*

Example 4:

Part of sales proceeds can be paid to exchanger: On May 17, 2003, Barb transfers a rental building to Carol. On the same day, Carol pays $10,000 to Barb and deposits $90,000 in escrow as security for Carol's obligation to perform under the agreement. The escrow agreement provides that Barb has no rights to receive, pledge, borrow, or otherwise obtain the benefits of the money in escrow before November 14, 2003, except that

1. if Barb fails to identify replacement property on or before July 1, 2003, Barb may demand the funds in escrow at any time after July 1, 2003, and
2. if Barb identifies and receives replacement property, then she may demand the balance of the remaining funds in escrow at any time after she has received the replacement property.

The funds in escrow may be used to purchase the replacement property. The escrow holder is not a disqualified person. Pursuant to the terms of the agreement, Barb identifies replacement property, and Carol purchases the replacement property using the funds in escrow and transfers the replacement property to Barb.

Tax result:

§1031 exchange available. Carol's obligation to transfer the replacement property to Barb is secured by cash held in a qualified escrow account because the escrow holder is not a disqualified person and the escrow agreement expressly limits Barb's rights to receive, pledge, borrow, or otherwise obtain the benefit of the money in escrow. In addition, Barb does not have the immediate ability or unrestricted right to receive money or other property in escrow before she actually receives the like-kind replacement property. Therefore, for purposes of §1031, Barb is determined not to be in actual or constructive receipt of the $90,000 held in escrow before she receives the like-kind replacement property. The transfer of the rental property by Barb and her acquisition of the replacement property qualify as an exchange under §1031. Of course, the $10,000 gain is considered boot and may be taxable [§1.1031(k)-1(g)(8) (Example 1)]. ▪

Safe harbor 3—Qualified accommodators. Sometimes buyers of real estate want only to pay their money and be done with the deal. They have little interest in, or are unable to fund, the purchase of replacement property for the exchanger. What happens if a buyer simply doesn't want to be bothered with this complication and starts looking for other property? In such cases, *intermediaries* and *accommodators* have sprung up to facilitate regular exchanges—and now deferred exchanges.

Safe harbor 3 uses a qualified accommodator's participation in the exchange to prevent the taxpayer from constructively receiving the purchase money. Deferred exchanges are permitted to be facilitated by the use of a *qualified intermediary* if the taxpayer's rights to receive the money or other property held by the accommodator are limited by the previously discussed rules on substantial limitations or restrictions [§1.1031(k)-1(g)(4)(vi)]. In this case the qualified accommodator is not considered the agent of the taxpayer (an agent is normally a disqualified person) [§1.1031(k)-1 (g)(4)(i)].

Example:

Using a qualified facilitator: On May 1, 2003, Barb enters into an agreement to sell (not exchange) to Carol a $100,000 rental building on May 17, 2003. Prior to closing, on May 16, Barb retains Acme Accommodators to facilitate a deferred exchange by entering into a deferred exchange agreement. Acme is a qualified accommodator and is not a disqualified person. Under the terms of the deferred exchange agreement, on May 17, 2003, Barb will transfer the rental property to Acme subject to Carol's right to purchase it for $100,000 on that date. Barb has to identify the replacement property by July 1, 2003, and Acme must purchase that identified property by November 13, 2003, and transfer it to Barb. Barb's rights are limited by the substantial limitations discussed above and she is not related to Acme. Barb pays $1,000 to Acme for facilitating this transaction.

Additional facts:

On May 17, 2003, Acme acquires the rental property from Barb and simultaneously transfers it to Carol in exchange for $100,000 cash. For reasons unrelated to the federal income tax, the rental property's legal title is transferred directly from Barb to Carol (permitted by §1.1031(k)-1(g)(4)(iv) and Rev. Rul. 90-34). On June 1, 2003, Barb identifies an office building as replacement property. On August 9, 2003, Acme purchases the office building for $100,000 and transfers it to Barb.

Tax result:

A §1031 exchange. The transfer of the rental property by Barb is a qualified §1031 exchange. Even though Acme acquires the rental property subject to Carol's right to purchase the property on prearranged terms and conditions, and similarly acquires the office building, they both are deemed legitimate acquisitions. Barb is deemed not to be in constructive receipt of the money before she receives the office building [§1.1031(a)-3(g)(7)(Example 3)]. ■

Who May Be an Accommodator in a Deferred Exchange?

A qualified accommodator is a person

1. who is not the taxpayer or a disqualified person (discussed in the next section) *and*
2. who acts to facilitate a deferred exchange by entering into a written agreement (called the *exchange agreement*), and, as required by the exchange agreement, *acquires* the relinquished property from the taxpayer, transfers the relinquished property, acquires the replacement property, and transfers the replacement property to the taxpayer [§1.1031(k)-1(g)(4)(iii)].

Caution

A legal document, generally called an *exchange agreement, must* exist evidencing the relationship between the exchanger and the accommodator.

Tax Tip

As previously discussed, the word *acquire* means either actual acquisition or assignment of the right to purchase.

Definition of a Disqualified Person

1. *Any agent of the taxpayer—within the past two years.* The person who is the agent of the taxpayer at the time of the transaction is a disqualified person. For this purpose, *a person who has acted as the taxpayer's employee, attorney, accountant, investment banker or broker, or real estate agent or broker within the two-year period* ending on the date of the transfer of the first of the relinquished properties *is treated as an agent of the taxpayer* at the time of the transaction.

   But the following will not be a disqualified agent:

   - *Putting together an exchange.* An agent providing services for the taxpayer with respect to exchanges of property intended to qualify for nonrecognition of gain or loss under §1031
   - *Routine financial, title insurance, escrow, or trust services* for the taxpayer by a financial institution, title insurance company, or escrow company, [§1.1031(k)-1(k)(2)]

Investor Hint

Most real estate agents putting together an exchange may be the accommodator as long as they have not represented the client in the last two years.

---

2. *A related party.* If a person and the taxpayer bear a relationship described in either §267(b) (e.g., family members, spouses, lineal descendants, a corporation and owner of 10% or more of the corporation, a fiduciary and beneficiary of a trust, a grantor and a fiduciary of a trust, etc.) or §707 (b) (e.g., a partnership and partner owning 10% or more of the partnership), determined by substituting in each section "10%" for "50%" each place it appears, he or she shall be a disqualified person [§1.1031(k)-1(k)(3)].

3. *A related agent.* If a person and a person who is an agent of the taxpayer at the time of the transaction bear a relationship described in §267(b) or §707(b), again substituting 10% for 50%, he or she shall be a disqualified person.

Examples:

Unless otherwise provided, in the next group of examples the following facts are assumed: On May 1, 2003, Larry enters into an exchange agreement with General Business Services (GBS) whereby Larry retains GBS to facilitate an exchange with respect to his office building. On May 17, 2003, pursuant to the agreement, Larry executes and delivers to GBS a deed conveying his office building to GBS.

Example 1:

Taxpayer's accountant: GBS is Larry's accountant and has rendered accounting services to Larry within the two-year period ending on May 17, 2003, in addition to counseling him about the exchange of this property to qualify for nonrecognition of gain or loss under §1031.

GBS is a disqualified person because GBS has acted as Larry's accountant within the two-year period ending on May 17, 2003.

If GBS had not acted as Larry's accountant within the two-year period ending on May 17, 2003, or if GBS had acted as Larry's accountant within that period only with respect to exchanges intended to qualify for nonrecognition of gain or loss under §1031, GBS would not have been a disqualified person [§1.1031(k)-1(k)(5)(Example 1)]. ▪

Example 2:

Escrow company: GBS, which is engaged in the trade or business of acting as an accommodator to facilitate deferred exchanges, is a wholly owned subsidiary of an escrow company that has performed routine escrow services for Larry in the past. GBS has previously been retained by Larry to act as an accommodator in prior §1031 exchanges.

GBS is not a disqualified person notwithstanding the accommodator services previously provided by GBS to Larry and notwithstanding the combination of GBS's relationship to the escrow company and the escrow services previously provided by the escrow company to Larry [§1.1031(k)-1(k)(5)(Example 2)]. ▪

Example 3:

Escrow company owned by exchanger's lawyer: GBS is a corporation that is only engaged in the trade or business of acting as an accommodator to facilitate deferred exchanges. Each of ten law firms owns 10% of the outstanding stock of GBS. One of the ten law firms that owns 10% of GBS is Snydley & Whiplash, Attorneys-at-Law. Barrister Bill is the managing partner of Snydley & Whiplash and is the president of GBS. Barrister Bill, in his capacity as a partner in Snydley & Whiplash, has also rendered legal advice to Larry within the two-year period ending on May 17, 2003, on matters other than exchanges intended to qualify for nonrecognition of gain or loss under §1031.

Barrister Bill and Snydley & Whiplash, Attorneys-at-Law, are disqualified persons. GBS, however, is not a disqualified person because neither Barrister Bill nor Snydley & Whiplash own, directly or indirectly, more than 10% of the stock of GBS. Similarly, Barrister Bill's participation in the management of GBS does not make GBS a disqualified person [§1.1031(k)-1(k)(5)(Ex 3)]. ▪

How the Interest Earned in the Escrow Is Handled

Can the interest earned while the cash is controlled by the accommodator be paid to the exchanger? To compensate for the time value of money for the period between transfer and receipt of the replacement property, the taxpayer may charge interest, sometimes called a *growth factor,* during the exchange period, but only if:

1. the previously mentioned *substantial limitations or restrictions* exist [§1.1031(k)-1(g)(5)],
2. the interest time period is only the time between transfer of the relinquished property and receipt of the replacement property [§1.1031(k)-1(h)(1)], *and*
3. it is taxable as interest income, whether paid in cash or other property, *including like-kind property* [§1.1031(k)-1(h)(2)].

The interest income is taxed to the exchanger/seller. In a typical deferred Starker exchange, the "seller" of a piece of real estate transfers it to an intermediary, who ultimately carries out the sale and then holds the proceeds until the seller identifies the replacement property to be purchased. Questions have arisen as to who is taxable on the interest earned on the seller's funds while they are held by the accommodator in a qualified settlement fund (QSF) are taxed to the seller. This is true even if part of the earnings are paid to the accommodator for exchange fees. The only exception is if the accommodator is entitled to all of the earnings [§1.1031(j)(2); §1.468b-1(k)6-90].

Investor Hint

The exchanger must include the interest (or growth factor) in income according to the exchanger's method of accounting, (e.g., a calendar-year exchanger would include the interest income earned through December 31 even though the exchanger cannot remove the interest from the trust account because of the access-to-the-cash limitation rules) [§1.1031(k)-1(h)(2)].

Investor Hint

Previously, small accommodators have retained any interest earned in escrow as partial compensation for services rendered. This new rule alerts the taxpayer(s), and their agents, that interest may be charged without risking the exchange, which will probably result in the more knowledgeable taxpayers requesting the interest for themselves. The effect of these regulations likely will be that either small accommodators will start charging flat fees or the majority of the work will be performed by banks and escrow companies.

Chapter 8

Minimum Requirements for an Exchange

HOW TO USE THIS CHAPTER

The reader now knows how to calculate the tax results of a like-kind exchange and can pull together the parties for an exchange. The three previous chapters make like-kind exchanges sound fun, and they are fun—up to a point.

At some time in every exchange comes a technical question so crucial that potentially it can blow up the exchange. This chapter is written to supply the answer to that all-important deal killer. This part is not written to be read as a novel, but it does supply the nitty-gritty of the exchange requirements. Once the problem surfaces, look for the answer in this chapter. Generally, the answer is supported by tax citations and/or court cases.

As previously mentioned, §1031 provides that no gain (or loss) is recognized if certain qualifying property is exchanged solely for like-kind property. However, property qualifying for the nontax treatment is limited to *property held for productive use in a trade or business or for investment,* so long as the property is specifically not excluded (e.g., inventory, stocks, and bonds cannot be traded tax-free) [§1031(a)(1)].

Six Basic Elements for an Exchange

To make searching for technical answers easier, this chapter has been divided into the six criteria necessary to meet the like-kind exchange prerequisites. Determine in what area your exchange question is and skip forward to find your answer.

The requirements of §1031(a)(1) involve the following six components:

1. *Property:* There must be property transferred and property received.
2. *Exchange:* There must be an "exchange" of properties.
3. *Qualified use:* Both the property transferred and the property received must be held for "productive use in a trade or business or for investment."
4. *Not excluded property:* The tax-free benefits of §1031 are not available to the transfers of stock-in-trade (e.g., inventory), stocks, bonds, notes, other securities or evidences of indebtedness or interest, interests in a partnership, certificates of trust or beneficial interests, or choses in action; and therefore exchanges of any of the enumerated properties are taxable transfers.
5. *Like kind:* The business or investment properties transferred must also be of a "like kind."
6. *No boot:* For the transaction to be entirely tax-free, the property received must be exchanged *solely* for qualified like-kind property.

1. The "Property" Requirement

Section 1031(a)(1) only applies "on the exchange of *property . . . for property,*" not an exchange of property for something else (e.g., prepaid rent or services to be rendered). If nonqualifying property is included, §1031 may be partially or totally unavailable. Here is a list of some unusual items that may or may not qualify as property for like-kind exchange purposes.

Leasehold. A taxpayer who transfers a 30-year, or longer, leasehold on real property (e.g., land or building) is considered to have transferred qualifying property [§1.1031(a)-1(c)]; optional renewal periods are included when calculating the 30 years [Rev. Rul. 78-72, 1978-1 CB 258]. Leaseholds with a remaining duration of less than 30 years are of like kind to each other only but not to any other real property [Rev. Rul. 76-301, 1976-2 CB 241].

Prepaid rent. A leasehold is not considered real property if below-market rent is paid or when property reverts back to the exchanger at the end of the 30-year-plus lease [Rev. Rul. 66-209, 1966-2 CB 299].

Life estate.   A taxpayer can exchange a life estate for real property so long as the property does not revert back to the exchanger. If the exchanger retains a remainder interest, the property received represents prepaid rent, not property [Rev. Rul. 72-601, 1972-2 CB 467].

Services to be rendered.   A taxpayer cannot exchange property for services, including brokerage fees or production services [§1.1031(e)(4)]. This may lead to some bizarre results, as seen in the next two examples.

1.   *The exchange of land for a building to be constructed on presently owned property* is not a qualified exchange. *Bloomington Coca-Cola Bottling Co.* [189 F2d 14 (9th Cir. 1950)] transferred property to a contractor in exchange for the construction of a building on some other Coca-Cola land. We know that the contractor cannot use §1031, but what about Coca-Cola? The court decided no exchange, as Coca-Cola was considered to have received building services and materials, not qualifying property. (However, LTR 8008113 held that an exchange of improvements in a shopping center for a fee interest qualified for §1031). On the other hand:

2.   *The exchange of land for a building to be constructed on a site not presently owned* is a qualified exchange [*J. H. Baird Publishing Co.* 39 TC 608 (1962), *acq.*, 1963-2 CB 4]. The taxpayer "sold" high-basis property to a contractor, then hired the contractor to build a building, and subsequently "traded" some low-basis property back to the same contractor—tax-free under §1031 (LTR 7823035)!

> ### Caution
>
> This so-called reverse-Starker exchange took place prior to the publishing of Revenue Procedure 2000-37, although, as explained below, it is doubtful DeCleene would have won in any event. So what went wrong? Incidentally, doesn't this sound exactly like the *J.H Baird Publishing Co.* case mentioned previously?

> ### Tax Tip
>
> As discussed previously in the "deferred exchange" rules, the taxpayer can clearly exchange existing property for property to be constructed but maybe not on their own property and definitely not for future services [§1.1031(e)].

Attempt to build "replacement property" on presently owned land fails.   Donald DeCleene was looking for land to move his growing Green Bay, Wisconsin trucking repair business located on McDonald Street. He *acquired* property on Lawrence Drive, found a buyer (WLC) for his old property, and then went to his accountant for tax advice. The accountant suggested that he could structure a like-kind exchange in which he would sell, via a quitclaim deed, the Lawrence Drive property to WLC, after which WLC would convey back to DeCleene the Lawrence Drive property with a new building built thereon to DeCleene's specifications, in exchange for the McDonald Street property.

"Burdens and benefits" of ownership found to have never passed.   The court found that WLC did not acquire any of the benefits and burdens of ownership of the Lawrence Drive property during the three-month period it held title to the property during the construction phase. According to the agreement between DeCleene and WLC, WLC had no exposure to real estate taxes that accrued while WLC held title and all such taxes were to be paid by DeCleene, the purported acquisition of the property was nonrecourse, no interest accrued or was paid during the period, the construction was financed by DeCleene, only DeCleene was financially "at risk," and WLC had no potential for or exposure to any economic gain or loss on its acquisition and disposition of title to the Lawrence Drive property. The court stated: "WLC merely served as an accommodation party, providing the parking place for legal title to the Lawrence Drive property, while [DeCleene] remained the beneficial owner before and after and throughout the 3-month focal period of the subject transactions."

Therefore, because the taxpayer never "actually" divested himself of beneficial ownership of the unimproved property, he could not reacquire it as replacement property in exchange for the relinquishment of his remaining property. Thus, the exchange was characterized as a sale of property *(Donald DeCleene v. Comm.,* 115 TC 457).

2. The "Exchange" Requirement

There must be an *exchange* of property, not a sale of property followed by a subsequent purchase of other property. Ordinarily, a transfer will be considered an exchange if there is a reciprocal transfer of property for property but not a transfer of property for money [§1.1002-1(d)].

No simultaneous purchases allowed.   The exchange requirement is not met when a cash sale of property is immediately followed by a cash purchase of like-kind property [*Halpern v. U.S.,* 286 F. Supp. 255 (N.D. GA. 1968)].

May an exchange be arranged even though a contract for sale between two parties has already been signed?   *Yes,* amazingly enough, by using an escrow arrangement. The Tax Court looks at the *form* of the transaction over its *substance.*

Example:

In *Leslie Q. Coupe* [52 TC 394 (1960)], even though a contract to sell for a stipulated price had been signed with a second party, it was arranged that the second party deposit the money into an escrow account with instructions to the escrow agent that it be paid to the title holders of Coupe's property. Coupe then exchanges his property for like-kind property owned by a third party. The third party sells the Coupe property to the second party for the cash in the escrow account. This transaction was not considered a sham but rather a perfectly legitimate tax-free exchange. ■

Some sales will be treated as exchanges—trade-ins.   A taxpayer may own property that has a basis higher than the trade-in value. Prudent tax planning would structure the transaction as a sale, followed with a subsequent purchase, to trigger the deductible loss. Tax planning professionals would *not* want to structure the transaction as an exchange, because this requires that the loss be currently nondeductible and adds the loss to the basis of the newly acquired property.

May a trade-in be structured as a sale? Probably not. If the sale and purchase is mutually dependent (i.e., both the sale and the purchase are from the same business—as is common in the automobile industry), the transaction may be deemed an exchange [Rev. Rul. 61-119, 1961-1 CB 395; *Redwing Carriers, Inc. v. Tomlinson,* (CA-5) 68-2 USTC ¶9540; 399 F2d 652].

Caution

Therefore, all documents used at closing must be *exchange documents* and not the typical purchase and sale agreements commonly associated with residential sales. It is not sufficient, in the author's opinion, to simply draw a line through the words *buy, sell, purchaser* and *seller* and substitute exchange verbiage, such as *exchanger* and *exchangee.*

Example:

George owns an apartment house with a central air conditioner that has a present depreciable basis of $12,000 (because it previously has only been allowed a depreciation rate of 27.5 years). This old air conditioner fails, and George decides to replace it with a new $42,000 Lennox. Dave (Lennox) allows a $2,000 trade-in on the old unit. Therefore, George's *loss* is $10,000 ($12,000 basis – $2,000 fair market value).

Tax problem:

Is the $10,000 loss deductible? *No.* This is a like-kind exchange, and losses on like-kind exchanges are never deductible [§1031(a)(1); also discussed in Chapter 5]. Losses on exchanges are added to the purchase price of the new asset *and now will have to be depreciated over another 27.5 years* (also discussed in Chapter 10 on depreciation)! This is a terrible result. Are there any alternatives?

Tax solution:

One of the six like-kind exchange elements must be avoided. The most common solution is to not have an exchange in the first place by junking (abandoning) the old air conditioner and asking Dave for a $2,000 reduction in price for a cash purchase. In this situation, the $12,000 loss is currently deductible as an abandonment loss, normally reportable on IRS Form 4797.

Some exchanges will be treated as sales—cash received may create a deemed sale and reinvestment. If the taxpayer *constructively* receives the cash and subsequently uses it to purchase property, a structured exchange is treated as a sale, especially where a step-transaction analysis indicates that the substance (over the form) of the transaction is a sale [*Carlton v. U.S.,* 385 F. 2d 238 (5th Cir. 1967); *Crenshaw v. U.S.,* 450 F. 2d 472 (5th Cir. 1971)]. These problems can be easily avoided by using *qualified accommodators* as discussed in Chapter 7 on deferred exchanges.

3. The "Qualified Use" Requirement—What Property Qualifies for a Tax-Free Exchange?

Requirement. As mentioned previously, *both* the property given up and the property received by the taxpayer must be held for *productive use in a trade or business* **or** for investment [§1031(A)(1)]. For confusion's sake, §1031 does not define *business* or *investment;* therefore, conventional wisdom assumes that the terms have the same meaning as elsewhere in the code, which is discussed below.

"Held for productive use in trade or business." Qualifying property must be used in a trade or business in which the taxpayer is engaged [§162; §1231].

Examples of trade or business property include buildings owned and used by a business, office buildings, apartment houses, machinery and equipment, business trucks, and automobiles.

Confusion reigns—rental units are business property. For tax and exchange purposes, rental units are considered to be business property, *not* investment property. Most investors think rentals are investments, which is not true. Investment property has the nega-

Investor Hint

The *qualified use* test is determined by the use of each property, both given and received, *in the taxpayer's hands.* Therefore, the use of either property in the hands of the other party involved in the exchange is irrelevant [Rev. Rul. 75-291].

tive result of creating a capital loss whereas business property creates a fully deductible ordinary loss (see Chapter 2 for more details). So what is included in the very limited definition of *investment* property?

"Held for investment."   This probably refers to property held for future use or future appreciation in value [§212].

Examples of investment property include unimproved raw land, recreational property, vacation homes, and condominiums.

Investor Hint

As will be discussed further under requirement 5, real estate business property (e.g., an apartment) may be exchanged for real estate investment property (e.g., raw land or a vacation home being held for appreciation).

Personal residences and certain vacation homes don't qualify.   A personal residence (or a vacation home not held for investment) is not *qualified use* property because it is being used for personal purposes, not *business or investment* purposes.

Personal residences cannot be included in an exchange: Therefore, when a personal residence is exchanged for any other property, the §121 residence exclusion rules apply (Chapter 3) and not the §1031 tax-free exchange rules.

Can we exchange a vacation home for a vacation home?   The question is, at the date of exchange is the vacation home being used primarily for personal purposes or is it being held for investment purposes (e.g., for future appreciation)? An exchange of a personal-use vacation home for anything, even another vacation home, cannot use the §1031 exchange rules (and therefore it would be a taxable exchange). On the other hand, a vacation home held for investment (appreciation) or as a vacation home rental would fully qualify for a like-kind exchange. The date to determine personal, business, or investment use is at the date of sale, and the previous use is relatively immaterial unless the conversion is for tax purposes only [*U.S. v. Winthrop,* 5 Cir. 1969, 417 F.2d 905; Rev. Rul. 82-26, 1982-1 CB 114].

Residence into investment property. In Rev. Rul. 57-244, 1957-1 CB 247, the IRS addressed the facts of three taxpayers who purchase property for the construction of homes and later abandon that purpose for clearly established reasons and continue to hold the property for investment purposes (i.e., for appreciation in value). A subsequent exchange is held to qualify under §1031. Property constituting the taxpayer's principal residence will not con-

Caution

Vacation homes used personally cannot use §121 residence exclusion rules (as the home is not being used as the taxpayer's *principal* residence) and cannot use the §1031 rules (as the home is not being used for business or investment property). Personal-use vacation homes are normally fully taxable when sold.

Tax Tip

Can we convert a personal residence into property qualified for an exchange? Sometimes it may be desirable to use §1031 on the transfer of a personal resi-dence, as when the taxpayer wishes to acquire, with separate funds, a less costly personal residence and the gain exceeds $250,000. Is it possible? Maybe, but with the changes to gains of sale on a principal residence and the ability to rent it for up to three years and still use the §121 exclusion, the law is unsettled in this area.

---

currently qualify as investment property [*Starker v. U.S.,* 602 F2d 1341 (9th Cir. 1979)], even when the taxpayer argues that the residence is being held for appreciation.

Residence into rental property. Converting a personal residence into a rental would also change the use to qualified use. Given that the burden of proving conversion is on the taxpayer, the success of this tactic depends upon how long the property is rented before exchange, the documentation of rental efforts (e.g., newspaper for-rent advertisements, written rental agreements, retention of property managers, etc.), and the substance of the transaction.

Property received in exchange and immediately resold is not "held for" correct purpose.

The purpose the taxpayer establishes for acquiring the property is important because property acquired by exchange for immediate sale is not *held for business or investment.* Rather it is acquired for resale (which is not one of the two qualified uses) and therefore cannot be exchanged tax-free. This is especially true when the taxpayer has entered into a binding contract *before the exchange* to sell the property after the exchange. The length of time the property must be held before sale or liquidation is uncertain [*Griffin v. Comm.,* 49 TC 253 (1967); *Black v. Comm.,* 35 TC 90 (1960); Rev. Rul. 75-291; Rev. Rul. 77-297].

Preexisting plan and contract. In one case, the taxpayer exchanged property for a commercial building and one month later initiated a plan of liquidation under which it would sell the building. The court held that the commercial building was *not* held for business or investment (but was held for trading or resale) and therefore the exchange did not qualify under §1031 [*Regals Realty Co. v. Comm.,* 43 BTA 194 (1940)].

Contributions or distributions involving corporations and partnerships. The law is unsettled concerning nonrecognition transfers to or from an entity soon before or after an exchange. The IRS argues that tax-free transfers (under §351 and §721) to the exchanger's own partnership or corporation soon before or after an exchange cause the taxpayer's exchange to fail the *holding for qualifying use* test [Rev. Rul. 75-292, 1975-2, CB 333; Rev. Rul. 77-337, 1977-2 CB 305].

In numerous cases, the Tax Court disagreed with the IRS's position in the previous paragraph and decided that each taxpayer *did meet* the holding-for-business-or-investment requirement. The court overruled the IRS opinion that the corporation or partnership will, by itself, have to reestablish business or investment use and could not attach the partner's/shareholder's use [*Magneson v. Comm.,* 81 TC 767 (1983), *aff'd* 753 F2d 1490 (9th Cir. 1985); *Bolker v. Comm.,* 81 TC 782 (1983), *aff'd* 760 F2d 1039 (9th Cir. 1985); *Mason v. Comm.,* 55 TCM 1134, *aff'd* 880 F2d 420 (11th Cir. 1989); and *Chase v. Comm.,* 92 TC 53 (1989); *Fredericks,* TC CCH Dec. 49,629(M), ¶47,543(M)(1994)].

Property acquired for exchange is also *not held* for correct purpose.   In the reverse of the above situation, if the purpose for acquisition is to use the property for a future exchange, it also cannot be exchanged tax-free as it is not being *held for business or investment,* but rather it is being acquired for a future exchange. The length of time the property must be held before an exchange is uncertain [Rev. Rul. 77-337, 1977-2 CB 305; Rev. Rul. 84-121, 1984-2 CB 168].

4. The "Specifically Excluded Property" Requirement

Section 1031(a)(2) specifically states that the tax-free benefits are not available to the transfers of stock-in-trade (e.g., inventory), stocks, bonds, notes, other securities or evidences of indebtedness or interest, interests in a partnership, certificates of trust or beneficial interests, or choses in action. If an exchange involves any of these items, it is nonqualifying property.

Example:

Dean exchanged his 40-acre farm for Mary's 200 shares of Texaco stock, a $100,000 Commonwealth bond, and a personal note for $100,000. As all three assets received are specifically nonqualified property, the total gain must be recognized. ▪

No like-kind exchange for "dealers" in real estate, as only "investors" qualify. Dealers in real estate may not use the like-kind exchange provisions regarding nonrecognition of gain or loss on exchange of real property because they hold real property as stock-in-trade (inventory), and not for productive use in business or for investment [§1031(a)(2)].

> ## Tax Tip
>
> Often recently subdivided real estate may not be traded tax-free for other real estate, subdivided or otherwise, as the property being traded is *property held primarily for sale* and therefore is nonqualifying property. Special rules allow the investor to subdivide property and be exempt from dealer status [§1237].

Who is a dealer? In determining whether a person is a *dealer* to any property (as opposed to an *investor*), the facts and circumstances of each situation must be analyzed. The dealer-versus-investor issue must be decided on a property-by-property basis and not an individual-by-individual basis. There are no specific factors, or even combinations of them, that are controlling for deciding the dealer-versus-investor issue. The courts have traditionally used the following tests [*Winthrop, Ada Belle v. Tomlinson,* ¶(CA-5) 69-2 USTC ¶9686, 417 F2d 905]:

1. The reason and purpose the property was acquired and/or disposed
2. The length of time the property was held
3. The number and frequency of sales, usually annually

4. The continuity of sales or sales-related activity over a period of time
5. Overall reluctance to sell the property
6. The substantiality of the gain obtained on the sale
7. The extent to which the taxpayer or his or her agents engaged in sales activities by developing or improving the property, soliciting customers, or advertising
8. The substantiality of sales when compared with other sources of the taxpayer's income
9. The desire to liquidate unexpectedly obtained land holdings (such as by inheritance)

May a REALTOR® *also be an investor?* Yes. It is possible for the same person to simultaneously be a dealer and an investor in real estate. A dealer in real estate must be distinguished from a REALTOR® or a real estate agent. A dealer has ownership interest in property whereas a real estate agent brings together a buyer and a seller of property for a fee or commission [*Williford v. Comm.,* TC Memo 1992-430].

May we convert "dealer" property into property qualified for an exchange? Dealers have, with difficulty, converted a portion of their real estate inventory into business or investment property, but they must prove that the dealer intent has been abandoned and the property thereafter has been held for investment. The length of time the property must be held before sale or liquidation is uncertain, and the difficult evidentiary burden of proof has not been analyzed in any recent exchange cases by the courts [*Maddux Construction Co.,* 54 TC 1278 (1970); *Silversmith v. U.S.,* 79-1 USTC ¶9117 (D. Colo. 1979)].

Trading of partnership interests. The like-kind exchange rules do *not* apply to any exchange of interests in a partnership of whether the interests exchanged are general or limited partnership interests or are interests in the same partnership or in different partnerships. The assets owned by the partnership are irrelevant [§1.1031(a)-(1)(a)(1)].

Example:

Edith owns a 50% partnership interest in a $500,000 rental office building in Syracuse and wishes to exchange it for a 50% partnership interest in a $500,000 rental office building in Orlando. Edith has been reporting her income or loss as partnership income or loss (Form K-1), and the rental office building has been reported on a partnership tax return, Form 1065. Edith's exchange would be a *taxable* exchange under these new regulations. ■

Tax Tip

Liquidation of a real estate partnership and transferral of the assets back into individual ownership allows Edith to use the like-kind exchange provisions. Therefore, if Edith first liquidated the partnership, she could use §1031 on her $250,000 half-interest in the rental office building.

Certain real estate joint ventures, and the like, are not considered partnerships. Mere co-ownership of property that is maintained, kept in repair, and rented or leased does not constitute a partnership. For example, if an individual owner or tenant in common of farm property lease it to a farmer for a cash rental or a share of the crops, he or she does not necessarily create a partnership [§1.761-1(a)].

Tenants-in-common, however, may be partners if they *actively* carry on a trade, business, financial operation, or venture and divide the profits from the enterprise. For example, a partnership exists if co-owners of an apartment building lease space *and in addition provide services to the occupants,* either directly or through an agent [§1.761-1(a)].

Example:

If Edith owns a 50% co-ownership interest in a $500,000 rental office building in Syracuse, she *could exchange tax-free* for a 50% co-ownership interest in a $500,000 rental office building in Orlando. If she really wants to protect herself, she could file a §1.761-2(b) election (discussed next) and not be considered a partnership. ■

Because a partnership interest in rental real estate cannot be traded tax-free under §1031 but a co-ownership interest, such as tenancy-in-common, of the same rental real estate can avail itself of the §1031 benefits, taxpayers have inundated the IRS with requests for ruling on the taxpayer's ownership interest. The central characteristic of a tenancy in common, one of the traditional concurrent estates in land, is that *each owner is deemed to own individually a physically undivided part of the entire parcel* of property. Each tenant in common is entitled to share with the other tenants the possession of the whole parcel and has the associated rights to a proportional share of rents or profits from the property, to transfer the interest, and to demand a partition of the property.

The different factors between co-ownership and partnership. Where a sponsor packages co-ownership interests for sale by acquiring property, negotiating a master lease on the property, and arranging for financing, the courts have looked at the relationships not only among the co-owners but also between the sponsor (or persons related to the sponsor) and the co-owners in determining whether the co-ownership gives rise to a partnership. For example, in *Bergford v. Comm.,* 12 F.3d 166 (9th Cir. 1993), 78 investors purchased "co-ownership" interests in computer equipment that was subject to a seven-year net lease. The court held that the co-ownership arrangement constituted a partnership for federal tax purposes. Among the factors that influenced the court's decision were the limitations on the co-owners' ability to sell, lease, or encumber either the co-ownership interest or the underlying property and the manager's effective participation in both profits (through the remarketing fee) and losses (through the advances). Where the parties to a venture join together capital or services with the intent of conducting a business or enterprise and of sharing the profits and losses from the venture, a partnership (or other business entity) is created.

When is an undivided fractional interest not a partnership? The IRS has specified the conditions under which it will consider a request for a ruling that an undivided fractional interest in rental real property (other than a mineral property as defined in §614) is not an interest in a business entity, within the meaning of §301.7701-2(a). The procedure applies to co-ownership of rental real property in an arrangement classified under local law as a tenancy-in-common. This reverses the previous announcement that the IRS would not issue advance rulings or determination letters on undivided fractional interests (see Rev. Proc. 2000-46).

The conditions for a ruling.   The IRS ordinarily will not consider a request for a ruling under this revenue procedure unless the conditions, described in synopsis form below, are satisfied:

1. Tenancy in common ownership required
2. No more than 35 co-owners
3. Co-ownership not a separate entity, e.g., property owned in partnership or corporate name
4. Limited co-ownership agreement permitted
5. Co-owners retain voting rights
6. Limited restrictions on co-owners' rights of alienation
7. On sale of property, liens must be satisfied before proceeds are shared
8. Profit and losses shared in proportion to co-owners' interest
9. Debt shared in proportion to co-owners interest .
10. Options must reflect fair market value
11. Co-owners limited to rental real estate repair and maintenance activities [see Rev. Rul. 75-374]
12. Property management agreement must contain certain provisions on management, fees, and disbursements
13. Leasing agreements must be bona fide
14. Lender may not be directly or indirectly related
15. Only fair market value payments, not percent of profit, to sponsor [Rev. Proc. 2002-22]

   Note: These conditions indicate the IRS's audit issues in deciding what property is unqualified for a §1031 exchange.

Election to be excluded from partnership provisions available.   An interest in certain investment and production partnerships that have made a valid §761(a) election [§1.761-2(b)] is excluded from the application of all of the partnership provisions and is treated as an interest in each of the assets of the partnership, not as an interest in a partnership [§1.1031(a)-(1)(a)(1)]. If the participants in the joint venture (1) purchase, retain, sell, or exchange investment property; (2) own the property as co-owners; (3) reserve the right separately to take or dispose of their shares of any property acquired or retained; and (4) do not actively conduct business or use certain agents, then the participants may elect to be excluded from the partnership provisions [§1.761-2(a)(2)].

Foreign real property.   Real property located in the United States and real property located outside the United States are *not* property of a like kind. But exchanges of foreign real estate for foreign real estate and domestic real estate for domestic real estate are still permitted [1031(h)].

> **Investor Hint**
>
> If the partnership has filed partnership returns for previous years, this election is probably not available as the election must be timely filed. When possible, consideration should be given to a partnership liquidation and a subsequent donation to a joint venture, which will timely file this election! The problem is that liquidation may be difficult.

5. The "Like-Kind" Requirement

As mentioned previously, only like-kind trade, business, or investment property owned and used may be traded for like-kind trade, business, or investment property. In §1031, the words *like kind* refer to the nature or character of the property (and not to its grade or quality). Accordingly, "one kind or class of property may not . . . be exchanged for property of a different kind or class" [§1.1031(a)-1(b)].

Example:

An exchange of a business office building (real property) for business machinery (personal property) will *not* qualify because the nature or character of the property is not like kind. ■

Like-kind real property exchanges. The Internal Revenue Service is quite liberal in interpreting that all real estate is similar in nature or character and does not have a different grade or quality. The fact that any real estate is improved or unimproved is not material. Also, unproductive real estate held for future use or appreciation in value is held for investment [§1.1031(a)-1(b)].

> **Tax Tip**
>
> Any business property for investment property qualifies. Therefore, any mixture of office buildings, apartment buildings, factory buildings, shopping centers, stores, hotels, motels, farms, ranches, and parking lots is permitted.

Fee simple transfers. Exchanging fee simple ownership in real estate is virtually always of *like kind* to other fee interests in realty. Fee simple property may even be exchanged for leases in excess of 30 years [§1.1031(a)-1(b),(c)].

Mineral interests. Mineral and nonmineral real estate interests may be exchanged on a like-kind basis, provided that the mineral interests are considered real property under state law and are of substantial equality with respect to the character and nature of title as the nonmineral property given. For example, oil and gas royalty rights are of like kind to ranch properties [Rev. Rul. 55-749, 1955-2 CB 95; LTR 7935126].

Leasehold. Thirty-year, or longer, leaseholds and real property (e.g., land or building) are considered to be like kind [§1.1031(a)-1(c)]. Optional renewal periods are included when calculating the 30 years [Rev. Rul. 78-72, 1978-1 CB 258]. Therefore, less-than-30-year leaseholds are not of like kind to a fee ownership in real estate [*Capri, Inc.,* 65 TC 162 (1975)]. Interestingly, leaseholds with a remaining duration of less than 30 years are of like kind to each other [Rev. Rul. 76-301, 1976-2 CB 241].

Sale coupled with a leaseback. A sale of property coupled with the seller leasing the property back for 30 years or longer is considered an exchange of like-kind property, according to the IRS [§1.1031(a)-1(c)(2)]. If the property being disposed of would have created a loss upon sale, this could be disastrous. The courts disagree with this regulation when both the sales price and the rent charged were fair market value [*Jordan Marsh Co. v. Comm.,* 269 F2d 452 (2d Cir. 1959), *nonacq.; Lesslie Co. v. Comm.,* 539 F2d 943 (3rd Cir. 1976), *nonacq.,* 1978-1 CB 3]. Losses have been allowed where the leaseback was for less than a 30-year term, as less-than-30-year leaseholds are not of like kind to fee estates [Rev. Rul. 78-72, 1978-1 CB 258; *Standard Envelope Manufacturing Co.,* 15 TC 41 (1950), *acq.,* 1950-2 CB 4].

Other examples of "like-kind" real property.

1. Commercial building for lots [*Burkhard Inv. Co. v. U.S.,* 100 F2d 642 (9th Cir 1938)]
2. City real estate for a farm or ranch [§1.1031(a)-1(c)]
3. Developed property for undeveloped property [§1.1031(a)-1(c)]
4. Land subject to a 99-year condominium lease [*Carl E. Koch,* 71 TC 54, 1978, *acq.*]
5. Improved real property for unimproved real property, regardless of the locations [§1.1031(a)-1(c)], with the exception of foreign real estate [§1031(h)]
6. Timberland for timberland [Rev. Rul. 72-515; Rev. Rul. 76-253]
7. A remainder interest in farmland for a remainder interest in other farmland [Rev. Rul. 78-4]
8. Perpetual water rights for a fee interest in land [Rev. Rul. 55-749]
9. Producing oil leases for a ranch [Rev. Rul. 68-331]
10. An easement on a farm for an unencumbered fee simple interest in another farm [PLR 9215049]
11. A conservation easement for a cattle ranch [LTR 200203033; 200203042; 200201007]
12. A cooperative leasehold interest for a condominium fee simple interest [LTR 200137032]

Like-kind personal property exchanges.

Normally, exchanges of real estate include furniture and fixtures. The exchange rules for personal property are much stricter than those for real property. Personal property used in a trade or business is considered exchanged for like-kind property *only if* the properties are either (1) like kind *or* (2) like class (e.g., one can't trade tax-free a business lawnmower for a business refrigerator, even though both are being used at the same rental).

Each personal property exchange must be reported separately. Reporting like-kind exchanges has become substantially more complicated because disclosure of the exchange now goes on Form 8824 instead of Form 4797 or on Line 9a of Schedule D. To make matters worse, the final regulations [TD 8343] tell taxpayers *how* to report the "trading in" of personal property (e.g., automobiles, over-the-road trucks, office furniture, and equipment) when replacing it with other similar personal property.

> *Investor Hint*
> _____
>
> The final regulations contain *no exceptions* for items of personal property that have de minimis or minimum value! Therefore, every time a landlord trades in an old $50 refrigerator for a new $500 refrigerator, this will require the filing of a different Form 8824. Similarly, each time the real estate agent trades in his or her business automobile, another Form 8824 must be created! Each trade is a reportable like-kind exchange, even though no tax may be due.

Multiple asset exchanges—analysis of underlying assets needed in business exchanges. When a taxpayer exchanges one business for a similar business, is the exchanged property the business for the other business? Can we exchange a Wendy's for a McDonald's, or a farm for a farm? According to the IRS, we cannot do a business-for-business exchange. It is an exchange of the separate assets of the businesses.

Example:

Dennis exchanges his laundry business, comprising a building and seven washer and dryer units (fair market value of $1,000 per unit), to Evelyn for her laundry business, comprising a building, five washer and dryer units (fair market value of $1,000 per unit), and an old pickup truck. Can Dennis consider the exchange to be entirely tax-free? No. ■

As a general rule, real property may continue to be exchanged as one group, but personal property must be segregated into specific like-kind groups [§1.1031 (j)-1(a)(1); (§1.1031(j)-1(b)(2)(i); Rev. Rul. 89-121; Rev. Rul. 72-151]. The separation of the properties transferred and the properties received into *exchange groups* involves matching up properties of a like kind or like class to the smallest extent possible [§1.1031(j)-1(a)(2)]. For example:

1. *Personal properties* are accumulated into separate exchange groups of the same General Asset Class *or* within the same Product Class [as defined in §1.1031(a)-2(b)].
2. *All real properties* belong to one exchange group as they are of a like kind.
3. *Not-like-kind property*—if property exists that cannot be matched up like kind (or is unqualified property), it must be placed in the *residual* group.

How do the §1031 exchange rules apply to these exchange groups? The §1031 exchange rules apply *separately* to each exchange group to determine the amount of gain recognized in the exchange [§1.1031(j)-1(a)(2)(i)].

Example (continued):

Dennis and Evelyn have a tax-deferred like-kind exchange only to the extent of the first exchange group, consisting of the five washers and dryers being traded for five washers and dryers (Product Class 3633). But *both* have taxable boot (a non-like-kind exchange) to the extent of the second exchange group—that is, Dennis's trade of two washers and dryers (Product Class 3633) for Evelyn's pickup truck (ADR 00.22). ■

Example:

Paige owns a ranch comprising of three separately purchased properties that are exchanged (one deed) with Tyson for 20 commercial lots (again via one deed). Even though this exchange involves 23 separate properties, it is *one* separate exchange group for §1031 purposes, and the §1031 exchange rules apply to the group, not to each separate property. ■

Like-kind exchanges—rules for exchanges of goodwill. The goodwill or going-concern value of a business is not of a like kind to the goodwill or going concern value of another business. Therefore, the trading of goodwill is taxable [§1.1031(a)-2(c)(2)].

Investor Hint

When exchanging business opportunities, the goodwill of either business is "boot" (or not-like-kind property) and could create taxable gain. The IRS's theory is that goodwill comes from a business's customer base, and since most businesses being exchanged are in different locations, it would be impossible to have the exact same customer base.

Tax Tip

When the different components of a business are being valued for exchange purposes, goodwill must also be identified and valued. In most cases, it would be desirable to establish the *lowest* fair market value. Establishing the lowest value would also be consistent with the §1060 regulations for valuing a business in non-like-kind exchanges, even though §1060 is not applicable to exchanges [Reg. §1.1031(d)-1T].

Like-kind exchanges of other intangible personal property and nondepreciable personal property. An exchange of intangible personal property or nondepreciable personal property qualifies for nonrecognition of gain or loss under §1031 only if the exchanged properties are of a like kind. No like classes are provided for these properties. Whether intangible personal property is of a like kind to other intangible personal property generally depends on the nature or character of the rights involved (e.g., a patent or a copyright) and also on the nature or character of the underlying property to which the intangible personal property relates [§1.1031(a)-2(c)(1)].

Example:

Stephen King exchanges a copyright on a novel for a copyright on a different novel. The properties exchanged are of a like kind [§1.1031(a)-2(c)(3) (Example 1)].

Example:

P. Diddy exchanges a copyright on a novel for a copyright on a song. The properties exchanged are not of a like kind [§1.1031(a)-2(c)(3)(Example 2)]. ■

Example:

Trading of a McDonald's franchise for another McDonald's franchise should be deemed like kind. ▪

RELATED PARTY EXCHANGES

If a taxpayer exchanges property with a related party (as defined below), the original exchange will not qualify for tax deferral if either of the exchanged properties is sold or disposed of within two years of the transfer. Interestingly, the postponed gain becomes taxable at the time of the disqualifying disposition. It is important to note that exchanges between related parties may still use the tax-free benefits of §1031, provided the two-year waiting period and other requirements listed below are met [§1031(f) and (g)].

Who is a related party?   Related parties include

1. *family members,* such as brothers, sisters, spouse, ancestors, and lineal descendants as well as C or S corporations and over 50% shareholders, corporate controlled members, and grantors and fiduciaries of trusts [§267(b)];
2. *partnership–partner.* The related party definition also includes over 50% partner-to-partnership attribution rules [§707(b)].

Two exceptions to the two-year rule.

1. *Dispositions due to death, involuntary conversion, or for non-tax-avoidance purposes* will not invalidate §1031 treatment. The Conference Report gives three examples of this non-tax-avoidance exception, which are (1) transactions involving certain exchanges of undivided interests in different properties that result in each taxpayer's holding either the entire interest in a single property or a larger undivided interest in any of the properties, (2) dispositions of property in a compulsory or involuntary conversion (e.g., §1033), and (3) transactions that do not involve the shifting of basis between properties [§1031(g)(2)].
2. *Risk of loss diminished.* In addition, the running of the two-year holding period will be suspended during any period when a party's risk of loss with respect to the property is substantially diminished by §1031(g)(2), such as (1) the holding of a put with respect to the property, (2) the holding by another person of a right to acquire the property, or (3) a short sale or any other transaction.

The penalty applies to both parties!

Example:

Dan and George, who are brothers, exchange like-kind property in a §1031 transaction. The realized gain on the exchange is postponed. Dan sells the property he received 18 months after the exchange. The result is that an *unqualified* like-kind exchange is deemed to have occurred—as of the date Dan sold the property. When Dan disposes of the property, it causes all of the postponed gain to be recognized as of the date of the disposition. Not only does Dan have to recognize the gain, but George also has to recognize the gain he postponed. What happens if Dan, 18 months after the exchange, enters into another

§1031 exchange with an unrelated party? Even in this case, the second §1031 exchange is treated as a sale and will cause Dan and George to recognize the postponed gain from the first exchange. ▪

Therefore, advance tax planning is required.   Stronger controls must exist between the related parties to prevent unexpected tax consequences created by the unilateral actions of just one of the parties. The legal documents should include a provision specifying that if either of the parties triggers the recognition of the postponed gain within the two-year period, the innocent party will be reimbursed for the tax consequences.

Ouch—related parties who exchange must file IRS Form 8824 for the next two years!   If the exchange is made with a related party, the taxpayer must file Exchange Form 8824 in the year of the exchange *and for the two following years* (Tax Management, Inc. (BNA) Portfolio, Vol. 61-5th, page C&A-2, A-31).

6. Boot—Receipt of Other Property or Money in Tax-Free Exchanges

May a tax-free exchange involve both qualifying and nonqualifying property?   Yes. A §1031 exchange is fully tax-free only if the taxpayer exchanges property *exclusively* for qualifying like-kind property. Nevertheless, if cash or any other type of nonqualifying property is received (commonly referred to as *receiving boot,* as in: "My property is worth more than yours and I will only trade you my apartment for your apartment if you give me $100,000 to boot"), this does not prevent the *partial* use of §1031, thereby finding part of the gain not currently taxable.

Definition of boot.   The amount of boot received is the sum of any money and the fair market value of other nonqualified property the exchanger receives. Therefore, boot consists of money, liabilities assumed (or attached to the property received in exchange), nonqualifying property (such as cash, inventory, or stocks and bonds), and property that does not meet the like-kind definition (such as trading business property for personal property) [§1031(b); §1.1031(b)-1]. It even includes cash received several years before the exchange for an option on the relinquished property, with the option money treated as boot during the year in which the exchange is completed [PLR 9413024]. However, there is a price to pay when receiving boot.

Receipt of boot—gain may be recognized to the lower of the gain or the boot. If nonqualifying property, or boot, is received in an exchange that otherwise consists of like-kind property, gain will be recognized (i.e., taxable) but not in excess of such money (and liabilities relieved of) and the fair market value of such other unlike property. This is basically saying that the taxpayer will not be required to pay more tax than would have been paid if the property had been sold for cash [§1031(b); §1.1031(b)-1(a)].

Example:

Jerry trades a building (fair market value of $500,000) and machinery (fair market value of $100,000) for Bill's building (fair market value of $600,000).

Jerry does not recognize any gain on the exchange as he *did not receive* any nonqualifying property. (But watch out for giving nonqualifying appreciated property in an exchange as discussed in "giving of boot.")

Bill, though, has a taxable gain, because he *did receive* nonqualifying property, the machinery. His gain is recognized but not in excess of the value of the machinery, $100,000 (unless Bill's realized gain is less than $100,000, e.g., if his adjusted basis were $550,000, the maximum taxable gain would, of course, be only $50,000). ■

Receipt of boot—but loss is not recognized. If a taxpayer receives, in addition to qualified like-kind property, either money or other property, any loss realized on the exchange is not recognized, that is, not deductible. This is true even if the loss on the exchange is created solely by the exchange brokerage commission. The loss is added to the fair market value of the property received (see basis-adjustment section for details on computation) [§1031(c); Rev. Rul. 72-456, 1972-2 CB 468].

Giving of boot—it's a regular sale for gain or loss purposes. Giving boot, or nonqualifying property (i.e., Jerry's machinery in the previous example), along with giving qualifying property in an exchange does not completely remove the transaction from §1031. Nevertheless, the transfer of non-money boot is treated as a sale of such property with respect to which any gain or loss is taxable. The taxpayer is deemed to receive in exchange for the nonqualifying property transferred an amount equal to its fair market value [§1.1031(a)-1(a); §1.1031(d)-1(e)].

Formula. Therefore, the gain (or loss) is calculated under the general reporting rules of §1001(c), using the following formula:

Gain on Boot (B1 through B4) Calculation

Fair market value of boot property given	B1	+
Less: Adjusted basis of boot property given	B2	−
Gain recognized on boot property given (1 − 2)	B3	
Loss recognized on boot property given (2 − 1)	B4	

Example:

Joe trades in his old delivery truck for a new one. In addition, he gives the auto dealer 100 shares of stock as boot. Joe originally paid $1,000 for the stock, but at the time of the trade-in, the stock is worth $3,000. Joe has a $2,000 taxable gain because he has used the stock as boot.

Fair market value of boot property given	B1	+	$3,000
Less: Adjusted basis of boot property given	B2	−	1,000
Gain recognized on boot property given (1 − 2)	B3		$2,000
Loss recognized on boot property given (2 − 1)	B4		

Netting boot. In certain circumstances, the taxpayer may net the (taxable) boot received by any boot given (such as the netting of liabilities), thereby lowering the gain to be recognized.

Liabilities assumed. As mortgage relief is considered boot and treated as if it is money received by the taxpayer in the exchange, this can result in a disastrous tax consequence. Any mortgage assumed, or taken subject to, creates taxable gain for the party being relieved of the debt . . . to the extent of the total gain [§1031(d); §1.1031(b)-1(a)].

Example:

Bob trades his $100,000 apartment house with a $60,000 mortgage (and a basis of $30,000) to Scott for a free and clear $40,000 bare lot. The $60,000 debt relief experienced by Bob is deemed *boot,* requiring that Bob pay tax on the gain to the extent of the boot. But Bob has no cash to pay the tax! ■

The mortgage napkin test. What happens if both parties bring a mortgage to the exchange? Fortunately, we can *net* the liabilities, as explained next. This calculation is similar to the computation used to balance equities when the transaction first started.

Mortgage given netted against mortgage received. If each exchange party assumes the liability of the other party, the parties are allowed to *net* their liabilities when calculating the amount of the taxable boot received. Even the issuance of the exchanger's own promissory note is considered boot given, which may be offset against mortgage relief. Therefore, only when taxpayers realize a *net* reduction in their debt do they experience taxable boot [§1.1031(b)-1(c); §1.1031(d)-2 (Example 2); Rev. Rul. 79-44, 1979-1 CB 265].

Example:

Zane exchanges property with a fair market value of $150,000, which is subject to a liability of $60,000, for Willow's property, which has a fair market value of $190,000 and is subject to a liability of $100,000. Zane receives no mortgage boot because he experiences a net increase in indebtedness. But Willow receives $40,000 of boot, as she receives a net reduction of liability.

Note: The numbers in front of the dollar amounts in this example refer to the like-kind exchange worksheet in Figure 5.1.

Mortgage Relief—Zane

Mortgage on property given	20	$ 60,000
Less: Mortgage on property received	21	– 100,000
Net mortgage relief (but not below zero)	22	0

Mortgage Relief—Willow

Mortgage on property given	20	$100,000
Less: mortgage on property received	21	– 60,000
Net mortgage relief (but not below zero)	22	$ 40,000

Tax Tip

Trade up in debt!

Cash (and other property) **given** *may be netted against mortgage* **received.** The giving of cash and the fair market value of other nonqualifying property (property boot) is also netted against any relief of liabilities [1.1031(d)-2 (Example 1); *Coleman v. Comm.,* 180 F2d 758 (8th Cir. 1950); Rev. Rul. 79-44].

Example:

Zane exchanges $50,000 cash, stock worth $50,000, and property with a fair market value of $300,000 subject to a liability of $200,000 for Willow's property, which has a fair market value of $250,000 subject to a liability of $50,000. Even though Zane has a net mortgage relief of $150,000, he only receives $50,000 of net boot.

Cash and Boot

Cash received	5	0		
FMV of other (boot) property received	6	0		
Net cash and other boot received			16	0
Cash given	10	$50,000		
FMV of other (boot) property given	11	50,000		
Net cash and other boot given			17	– $100,000
Exchange expenses			18	– 0
Net cash and other boot received (16 – 17 + 18)			19	– $100,000
Mortgage on property given			20	$200,000
Less: mortgage on property received			21	– $ 50,000
Net mortgage relief (but not below zero)			22	$150,000
Net Boot (Line 22 ± 19)				$ 50,000

But cash (and other property) **received cannot** be offset against mortgage given. Receipt of cash or other nonqualified property in a §1031 exchange *cannot* be offset by the assumption of liabilities. Therefore, the IRS prohibits netting when the exchanger both receives cash and receives a mortgage debt from the other party [§1.1031(d)-2 (Example 2)].

Tax Tip

Rather than receiving equalizing cash, it may be smarter to pay down each party's liabilities prior to the exchange. The cash received may also be used to pay exchange expenses.

Example:

Zane exchanges property with a fair market value of $350,000 and subject to a liability of $150,000 for Willow's $100,000 cash plus property, which has a fair market value of $300,000 and is subject to a liability of $200,000. Zane receives $100,000 of boot because of the cash received. Although Zane may net boot given against boot received in the form of indebtedness, the increased debt cannot be offset by cash or property boot received.

Cash and Boot

Cash received	5	$100,000		
FMV of other (boot) property received	6	0		
Net cash and other boot received			16	$100,000
Cash given	10	0		
FMV of other (boot) property given	11	0		
Net cash and other boot given			17 –	0
Exchange expenses			18 –	0
Net cash and other boot received (16 – 17 + 18)			19	$100,000
Mortgage on property given			20	$150,000
Less: mortgage on property received			21 –	$200,000
Net mortgage relief (but not below zero)			22	0
Net Boot (Line 22 ± 19)				$100,000

Note: For the opposite result, see *Barker v. Comm.,* 74 TC 555 (1980), in which a concurrent payoff through escrow of liabilities *was not* treated as cash received. The court stressed that there was an obligation to use the cash to pay off the mortgage, and hence the taxpayer did not at any time have the unfettered use of the cash. ■

What about netting cash given against cash received or other property given against other property received?   Even though many exchanger parties make the assumption that this netting is permitted, it is uncertain whether, or to what extent, money (or other nonqualified property) given may be netted against money (or other nonqualified property) received, as no cases or IRS pronouncements currently give guidance.

Exchange expenses.   Certain transaction expenses of the §1031 exchange, such as brokerage commissions paid, reduce the total consideration received and increase the basis of the exchange property received [Rev. Rul. 72-456, 1972-2 CB 468]. In *Westall v. Comm.,* 56 TCM 66 (1988), the court held that the taxpayer's cash received was offset by *all* the taxpayer's selling expenses and did not delineate the type of selling expenses involved.

Investor Hint

May exchangers create liabilities in anticipation of the exchange? The 1991 final regulations *do not include* the proposed amendment that liabilities incurred by the taxpayer in anticipation of a §1031 exchange will be considered taxable boot (i.e., §1031(b) "other property or money"). Whew! Therefore:

May We Refinance Just Prior to the Exchange?

Planning that the IRS doesn't like.   In order to equalize their net equities, taxpayers sometimes place a mortgage on their property just prior to closing, with the result that they put cash in their pocket, tax-free. If the cash were paid at closing to that same taxpayer, the cash would be considered taxable boot. Needless to say, this "tax-planning device" is not favorably viewed by the IRS [Rev. Rul. 73-555, 1973-2 CB 159; *Long v. Comm.,* 77 TC 1045 (1981); PLR 8434015]. But can the IRS do anything but yell? See the following:

Refinancing before or after is OK.   The Tax Court held, with an IRS acquiescence (i.e., complying without protest), that the assumption of a liability by a taxpayer in a like-kind exchange will be recognized even though the liability was placed on the property immediately *before* the exchange at the taxpayer's prompting so as to avoid the recognition of gain under the mortgage netting rule [*Garcia v. Comm.,* 80 TC 491 (1983), *acq.,* 1984-1 CB 1; PLR 8248039]. Any refinancing *after* the exchange should also be permitted [*Carlton v. U.S.,* 385 F2d 238 (5th Cir.) 1967].

Refinancing is extremely helpful in the multiple (three or more) party exchanges, as illustrated in the next example.

Example:

In an otherwise qualified exchange, Edwina wishes to exchange tax-free her free-and-clear (of debt) office building that has a fair market value of $400,000 for Sandy's office building that has a fair market value of $700,000 subject to a $300,000 mortgage. Sandy wants to sell, not exchange, her office building as she needs $400,000 cash (she is willing to pay the tax due). Bobby has $100,000 cash and wishes to purchase Edwina's property.

Problem:

Bobby does not have enough cash to buy Sandy's office building, which Bobby would subsequently exchange for Edwina's office building.

Solution:

Bobby secures a new loan commitment on Edwina's property for the other $300,000, with Edwina having no immediate right to the money. The loan proceeds are then added to Bobby's existing $100,000 cash (i.e., now $400,000) and, coupled with the assumption of the existing loan, he can acquire Sandy's property through a cash-out (which is what Sandy wants). Bobby then exchanges his newly acquired property with Edwina. The result is that Bobby ends up with what he wants (i.e., Edwina's office building) and Edwina ends up with what she wants (i.e., Sandy's office building), acquired by using a tax-free exchange! ■

What about this new loan commitment?   Many lenders realize that since Bobby will ultimately own Edwina's property and be responsible for paying off the mortgage, he can apply for the loan. This becomes clearer to the lender if all transactions are closed simultaneously in the lender's escrow department!

Reporting Gain on Boot—The Installment Method Is Available

Coordinating the exchange (§1031) and installment (§453) rules.   When a taxpayer receives a promissory note instead of cash in addition to receiving like-kind property, the gain recognized in the like-kind exchange may be reported on the installment method (if the transaction otherwise qualifies as an installment sale). Furthermore, the like-kind property received in the exchange is not considered an installment payment in the year of sale [§453(f)(6)(C); §1.1031(k)-1(j)(2)].

> **Caution**
>
> Refinancing *during* the exchange, if the taxpayer is allowed to touch the cash (i.e., be in actual or constructive receipt of the money), is not a safe option.

Use escrows to hold installment note. The safe harbors relating to qualified escrow accounts, trusts, and intermediaries apply for purposes of determining whether a taxpayer is in receipt of payment under the installment sale rules of section 453 [§1.1031(k)-1(j)(2)(i),(ii)].

Bona fide intent requirement. If at the beginning of the exchange period the taxpayer had a *bona fide intent* to enter into a deferred exchange and meets the safe-harbor rules of section 1031, the taxpayer then may report any gain recognized in the exchange under the installment method. A taxpayer will be treated as having a "bona fide intent" only if it is "reasonable to believe, based on all the facts and circumstances as of the beginning of the exchange period, that like-kind replacement property will be acquired before the end of the exchange period" [§1.1031(k)-1(j)(2)(iv)].

Certain other limitations also apply.

1. The gross profit from the exchange is reduced by the gain not recognized because of the exchange rules. Therefore, the gross profit is limited to the amount of the gain that would be recognized on the exchange if the installment obligation had to be satisfied at its face value [§453(f)(6)(B)].

2. In addition, the total contract price does not include the value of the like-kind property. Therefore, the contract price will consist only of the money, face amount of the installment obligation, and fair market value of the other boot received [§453(f)(6)(A)].

The taxpayer's basis in the property put into the exchange is allocated first to the like-kind property received to the extent of its fair market value. The effect of this allocation is to maximize the percentage of each payment received on the installment obligation to be reported as gain from an installment sale. Any remaining basis is used to calculate the gross profit ratio [§1.453(f)].

Investor Hint

As a result of the above rule, if the property exchanged has a lower basis than the fair market value of the property received, the gross profit ratio will be 100%, and all payments on any installment obligation will be fully taxable. A more economically reasonable IRS alternative would have been to allocate the basis based on each property's relative fair market value.

Example:

Dwight exchanges an office building with a fair market value of $1,000,000 and a basis of $200,000 for Jack's office building with a fair market value of $300,000 and Jack's note of $700,000. The sum of $100,000 is to be paid on the installment note each year, starting one year after the sale.

Even though the purported sales price is $1,000,000, the contract price for installment reporting purposes is $700,000 (because the fair market value of the like-kind property is ignored). The gross profit is also $700,000 because the realized gain of $800,000 is reduced by the $100,000 gain not recognized because of the exchange rules ($300,000 building received less $200,000 basis of the property given). Now the gross profit ratio is 100%, but as no "payment" is received in the year of the sale, no gain is recognized. Thereafter, 100% of each future payment must be included in income as gain! ▪

Timing of gain recognition when exchange fails after cash deposited into escrow.

From reading the above regulations, if a delayed exchange falls through, when is the gain from the sale of the relinquished property taxable? Is the gain taxable in the year of sale or in the year that money is received from the intermediary?

Example:

Sharon transfers her apartment building to an exchange accommodator in 2003. The accommodator sells the property to a waiting buyer and holds the funds until Sharon can identify a replacement property. Sharon properly identifies a new property within 45 days but is unable to close the exchange within the required 180 days. Because the exchange fell through, the accommodator hands Sharon in 2004 all of the cash it held from the sale of the old property.

Tax Result:

Because Sharon always intended to exchange, the sale is reported in 2003 but the gain is taxable as an installment sale with proceeds received in 2004. ▪

What if the taxpayer does not want installment sales treatment? Sharon in the

above example may prefer to have the gain taxable in 2003. Can she? Yes, by electing out of installment sales reporting. Remember that the exchange must be completed by the earlier of the due date of Sharon's return for the year of the exchange or 180 days from when she relinquished her property. If replacement property has not been found by the due date of Sharon's 2003 return, she must extend. The election out of installment sales reporting must be made on a timely filed return, including extensions. Regulation §15A.453-1(d)(3)(ii) states that late elections out of the installment method "will be permitted only in those rare circumstances when the IRS concludes the taxpayer had good cause for failing to make a timely election."

Exchanger receives a note. If the intermediary receives a note from the buyer of the

relinquished property, can the note be passed on to the exchanger as a qualifying §453 installment obligation?

Example:

Laura has a buyer, Beth, for Blueacre, but Laura has not yet found a replacement property. Laura transfers Blueacre, pursuant to an exchange agreement, to a qualified intermediary, who then transfers it to Beth for $80,000 in cash and Beth's ten-year installment obligation for $20,000. Laura does not have an immediate ability or an unrestricted right to receive, pledge, borrow, or otherwise obtain the benefits of the cash held by the qualified intermediary until the earlier of the date the replacement property is delivered to her or the end of the exchange period. Beth's obligation bears adequate stated interest and is not payable on demand or readily tradeable. Within 180 days the qualified intermediary acquires replacement property worth $80,000 and delivers it, along with the $20,000 installment obligation, to Laura.

Is Laura's receipt of Beth's installment obligation considered a current payment under the installment sale rules because Beth is not the person who acquired the property from the taxpayer (the qualified intermediary is)? No.

Regulation §15A.453-1(b)(3)(i) provides that the term payment does not include the receipt of evidence of indebtedness of the person acquiring the property. Furthermore, the regulations state that payment does include evidence of indebtedness of a person other than the person acquiring the property from the taxpayer.

The regulations provide that, for purposes of the installment rules, the receipt of an installment obligation from the qualified intermediary's transferee is treated as the receipt of an installment obligation of the person acquiring the relinquished property.

BASIS, DEPRECIATION RECAPTURE, AND HOLDING PERIOD

The basis of property received.   Computing the basis on the new property is simple when the exchange involves only property for like-kind property. The new basis of the property received in a tax-free exchange is the basis of the old property surrendered. This new *unadjusted basis* is known as the property's *substituted basis* and preserves the potential gain (or loss) on the disposed building for future recognition [§1031(d); §1.1031(d)-1(a)].

Example:

Straight exchange. Jennifer trades her office building, with a fair market value of $625,500 and an adjusted basis of $341,000, *straight across* for Hilary's office building. Jennifer's old remaining basis of $341,000 becomes her *substituted basis* in the new property.

This substituted-basis rule becomes complicated, though, when the exchange involves the paying or receiving of cash, netting of liabilities, giving or receiving of other boot, or if a loss is recognized because unlike property is transferred in the exchange along with the like-kind property.

The technical formula to calculate basis of property received.   In a tax-free exchange, the new basis is the basis of the old property surrendered, increased by any money (including debt) given and the amount of any gain recognized, and decreased by the amount of money (including debt) received and any loss recognized on the exchange. Therefore, payment of cash and net mortgage debt assumed increases the new basis. Any brokerage commissions and other exchange expenses paid by the exchanger also increase basis [§1031(d); §1.1031(d)-1; Rev. Rul. 72-456, 1972-2 CB 468; *Westall v. Comm.,* 56 TCM 66 (1988)].

Investor Hint

Said another way, if the exchange is tax-free, the exchanger's old basis is reduced by the cash received and mortgage relief (i.e., "cashed out") *and* increased by the cash given and the mortgage acquired (i.e., "cash in").

Note: In the following formula, the numbers in front of the dollar amounts refer to the like-kind exchange worksheet in Figure 5.1; B1-4 is the gain calculation on sale of boot property discussed previously in this chapter. "LKE" means like-kind exchange.

Formula for Calculating the Basis of the New Property

Adjusted basis of LKE property given	03 +	
Adjusted basis of boot property given	B2 +	
Cash given	10 +	
Mortgage assumed on property	12 +	
Subtotal (Plus)		28 +
Cash received	05 +	
Mortgage on property given	07 +	
Subtotal (Minus)		31 –
Plus: Gain recognized on exchange		23 +
Plus: Gain recognized on boot given		B3 +
Less: Loss recognized on boot		B4 –
Exchange expenses		13 +
BASIS OF ALL NEW PROPERTY RECEIVED		
(28, 31, 32, B, 35)		36 = $
BASIS OF BOOT PROPERTY RECEIVED		
(FMV) (Line 6)		37 = $
BASIS OF LIKE-KIND PROPERTY FECEIVED	36–37= $	

Proving the basis of the new property: The "rule-of-thumb" proof to determine if the basis calculation has been properly computed is:

Fair market value of property received	E1	$
Less: Gain not taxed	15–23 –	
New basis	34	= $

Basis when boot is given.   As mentioned previously, the basis of the new property received in a tax-free exchange is the basis of the old property surrendered, increased by any money (including debt) given [§1031(d); §1.1031(d)-1].

Example:

Giving of boot. Jennifer trades her $625,500 office building and $100,000 cash for Hilary's office building. Jennifer's new substituted basis is her old remaining basis of $341,000 *plus* the $100,000 cash for a new substituted basis of $441,000 [§1.1031(d)-1(a)].

Basis when *cash* boot is received and gain is recognized.   In a tax-free exchange, the exchanger's new basis is the basis of the old property surrendered, increased by any money (including debt) given plus the amount of any gain recognized and decreased by the amount of any money (including debt) received [§1031(d); §1.1031(d)-1].

Formula for Calculating the Basis of the New Property

Adjusted basis of LKE property given	03 +	$341,000		
Adjusted basis of boot property given	B2 +			
Cash given	10 +	$100,000		
Mortgage assumed on property	12 +			
Subtotal (Plus)			28 +	$441,000
Cash received	05 +	$		
Mortgage on property given	07 +			
Subtotal (Minus)			31 –	
Plus: Gain recognized on exchange			23 +	
Plus: Gain recognized on boot given			B3 +	
Less: Loss recognized on boot			B4 –	
Exchange expenses			13 +	
BASIS OF ALL NEW PROPERTY RECEIVED (28, 31, 32, B, 35)			36 =	$441,000
BASIS OF BOOT PROPERTY RECEIVED (FMV) (Line 6)			37 =	$
BASIS OF LIKE-KIND PROPERTY RECEIVED			36–37 =	$441,000

Example:

Receiving boot. Jennifer trades her $625,500 office building for Hilary's office building and Hilary adds $50,000 cash. Jennifer's new *substituted basis* is her old remaining basis of $341,000 decreased by the $50,000 cash and increased by the $50,000 gain recognized [§1.1031(d)-1(b)]. ■

Allocating basis when *property* boot is received and gain recognized. When the exchanger receives boot property and gain is recognized because of the receipt of the boot, the adjusted basis of the property given, decreased by the amount of cash received and increased by the amount of gain recognized, must be allocated to the properties (other than money) received on the exchange. The basis is *first* allocated to the boot property to the extent of the boot property's fair market value [§1.1031(d)-1(c)].

Example:

Receiving boot. Del trades her office building with a $125,000 fair market value but an adjusted basis of $100,000 for Hilary's $90,000 office building, an auto with a fair market value of $10,000, and $25,000 cash. Del realizes $25,000 of gain (smaller of the $35,000 boot received or the total gain of $25,000), all of which is taxable [§1.1031(d)-1(c) (Example)]. ■

Allocating basis when boot is received and nondeductible loss exists. No loss is recognized even when other property or money is received. The basis of the property(ies) (other than cash) received is the adjusted basis of the property given, decreased by the amount of money received. This basis is allocated to the properties received, and there must be allocated to such other property an amount of such basis equivalent to its fair market value [§1.1031(d)-1(d)].

Formula for Calculating the Basis of the New Property

Adjusted basis of LKE property given	03 + $341,000	
Adjusted basis of boot property given	B2 +	
Cash given	10 +	
Mortgage assumed on property	12 +	
Subtotal (Plus)		28 + $341,000
Cash received	05 + $ 50,000	
Mortgage on property given	07 +	
Subtotal (Minus)		31 – $ 50,000
Plus: Gain recognized on exchange		23 + $ 50,000
Plus: Gain recognized on boot given		B3 +
Less: Loss recognized on boot		B4 –
Exchange expenses		13 +
BASIS OF ALL NEW PROPERTY RECEIVED		
(28, 31, 32, B, 35)		36 = $341,000
BASIS OF BOOT PROPERTY RECEIVED		
(FMV) (Line 6)		37 = $
BASIS OF LIKE-KIND PROPERTY RECEIVED	36–37 =	$341,000

Formula for Calculating the Basis of the New Property

Adjusted basis of LKE property given	03 + $100,000	
Adjusted basis of boot property given	B2 +	
Cash given	10 +	
Mortgage assumed on property	12 +	
Subtotal (Plus)		28 + $100,000
Cash received	05 + $ 25,000	
Mortgage on property given	07 +	
Subtotal (Minus)		31 – $ 25,000
Plus: Gain recognized on exchange		23 + $ 25,000
Plus: Gain recognized on boot given		B3 +
Less: Loss recognized on boot		B4 –
Exchange expenses		13 +
BASIS OF ALL NEW PROPERTY RECEIVED		
(28, 31, 32, B, 35)		36 = $ 100,000
BASIS OF BOOT PROPERTY RECEIVED		
(FMV) (Line 6)		37 = $ 10,000
BASIS OF LIKE-KIND PROPERTY RECEIVED	36–37 =	$ 90,000

Allocating basis when gain or loss on boot property is recognized.   When an exchanger exchanges boot property and the boot property creates the recognized gain or loss (§1002), basis is first allocated to the boot property (other than money or liabilities) to the extent of its relative fair market on the date of the exchange, and the balance is allocated among the qualifying property received, based on its relative fair market value on the date of the exchange [§1.1031(d)-1(e)].

Example:

Recognizing loss. Angela exchanges raw land plus stock for a vacation home to be held for appreciation. The raw land has an adjusted basis of $100,000 and a fair market value of $110,000. The stock transferred has an adjusted basis of $40,000 and a fair market value of $20,000. The vacation home acquired has a fair market value of $130,000. Angela is deemed to have received a $20,000 portion of the acquired real estate in exchange for the stock since $20,000 is the fair market value of the stock at the time of the exchange. A $20,000 loss is recognized under §1002 on the exchange of the stock for real estate. No gain or loss is recognized on the exchange of the real estate since the property received is of the type permitted to be received without recognition of gain or loss. The basis of the vacation home is determined as follows [§1.1031(d)-1(e), Example]:

Formula for Calculating the Basis of the New Property

Adjusted basis of LKE property given	03	+ $100,000		
Adjusted basis of boot property given	B2	+ $ 40,000		
Cash given	10	+		
Mortgage assumed on property	12	+		
Subtotal (Plus)			28 +	$140,000
Cash received	05	+ $		
Mortgage on property given	07	+		
Subtotal (Minus)			31 –	$
Plus: Gain recognized on exchange			23 +	$
Plus: Gain recognized on boot given			B3 +	
Less: Loss recognized on boot			B4 –	
Exchange expenses			13 +	
BASIS OF ALL NEW PROPERTY RECEIVED (28, 31, 32, B, 35)			36 =	$ 20,000
BASIS OF BOOT PROPERTY RECEIVED (FMV) (Line 6)			37 =	$120,000
BASIS OF LIKE-KIND PROPERTY RECEIVED		36–37=		$120,000

Loss on not-like-kind property given.   Where loss is recognized on a partially tax-free exchange because unlike property is transferred by the taxpayer as part of the exchange, the recognized loss decreases the basis of the property received. For purposes of this rule, the amount regarded as having been received in exchange for the "other" property is its fair market value on the date of the exchange [§1.1031(d)-1(e)].

Example:

Dave exchanges a parking lot with an adjusted basis of $15,000, together with equipment having a basis of $3,000 and worth $2,000, for farmland worth $17,000. His $1,000 loss on the exchange is recognized because he has transferred property that is not of a like kind. His basis for the farmland is $17,000, that is, the $18,000 basis of the properties transferred minus the $1,000 recognized loss.

Formula for Calculating the Basis of the New Property

Adjusted basis of LKE property given	03 + $15,000		
Adjusted basis of boot property given	B2 + $15,000		
Cash given	10 +		
Mortgage assumed on property	12 +		
Subtotal (Plus)		28 +	$ 18,000
Cash received	05 + $		
Mortgage on property given	07 +		
Subtotal (Minus)		31 – $	
Plus: Gain recognized on exchange		23 + $	
Plus: Gain recognized on boot given		B3 +	
Less: Loss recognized on boot		B4 – $	1,000
Exchange expenses		13 +	
BASIS OF ALL NEW PROPERTY RECEIVED (28, 31, 32, B, 35)		36	=$ 17,000
BASIS OF BOOT PROPERTY RECEIVED (FMV) (Line 6)		37	=$
BASIS OF LIKE-KIND PROPERTY RECEIVED		36–37=	$ 17,000

Allocation of basis when more than one property received. If more than one property is received in the exchange, the basis of the property given is allocated to the properties received in proportion to their fair market values on the date of the exchange [Rev. Rul. 68-36, 68-1 CB 357; §1.1031(j)-1(c); *Laster v. Comm.,* 43 BTA 159 (1940)].

Example:

Natalie trades her office building worth $675,000, but with an adjusted basis of $140,000, for five residential rental properties. The $140,000 is spread among the five properties according to *their* fair market values. ■

What is done with the land in an exchange? The basis allocated to *each* rental must subsequently be allocated between the land and building, again on the basis of their relative fair market values [§1.61-6(a)].

Description	Fair Market Value	Percent	Basis Allocation
Rental A	$261,000	38.67%	$ 54,138
Rental B	$140,000	20.74%	$ 29,036
Rental C	$ 88,000	13.04%	$ 18,256
Rental D	$ 64,000	9.48%	$ 13,272
Rental E	$122,000	18.07%	$ 25,298
Total:	$675,000	100.00%	$140,000

Example:

Natalie, in the previous example, determines that the land in Rental A is worth 20% of the entire fair market value (probably by using the property tax appraisal report). Therefore, $10,828 of the $54,138 is not depreciable, with the remaining $43,310 depreciable over 27.5 years. A similar allocation is made with properties B through E. ▪

Allocation of basis when personal residence included. When an exchanger gives a personal residence as part of the boot in an exchange, the residence is treated separately from the exchange of the qualifying property. The basis in the personal residence is calculated under the §1034 rollover rules, not the §1031 like-kind exchange rules [Rev. Rul. 59-229, 59-2 CB 180].

Depreciation recapture. Real property capital gain may be converted into ordinary income if §1250 requires the taxpayer to calculate depreciation recapture. Under §1250, all realized gain is recognized as ordinary income to the extent that depreciation deductions exceed the allowable deduction under the straight-line method (or if the property is disposed of less than 12 months after acquisition).

No depreciation recapture exists if the real property is depreciated on a straight-line basis. Therefore, no depreciation recapture exists for property purchased and placed in service after 1986, as all residential and commercial real property must be depreciated on a straight-line basis. However, a taxpayer exchanging property purchased between 1981 through 1986 (Accelerated Cost Recovery System property) using an accelerated (faster than straight-line) method may have depreciation recapture.

Section 1250(d)(4) provides that the amount of realized gain recognized under §1250 is limited to the greater of the gain recognized under §1031 or the *excess* of the recapturable amount over the fair market value of any §1250 property acquired. Thus, when sufficient improved property (qualified as "§1250 property") is acquired, recapture does not occur. However, the recapture potential is transferred to the new property [§1250(d)(4)(A); §1.1250-3(d)(1)].

Depreciation on Property Received in Exchange

Break for older property! In determining the depreciation allowable for Modified Accelerated Cost Recovery System (MACRS) real (e.g., real estate rentals) and personal (e.g., automobiles and computers) property acquired in an exchange of MACRS property under §1031 (like-kind exchanges) or §1033 (involuntary conversions), the acquired MACRS property is

1. depreciated over the *remaining recovery period,*
2. *using the same depreciation method* and convention as that of the exchanged MACRS property, and
3. any excess of the basis in the acquired MACRS property over the adjusted basis in the exchanged MACRS property *is treated as newly purchased MACRS property* [IRS Notice 2000-4].

Investor Hint

The result of this change by the IRS is that to the extent of old basis, the taxpayer will continue to depreciate property as he/she did. To the extent of new basis in the acquired property, the taxpayer will depreciate the property as if it was a newly acquired property.

For exchanges after January 3, 2000. *This provision is effective, and must be followed,* for acquired MACRS property placed in service on or after January 3, 2000, in a like-kind exchange of MACRS property under §1031. Notice 2000-4 is to be used until the IRS issues §168 Regulations addressing these transactions, but is consistent with PR §1.168-5(f) published in 1984.

Example

Duane purchased a residential rental apartment building on January 1, 1995, for $400,000. On January 4, 2001 (after taking $100,000 of depreciation in those six years), he had the choice of selling it for $600,000 or exchanging his property. He plans to use the proceeds to acquire a $750,000 commercial building.

Sell Residential Rental		Give Residental Rental in Exchange	
Sales Price	$600,000	Fair Market Value	$600,000
Original Purchase Price	400,000	Original Purchase Price	400,000
Accumulated Depreciation	– 100,000	Accumulated Depreciation	– 100,000
Less: Adjusted Basis	$300,000	Less: Adjusted Basis	$300,000
Gain:	$300,000	Gain:	$300,000

Buy Commercial Property		Receive in Exchange Commercial Property	
Purchase	$750,000	Fair Market Value	$750,000
		Less: Deferred Gain	$300,000
Depreciable Basis	$750,000	Depreciable Basis	$450,000
Life: 27.5 years	None	Life: 27.5 years	$300,000
Life: 39.0 years	$750,000	Life: 39.0 years	$150,000

> **Investor Hint**
>
> If an apartment building is exchanged for a commercial building, presumably the depreciation of the old basis would still be calculated using residential real estate rules and only the new portion of the basis would be depreciated at the longer commercial recovery periods. This means that a commercial building may end up with a part of its basis depreciated at 27.5 years (to the extent of the old residential rental building's basis) and part at 39.5 years (to the extent of the "new basis" in the acquired property).

For exchanges before January 4, 2000—taxpayer has a choice. As taxpayers have previously been inconsistent, some having treating the acquired property as new property and others depreciating the remaining basis in the acquired property over the remaining recovery period, the IRS is allowing MACRS acquired property placed in property before January 3, 2000, a choice.

Stay with the old method: The IRS will allow a taxpayer to continue to use its present method of depreciating the acquired property and treat these methods as allowable methods of depreciation.

> **Investor Hint**
>
> The difference may be material if the taxpayer started the depreciation over at 39.5 years instead of continuing with the remaining life. If it is material, see the next option.

Caution

The new IRS requirement to separately state the old basis will force the taxpayer to clearly spell out accumulated depreciation. This means that the IRS will have a better chance of getting the correct (and higher) tax rates on "unrecaptured section 1250 depreciation" as well as section 1245 and 1250 recapture that are presently hidden in "deferred gain."

Or change to the new method if exchange within the past two years: However, a taxpayer present-ly treating the acquired property as newly purchased MACRS property may change to treating the property under these new principles, provided the property has been treated by the taxpayer as acquired in a §1031 like-kind exchange or §1033 involuntary conversion and the change is made for the first or second taxable year ending after January 3, 2000.

Form 3115 required—It's a change in method of accounting. Those who qualify and wish to change to the method in Notice 2000-4 must treat it as a change in a §446 and §481 method of accounting. Rev. Proc. 2002-9, which must be followed, deals with this as an automatic change in accounting method.

Calculation worksheet. To help you with this computation, we have included a depreciation recapture worksheet, Figure 8.5, at the end of this chapter. An extensive example can be found at IRS Regulations §1.1250-3(d)(1)(Example).

HOLDING PERIOD

The holding period of the new property acquired in a like-kind exchange *tacks,* or adds, onto the holding period of the property given, provided that (1) the property transferred was either a capital asset or §1231 trade or business property and (2) the basis of the property acquired is determined in whole or in part by the basis of the property exchanged [§1223(l)].

REMAINING CALCULATION AND REPORTING REQUIREMENTS

As previously shown in Chapter 5, the like-kind exchange worksheet is divided into five parts:

1. Equity calculation
2. Part I—Basis of property conveyed
3. Part II—Total realized gain (or loss)
4. Part III—Recognized (taxable) gain
5. Part IV—Basis of new property

We are now ready to calculate Parts II, III, and IV. (The equity calculation and the basis of property conveyed were discussed in the previous chapter.) Again we will use a difficult IRS example to demonstrate how easy this computation is.

Example:

Bonnie owns an apartment house with a fair market value of $800,000, and an adjusted basis in her hands of $500,000, but it is subject to a mortgage of $150,000. Bonnie transfers the apartment house to Charlie, receiving in exchange $50,000 in cash and an office building with a fair market value of $600,000. The transfer to Charlie is made subject to the $150,000 mortgage. Bonnie pays $50,000 in exchange expenses. Bonnie realizes a gain of $250,000 on the exchange, computed as follows [§1.1031(d)-2 (Example 1)]:

1. Equity Calculation

		Bonnie Gives Bonnie's Apt.	and Receives Charlie's Apt.
E1. FMV of property exchanged	E1	$800,000	$600,000
E2. Less: Existing mortgages	E2	− 150,000	0
Equity (1 − 2)		$650,000	$600,000
E3. Net boot added (Plug figure**)	E3	0*	$ 50,000#
(**Difference between equities)			
Do equities balance? (1 − 2 + 3) [G = R]		$650,000 =	$650,000
Detail of boot added		*	#
E4. Cash	E4	0	$ 50,000
E5. Other financing	E5	0	0
E6. Other unlike property (B1)	E6	0	0

A $50,000 "sweetener" or "evener" is required to balance the exchange economically (line E3). Once the equity calculation is completed, the only other information needed for the exchange calculation is

1. the exchange expenses and
2. the adjusted basis of the property given.

2. Part I—Compute the Adjusted Basis of the Property Being Given

Exchange—Adjusted Basis Computation

Adjusted basis:

	Original cost (or basis)	+		$680,889
Equals:	Cost (or other basis) of property given	=	1	$680,889
	Less: Accumulated depreciation	−	2	$180,889
Total Adjusted Basis (1 − 2)		=	3	$500,000

Note: The numbers in front of the dollar amounts refer to the like-kind exchange worksheet in Figure 5.1.

3. Part II—Calculate the Total Realized Gain or Loss

The taxpayer must calculate the total gain on the property given before determining the amount of that gain that is not taxable and thereby determining the adjustment, if any, required to be made to the basis of the new property. Realized gain (Part II) is the profit on the property being exchanged as if the property had been sold for cash. Recognized gain (Part III) is the portion of the Part II realized gain that is taxable.

Formula for Calculating Realized Gain (Loss)

FMV of LKE property received	4 + $	
Cash received	5 +	
FMV of non-LKE boot property received	6 +	
Mortgage on property given	7 +	
Total consideration received (add lines 4 through 7)		8 + $
Less:		
Adjusted basis of LKE property given	9 + $	
Cash given	10 +	
FMV of non-LKE boot property given	11 +	
Mortgage assumed on property received	12 +	
Exchange expenses	13 +	
Total consideration given (add lines 9 through 13)		14 − $
Gain Realized on Exchange (line 8 − line 14)		15 $

Example (continued):

Bonnie's gain would be:

Formula for Calculating Realized Gain (Loss)

FMV of LKE property received	4 + $600,000	
Cash received	5 + 50,000	
FMV of non-LKE boot property received	6 +	
Mortgage on property given	7 + $150,000	
Total consideration received (add lines 4 through 7)		8 + $800,000
Less:		
Adjusted basis of LKE property given	9 + $500,000	
Cash given	10 +	
FMV of non-LKE boot property given	11 +	
Mortgage assumed on property received	12 +	
Exchange expenses	13 + 50,000	
Total consideration given (add lines 9 through 13)		14 − $550,000
Gain Realized on Exchange (line 8 − line 14)		15 $250,000

The information required for Part II is very similar to the gain or loss formula found in Chapter 2. We use the formula below to prove that the information entered in Part II of our worksheet is correct.

Proof for Gain or Loss Computation

Fair market value of property given		E1 + $800,000	
Less:	Exchange expenses	13 − $ 50,000	
Equals:	Net selling price	= $750,000	
Less:	Adjusted basis		
	Original cost (or basis)	+ $500,000	
	Plus: Purchase expenses	+	
	Plus: Improvements	+	
	Less: Accumulated depreciation	−	
Equals:	Total adjusted basis	9 − $500,000	
Net Gain (or Loss) Realized on Exchange		15 = $250,000	

4. Part III—Calculate the Recognized Taxable Gain (If Any)

As mentioned in the discussion of "receipt of boot," the amount of the gain that will be taxable is the smaller of the net gain or the boot received. Part III simply ascertains which one is smaller, the boot (calculated below) or the gain (line 15, above), and thereby establishes the amount of the gain taxable because of the exchange.

Formula for Calculating Recognized Taxable Gain

Cash and Boot

Cash and boot received (lines 5 and 6)	16 +	
Cash and boot given (lines 10 and 11)	17 –	
Exchange expenses (line 13)	18	
Net cash and boot received (line 16 less 17 & 18)		19 ±

(can be negative)

Mortgage Relief

Mortgage on property given (line 7)	20 $	
Mortgage on property received (line 12)	21 –	
NET MORTGAGE RELIEF (line 20 less 21, but not below zero)		22
GAIN RECOGNIZED (line 22 +/–line 19, but not in excess of actual gain [line 15]; if negative, put zero)		23

Example (continued):

Receiving cash and net debt relief. Assuming $50,000 of exchange expenses, of the total $250,000 gain realized in Part II, Line 15, Bonnie's recognized gain (because of the $50,000 cash received and the $150,000 net mortgage relief) is as follows:

Recognized Taxable Gain

Cash and Boot

Cash and boot received (lines 5 and 6)	16 +	$50,000
Cash and boot given (lines 10 and 11)	17 –	
Exchange expenses (line 13)	18 –	$50,000
Net cash and boot received (line 16 less 17 and 18)		19 ± 0

(can be negative)

Mortgage Relief

Mortgage on property given (line 7)	20	$150,000	
Mortgage on property received (line 12)	21 –		
NET MORTGAGE RELIEF (line 20 less 21, but not below zero)		22	$150,000
GAIN RECOGNIZED (line 22 +/–line 19, but not in excess of actual gain [line 15]; if negative, put zero)		23	$150,000

5. Part IV—Calculate the Substituted Basis of the New Property

The technical formula to calculate the basis of property received in a tax-free exchange is the basis of the old property surrendered, increased by any money (including debt) given and the amount of any gain recognized and decreased by the amount of money (including debt) received and any loss recognized on the exchange [§1031(d); §1.1031(d)-1]. The formula for calculating the basis of the new property was discussed earlier in this chapter.

Example (continued):

Bonnie's new substituted basis is her old basis less the $50,000 cash received and the $150,000 net mortgage relief plus the exchange expenses and the $200,000 gain recognized.

Formula for Calculating the Basis of the New Property

Adjusted basis of LKE property given	03 +	$500,000		
Adjusted basis of boot property given	B2 +			
Cash given	10 +			
Mortgage assumed on property	12 +			
Subtotal (Plus)			28 +	$500,000
Cash received	05 +	$ 50,000		
Mortgage on property given	07 +	$150,000		
Subtotal (Minus)			31 −	$200,000
Plus: Gain recognized on exchange			23 +	$150,000
Plus: Gain recognized on boot given			B3 +	
Less: Loss recognized on boot			B4 −	
Exchange expenses			13 +	$ 50,000
BASIS OF ALL NEW PROPERTY RECEIVED (28, 31, 32, B, 35)			36 =	$500,000
BASIS OF BOOT PROPERTY RECEIVED (FMV) (Line 6)			37 =	
BASIS OF LIKE-KIND PROPERTY RECEIVED			36–37 =	$500,000

The proof to determine if the basis calculation has been properly computed is

Proof for Basis of New Property

Fair market value of property received	E1	$600,000
Less: Gain not taxed	15-23 −	$100,000
NEW BASIS	34 =	$500,000

(See Figure 8.1 and Figure 8.2.)

Lowering gain created by debt relief with other boot given. This example highlights the interaction of receiving cash and assuming liabilities. It also discloses the impact of mixing unlike property with like property in a tax-free exchange. Again we will use a difficult IRS example to demonstrate how easy this computation is. It is important to realize that a negative number is possible on line 19, the significance being that cash given can lower the amount of mortgage relief for gain purposes!

Example:

Giving cash and boot but receiving debt relief. Zane exchanges $50,000 cash, stock worth $50,000 (with a basis to Zane of $30,000) and real property with a fair market value of $300,000 subject to a liability of $200,000 for Willow's property, which has a fair market value of $250,000 subject to a liability of $50,000. Even though Zane has a net mortgage relief of $150,000, he only receives $50,000 of net boot.

Formula for Calculating Realized Taxable Gain

Cash and Boot

Cash and boot received (lines 5 and 6)	16 +			
Cash given	10 +	$50,000		
FMV of other boot given	11 +	$50,000		
Cash and boot given (lines 10 and 10)			17 −	$100,000
Exchange expenses (line 13)			18 −	
Net cash and boot received				19 − $100,000
(line 16 less 17 and 18)				(can be negative)

Mortgage Relief

Mortgage on property given (line 7)	20	$200,000
Mortgage on property received (line 12)	21 −	$ 50,000
NET MORTGAGE RELIEF (line 20 less 21, but not below zero)	22	$150,000
GAIN RECOGNIZED (line 22 +/−line 19, but not in excess of actual gain [line 15]; if negative, put zero)	23	$ 50,000

Zane's tax preparer e-mails us the information that Zane originally purchased the property for $200,000 and has accumulated depreciation of $80,000. Only $50,000 of Zane's entire $180,000 gain is taxable! Remember, the stock is unlike property and therefore it is considered a taxable exchange! ▪

See Figure 8.3 and Figure 8.4 for the entire solution.

REPORTING AN EXCHANGE TO THE IRS—FORM 8824

The Internal Revenue Service has issued Form 8824 for reporting like-kind exchanges. As the form is clumsy and confusing to prepare, we use the previously discussed worksheet (Figure 8.5). After completing the worksheet, we simply transfer the information to Form 8824. Form 8824 directs the taxpayer to transfer the taxable gain to the next appropriate form, either Form 4797, or directly to Form 1040, Schedule D.

FIGURE 8.1 Sample Section 1031 Tax-Free Exchange of Property Worksheet

Copyright - Hoven - 2003

SECTION 1031 TAX-FREE EXCHANGE OF PROPERTY
———
WORKSHEET
exchange1.pm5

EQUITY CALCULATION	Form 8.1	BONNIE Gives	CHARLIE Receives
E1. FMV of property exchanged E1		+$ 800,000	+$ 600,000
E2. Less: Existing mortgages E2		− 150,000	−
Equity (1 - 2).		= 650,000	= 600,000
E3. Net boot added (plug figure**). E3		+ *	+ 50,000#
(**Difference between equities)			
Do equities balance? (1-2+3) [G = R]		= 650,000	= 650,000
Detail of boot added			
Cash E4		*	# 50,000
Other financing. E5		*	#
Other unlike property E6		*	#

PART I - BASIS OF PROPERTY GIVEN EXCHANGE DATE: 1/1/98

Description: BONNIE'S APARTMENT HOUSE

1. Cost (or other basis) of property given - [date purchased: 1/1/87] 1	+$ 680,889
2. Depreciation allowed or allowable 2	− 180,889
3. Adjusted basis of property given up (line 1 less line 2). 3	$ 500,000

PART II - REALIZED GAIN (LOSS)

4. FMV of qualifying property received (line E1-R) (Form 8824, Line 16) 4	$ 600,000
5. Cash received (line E4-R) 5	+$ 50,000
6. Less: Cash given (line E4-G) 6	−
7. Fair market value of other (boot) received (line E6-R) 7	+
8. Less: FMV of boot (other than cash) given up (line E6-G) 8	−
9. Net liabilities assumed by other party (line E2-G less E2-R but not < zero) 9	+ 150,000
10. Exchange expenses. 10	− 50,000
11.Total consideration received (add lines 5 thru 10) (Form 8824, Line 15) 11	$ 150,000
LESS:	
12. Adjusted basis of qualified property given up (line 3) 12	+$ 500,000
13. Net liabilities assumed by taxpayer (line E2-R less E2-G but not < zero) 13	+
14. Total consideration given (add lines 12 and 13). . . . . (Form 8824, Line 18) . . .14	$ 500,000
15. GAIN REALIZED ON EXCHANGE (line 4 plus line 11 less line 14) (Form 8824, Line 19) 15	$ 250,000

Proof: A Simple Check
FMV of Prop Exch: 800,000
Less: Adj. Basis: 550,000
Gain (if sold): 250,000

PART III - RECOGNIZED TAXABLE GAIN

CASH AND BOOT

16. Cash and boot (other than cash) received (add lines 5 and 7) . . 16	+$ 50,000
17. Cash and boot (other than cash) given (add lines 6 and 8) 17	−
18. Exchange expenses (line 10). 18	− 50,000
19. Net cash and boot (other than cash) received (line 16 less lines 17 and 18) . . . 19	+/-$ -0-

MORTGAGE RELIEF

20. Mortgage on property given (line E2-G) 20	+$ 150,000
21. Mortgage assumed on property received (line E2-R) 21	−
22. Net mortgage relief (line 20 less line 21; if less than zero, enter zero). 22	+$ 150,000
23 GAIN RECOGNIZED (line 22 +/- line 19; line 23 cannot exceed) . . . . (Form 8824, Line 20). . . 23	$ 150,000
line 15; if less than zero, enter zero	

PART IV - BASIS OF NEW PROPERTY Description: CHARLIE'S APARTMENT

24. Adjusted basis of LKE property given (line 3). 24	+$ 500,000
25. Adjusted basis of boot property given (Form 8824, Line 13). . . . 25	+
26. Cash given (line 6). 26	+
27. Mortgage assumed on property received (line E2-R) 27	+
28. Subtotal (Plus) 28	+$ 500,000
29. Cash received (line 5) 29	+$ 50,000
30 Mortgage on property given (line E2-G). 30	+ 150,000
31. Subtotal (Minus) 31	−$ 200,000
32. Plus: Gain recognized on exchange (line 23) 32	+ 150,000
33. Plus: Gain recognized on boot given (line 8 less line 25 but not < zero) (Form 8824, Line 14) 33	+
34. Less: Loss recognized on boot given (line 25 less line 8 but not < zero) (Form 8824, Line 14) 34	−
35. Exchange expenses (line 10) 35	+ 50,000
36. BASIS OF ALL NEW PROPERTY RECEIVED (28,31,32,33,34,35) 36	150,000
37. BASIS OF BOOT PROPERTY RECEIVED (FMV) (LINE 7) 37	
38. BASIS OF LIKE-KIND PROPERTY RECEIVED (LINE 36 LESS LINE 37) (Form 8824, Line 25) . 38	$ 500,000

Proof: A Simple Check
FMV of Prop Rec'd: 800,000
Less: Gain *not* taxed: 100,000
New Basis: 500,000

FIGURE 8.2 **Sample IRS Form 8824**

Form **8824**

Department of the Treasury
Internal Revenue Service

Like-Kind Exchanges
(and section 1043 conflict-of-interest sales)
► Attach to your tax return.

OMB No. 1545-1190

200
109

Name(s) shown on tax return | Identifying number
517-

| | Part I | **Information on the Like-Kind Exchange** |

Note: *If the property described on line 1 or line 2 is real or personal property located outside the United States, indicate the country.*

1 Description of like-kind property given up ► BONNIE'S APARTMENT

2 Description of like-kind property received ► CHARLIE'S APARTMENT

3	Date like-kind property given up was originally acquired (month, day, year)	3	1/01/92
4	Date you actually transferred your property to other party (month, day, year)	4	1/01/02
5	Date like-kind property you received was identified (month, day, year) (see instructions)	5	1/01/02
6	Date you actually received the like-kind property from other party (month, day, year)	6	1/01/02

7 Was the exchange made with a related party (see instructions)? If 'Yes', complete Part II. If 'No', go to Part III.
a ☐ Yes, in this tax year   **b** ☐ Yes, in a prior tax year   **c** ☒ No

Part II **Related Party Exchange Information**

8 Name of related party | Related party's identifying number

Address (number, street, and apartment, room, or suite number)

City or town | State | ZIP code | Relationship to you

9 During this tax year (and before the date that is 2 years after the last transfer of property that was part of the exchange), did the related party sell or dispose of the like-kind property received from you in the exchange? ☐ Yes ☐ No

10 During this tax year (and before the date that is 2 years after the last transfer of property that was part of the exchange), did you sell or dispose of the like-kind property you received? ☐ Yes ☐ No

If both lines 9 and 10 are 'No' and this is the year of the exchange, go to Part III. If both lines 9 and 10 are 'No' and this is *not* the year of the exchange, stop here. If either line 9 or line 10 is 'Yes,' complete Part III and report on this year's tax return the deferred gain or (loss) from line 24 *unless* one of the exceptions on line 11 applies. See *Related party exchanges* in the instructions.

11 If one of the exceptions below applies to the disposition, check the applicable box:
a ☐ The disposition was after the death of either of the related parties.
b ☐ The disposition was an involuntary conversion, and the threat of conversion occurred after the exchange.
c ☐ You can establish to the satisfaction of the IRS that neither the exchange nor the disposition had tax avoidance as its principal purpose. If this box is checked, attach an explanation (see instructions).

Part III **Realized Gain or (Loss), Recognized Gain, and Basis of Like-Kind Property Received**

Caution: *If you transferred and received (a) more than one group of like-kind properties or (b) cash or other (not like-kind) property, see Reporting of multi-asset exchanges in the instructions.*

Note: *Complete lines 12 through 14 only if you gave up property that was not like-kind. Otherwise, go to line 15.*

12	Fair market value (FMV) of other property given up	12			
13	Adjusted basis of other property given up	13			
14	Gain or (loss) recognized on other property given up. Subtract line 13 from line 12. Report the gain or (loss) in the same manner as if the exchange had been a sale	14		
15	Cash received, FMV of other property received, plus net liabilities assumed by other party, reduced (but not below zero) by any exchange expenses you incurred (see instructions)	15	150,000.
16	FMV of like-kind property you received	16	600,000.
17	Add lines 15 and 16	17	750,000.
18	Adjusted basis of like-kind property you gave up, net amounts paid to other party, plus any exchange expenses **not** used on line 15 (see instructions)	18	500,000.
19	**Realized gain or (loss).** Subtract line 18 from line 17	19	250,000.
20	Enter the smaller of line 15 or line 19, but not less than zero	20	150,000.
21	Ordinary income under recapture rules. Enter here and on Form 4797, line 16 (see instructions)	21	0.
22	Subtract line 21 from line 20. If zero or less, enter -0-. If more than zero, enter here and on Schedule D or Form 4797, unless the installment method applies (see instructions)	22	150,000.
23	**Recognized gain.** Add lines 21 and 22	23	150,000.
24	Deferred gain or (loss). Subtract line 23 from line 19. If a related party exchange, see instructions	24	100,000.
25	**Basis of like-kind property received.** Subtract line 15 from the sum of lines 18 and 23	25	500,000.

BAA **For Paperwork Reduction Act Notice, see separate instructions.**   FDIZ2112L 12/05/02   Form **8824** (2002)

FIGURE 8.3   **Sample Section 1031 Tax-Free Exchange of Property Worksheet**

Copyright - Hoven - 2003

**SECTION 1031
TAX-FREE
EXCHANGE
OF PROPERTY**
———
WORKSHEET
exchange3.pm5

EQUITY CALCULATION Form 8.3		ZANE Gives	WILLOW Receives
E1. FMV of property exchanged E1	+$	+$ 300,000	+$ 250,000
E2. Less: Existing mortgages E2	–	200,000	50,000
Equity (1 - 2).	=	100,000	= 200,000
E3. Net boot added (plug figure**). E3	+	100,000 *	+ #
(**Difference between equities)			
Do equities balance? (1-2+3) [G = R]	=	200,000	= 200,000
Detail of boot added			
Cash E4	*	50,000	#
Other financing. E5	*		#
Other unlike property E6	*	50,000	#

PART I - BASIS OF PROPERTY GIVEN   EXCHANGE DATE: 1/1/98

Description: ZANE'S APARTMENT		
1. Cost (or other basis) of property given - [date purchased: 1/1/87] 1	+$ 200,000	
2. Depreciation allowed or allowable 2	– 80,000	
3. Adjusted basis of property given up (line 1 less line 2). 3	$ 120,000	

PART II - REALIZED GAIN (LOSS)

4. FMV of qualifying property received (line E1-R) (Form 8824, Line 16) 4	$ 250,000	
5. Cash received (line E4-R) 5	+$	
6. Less: Cash given (line E4-G) 6	– 50,000	**Proof: A Simple Check**
7. Fair market value of other (boot) received (line E6-R) 7	+	FMV of Prop Exch:300,000
8. Less: FMV of boot (other than cash) given up (line E6-G) 8	– 50,000	Less: Adj. Basis: 120,000
9. Net liabilities assumed by other party (line E2-G less E2-R but not < zero) 9	+ 150,000	Gain (if sold): 180,000
10. Exchange expenses. 10	–	
11.Total consideration received (add lines 5 thru 10) (Form 8824, Line 15) 11	$ 50,000	
LESS:		
12. Adjusted basis of qualified property given up (line 3) 12	+$ 120,000	
13. Net liabilities assumed by taxpayer (line E2-R less E2-G but not < zero) 13	+	
14. Total consideration given (add lines 12 and 13). . . . . . (Form 8824, Line 18) . . . 14	$ 120,000	
15. GAIN REALIZED ON EXCHANGE (line 4 plus line 11 less line 14) (Form 8824, Line 19) 15	$ 180,000	

PART III - RECOGNIZED TAXABLE GAIN

CASH AND BOOT		
16. Cash and boot (other than cash) received (add lines 5 and 7) . . 16	+$	
17. Cash and boot (other than cash) given (add lines 6 and 8) 17	– 100,000	
18. Exchange expenses (line 10). 18	–	
19. Net cash and boot (other than cash) received (line 16 less lines 17 and 18) . . . 19	+/-$ 100,000	
MORTGAGE RELIEF		
20. Mortgage on property given (line E2-G) 20	+$ 200,000	
21. Mortgage assumed on property received (line E2-R) 21	– 50,000	
22. Net mortgage relief (line 20 less line 21; if less than zero, enter zero). 22	+$ 150,000	
23 GAIN RECOGNIZED (line 22 +/- line 19; line 23 cannot exceed) . . . . (Form 8824, Line 20) . . . 23 line 15; if less than zero, enter zero	$ 50,000	

PART IV - BASIS OF NEW PROPERTY   Description: WILLOW'S APARTMENT

24. Adjusted basis of LKE property given (line 3) 24	+$ 120,000	**Proof: A Simple Check**
25. Adjusted basis of boot property given (Form 8824, Line 13) . . 25	+ 30,000	FMV of Prop Rec'd: 250,000
26. Cash given (line 6). 26	+ 50,000	Less: Gain not taxed:130,000
27. Mortgage assumed on property received (line E2-R) 27	+ 50,000	New Basis: 120,000
28. Subtotal (Plus) 28	+$ 250,000	
29. Cash received (line 5) 29	+$	
30 Mortgage on property given (line E2-G). 30	+ 200,000	
31. Subtotal (Minus) 31	–$ 200,000	
32. Plus: Gain recognized on exchange (line 23) 32	+ 50,000	
33. Plus: Gain recognized on boot given (line 8 less line 25 but not < zero) (Form 8824, Line 14) 33	+ 20,000	
34. Less: Loss recognized on boot given (line 25 less line 8 but not < zero) (Form 8824, Line 14) 34	–	
35. Exchange expenses (line 10) 35	+	
36. BASIS OF ALL NEW PROPERTY RECEIVED (28,31,32,33,34,35) 36		120,000
37. BASIS OF BOOT PROPERTY RECEIVED (FMV) (LINE 7) 37		
38. BASIS OF LIKE-KIND PROPERTY RECEIVED (LINE 36 LESS LINE 37) (Form 8824, Line 25) . 38	$ 120,000	

FIGURE 8.4 **Sample IRS Form 8824**

Form **8824**	**Like-Kind Exchanges** (and section 1043 conflict-of-interest sales) ► Attach to your tax return.	OMB No. 1545-1190 **200** **109**
Department of the Treasury Internal Revenue Service		

Name(s) shown on tax return	Identifying number 517–

Part I **Information on the Like-Kind Exchange**

Note: *If the property described on line 1 or line 2 is real or personal property located outside the United States, indicate the country.*

1 Description of like-kind property given up ► ZANE'S APARTMENT

2 Description of like-kind property received ► WILLOW'S APARTMENT

3	Date like-kind property given up was originally acquired (month, day, year)	**3**	1/01/87
4	Date you actually transferred your property to other party (month, day, year)	**4**	1/01/02
5	Date like-kind property you received was identified (month, day, year) (see instructions)	**5**	1/01/02
6	Date you actually received the like-kind property from other party (month, day, year)	**6**	1/01/02

7 Was the exchange made with a related party (see instructions)? If 'Yes', complete Part II. If 'No', go to Part III.

  a ☐ Yes, in this tax year   **b** ☐ Yes, in a prior tax year   **c** ☒ No

Part II **Related Party Exchange Information**

8 Name of related party	Related party's identifying number

Address (number, street, and apartment, room, or suite number)		
City or town	State ZIP code	Relationship to you

9 During this tax year (and before the date that is 2 years after the last transfer of property that was part of the exchange), did the related party sell or dispose of the like-kind property received from you in the exchange? ☐ Yes ☐ No

10 During this tax year (and before the date that is 2 years after the last transfer of property that was part of the exchange), did you sell or dispose of the like-kind property you received? ☐ Yes ☐ No

*If both lines 9 and 10 are 'No' and this is the year of the exchange, go to Part III. If both lines 9 and 10 are 'No' and this is **not** the year of the exchange, stop here. If either line 9 or line 10 is 'Yes,' complete Part III and report on this year's tax return the deferred gain or (loss) from line 24 **unless** one of the exceptions on line 11 applies. See **Related party exchanges** in the instructions.*

11 If one of the exceptions below applies to the disposition, check the applicable box:

  a ☐ The disposition was after the death of either of the related parties.

  b ☐ The disposition was an involuntary conversion, and the threat of conversion occurred after the exchange.

  c ☐ You can establish to the satisfaction of the IRS that neither the exchange nor the disposition had tax avoidance as its principal purpose. If this box is checked, attach an explanation (see instructions).

Part III **Realized Gain or (Loss), Recognized Gain, and Basis of Like-Kind Property Received**

Caution: *If you transferred **and** received **(a)** more than one group of like-kind properties or **(b)** cash or other (not like-kind) property, see **Reporting of multi-asset exchanges** in the instructions.*

Note: *Complete lines 12 through 14 **only** if you gave up property that was not like-kind. Otherwise, go to line 15.*

12	Fair market value (FMV) of other property given up	**12**	50,000.	
13	Adjusted basis of other property given up	**13**	30,000.	
14	Gain or (loss) recognized on other property given up. Subtract line 13 from line 12. Report the gain or (loss) in the same manner as if the exchange had been a sale	**14**		20,000.
15	Cash received, FMV of other property received, plus net liabilities assumed by other party, reduced (but not below zero) by any exchange expenses you incurred (see instructions)	**15**		50,000.
16	FMV of like-kind property you received	**16**		250,000.
17	Add lines 15 and 16	**17**		300,000.
18	Adjusted basis of like-kind property you gave up, net amounts paid to other party, plus any exchange expenses **not** used on line 15 (see instructions)	**18**		120,000.
19	**Realized gain or (loss).** Subtract line 18 from line 17	**19**		180,000.
20	Enter the smaller of line 15 or line 19, but not less than zero	**20**		50,000.
21	Ordinary income under recapture rules. Enter here and on Form 4797, line 16 (see instructions)	**21**		0.
22	Subtract line 21 from line 20. If zero or less, enter -0-. If more than zero, enter here and on Schedule D or Form 4797, unless the installment method applies (see instructions)	**22**		50,000.
23	**Recognized gain.** Add lines 21 and 22	**23**		50,000.
24	Deferred gain or (loss). Subtract line 23 from line 19. If a related party exchange, see instructions	**24**		130,000.
25	**Basis of like-kind property received.** Subtract line 15 from the sum of lines 18 and 23	**25**		120,000.

BAA **For Paperwork Reduction Act Notice, see separate instructions.**   FDIZ2112L 12/05/02   Form **8824** (2002)

FIGURE 8.5   **Like-Kind Exchange Depreciation Recapture Worksheet**

LIKE - KIND EXCHANGE
DEPRECIATION RECAPTURE

Test #1: If straight-line depreciation has been used on the old like kind property, enter zero at Items g and l and go to the next schedule.

 a. Gain recognized on like kind property. $

 b. Gain recognized on non-like kind property given up. $

 c. Total Gain Recognized on the Exchange (a + b). $

Test #2: If the old like kind property is residential and accelerated depreciation or ACRS was used, fill out Part I. However, if the old like kind property is commercial and accelerated depreciation or ACRS was used, fill out Part II.

PART I - RESIDENTIAL PROPERTY RECAPTURE UNDER ß1250

 d. Amount of ß1250 recapture (determined as if the property had been sold). $

 e. Fair market value (at the date of the exchange) of ß1250 property received in the exchange. $

 f. Excess of recapture over FMV of ß1250 property received (d - e, but not less than zero). $

 g. Section 1250 recapture recognized (as ordinary income) in the exchange (greater of c and f, but not in excess of d). $

PART II - COMMERCIAL PROPERTY RECAPTURE UNDER ß1245

 h. Amount of ß1245 recapture (determined as if property had been sold). $

 i. Fair market value of property received that is not ß1245 property. $

 j. Total gain recognized on exchange (Item c above). $

 k. Gain recognized plus FMV of non-ß1245 property received (i + j). $

 l. Section 1245 recapture recognized (as ordinary income) in the exchange (h - k, but not less than zero). $

Chapter

The Home Mortgage Interest Deduction

For most taxpayers, all mortgage interest expenses on the first and second personal residences remain fully deductible in spite of the elimination of the deduction for other personal interest expenses (e.g., interest on credit card purchases or personal automobile purchases).

Home mortgage debt must be secured by a security interest perfected under local law on the *qualified residence(s)*. In addition, the deductible portion of home mortgage interest is limited to the taxpayer's *qualified residence interest*. That is, the debt (within limits) must be incurred to buy, build, or substantially improve these qualified residences [§163(h)(3)].

Because of the Tax Reform Act of 1986, home equity loans came into vogue. These loans allow the taxpayer to deduct interest on a loan secured by a principal residence, even though it has no relation to the acquisition or substantial improvement of the residence.

FIGURE 9.1   Qualified-Residence Interest Deduction

Interest paid on *acquisition debt (1 below)*	+	_____
Plus: Interest paid on *home equity debt (2 below)*	+	_____
Equals: Qualified-residence interest deduction	=	_____

(1) What is acquisition debt?

Pre-10/13/87 grandfathered debt (no dollar limitation)		+	_____
Plus			
Post-10/12/87 acquisition (or construction) debt	+	_____	
Substantial improvement debt	+	_____	
Divorce debt	+	_____	
Subtotal (cannot exceed $1,000,000 less grand- fathered debt, but not below zero)		+	_____
Equals: **Acquisition debt**		=	_____

(2) What is home equity debt?

Fair market value of residence	+	_____
Less: Acquisition debt (above)	–	_____
Equals: **Home equity debt (cannot exceed $100,000)**	=	_____

Example:

Terry purchases a personal automobile on an installment contract and gives his home, instead of the automobile, as collateral. This converts a nondeductible personal interest expense to a deductible home mortgage interest expense. ■

The limitation on residential interest expense. To prevent abuse, as illustrated in the above example, "qualified residence interest" includes the aggregate amount of acquisition indebtedness not exceeding $1 million and the aggregate amount of home equity indebtedness not exceeding $100,000. This provision applies cumulatively to *both* the principal and the second residence of the taxpayer [§163(h)(3)].

The fill-in-the-blank formula in Figure 9.1, which helps arrive at the deductible portion of home mortgage interest, acts as a starting point for defining the new terms *acquisition* and *home equity indebtedness*. A line-by-line explanation follows.

WHAT IS ACQUISITION INDEBTEDNESS?

Acquiring or constructing a residence. Acquisition indebtedness is debt that is incurred in acquiring, constructing, or substantially improving the principal residence or a second residence of the taxpayer *and* is secured by such property.

"Substantially improving" a residence. This term is not defined either by statute or by the Conference Report. It is hoped that future regulations will stipulate when an improvement is "substantial." Until then, uncertainty exists.

Investor Hint

The word *substantial* as used in other Internal Revenue Code sections ranges in meaning from 15% to 35% or more of the fair market value. This would be unconscionable if applied to home loans; for a homeowner to deduct the interest on a home improvement loan, for example, the loan on a $100,000 home would have to exceed $15,000 to $35,000 or more. Most home improvement loans are not that large, and therefore *all* interest on the home improvement would not be deductible when using this definition; it would be a personal interest expense unless it qualifies as a home equity loan. The IRS will, it is hoped, be lenient in its future defining of the word *substantial*.

$1 million cap on level of acquisition debt. The total amount of acquisition debt that can give rise to qualified residence interest is $1,000,000. This cap applies to the combined debt on the principal and second residence. In the case of married persons filing a separate return, the limit is $500,000. Secured indebtedness created prior to October 14, 1987 is grandfathered and exempt from this limitation even if subsequently refinanced. For refinanced grandfathered debt to be considered pre-October 14, 1987 debt, the remaining term of the loan cannot be extended [§163(h)(3)(B),(D)].

A real problem for future refinancing. Acquisition indebtedness decreases as payments are made, and it cannot be increased if the loan is refinanced. In other words, a taxpayer's acquisition indebtedness eventually reduces to zero if the property remains the taxpayer's principal residence for the term of the mortgage.

Example:

Don purchases a principal residence for $250,000 in 2003, borrowing $200,000 on a 20-year mortgage note. In 2003, Don's acquisition indebtedness is $200,000, and the interest expense on that $200,000 is fully deductible. As Don amortizes his mortgage, the deductible amount of interest expense also decreases. In 2023 (20 years later), Don's acquisition indebtedness is zero, and any interest expense paid by Don on his home is nondeductible (with the exception of the interest expense on the home equity indebtedness). ▪

Refinanced acquisition debt causes another problem. This is treated as acquisition debt *only* to the extent that it does not exceed the principal amount of acquisition debt *immediately before* the refinancing. In other words, the refinanced debt in excess of the debt just prior to refinancing is not qualified residence debt, and the interest expense created by the excess debt is generally not deductible (with the exception that it might qualify as home equity debt, business debt, or investment debt).

Example:

Bill incurs $85,000 of acquisition indebtedness to acquire his principal residence and pays the debt down to $60,000. His acquisition indebtedness with respect to that residence cannot thereafter be increased above $60,000 (except for indebtedness incurred to substantially improve the residence). ▨

Example:

Bill purchases a principal residence for $250,000 cash, and one year later needs to refinance $200,000. The acquisition debt *immediately before* the refinance is zero; therefore, the full $200,000 is excess debt, with only $100,000 eligible for home equity debt. Bill can only deduct 50% of his interest expense. Prior planning prevents poor performance. ▨

Tax Tip

This law is economically strange as it creates a tax incentive for homeowners to (1) buy a new residence rather than improve an existing residence, (2) choose not to live and occupy their homes for long periods of time, (3) create as lengthy a loan as possible, and (4) invest a minimal down payment. It is a pro-purchase, pro-borrowing but antisavings tax provision.

Relief for debt created at divorce. At divorce, it is often required that one spouse purchase the interest of the other spouse in the residence. The payor spouse must often create a second mortgage to accumulate the necessary funds. The problem is that the mortgage is not created at the time the home is purchased (not the typical acquisition debt), and it is not a typical substantial improvement loan (although the author has had taxpayers disagree with him on this as they think throwing out the spouse is a very substantial improvement). This new debt, even though not created at the original acquisition date, is also considered acquisition debt.

If an individual acquires the interest of a spouse in a qualified residence incident to a divorce, and such individual incurs indebtedness that is secured by such qualified residence, the individual's debt in such qualified residence may be increased by the amount of secured indebtedness incurred by the individual in connection with the acquisition of the spouse's interest in the residence. The amount of such debt, however, shall not exceed the fair market value of the interest in the residence that is being acquired [TAMRA of 1988, P.L. 100-203; Act. Sec. 1005(c)(14); also see House Committee Report].

WHAT IS HOME EQUITY INDEBTEDNESS?

Home equity indebtedness is debt (other than acquisition indebtedness) that is secured by the taxpayer's principal or second residence and does not exceed the fair market value of such qualified residence reduced by the amount of acquisition indebtedness for such residence(s) [§163(h)(3)(C)(I)].

In the following example, interest on qualifying home equity debt is deductible even though the money is used for personal expenses, such as purchasing a personal automobile.

Example:

Lynn has a principal and second residence with fair market values and acquisition indebtedness as follows:

	Principal Home	*Second Home*
Fair market value	$150,000	$100,000
Less: Acquisition debt	− 100,000	− 75,000
Equals: Home equity	$ 50,000	$ 25,000

Lynn has a maximum of $75,000 of home equity indebtedness available to her under this provision. If she purchases a BMW for $75,000 in 1998 and gives her two residences as collateral on the loan, she converts a nondeductible personal loan to a deductible qualified-residence interest loan.

What is fair market value? It is the price at which the property would change hands between a willing buyer and a willing seller, neither being under any compulsion to buy or sell.

$100,000 cap on home equity indebtedness. The amount of home equity indebtedness on which interest is treated as deductible qualified-residence interest may not exceed $100,000 ($50,000 for married persons filing separate returns). The amounts borrowed for educational or medical expenditures are included in the $100,000 limitation [§163(h)(3)(C)(ii)].

WHAT IS A RESIDENCE?

A residence *generally* includes a house, condominium, mobile home, boat, or house trailer that contains sleeping space and toilet and cooking facilities. But whether a specific property qualifies as a residence shall be solely determined by all the facts and circumstances, including the good faith of the taxpayer [§1.163-10T(p)(3)(ii)].

Investor Hint

Does this mean a fishing cabin in the Rocky Mountains does not qualify as a second dwelling unit if it has only an outdoor toilet? The word *generally* might give relief, no pun intended. Most certainly, the primary residence with outdoor plumbing still qualifies as the principal residence.

Do motor homes qualify? Yes, motor homes have previously been held by the courts to be dwelling units [*R. L. Haberkorn,* 75 TC 259, Dec. 37,392; *J. O. Loughlin,* DC-Minn, 82-2 USTC ¶9543].

How many residences qualify? Only *qualified residences* are allowed a home mortgage interest deduction. The term *qualified residences* means the taxpayer's principal residence and/or the taxpayer's second residence [§163(h)(5)].

What is a principal residence? A taxpayer's principal residence is the land and building where the taxpayer principally domiciles, based upon all the facts and circumstances in each case, including the good faith of the taxpayer. The home must qualify for the exclusion provisions (see Chapter 3). It normally will be the home in the area where the taxpayer works; if retired or not working, it is usually where the taxpayer spends the most amount of time, votes, pays taxes, files his or her tax return, and the like. A taxpayer cannot have more than one principal residence at any one time [§1.163-10T(p)(2)].

What is a second residence? The second home, or vacation home, must (1) be a "dwelling unit" that (2) qualifies as a residence under the "use" requirements of §280A and that (3) the taxpayer elects to treat as a second residence [§163(h)(5)(A)(I),(II); §1.163-10T(p)(3)].

What qualifies as a second "dwelling unit"? A house, apartment, condominium, mobile home, boat, or similar property qualifies as a dwelling unit. A dwelling unit does not include personal property, such as furniture or a television, that, in accordance with the applicable local law, is not a fixture [§280(f)(1); §1.163-10T(p)(3)(ii)].

Tax Tip

This definition allows the interest expense associated with the purchase of a yacht or motor home to be deductible if the taxpayer wishes to treat the yacht or motor home as a dwelling unit.

How much "use" must the taxpayer make of the vacation home? For a residence to qualify as a second dwelling unit, the taxpayer must either (1) not rent it out to anyone during the year or (2) personally use it at least two weeks a year or 10% of the number of days the residence is rented out to others, whichever period is greater. A residence will be deemed to be rented during any period that the taxpayer holds the residence out for rental, resale, or repairs or renovates the residence with the intention of holding it out for rental or resale [§280A(d)(1); §1.163-10T(p)(3)(iii)].

Investor Hint

Interestingly enough, this 14-day use period could eliminate some or all of the vacation home expenses in excess of income, a catch-22 problem [§280A].

The taxpayer elects the two homes, not the IRS! In the case of a taxpayer who owns more than two residences, the taxpayer may designate *each year* which residence (other than the taxpayer's principal residence) is to be treated as the second residence. This election need not be disclosed to the IRS.

Exceptions to the "only-two-in-a-year" rule. A taxpayer may not elect different residences as second residences at different times of the same taxable year except as provided below [§1.163-10T(p)(3)(iv)]:

1. *Owning two homes and purchasing another.* If the taxpayer acquires a new residence during the taxable year, the taxpayer may elect the new residence as the taxpayer's second residence as of the date acquired.

Example:

Jeff owns vacation home A for the entire year and pays $3,000 interest expense. He acquires vacation home B on July 1 and pays $4,000 interest expense through December 31. Jeff may elect vacation home A as his second residence for the first half of the year (approximately $1,500 of interest) and vacation home B as his second residence for the second half of the year (the entire $4,000 of interest). ■

2. *Converting principal home into vacation home.* If a taxpayer moves out of his or her principal residence and converts it into a vacation home, the new vacation home becomes eligible as a second residence for interest deduction purposes.

Example:

On July 1, Jeff decides to move out of his principal residence on St. Thomas, Virgin Islands, and purchase a principal residence in Aspen. The interest expense for the year on his St. Thomas home is $9,000 and for the half-year on his Aspen home is $4,000. Assuming Jeff does not convert the property into a rental, he may elect the St. Thomas home as a qualified second residence for the second half of the year. The tax result is that all $13,000 interest expense is deductible. ■

3. *Owning three homes and selling one in middle of year.* If property that was the taxpayer's second residence is sold during the taxable year or becomes the taxpayer's principal residence, the taxpayer may elect a new second residence as of that day.

Example:

Jeff sold vacation home A on July 1, paying $4,000 interest expense from January 1 through the sale date. He elects A as his qualified second residence for the first half of the year. Jeff also owns vacation home B, paying $7,000 interest expense for the entire year. Jeff may elect vacation home B as his new second qualified residence starting July 1. ■

If the residence is also used for business, interest must be prorated. The interest expense must be allocated, based on their fair market values, between the residential use and the nonresidential use (e.g., business, rental, or investment use) with the exception discussed below given to "certain residential rentals" [§1.163-10T(p)(4)].

> ### Caution
>
> See *secured* debt, discussed later, for a potential problem. Secured debt overrides the direct tracing rules. This requires that Tom deduct the 10% normal business expense as qualified-residence interest, an itemized deduction [§1.163-

Example:

Tom uses 10% of his residence as an office in his trade or business. That portion does not qualify as a residence. Therefore, 10% of the interest *may* be deductible as business interest expense. ▪

Special rule for "certain residential rentals." If the taxpayer rents out a portion of the principal or second residence, that portion may still be treated as residential use if

1. the tenant uses the rented portion primarily for residential purposes;
2. the rented portion is not a self-contained residential unit containing separate sleeping space and toilet and cooking facilities; and
3. the total number of tenants renting (directly or by sublease) the same or different portions of the residence at any time during the taxable year does not exceed two. If two persons (and their dependents) share the same sleeping quarters, they are treated as a single tenant [§1.163-10T(p)(4)(ii)].

The most common tax question—deducting interest on a residence under construction. A taxpayer may treat a residence under construction as a qualified residence for up to 24 months, but only if the residence becomes a qualified residence at the time the residence is ready for occupancy. This is an exception to the basic rule that the property must be *used* by the taxpayer as a residence [§1.163-10T(p)(5)].

Interest on a vacant lot may be nondeductible. Frances Garrison's vacant lot, located in a recreational area, was determined to be neither the taxpayer's principal residence nor a second home; therefore, the interest on the debt was not qualified residence interest. Although the Garrisons never built a home on this property, they did avail themselves of camping privileges each year. The Tax Court cited Temporary Regulation §1.163-10T(p)(3)(A), which requires that a second residence generally include a house, condominium, mobile home, boat, or house trailer containing sleeping space and toilet and cooking facilities (which this vacant lot did not). As the taxpayer didn't make the argument that the property was an investment because it was principally used as recreational property, Garrison's interest was treated as nondeductible personal interest [*Frances B. Garrison,* 67 TCM 2896; TC Memo. 1994-200].

Deducting interest on time-share purchases. Time-sharing arrangements are considered qualified residences as long as the taxpayer does not lease their use [§1.163-10T(p)(6)].

> **Investor Hint**
>
> Therefore, swapping personal-use time-share units should not jeopardize the qualified-residence status.

Joint return. In the case of a joint return, a residence includes property used by the taxpayer or spouse and is owned by either or both spouses.

> **Caution**
>
> If construction takes more than 24 months to complete, the interest after the 24th month and before occupancy is *not* deductible. The interest becomes deductible again as residence interest only after occupancy. What a strange regulation!

> **Caution**
>
> Make sure that the debt is also "secured" by the residence or this "relief" is irrelevant.

> **Caution (for newlyweds)**
>
> Be careful with newlyweds if both previously owned personal residences and one also owned a vacation home! They did own two deductible homes but now own one nondeductible home.

PROVING LOAN IS TAXPAYER'S DEBT

Interest deductible by legal "or equitable" owner only! Deductible qualified residence interest is defined as any interest paid or accrued during the taxable year on "acquisition indebtedness with respect to any qualified residence of the taxpayer" [§163(h)(3)(A)(i)]. This "indebtedness" must, in general, be an obligation of the taxpayer and not an obligation of another [*Golder v. Comm.*, 604 F.2d 34, 35 (9th Cir. 1979), *affg.* T.C. Memo. 1976-150). However, the IRS Regulations provide: "interest paid by the taxpayer on a mortgage upon real estate of which he is the legal or equitable owner, even though the taxpayer is not directly liable upon the bond or note secured by such mortgage, may be deducted as interest on his indebtedness" [§1.163-1(b)]. Where the taxpayer has not established legal, equitable, or beneficial ownership of mortgaged property, the courts generally have disallowed the taxpayer a deduction for the mortgage interest [*Song v. Comm,* T.C. Memo. 1994-446; *Bonkowski v. Comm.,* T.C. Memo. 1970-340, *affd.* 458 F.2d 709 (7th Cir. 1972)].

Look to state law to determine who is owner. State law determines the nature of property rights, and Federal law determines the appropriate tax treatment of those rights [*United States v. Natl. Bank of Commerce,* 472 U.S. 713, 722 (1985)]. For example, it is presumed under California law that the owner of legal title is the owner of the full beneficial title. This presumption may be rebutted only by clear and convincing proof.

Deductions denied for mortgage interest and real estate taxes paid for residence owned by sister. H. H. Hackley didn't qualify for a loan to purchase a Los Angeles residence and asked his sister, Ms. Orum, to "get the property in her name." Hackley's name was not on the deed, but he made the mortgage payments directly to the lender, Countrywide Home Loans, and also paid for all real estate taxes, homeowner's insurance, repairs, and maintenance. He lived alone in the property and did not pay rent to his sister. The court found there was, outside of Hackley's testimony, no objective evidence to persuade the court that he had equitable ownership of the L.A. residence. His testimony, without more independent testimony, was insufficient (also see *Loria v. Comm,* T.C. Memo. 1995-420, where taxpayer's attempt to establish equitable ownership with his sole testimony is insufficient).

Investor Hint

Why he didn't bring his sister, Ms. Orum, to court to testify on his behalf is a mystery to this author. Hackley should have won the case!

Prior cases on point. In *Uslu v. Comm.,* (T.C. Memo. 1997-551), Mr. and Mrs. Uslu made mortgage payments on a residence for which legal title was held by Mr. Uslu's brother and sister-in-law. The court found in Uslu that the taxpayers "exclusively held the benefits and burdens of ownership," and therefore, were the equitable and beneficial owners of the residence. However, in *Song v. Comm.,* (T.C Memo. 1995-446), where legal title was held by the taxpayer's brother, the court found that the taxpayer failed to prove that she had any equitable or beneficial ownership in the residence. An important distinction between *Uslu* and *Song* was the completeness of the record and the credibility of the legal title holder of the residence: Mr. Uslu's brother and sister-in-law in *Uslu,* and the taxpayer's brother in *Song.*

HOW DOES A DEBT BECOME "SECURED DEBT"?

What does "secured" mean? In order for any interest to be deductible as *qualified-residence indebtedness interest,* the debt is required to be *secured by such residence.* The term *secured debt* means a debt connected with a security instrument (such as a mortgage, deed of trust, or land contract), and

1. the qualified residence is specific security for the payment of the debt;
2. in the event of default, the residence *could* be subjected to the satisfaction of the debt; and
3. *it is recorded* (or otherwise perfected under local or Texas law) [§1.163-10T(j)(1); §1.163-10T(o)(1)]. *(Observe the tax sucker-punch this administrative hassle causes, as illustrated in the next example!)*

Collateral must be correct. The "specific security" requirement compels the purchased property be pledged as collateral against the loan.

Example:

The John Sununu provision. As reported by the Wall Street Journal, the ex-governor of New Hampshire purchased a home in Georgetown for more than $400,000 when he became the President's chief of staff. He borrowed the $400,000 from a Republican banker, giving the banker *his New Hampshire home* as collateral. A mistake, John! The loan must be "specific security," therefore, the Georgetown home must secure the Georgetown loan. The estimated $40,000 per year interest is not deductible by John as it is personal interest! Query: how many think John amended his returns? ▪

Tax Tip

Is this common? Yes! We have found numerous taxpayers purchasing vacation homes with loans secured by their primary residences. The result is that a loan normally considered acquisition debt of a second residence is now considered home equity debt of the primary residence. *Bad tax planning!*

Example:

Winning with a *home equity* **debt.** Terry purchases a $75,000 BMW on an installment contract from the auto dealer and gives his home, in addition to the automobile, as collateral. This converts a nondeductible personal interest expense to a deductible home mortgage interest expense *if* the auto dealer records the house lien, along with the auto lien, with the local registrar. ■

Commercial property pledged against home loan. Borrowed money used to purchase a personal residence but secured by a commercial rental property is *not properly secured,* and therefore the interest is nondeductible personal interest [TAM 9418001].

Home pledged against commercial loan. Debt secured by a personal residence but used for business purposes is deductible as an itemized deduction, not a business expense. When the security for the borrowed funds is a mortgage on a first or second home, *the security,* not the way the funds are used, controls the treatment of the interest. This is the only exception to the rule that interest expense is deducted by tracing how the underlying debt is used [§1.163-8T(m)(3)].

> **Caution**
>
> The IRS gets the taxpayer coming and going with this technical requirement!

Example:

Dennis took out a $20,000 loan to purchase office furniture and computer equipment for his new business. The bank requires that Dennis give them a second mortgage on his personal residence as additional collateral. During the year, Dennis earns $2,400 of income before deducting the $2,400 interest expense he paid on the home equity loan. Regulation §1.163-8T(m)(3) requires that Dennis report $2,400 of income on his business tax return and subsequently to pay $367.20 self-employment tax (15.3% of $2,400). The $2,400 interest expense is deductible on his Schedule A as an itemized personal deduction. But he is still out $367.20 for self-employment taxes. Dennis attaches to his tax return a §1.163-10T (o)(5) election out. He traces the use of the $20,000 loan to the purchase of the business furniture and computer equipment, thereby legally deducting the interest expense on his business tax return [§1.161-8T(c)(1)]. The tax result is that the $2,400 of income is offset by the $2,400 interest expense and therefore no self-employment tax is due. A savings of $367! ■

> **Tax Tip**
>
> ***Can an election be made to treat the debt on a qualified residence as not "qualified-residence interest"?*** Yes, by attaching to the taxpayer's tax return a *§1.163-10T(o)(5) election out* of the qualified-residence interest rules. This election is effective for that taxable year and for all subsequent taxable years unless revoked with the consent of the Commissioner.

Example:

Pat owns a principal residence having a fair market value of $75,000 with an acquisition indebtedness of $45,000. She borrows an additional $25,000 to be used as a business loan, giving a second mortgage on her home to the lender. Later she borrows another $15,000 to purchase a personal automobile, giving both her home and the automobile as collateral. In the absence of an election to treat the business loan as unsecured, the applicable debt limit for the automobile loan would be only $5,000, the limit of her home equity amount (Option 1). A §1.163-10T(o)(5) election out would allow Pat to deduct all the business interest on her business tax return and all the interest on the automobile loan as qualified-residence interest (Option 1).

	Option 1	Option 2
Fair Market Value	$75,000	$75,000
Debt:		
Acquisition Debt	− $45,000	− $45,000
Business Loan	− 25,000	− 0
Automobile Loan	− 5,000	− 15,000
Home Equity Amount	$ 0	$ 15,000

Example:

Avoiding a tax problem with related-party loans. On January 1, 2004, Chuck, Sr., sells to Chuck, Jr., the lake cabin for $65,000 on the installment plan with $1,000 down and the balance due over a 20-year contract. Chuck, Sr., does not record the sale as he doesn't want his son to think he doesn't trust him. As a result, Chuck, Jr., doesn't have an interest deduction on his second dwelling unit! ▨

When is the debt treated as secured? A debt is treated as secured as of the date on which each of the three requirements detailed previously are satisfied, *regardless of when amounts are actually borrowed with respect to the debt.*

Example: (continued)

On July 1, 2004, Chuck, Sr., records the above lake cabin contract. Chuck, Jr., would be able to deduct only the interest paid for the last half of the year. ▨

Unsecured liens, mechanics liens, and general asset liens do not qualify. A debt will not be considered to be secured by a qualified residence if it is secured solely by virtue of a lien upon the general assets of the taxpayer or by a security interest, such as a mechanic's lien or judgment lien, that attaches to the property without the consent of the debtor.

GENERAL REQUIREMENTS FOR HOME MORTGAGE INTEREST AND POINTS TO BE DEDUCTIBLE

Interest is anything paid as compensation for the use of money. In order for interest to be deductible, though, there must be an existing, valid, and enforceable obligation for the individual to pay a principal sum and to pay interest on it [§163; §461].

Cash-basis taxpayers can't deduct prepaid interest. They are automatically placed on the accrual basis. Taxpayers may only deduct interest in the year the interest represents a cost of using the borrowed money. Even if paid in cash in advance, it can never be fully deducted and must be charged to a capital account and deducted in the period to which it applies [§461(g)(1)].

Example:

Shane buys a piece of property for $50,000, paying $10,000 as a cash down payment and assuming the mortgage of $40,000. He also pays five years of interest in advance at the time of purchase, amounting to $20,000. Shane must deduct the interest expense *monthly* over the next five years, approximately $4,000 per year. On the other side of the transaction, the seller must report the entire $20,000 as interest income in the year of the sale!

Points are deductible over the loan term. On the whole, points paid, generally at the time of purchase or refinance, are considered similar to a prepayment of interest and are to be treated as paid over the term of the loan. This also applies to charges that are similar to points, such as loan origination fees, loan-processing fees, or premium charges, provided that they are to be paid for the use of the lender's money. Such payments are viewed as a substitute for a higher-stated interest rate [§461(g)].

Example:

Susannah paid $2,400 in points on a 20-year loan involving 240 monthly payments. Susannah may deduct only $10 for each payment that is due during the tax year. The remaining amount must be capitalized and deducted monthly over the remaining loan period.

What expenses are considered points? *Loan-processing-fee* points paid by a mortgagor-borrower as compensation to a lender solely for the use or forbearance of money is considered to be interest. *Loan-origination-fee points* paid by a borrower obtaining an FHA loan are normally considered deductible interest points [Rev. Rul. 69-188, 1969-1 CB 54, as amended by Rev. Rul. 69-582, 1969-2 CB 29].

What are not considered points? Charges for services, including the lender's services (such as appraisal fees, the cost of preparing the note and mortgage or deed of trust, settlement fees, etc.) are not interest. They are similar to acquisition costs even though the lender may characterize or refer to them as "points" [Rev. Rul. 67-297, 1967-2 CB 87].

In addition, items such as appraisal fees, inspection fees, title fees, attorney fees, property taxes, mortgage insurance premiums, and other amounts ordinarily charged separately on the settlement statement cannot be disguised as points [Rev. Rul. 92-2].

But home mortgage points can be currently deducted. The entire amount of points paid for a mortgage note may be deducted in the year of payment if

1. the loan is incurred in connection with the purchase or improvement of a principal residence and the indebtedness is secured by that home;
2. the payments of points is an established business practice in the area where the debt is created; and
3. the points do not exceed the amount generally charged in the area [§461(g)(2)].

Example:

Susannah paid $2,400 in points on a 20-year loan involving 240 monthly payments when purchasing a principal residence. Susannah may deduct all $2,400 in the year of the payment of the home mortgage points. ▪

The points paid on a loan in excess of the $1,000,000 qualified acquisition-indebtedness cap would not qualify [Rev. Rul. 92-2; Rev. Proc. 92-12].

Closing statement should designate points. The IRS, "as a matter of administrative practice," permits the current deduction of points incurred when purchasing a principal residence if the following conditions are satisfied:

1. The above three rules of §461(g)(2) are met.
2. The Uniform Settlement Statement, HUD Form 1, clearly designates the amounts as "points" incurred to procure the loan. Therefore, labels such as *loan origination fees, loan discounts, discount points, points,* service fee points, and commissions paid to a mortgage broker for arranging financing are acceptable [Rev. Rul. 92-2]. Loan-origination-fee points paid by the borrower to obtain a VA or FHA mortgage are now also deductible as interest.
3. The points must be stated as a percentage of the principal amount borrowed.
4. The amount must be paid directly by the taxpayer [Rev. Proc. 92-12, IRB 1992-26].

Points paid by seller are deductible by both buyer and seller! The IRS ruled that when a seller pays "points" on the sale of a principal residence, the *buyer* may deduct those points as interest, but both must subtract these points from the sales/purchase price. Seller-paid points are viewed as an adjustment to the purchase price of the home when certain requirements are met. This pro-homebuyer rule is retroactive for points paid by the seller after December 31, 1990 [Rev. Proc. 94-27; Reg. §1.1273-2(g)(5) (Example 3)]!

Example:

Danny Seller sells Roberta Buyer his principal residence for $101,600 and also agrees to pay two of the four points on Roberta's new $80,000 mortgage ($1,600.00). Danny must decrease his net sales price to $100,000 (which decreases his gain by $1,600). Roberta's purchase price is $100,000 and she gets to deduct all $3,200 of the mortgage points, just as if she had paid it personally! ▪

The IRS requirements. So long as the previously mentioned requirements are met (i.e., computed as percentage, established business practice, not excessive, purchase points only, and paid directly), the deductible amount designated as mortgage discount points on HUD Form 1 may be shown as paid from either the borrower's or the seller's funds at closing!

Tax Tip

Points paid by the seller (including points charged to the seller) in connection with the buyer's loan will be treated as paid directly by the buyer from funds that have not been borrowed!

Tax Tip

For substantiation purposes, this requires that the buyer receive the seller's closing statement along with the buyer's closing statement, something generally not given to the buyer with the exception of HUD Form 1.

Tax Tip

Make sure the points are paid in cash. In order for points to be deductible, they must be paid from separate funds at the time of loan closing. They cannot be paid from borrowed funds. Points withheld by a lender from loan proceeds may not be deducted by a borrower in the year the points were withheld, because the withholding does not constitute payment within that tax year. Such withholding reduces the issue price of the loan, and thereby the amount of the deduction is governed by the original issue discount rules [§1271-1274] [*R. A. Schubel*, 77 TC 701, Dec. 38, 388 (1981)].

Points can be paid out of the earnest money deposit. So long as the funds are not borrowed, points may be deducted if they do not exceed the down payment, escrow deposit, earnest money applied at closing and other funds actually paid over at closing [Rev. Proc. 92-12; Rev. Rul. 92-2].

> ## Tax Tip
>
> Therefore, points do *not* have to be paid in cash at closing as long as the earnest money deposit exceeds the points.

Rental of large portion of residence does not hinder write-off of points. Russell rented a substantial portion of his principal residence (85%). The points he incurred to acquire the mortgage on the residence did not have to be amortized merely because the principal residence was also partially used for rental purposes. The Tax Court determined that there is "no exception in Code Section 461(g) for a principal residence which is also used (partly or substantially) for rental purposes." Therefore, the court held that the points Russell paid were deductible on Schedule A under Code Sections 163 and 461(g)(2) [*Russell,* TC Memo, 1994-96, 67 TCM 2347].

A big tax problem—points paid when refinancing are never currently deductible. Points paid in refinancing a mortgage are not deductible in full in the year paid, regardless of how the taxpayer arranges to pay for them. This is true even if the new mortgage is secured by the taxpayer's principal residence. According to the IRS, points paid to refinance an existing home mortgage are for repaying the taxpayer's existing indebtedness, and they are not paid *"in connection with"* the purchase or improvement of the home.

Therefore, taxpayers must deduct refinance points over the loan period. The IRS requires taxpayers to deduct these points monthly over the term of the loan. If part of the proceeds from the refinancing are used to improve the personal residence, the taxpayer may deduct a portion of the points in the tax year paid [IRS News Rel. IR-86-68, May 13, 1986; Rev. Rul. 87-22, IRB 1987-14, 41].

> ## Tax Tip
>
> The Tax Court's logic should also extend to a principal residence with a home office. The home office should not affect the write-off of the points.
>
> This rule would not apply to the purchase of a duplex with one unit being used personally as that represents the purchase of two assets, a personal home and a business rental.

Example:

Susannah paid $2,400 in points on refinancing a 20-year loan involving 240 monthly payments on her principal residence. Susannah may only deduct $10 for each payment that is due during the tax year. ■

Points paid to refinance a home mortgage loan may be currently deductible *if* advance planned—IRS doesn't agree. James and Zenith Huntsman bought a principal residence financed by a $122,000 mortgage loan with a balloon payment due in three years. Shortly thereafter, they obtained a $22,000 home improvement loan secured by a second mortgage. Within the three years, the Huntsmans obtained a 30-year variable-rate mortgage of $148,000 and paid off the prior loans with the proceeds.

When obtaining their new mortgage, the Huntsmans paid $4,440 in points and immediately deducted it as points paid *"in connection with"* the purchase of a principal residence [see the exact wording of §461(g)(2)]. In disagreeing with the IRS's and the Tax Court's disallowance of the current deduction, the U.S. Court of Appeals for the Eighth Circuit stated that "obtaining the short-term financing was merely an integrated step in securing the permanent financing to purchase the home." Judge Lay concluded that the statement *"in connection with"* should be "broadly construed" [*James Richard Huntsman v. Comm.,* CA-8 (rev'gTC) 90-2USTC ¶50,340; 91TC917].

Tax Tip

This requires that the taxpayer plan the refinancing at the time of acquisition.

IRS nonacquiesces. The IRS has announced that it will *not* follow the *Huntsman* decision outside of the Eighth Circuit. The service warns that the test created by the Eighth Circuit requires an examination of the facts of each case to determine whether a refinancing is sufficiently connected with the purchase or improvement of a principal residence. The IRS states that Congress enacted §461(g)(2) to eliminate the case-by-case approach to the deductibility of points [AOD No. 1991-02].

Caution

Any fact pattern other than the facts in *Huntsman* will probably *not* be considered acquisition points. This includes refinancing to lower the interest rates [*Kelly v. Comm.,* TC Memo 1991-605, 62TCM 1406; *Dodd v. Comm.,* TC Memo 1992-341].

Tax Tip

This means that taxpayers should be warned of a possible disallowance at audit but not necessarily loss of deduction—if they are willing to go to court!

A tax pain—how to allocate points on home mortgages when they cannot be deducted in the year paid. The IRS provides for a monthly straight-line allocation of residential points over the loan period for those taxpayers who qualify. Generally, the method applies to an individual cash-basis taxpayer who is charged points on a loan secured by his or her principal residence if the loan period is no greater than 30 years. There are additional restrictions on loan amounts and number of points charged [Rev. Proc. 87-15; IRB 1987-14].

What happens to the points if the home is sold before the loan is paid off? They are fully deductible in the year of the sale. Whenever the property is sold or disposed of, any unamortized part of the financing expense can be charged off and deducted as interest expense. It makes no difference whether the purchaser assumes the mortgage, the property is simply sold subject to the mortgage, or it is paid off by the seller at the time of the sale.

Example:

David S. places a ten-year mortgage on an apartment building on July 1, 2003, using the proceeds to pay off an existing mortgage and to pay for repairs and operating expenses. He pays $1,000 in points at closing, of which only $50 is deductible in 2003 ($1,000 ÷ 10 years × .5 year). David sells the property on July 1, 2005. The remaining capitalized interest of $650 is triggered and becomes totally deductible as an interest expense in 2005. This would be true whether the mortgage is paid off at closing or the property is sold subject to the mortgage. ▪

What happens to the points if the borrower prepays the loan? *The points become fully deductible in the year of the payment of the loan. Refinancing, however, will not trigger this option. The loan must be paid off in cash or its equivalent [B. L. Battlestein, CA-5, 80-1, USTC ¶9225].* (But the IRS disagrees; see PLR 8632058.)

Points paid by the seller to help the buyer get financing. A loan charge of points or a loan replacement fee, paid by the seller of a residence as a condition to the arrangement of an FHA financing term for the buyer, is not deductible as interest; this charge is a selling expense that reduces the amount realized [Rev. Rul. 68-650, 1968-2 CB 78; Rev. Proc. 92-12A, IRB 1992-26].

FHA mortgage insurance premium (MIP) points. The IRS maintains that the insurance premiums on FHA loans are not interest. They are insurance and are therefore not deductible as interest.

CONCLUSION

Home mortgage interest is often the largest tax deduction for the average taxpayer. As this chapter showed, many technical traps exist that cause the homeowner to lose this valuable deduction. The material here helps the investor to maintain a legal deduction in case of an IRS audit.

Depreciation

Depreciation expense is one of the major items of consideration when evaluating potential equipment or real estate acquisitions, as it allows the investor to take an "imaginary" deduction even though the property may actually be *appreciating* in value. Depreciation is the periodic expending of an asset over the property's theoretical economic life. This tax deduction is intended to recognize the decrease in value caused by wear and tear, outdated interior improvements, and neighborhood problems. Depreciation also provides a method of matching the income and related expense.

DEPRECIATION IS MANDATORY

If property qualifies for the depreciation expense deduction, the cost or other basis of property *shall* be decreased for depreciation at the end of each taxable year. This can create a financial disaster for the taxpayer.

Example:

A tax problem. Scott purchases a $100,000 rental building in 1998 (on leased land). He instructs his accountant not to take any depreciation on the building; he already has enough deductions to offset his income. In other words, he has no tax use for the depreciation deduction from the building. After holding the property for 39 years, he sells the building to Martin for $100,000. He reports to the IRS no gain on the sale because he never received any economic benefit from depreciation while owning the building. Wrong! He must report a $100,000 gain. Depreciation allowed *or allowable* is required in the capital gains computation.

Gain or Loss Computation

Sales price				$100,000
Less:	Adjusted basis			
	Original cost (or basis)	+	$100,000	
	Less: Accumulated depreciation	–	$100,000*	
	Equals: Total adjusted basis:		–	0
Net gain (or loss) on sale			=	$100,000

* Depreciation allowed or allowable [§1.1016-3].

MISSED DEPRECIATION

"Missed Depreciation" Can Be Claimed Later—If Form 3115 Filed by December 31!

Allowable depreciation not taken? It is sometimes discovered, generally at the time of sale or the switching of tax preparers, that the taxpayer has deducted less depreciation than he or she is entitled to, either because an asset was misclassified into a longer-life category (e.g., 15-year land improvements misclassified as 39-year commercial real property) or never placed on the return. The taxpayer cannot simply correct the mistake and take the missing depreciation without the IRS Commissioner's permission. The change in accounting method election, Form 3115, is required, as miscalculating depreciation for two or more years is not an error, it is an accounting method, albeit an erroneous one [§1.167(e)-1(a); §1.446-1(e)(2)(ii)(b); Rev. Rul. 72-491].

Depreciation allowed or allowable increases gain. Even worse, the IRS requires the taxpayer to calculate the gain upon sale by subtracting from the basis the greater of accumulated depreciation allowed *or allowable* [IRC §1016(a)(2) and Regulation §1.1016-3]. Under this calculation, the taxpayer who improperly computes depreciation deductions may upon sale of the property end up paying tax on gain increased by a benefit never received (the prior depreciation).

Example:

Elizabeth purchased a new apartment building (27.5 year life) on January 1, 1993, for $130,000, with the land value estimated at $30,000. Although the building was listed on her 1993 through 2000 depreciation schedules, no depreciation expense was taken because of a computer input error in her tax preparation software.

Year	Actual Depreciation	Allowable Depreciation	Accumulated Depreciation	Remaining Depreciation Basis
Purchase:				$100,000
1993	$–0–	$3,485	$3,485	$96,515
1994	$–0–	$3,636	$7,121	$92,879
1995	$–0–	$3,636	$10,757	$89,243
1996	$–0–	$3,636	$14,393	$85,607
1997	$–0–	$3,636	$18,029	$81,971
1998	$–0–	$3,636	$21,665	$78,335
1999	$–0–	$3,636	$25,301	$74,699
2000	$–0–	$3,636	$28,937	$71,063
2001	$3,636	$3,636	$32,573	$67,427
2002	$3,636	$3,637	$36,210	$63,790
2003	$3,636	$3,636	$39,846	$60,154

Catch-up depreciation in later years allowed. A taxpayer who has claimed less than or none of the otherwise allowable depreciation (or amortization) can take a "catch-up" current year deduction [as a §481(a) adjustment] for the understated amount, *including closed years,* by automatically electing (i.e., automatic IRS consent) to change his or her accounting method for that asset. [Rev. Proc. 2002-9, App, Sec. 2.01].

Example (continued):

Elizabeth's unclaimed accumulated depreciation from 1993 through 2000 is $28,937. If she timely files Form 3115, she can claim the entire $28,937 as a §481(a) adjustment on her 2003 tax return, in addition to deducting her annual depreciation of $3,636. If the error is discovered in 2000, the $28,937 would have to be deducted on her 2000 return after filing Form 3115. ▪

To obtain automatic IRS consent to catch up understated depreciation. File form 3115 with the IRS National Office at *any time* during the year. [§1.446-1t(e)(3)(i)(b); Rev. Proc. 2002-9]. No user fee is required to be paid. In addition, attach copy of Form 3115 to tax return claiming catch-up deduction.

> *Tax Tip*
>
> Don't sell unless the election has been made. This means that if property is sold and no
> election has been made by December 31 (which will be a very common occurrence that will
> trap many an unwary taxpayer; e.g., tax preparers find out from their clients what assets
> were sold just before April 15 of the *next* year!), no catch-up depreciation is available.

PROPERTY BECOMES DEPRECIABLE WHEN PLACED IN SERVICE, NOT WHEN PURCHASED!

Depreciation begins when the asset is *placed in service,* not necessarily when it is obtained.
Depreciable real property usually is considered to be placed in service when it has been
completed and is ready for occupancy [§1.167(A)-10(B)]. Business assets are not depreciable while out of service [W. J. Walsh, 55 TCM 994].

WHAT KIND OF PROPERTY IS DEPRECIABLE?

Generally, depreciable property is

1. a capital expenditure in depreciable property,
2. used in a trade or business or held for the production of income, and
3. has a definite useful life of more than one year (§167, 168).

Requirement 1: Capital expenditures in property. Capital expenditures include the
acquisition costs of property as well as subsequent improvements that increase the property's value or prolong its useful life.

**Requirement 2: Property used in a trade or business or for the production of
income.** Depreciation is allowed only for property that is used in a trade or business or
that is held for the production of income [§167(a)]. Therefore, personal property, such
as a personal residence or personal automobile, may not be depreciated.

Requirement 3: Useful life of more than one year. The useful life of an asset is the
period over which the asset is reasonably expected to be useful in a trade or business or
for the production of income. In order to be depreciable, an asset must have a useful
life of more than one year. If the life is one year or less, it is to be expended in the year
placed into service (normally the year of acquisition).

**The tests to determine if a future replacement or improvement is to be expended (as
repairs) or depreciated (as capital expenditures) are**

1. does it materially add to the property's value? or
2. does it prolong the property's useful life [§1.263(a)-1(b)] unless

3. substantial future benefit occurs (a facts and circumstances test) [*INDOPCO, Inc.* SCt (*aff'g* CA-3), 92-1 USTC ¶50,133; 112 SCt 1039]. *INDOPCO* doesn't apply to repair or maintenance expenditures (Rev. Rul. 94-12).

Incidental repairs. Improvements that have a more or less permanent value are capital expenditures that must be depreciated. Repairs, on the other hand, maintain the property in efficient operating condition and must be currently deducted [§1.162-4; §1.263(a)-1(b)]. The cost of replacement may be currently deductible as a repair or may have to be depreciated as a capital expenditure, depending on whether the replacement arrests deterioration and appreciably prolongs the life of the property.

The Plainfield-Union Water Co. standard. "An expenditure which returns property to the state it was in before the situation prompting the expenditure arose, and which does not make the relevant property more valuable, more useful, or longer-lived, is usually deemed a deductible repair. A capital expenditure is generally considered to be a more permanent increment in the longevity, utility, or worth of the property" (*Plainfield-Union Water Co. v. Comm.,* 39 TC 333).

Examples of deductible repair expenditures and nondeductible capital expenditures:

	Repair	**Capital Expenditures**
Machine and Equipment	Replacing small worn parts (Libby & Blouin, *Ltd. vs. Comm.,* 4 BTA 910)	Reconditioning fully depreciated machine and extending its useful life (*Claussner Hosiery Co., vs. Comm.,* 9 TCM 891); rebuilding a boiler (*Camilla Cotton Oil Co., vs. Comm.,* 31 TC 560)
Roof	Replacing roofing sheets blown away and stopping leaks (*Knoxville Iron Co. vs. Comm.,* TC Memo 1959-54); reroofing with same materials as before (*Thurner vs. Comm.,* 11 TCM 24); replacing the old roof with different materials to prevent leaks (*Oberman Mfg. Co. vs. Comm.,* 47 TC 471)	Replacing or recovering a roof (*Pierce Estates, Inc. vs. Comm.,* 16 TC 1020); reinforcing or shoring up roof (*Levy vs. Comm.,* 212 Fed 552; *Mountain States Steel Foundries, Inc. vs. Comm.,* TC Memo 1959-59)
Floor	Patching and repairing (*Libby & Blouin, Ltd. v. Comm.,* 4 BTA 910); reinforcing sagging floors (*Farmer's Creamery Co. v. Comm.,* 14 TC 879)	Replacing or recovering a floor (*Phillips & Easton Supply Co. v. Comm.,* 20 TC 455); replacing wood floor with cement floor (*Best v. Comm.,* TC Memo 1954-170); lowering a basement floor (*Difco Labs, Inc. v. Comm.,* 10 TC 660); raising floor above high flood level [*Black Hardware Co., v. Comm.,* 39 F2d 460 (5th Cir.)]

	Repair	**Capital Expenditures**
Painting	Painting and decorating show-room (*Luce Furniture Co. vs. Comm.*, 9 BTA 1413); painting of company-owned homes (*Chesapeake Corp. vs. Comm.*, 17 TC 668)	Painting house to make ready for rental *(Pryor v. Comm.*, TC Memo 1954-60)
Parking lot and driveway	Resurfacing [*Toledo Home Fed Sav & Loan Assn v. U.S.*, 203 F. Supp 491 (ND Ohio 1962], patching on asphalt driveway (*Knoxville Iron Co. v. Comm.*, TC Memo 1959-54)	Replacing gravel with cement [*Jones v. Comm*, 259 F2d 300 (5th Cir. 1958)]; grading, seeding, and shrubbery (*Knoxville Iron Co. v. Comm.*, TC Memo 1959-54)
Other Building Expenses	Plastering, plumbing and repairing glass [*Rose V. W Haverty Furniture Co.*, 15 F2d 345 (5th Cir)]; lining basement to prevent seepage (*Midland Empire Packing Co. v. Comm.*, 14 TC 635); filling and grading to prevent water seepage from nearby construction (*Southern Ford Tractor Corp. v. Comm.*, 29 TC 833); painting wood, repounding nails, replacing a small number of tin roof sheets, sealing nail holes, and painting roofs of farm buildings (*H.S. Schroeder,* TC Memo 1996-336)	Altering foundations [*Crocker First Natl Bank v. Comm.*, 59 F2d 37 (9th Cir.)]; adding new concrete cellar (*Foer Wallpaper Co. v. Comm.*, 9 BTA 377); reconditioning elevators (*HS Crocker Co. v. Comm.*, 15 BTA 175); replastering ceilings and walls (*Knoxville Iron Co. v. Comm.*, TC Memo 1959-54); installing air conditioner or heating system (*Plaza Inv Co. v. Comm.*, TC 1295; *Boddie v. Comm.*, TC Memo 1961-72); insulation (*Jamieson v. Comm.*, 8 TCM 961); replacing office book shelves [*Beaudry v. Comm.*, 150 F2d 20 (2d Cir)]

Is an $8,000 new roof deductible or depreciable?

Nevia Campbell was entitled to deduct the cost of removing and replacing the roof-covering material on her Long Beach, California, residential rental house as a trade or business expense. A quote from the case: *"The tenant complained to (Campbell) and, as (Campbell) put it in lay person's terms: 'So we had to get it repaired.' She could not have continued to rent the house if the roof had continued to leak."* The contractors removed the existing top layers of the roof and recovered it with fiberglass sheets and hot asphalt. They made no structural changes to the roof. The $8,000 cost of removing and replacing the roof-covering material on the roof of the rental house is the amount in issue. Campbell claimed it was a deductible expense; the IRS argued it was a capital expense.

> ### Investor Hint
>
> When "she could not have continued to rent the house if the roof had continued to leak" is heard by the IRS auditor, it results in the determination that the expenses "prolonged the useful life" of the property from zero (i.e., "Well, it didn't have any future life just before you replaced the roof!") to some extended life, resulting in the expense being recharacterized as a capital improvement. This may be an erroneous conclusion by the IRS agent if the expense was incurred to enable the owner to achieve the property's original economic useful life (see *Ingram Industries, Inc. v. Comm.*, TC. Memo 2000-323).

New roof "kept rental house in an operating condition"! The Court, following *Oberman Manufacturing Co v. Comm.,* [47 T.C. 471 (1967)], observed that Campbell's only purpose for the expense was to prevent leakage and keep her rental house in an operating condition over its probable useful life and not to prolong the life of the property, increase its value, or make it adaptable to another use. As in Oberman Manufacturing Co., there was no replacement or substitution of the roof (*Nevia Campbell v. Comm.,* TCS 2002-117).

> ### Tax Tip
>
> **"To the truss" is a repair, but "through the truss" is a capital improvement.** This argument should generally be successful when used on commercial roof expenditures (but no structural expenditures) because new roofs, by themselves, generally neither materially add to the value of the property nor extend the property's useful life beyond 39 years. If trusses are replaced, the courts often conclude that a structural expenditure has occurred (*George and Drousoula Tsakopoulos v. Comm.,* TC Memo 2002-8)

LAND IS NOT DEPRECIABLE

Land cannot be depreciated because the taxpayers cannot calculate, with reasonable certainty, what would be the life of land.

Allocating purchase price between land and building. When improved property is purchased, the taxpayer *must* allocate the purchase price between the land, building and other improvements [§1.167(a)-5]. The allocation must be done in a fair and equitable manner, *based on the relative fair market values* at the time of purchase [§1.61-6(a)]. In other words, when improved real property is purchased, the lump sum price is divided between the depreciable property and the land in the same proportion of each to the total cost.

Example:

Randy acquires a piece of property for a $100,000 lump sum purchase price. An appraisal shows the land to be worth $50,000 and the building to be worth $150,000. The $100,000 is allocated as follows:

Land:

$$\frac{\$50,000}{(50,000 + \$150,000)} \times \$100,000 = \$\ 25,000$$

Building:

$$\frac{\$150,000}{(50,000 + \$150,000)} \times \$100,000 = \$\ 75,000$$

Total $100,000

DEPRECIATION METHODS

Historically, the calculation of depreciation has been determined under one of the following three methods: (1) economic life, (2) ACRS, or (3) MACRS. As the acquisition date of the property determines which of the methods are available, below are the alternative depreciation methods and related depreciable lives available to investors.

Real Property Placed in Service Date Between:	The Depreciable Life Is:
February 12, 1913, and December 31, 1980	Economic Life
January 1, 1981, and March 14, 1984	15 years—ACRS
March 15, 1985, and May 8, 1985	18 years—ACRS
May 9, 1985, and December 31, 1986	19 years—ACRS
January 1, 1987, and May 12, 1993	27.5/31.5 years*—MACRS
May 13, 1993, to present	27.5/39 years*—MACRS

*First life is for residential rental real estate; second life is for commercial real estate.

Tax Tip

Investors may be required to use all six methods. Taxpayers who have depreciable property placed in service before January 1, 1981, must continue to apply the economic-life depreciation method during their period of ownership. They cannot start using the ACRS method on property placed in service before January 1, 1981. As a result, both the economic-life method, for pre-1981 acquisitions, and the following ACRS and MACRS methods, for post-1980 acquisitions, are being used by most taxpayers.

The Economic Life Theory: Acquisitions Between 1913–1980

For assets placed in service before 1981, and for assets not eligible for ACRS or MACRS, property is depreciated over the asset's economically useful life (i.e., how long that asset is economically profitable) [§167].

Straight-line depreciation. This term means that the property is expensed evenly over the life of the property (e.g., a $100,000 building with an estimated life of 50 years would be depreciated at the rate of $2,000 each year).

Useful economic life is determined by all the facts and circumstances in each case. For eligible properties, depreciation expense is generally calculated by the intermixing of three major elements:

1. The method of depreciation to be used (e.g., straight-line, declining balance, sum-of-the-year's digits)
2. The value of the property that is depreciable (land and salvage value is required to be subtracted)
3. The economic life of the property (buildings can be depreciated up to 60 years in length, depending upon the facts and circumstances)

As can be easily surmised, these three elements create many disagreements between the IRS and real estate investors.

The Accelerated Cost Recovery System (ACRS): Acquisitions Between 1981–1986

In an attempt to stop the disagreements about economic life, Congress completely revamped the depreciation calculation in the Economic Recovery Tax Act of 1981 (ERTA). Under ERTA, prior depreciation rules were discarded and replaced by a new simplified Accelerated Cost Recovery System (ACRS) for all property placed in service after December 31, 1980 (§168). This method is so radically different from the past that Congress even changed the word *depreciation* to *cost recovery*. Subsequently, Congress passed numerous changes that repeal, limit, and alter numerous ACRS deductions.

Investor Hint

Real estate investors have experienced *five* different depreciation changes since the enactment of ACRS in 1981, averaging a different depreciation alternative every *four* years. Multiple changes create investor uncertainty, which directly impacts value. These changes clearly illustrate the problem when Congress continually interferes in the economic process, trying to mandate how long an asset will be economically usable. Congress's ACRS may be simple, but it isn't always fair!

The classes. ACRS places depreciable or recovery property into four classes with useful lives of 3, 5, or 10 years for personal property and 15, 18, or 19 years for real property. The useful life for real property depends on the date the real property was placed into service.

Life. Under ACRS, investors have the choice of using one of two methods, a prescribed accelerated method using the regular recover period or the straight-line method, over either the ACRS-assigned life or an extended-class life.

New versus used acquisitions. The ACRS abandons the "useful life" rules, the "salvage value" rules and even the "new versus used" rules for property placed in service after 1980. Therefore, it is irrelevant if the property is new or used. The percentage depreciation rate is exactly the same for both a new building and a newly acquired 50-year-old building.

Depreciation recapture—the wisdom of using the straight-line election for commercial real estate. Taxpayers were able to use the straight-line method of depreciation instead of the accelerated method for 15/18/19 real property. Most owners of nonresidential (commercial) real estate made this election rather than the regular accelerated method. If they didn't, *all* accumulated depreciation (to the extent of the gain) would be subject to recapture as ordinary income *regardless* of how long the property is held and how the property is subsequently sold or exchanged. By electing the straight-line method of depreciation on the commercial real estate, *no* depreciation recapture is required. The depreciation recapture on residential real estate retains the §1250 rules—the amount of depreciation in excess of straight-line is recaptured as ordinary income in the year of the sale [§1245(a)(5)].

Rates. The rates used in computing depreciation for 3/5/10 property under the prescribed method is based on the 150% declining-balance method, switching to straight-line depreciation at the optimum time. For 18- and 19-year real property, the applicable percentage is based on the 175% declining-balance, switching to straight-line method using a month-by-month convention. Before the enactment of TRA '84, a building placed in service during any part of the month was entitled to a full month of depreciation. However, TRA '84 changes this rule so that 18- or 19-year property in service for any part of a month receives only one-half-month cost recovery for that month.

IRS tables make calculating depreciation easy. IRS Publication 534 and IRS Form 4562 illustrate the applicable ACRS percentage rates for both personal and real property. If real property is not purchased in the first month, the first and last years' depreciation expense is based on the number of months the property was actually used.

THE MODIFIED ACCELERATED COST RECOVERY SYSTEM (MACRS) ACQUISITIONS AFTER 1986

The Tax Reform Act of 1986 (billed as tax reform for fairness, growth, and *simplicity*) substantially revises the ACRS for both personal and real property. In addition, it repeals the investment tax credit (ITC).

Beginning January 1, 1987, all tangible depreciable property purchased and used (placed in service) is expended using a straight-line or accelerated depreciation method over normally longer predetermined recovery periods [§168].

The eight MACRS classes. All property is assigned to eight Modified Accelerated Cost Recovery System (MACRS) classes. The eight classes are titled for the number of years the property is to be depreciated.

Caution

This is a hidden tax rate increase. This Modified ACRS Method (MACRS) results in real property being depreciated at a substantially slower rate than in the past—as long as 27.5 to 39 years. Alternatively, investors and taxpayers may elect to use a 40-year recovery life on real property.

> ### Tax Tip
>
> **Don't change the method previously used.** These rules apply only to property placed into service after December 31, 1986. Investors continue with the depreciation method they started with when first placing the property on their depreciation schedule (e.g., commercial property purchased on December 31, 1986, would continue using a 19-year ACRS life in 1987 and thereafter. However, if that same property were purchased on May 13, 1993, the investor must use a 39-year MACRS life)! (And Congress wonders why real estate took such a nosedive starting in 1987!)

The Internal Revenue Service prescribes the depreciation percentages to be applied to both personal and real property. A specially computed percentage is applied to these classes. These percentages, with the applicable half-year and half-month conventions, the declining balance percentages, and the conversions to straight-line built in, are illustrated in Figure 10.1 and 10.2 reprinted from Rev. Proc. 87-57 [IRB 1987-42, 17].

Example:

The MACRS system. John purchases an office building on January 1, 2003, for $500,000 with land valued at $50,000, leaving a depreciable basis of $450,000. His allowable depreciation expense for the first two years is:

Year	Unadjusted Basis	×	MACRS Percentage	=	Depreciation Expense
2003	$450,000		2.461%	=	$11,075

In the second year of ownership, John's depreciation expense is:

Year	Unadjusted Basis	×	MACRS Percentage	=	Depreciation Expense
2004	$450,000	×	2.564%	=	$11,538

John finds his MACRS depreciation percentage by first determining the MACRS class (39-year class in this case) and then finding the proper MACRS Table (39-year Nonresidential Real Property Table). Both the MACRS classes and MACRS Tables are explained below.

As mentioned previously, the Tax Reform Act of 1986 creates eight MACRS classes: six classes for depreciable personal property and two classes for real property.

MACRS classes for personal property. The first six MACRS classes—3, 5, 7, 10, 15, and 20 year—are the personal property classes.

Check IRS guidelines first. To determine property classifications within these six classes, the taxpayer must first refer to the properties "Class Life (in years)" under the IRS's Asset Depreciation Range (ADR) system [Rev. Proc. 87-56, IRB 1987-42,4]. This class life is the property's midpoint life and indicates the average useful life of an asset. The average lives are based on prior IRS research of broad industry classes of assets. The purpose of the class-life ADR system is to keep conflicts over individual useful lives at a minimum. In the past, ADR was an option.

FIGURE 10.1 Straight-Line Depreciation Percentages for "Real Estate"[1]

TABLE 1: **27.5 YEAR RESIDENTIAL REAL PROPERTY**

The applicable percentage is: (Use the column for the
Month in the First Year the Property is Placed in Service)

Recovery Year(s)	1	2	3	4	5	6	7	8	9	10	11	12
1	3.485	3.182	2.879	2.576	2.273	1.970	1.667	1.364	1.061	0.758	0.455	0.152
2–9	3.636	3.636	3.636	3.636	3.636	3.636	3.636	3.636	3.636	3.636	3.636	3.636
10,12, . . . 26	3.637	3.637	3.637	3.637	3.637	3.367	3.636	3.636	3.636	3.636	3.636	3.636
11,13, . . . 27	3.636	3.636	3.637	3.636	3.636	3.636	3.637	3.637	3.637	3.637	3.637	3.637
28	1.970	2.273	2.576	2.879	3.182	3.485	3.636	3.636	3.636	3.636	3.636	3.636
29	0.000	0.000	0.000	0.000	0.000	0.000	0.152	0.455	0.758	1.061	1.061	1.667
Total	100	100	100	100	100	100	100	100	100	100	100	100

TABLE 2: **31.5 YEAR NON-RESIDENTIAL REAL PROPERTY**

The applicable percentage is: (Use the column for the
Month in the First Year the Property is Placed in Service)

Recovery Year(s)	1	2	3	4	5	6	7	8	9	10	11	12
1	3.042	2.778	2.513	2.249	1.984	1.720	1.455	1.190	0.926	0.661	0.397	0.132
2–7	3.175	3.175	3.175	3.175	3.175	3.175	3.175	3.175	3.175	3.175	3.175	3.175
8,10	3.175	3.174	3.175	3.174	3.175	3.174	3.175	3.175	3.175	3.175	3.175	3.175
9,11, . . . 31	3.174	3.175	3.174	3.175	3.174	3.175	3.174	3.175	3.174	3.175	3.174	3.175
12,14, . . . 30	3.175	3.174	3.175	3.174	3.175	3.174	3.175	3.174	3.175	3.174	3.175	3.174
32	1.720	1.984	2.249	2.513	2.778	3.042	3.175	3.174	3.175	3.174	3.175	3.174
33	0.000	0.000	0.000	0.000	0.000	0.000	0.132	0.396	0.661	0.925	1.190	1.454
Total	100	100	100	100	100	100	100	100	100	100	100	100

[1]Multiply depreciation percentages by original depreciation base.

Source: Rev. Proc. 87-57.

FIGURE 10.2 Straight-Line Depreciation Percentages for "Real Estate"[1]

TABLE 1: **39 YEAR NON-RESIDENTIAL REAL PROPERTY**

The applicable percentage is: (Use the column for the
Month in the First Year the Property is Placed in Service)

Recovery Year(s)	1	2	3	4	5	6	7	8	9	10	11	12
1	2.461	2.247	2.033	1.819	1.605	1.391	1.177	0.963	0.749	0.535	0.321	0.107
2–39	2.564	2.564	2.564	2.564	2.564	2.564	2.564	2.564	2.564	2.564	2.564	2.564
40	0.107	0.321	0.535	0.749	0.963	1.177	1.391	1.605	1.819	2.033	2.247	2.461

[1]Multiply depreciation percentages by original depreciation base.

Source: Rev. Proc. 87-57.

A simplified finding list. The following list provides a quick synopsis of which ADR properties belong to which MACRS classes. It also indicates the depreciable life for each property for alternative minimum tax (AMT) purposes.

Items of depreciable property worth noting under MACRS: For investors in real estate, some items of real property are not real estate for purposes of the revised MACRS but instead receive the benefit of the substantially faster personal property depreciation rates. Real estate investors often use some of the below-listed personal property items.

- *Stoves, refrigerators, apartment furniture, and similar items* are depreciable in the 5-year MACRS class (see 57.0 asset guideline ADR class).
- *Computers, adding machines, typewriters, and photocopy machines* are depreciable in the 5-year MACRS class (see 00.12 and 00.13 ADR class).
- *Office furniture, fixtures, and equipment* are depreciable in the 7-year MACRS class (see 00.11 ADR class).
- *Agriculture machinery and equipment* are depreciable in the 7-year MACRS class using the 150% declining-balance rate (see 01.1 ADR class).
- *Construction equipment* is depreciable in the 5-year MACRS class (see 15.0 ADR class).
- *Single-use agricultural buildings* (such as grain bins and silos) are in the 10-year MACRS class because of specific legislation (see 01.4 ADR class).
- *Land improvements* are in the 15-year 150% declining MACRS class and are described in ADR class 00.3 as follows: "includes improvements directly to or added to land, whether such improvements are section 1245 property or section 1250 property, provided such improvements are depreciable. *Examples of such assets might include sidewalks, roads (paving), canals, waterways, drainage facilities, sewers (not including municipal sewers in Class 51), wharves and docks, bridges, fences, landscaping, shrubbery, or radio and television transmitting towers*" (emphasis added).
- Farm buildings (but not special purpose) are in the 20-year class (see ADR class 1.3).
- *Municipal sewer pipes* are in the 20-year class (ADR class 51).

The ADR Class Life System allows the investor a certain amount of "component" depreciation.

Example:

Planning for a tax "loophole." Zane wishes to purchase a piece of office property for $200,000. Zane has two options.

	Investor		
Asset Breakdown	**Sophisticated**	**Unsophisticated**	**Life**
Building	$100,000	$150,000	39-year Straight-line
Municipal Sewer	$ 5,000	0	20-year Accelerated
Land Improvements	$ 35,000	0	15-year Accelerated
Personal Property	$ 10,000	0	5-year Accelerated
Land	$ 50,000	$ 50,000	Not depreciable
Total	$200,000	$200,000	

Note: *Allocating $50,000 of depreciable assets from 39-year straight-line depreciation to substantially faster 5-year to 20-year accelerated depreciation greatly changes the attractiveness of purchasing real property.*

> ### Tax Tip
>
> The biggest problem with "component" acquisitions is proving to the IRS auditor that the allocation of the purchase price is fairly presented. It is recommended that the buyer break down the purchase price in the purchase-and-sale agreement. "Arm's-length" negotiations between buyer and seller are considered adequate evidence of value in many cases. Otherwise the IRS auditor can simply "reallocate" the purchase price to the detriment of the buyer.

> ### Tax Tip
>
> Investors can easily determine the value of components from professional appraisal books, such as Marshall & Swift's. Contact your local appraiser.

Real estate categories: The last two MACRS classes are for (1) residential rental real property and (2) nonresidential rental (commercial) real property.

27.5-year (straight-line) residential rental real property class. The IRS defines the property to be included in this class as residential rental property such as duplexes, apartment houses, condominium units, and cooperative units used as personal residences, and the like. It specifically does NOT include hotels and motels [§168(b)(3),(c)].

Tax problem: One building containing both residential and commercial rentals must use the 80% gross rent test. The technical definition of residential rental property is a building in which 80% or more of the gross rental income comes from *dwelling units* [§167(j)(2)(B)]. The term *dwelling unit* is defined as a house or apartment used to provide living accommodations, but does not include a unit in a hotel, motor inn, or other establishment in which more than one-half of the units are used on a transient basis [§167(k)(3)(C)].

> ### Investor Hint
>
> Many tax preparers erroneously think that a dual-use property is considered two properties. This is not true, as illustrated in the next example.

Example:

Melvin owns a five-floor apartment complex with a grocery store on the first floor. In 2003, the residential tenants pay him $150,000 a year gross rent, and the commercial tenant pays him $50,000. Even though the residential portion of the building comprises 80% of the total floor space, it is irrelevant. The *total* building must be depreciated as a 39-year commercial building as the residential tenants' gross rent comprises only 75% of the total rental income. Better luck next year, Melvin! ■

> ### Investor Hint
>
> This is a year-by-year test and could result in the taxpayer's being required to switch to the faster 27.5-year residential property method for those taxable years when the 80% test is met!

> ### Tax Tip
>
> For dual-use buildings, the use of "net, net, net leases" for commercial tenants coupled with "gross, gross, gross leases" for the residential tenants many times solves this problem and is becoming more common.

Example:

The author is familiar with a large apartment complex that opened in Minneapolis recently with an exclusive health spa in the basement. All tenants received "free" membership (valued at $100 a month) in the spa *after* the landlord raised everyone's rent $100 per month. Their accountant had calculated that the spa's lease (with percentage lease payments) would exceed 20% of the annual gross rent from the building without this manipulation. [See Reg. §1.163(j)-(3)(b)(2) for the IRS's position on this "tax shelter."]

If any portion of a building or structure is occupied by the taxpayer, the gross rental income from such property shall include the rental value of the portion so occupied [§167(j)(2)(B)].

31.5-year or 39-year (straight-line) commercial real property class. Nonresidential real property is real property that is not residential rental property and that either has no ADR midpoint or does not have an ADR midpoint of less than 27.5 years [§168(b)(3),(c)].

Example:

Commercial property. This category includes office buildings, shopping centers, and residential rental property failing the above-mentioned 80% test or dwelling unit test.

31.5-year life. For acquisitions between January 1, 1987, and May 13, 1993, this commercial (nonresidential) real estate must be depreciated over 31.5 years using the straight-line method.

39-year life. Effective for purchases after May 12, 1993, commercial real property must be depreciated over 39 years using the straight-line method. The alternative minimum tax depreciation rate of 40 years is unchanged.

Effective date. This law generally affects property placed in service on or after May 13, 1993. A transition rule exists: The 39-year rule does not apply to property placed in service before January 1, 1994, if (1) the taxpayer, or a qualified person, entered into a binding contract to purchase or construct the property before May 13, 1993, or (2) construction of the property commenced by or for the taxpayer, or a qualified person, before May 13, 1993. (A qualified person is anyone who transfers rights in such a contract or such property to the taxpayer without first placing the property in service.)

Tax Tip

Residential rental property stays at 27.5 years. Only commercial property was extended to 39 years.

Tax Tip

Investors must continue with the depreciation method used in the first year the property is placed into service. They are not required to switch to the 39-year life for property purchased before May 13, 1993. The useful life for real property depends on the date the real property was placed into service.

The depreciation rates—tables. Figure 10.1 and Figure 10.2 illustrate the applicable MACRS percentage rates for both personal and real property [Rev. Proc. 87-57, IRB 1987-42,17].

Improvements and Components—ACRS and MACRS

After investors reluctantly concede that an expenditure is a depreciable improvement and not a currently deductible repair, they want the improvement to be depreciated over the shortest period of time.

Component depreciation is no longer an advantage. The benefits of component depreciation used on personal or real property were eliminated by ERTA in 1981. *The depreciation expense on any component shall be computed in the same manner as the asset itself is being computed.*

Example:

Pete purchases a used commercial building for $500,000. He immediately rewires the building for $80,000 and replumbs it for $70,000. The $150,000 in improvements must use the same 39-year MACRS method as the building itself.

Example:

Maurice purchases a used commercial building for $250,000 in 2003, buying the components of the property for the following prices:

Building	$200,000
Land	39,100
Air conditioner (a fixture)	3,900
Personal property	7,000
Total	**$250,000**

Because the building is being depreciated over 39 years, the air conditioner must also be depreciated over 39 years, as it is a structural component of the building. Any personal property, (e.g., refrigerators and furniture) could be depreciated over five years. ▇

Added improvements must be depreciated as if they are a new building. The life of any component of a building added after the acquisition shall be the same as the building, but the depreciation shall begin as of either the date the component starts to be used or the date the building starts to be used, whichever is later.

Example (continued):

Maurice, in the above example, is forced to replace the old air conditioner in 2006, after three years, and purchases a new air-conditioning system for $7,800. What is the depreciable life of the new air conditioner?

Answer:

The new air conditioner, being a structural component, is considered a new building, not personal property. Therefore it must be depreciated as if Maurice purchased another building in that year. After May 12, 1993, acquisitions must be depreciated using a 39-year life! ▇

Lessee leasehold improvements. Starting in 1987, leasehold improvements must be depreciated over the life of the property using the MACRS method and not over the life of the lease [§168(i)(6)].

Example:

A terrible tax problem. Hayes leases bare office space in downtown Chicago for a five-year period, with no renewals, and spends $39,000 on improvements before occupancy. Hayes' amortization of the leasehold improvements is as follows:

	Under MACRS	Under ACRS
Year 1	$1,000	$7,800
Year 2	1,000	7,800
Year 3	1,000	7,800
Year 4	1,000	7,800
Year 5	35,000	7,800
Total	$39,000	$39,000

Note. The reason for the $35,000 in year 5 is that Hayes gets his normal $1,000 MACRS plus a $34,000 loss on abandoning his leasehold improvements! This is not a good deal! Economically, Hayes has prepaid his taxes for years 1 through 4, and gets the prepaid taxes back in year 5. ▇

THE ALTERNATIVE DEPRECIATION SYSTEM (ADS) FOR CERTAIN PROPERTY

This optional depreciation system, required for some types of property and electable by all taxpayers, is a straight-line method using substantially longer lives (with the half-month and half-year convention applicable and without regard to a salvage value) [§168(g)].

The ADS recovery period. Generally, the ADS class lives for most property will be as shown below:

In the Case of:	The Straight-Line Recovery Period Shall Be:
(1) Nonresidential real and residential rental property	40 years
(2) Personal property with no class lives	12 years
(3) Property not mentioned in (1) or (2) above	ADR midpoint*

*See column titled "Class Life (in years)" at Rev. Proc. 87-57, IRB 1987,42.

AT-RISK LIMITATIONS EXTENDED TO REAL ESTATE

General rule. The at-risk rules extend to real estate activities for all property placed in service after December 31, 1986. The at-risk rules will continue to be applicable only to individuals and certain activities of closely held corporations.

What are the at-risk rules? The at-risk rules of the current law reflect that, as an economic matter, an investor cannot lose more than the amount that he or she has directly invested plus any additional amount for which the investor is liable. The purpose of the at-risk rules is generally to restrict the use of limited-risk transactions by individual taxpayers who artificially shelter their income from other sources.

Example:

Pat purchases a $100,000 building on leased land, paying a $5,000 cash down payment and giving the seller a $95,000 *nonrecourse* mortgage note for the remainder. At the end of five years, Pat pays another $5,000 on the principal. Assuming a 39-year life, Pat could have a total depreciation expense of $12,824 for the first five years. (Assume a zero cash flow and that the depreciation creates the total rental loss.) Since Pat has only *paid-in-cash or cash-like* $10,000 of the $100,000 owed, Pat's $12,824 depreciation deduction is limited to the *amount invested*—$10,000. If Pat had purchased the building with a $95,000 *recourse* note, he could have added the mortgage to the cash for a total amount invested of $100,000. In that case, the at-risk rules would not have limited any of the $12,824 depreciation deduction. Recourse notes are considered personal obligations and, therefore, for at-risk purposes can be added to the property's basis. ■

A real problem—trust deeds and contracts for deeds. In many states, trust deeds and contracts for deeds are considered nonrecourse financing. In case of default, the holder of the financing instrument can look only to the property for financial protection and cannot get a deficiency judgment in case of foreclosure.

> ### Tax Tip
>
> This makes trust deeds and contracts for deeds risky financing instruments to use in purchasing real estate. Even Congress admits, in the TRA 86 committee reports, that this tax change will require some states to statutorily change the legal concept of both these financing methods. Some states already make trust deeds recourse financing.
>
> This will radically change the way farms and ranches will be sold in the future. To make trust deeds and contracts for deeds unavailable will eliminate most owner-financed sales.

Potential exception—third-party nonrecourse debt. A taxpayer is considered at risk for certain unrelated third-party nonrecourse debt incurred with respect to real estate. This should help large banks but not owner financing.

CONCLUSION

Depreciation is often calculated on property that is appreciating in value. It is one of the remaining tax shelters as it allows the investor to deduct a *phantom* expense against rental income. (But consult Chapter 12 on passive losses when a resulting loss is created.) This chapter illustrates that the depreciation computation, both annually and for the total amount accumulated during ownership, is ascertained simply by consulting a one-page tax rate schedule. Advance planning allows the investor to maximize the depreciation deduction even in light of the negative 39-year life.

11

Office-in-Home Rules

A TAXPAYER MAY WORK OUT OF HIS OR HER HOME

A new nontraditional trend in the business community finds many taxpayers working out of their personal residences. When a portion of a home is used for business purposes, a percentage of the total housing costs of these normally nondeductible personal expenses may be deducted as business expenses by a taxpayer who is an individual or an S corporation.

The purpose of this chapter is to provide the taxpayer with information on calculating and claiming the deduction for business use of home and will help determine:

- whether the taxpayer qualifies to deduct expenses for the business use of home,
- what types of expenses can be deducted,
- how to figure the deduction,
- what records should be kept, and
- where to deduct the expense.

But there are limitations. As Congress feels it is necessary to prevent taxpayers from misusing the office-in-home deduction, it passed a general limitation that disallows *all* business deductions of the taxpayer's residence and then created narrow exceptions that require stringent "exclusive, regular, and principal" rules to be followed before this deduction is permitted.

Investor Hint

No regulations presently exist interpreting the office-in-home deduction. On May 20, 1994, LR-261-76 withdrew Reg. 1.280A-2(b)(2) and (b)(3) and §1.280A-2(B), as proposed on July 21, 1983. These proposed regulations explained the deductibility of expenses attributable to business use of a dwelling unit used as a residence.

STRICT OFFICE-IN-HOME RULES PREVENT ABUSE

To deduct expenses related to the business use of part of the home, the taxpayer must meet specific requirements. Even then, the deduction may be limited. For home office expenses to qualify for a deduction, the portion of the home that is used for business must

1. be used *exclusively* (however, exceptions exist),
2. on a *regular* basis,
3. in connection with a *trade or business*, AND

*in **one** of the following ways:*

4. as the *principal place of business* for any of the taxpayer's trade or business; or
5. as a place of business for meeting or dealing with patients, clients, or customers in the ordinary course of business; *or*
6. in connection with the taxpayer's trade or business if the taxpayer is using a separate structure that is not attached to the dwelling [§280A(c)(1)].

The term *home* includes a house, apartment, condominium, mobile home, or boat. It also includes structures on the property, such as an unattached garage, studio, barn, or greenhouse. However, it does not include any part of the property used exclusively as a hotel or inn.

ADDITIONAL TESTS FOR EMPLOYEES

Two more limitation rules apply to employees. In the case of a home office used by an employee, the employee must also establish that (1) the use of the home office is for the convenience of his or her employer [§280A(c)(1)(flush)] and (2) the employee **does not** rent all or part of the home to the employer and use the rented portion to perform services as an employee [§280A(c)(6)].

1. *The "convenience of employer" rule.* Whether the home's business use is for the employer's convenience depends on all the facts and circumstances. However, business use is not considered for the employer's convenience merely because it is appropriate and helpful.

2. *Employee renting office-in-home to employer doesn't work.* Code Sec. 280A specifically disallows the deduction of any expenses incurred when an employee rents a personal residence to his employer for business purposes [*L. A. Roy,* TC Memo 1998-125]. Therefore, even a home office deduction is barred when an employee leases a portion of his or her home to the employer at fair market value. This rule also extends to an independent contractor who attempts to lease to the party for whom he or she performs services (e.g., a real estate agent should not lease office space located at home to his or her broker/owner) [§280A(c)(6)].

Why would any shareholder/employee lease to his or her employer? To save on self-employment taxes! Despite having a "naked" Schedule E showing nothing other than the rental income, this type of arrangement can still have some positive tax benefits. First, it obviously gets some non-FICA dollars out of the company (i.e., especially where an owner/employee is involved) at a time when the FICA cap is projected to be surpassed, i.e., $87,000 in 2003. This might also lessen the amount that an owner/employee of an S corporation might otherwise have to pay in "salary" to avoid attack by the IRS for setting the payroll at a too "unreasonably low" level.

Self-employment tax is specifically not to be applied where personal property is rented in connection with real property rentals. Many owner/employees could further extend the means by which they seek to get non-FICA dollars out of their C or S corporations by leasing office equipment along with other personal property to their companies. The IRS would like to subject these personal property rentals to Schedule C treatment and, therefore, self-employment tax. Yet, given that the personalty was leased in connection with a legitimate real property rental, this should not be an issue [§1.1402(a)].

Investor Hint

The downside of this strategy might be that the owner/employee would lose the immediate §179 write-off (e.g., $25,000 in 2003) because of his or her status as a "noncorporate lessor" unless certain tests were met to overcome this prohibition.

The Exclusive Rule: The Room Must Be Exclusively Used for Business

What does "exclusive use" mean? Exclusive use of a portion of a taxpayer's dwelling unit means that the taxpayer must use a specific part of the dwelling unit *solely* for the purpose of carrying on his or her trade or business. Therefore, to qualify for business use of the home deduction, there must be a specific room or area that is set aside and used *exclusively* (no personal use at any time during the year, including storage of personal items) on a regular basis as the principal place of any business. The use of a portion of the dwelling unit for both personal purposes and for the carrying on of a trade or business does not meet the exclusive use test [see *Gomez v. Comm.*, TC Memo. 1980-565].

Example:

Joan, a real estate agent, also operates an advertising agency from her personal residence. She may *not* make real estate brokerage calls from her advertising agency home office. ▪

Operating two or more businesses simultaneously out of the same home office.

The judge in *Hamacher* makes clear that two businesses may be exclusively operated out of the same office-in-home. But *each* activity must satisfy all the statutory requirements. For example, real estate brokers or businesspersons with a home office and a second business as a property manager for managing property owned by themselves or others *may* be able to deduct an office-in-home.

> ### *Tax Tip*
>
> If any deduction, such as a home office, is first determined personal, and hence nondeductible, the taxpayer cannot subsequently deduct any business office expenses. Unfortunately, there is not a clear dividing line between deductible business expenses that render passing personal benefits *and* nondeductible personal expenses that incidentally benefit business purposes [*S. A. Bodzin*, CA-4, 75-1 USTC ¶9190].

> ### *Caution*
>
> **Don't take work home.** Work from one business (e.g., college professor correcting student tests) brought home and taken into the office-in-home (that was the sole office of the professor's other business of being an actor) taints the room as a nonexclusive, and therefore a non-business, room [*A. W. Hamacher v. Comm*, 94 TC 348, No. 21].

Space doesn't need to be marked by permanent partition.

The mere absence of a wall, partition, curtain, or the like does not negate this deduction but does raise the level of inquiry by the IRS agent. Also, the act of walking through the home office to another room is not a violation of this rule [PR §1.280A-2(g); *Weightman*, 42 TCM 104, 1981-301; §1.280A-2(g)(1); *C. D. Hughes*, 41 TCM 1153, 1981-140; *Williams v. Comm.*, TC Memo. 1991-567; *Jack Chien Ching Zhuang v. Comm.*, TCS 2002-93].

Exclusive use rule exceptions: Office-in-Home deduction for day care and for storage of inventory and product samples.

The exclusive use requirement does not apply when the home is used for qualified *day care* of children, handicapped, or the elderly (discussed later under *Day-Care Facilities*), and to wholesale or retail sellers *regularly storing inventory or product samples in the home* (e.g., part-time Mary Kay or Shaklee salespeople) [§280A(c)(4); §280A(c)(2); §1.280A-2(e)].

Rules when storing inventory or product samples. When part of the home is used for the storage of inventory or product samples, the exclusive use test does not apply. However, the home worker must meet all the following five tests:

1. The inventory or product samples are kept for use in a trade or business.
2. The business is the selling of products at wholesale or retail.
3. The home is the only fixed location of that trade or business.
4. The storage space is used on a regular basis.
5. The storage space is *separately identifiable space* suitable for storage [§280A(c)(2)].

Example:

Rhonda's home is the sole fixed location of her business of selling mechanics' tools at retail. She regularly uses half of her basement for storage of inventory and product samples. She sometimes uses the area for personal purposes. The expenses for the storage space are deductible even though she does not use this part of her basement exclusively for business.

Example:

Barrister Bill and Dr. Bob store business records at their home. They *cannot* satisfy the storage requirements, as they would fail the "selling a product" requirement and the material being stored is not "inventory or product samples."

How is the "separately identifiable space" requirement met? There is an absence of judicial or IRS guidance on this requirement. Barriers would clearly satisfy, but would lines painted on the basement floor?

The Regular Use Test

Even though no home office case specifically defines regular use, this test implies that the home office is being used systematically throughout the year. Occasional or incidental business use of the home office will not be sufficient, even though the room meets the exclusivity requirement.

Trade or business use. To qualify under the trade or business use test, the homeworker must use part of his or her home in connection with a trade or business. If the home is used for a profit-seeking activity that is not a trade or business, a deduction for its business use cannot be taken.

Meeting patients, clients, or customers at home. Even though the homeworker also carries on business at another location, a deduction for home office will *not* be denied when a taxpayer

- in the normal course of his or her business,
- *physically meets or deals* with patients, clients, or customers in his or her home, and
- their use of the home is substantial and integral to the conduct of the business,

as long as the space is used exclusively and regularly for this business activity [PR §1.280A-2(c)].

> **Caution**
>
> **Make it a sensible percentage.** A tattooer's office occupying 59% of her home, including her entire living room and dining room, her entire bathroom, and the portion of the kitchen containing the sink, was found implausible by the court [*Karan M. Hintze v. Comm.*, TC Memo 2001-70]. A psychologist's 400-square-foot apartment in San Francisco was considered too small to have any space used exclusively to meet patients [*Erin Mullin v. Comm.*, T.C. Memo 2001-121].

> **Caution**
>
> **No "Passive Business" Offices.** These rules makes personal investment activities (e.g., reading financial periodicals, clipping bond coupons, etc.) ineligible for home-office deductions as they don't rise to the level of a "business" activity [*J. A. Moller*, CA-FC 83-2 USTC ¶9698, 721 F.2d 810].

Investor Hint

This requirement may be easier to satisfy than the more demanding "principal place of business" requirement!

The IRS emphasizes that this "physically meets or deals" exception applies only when the taxpayer is actually visited by clients or patients, and will not apply to a room where only phone calls are received and occasional meetings are conducted [§280A(c)(1)(B); *J. W. Green,* CA-9, 83-1 USTC ¶9387]. Many commentators feel the word deal should allow communicating with patients and clients through computers, e-mail, and faxes without the other parties being physically present in the home.

Example:

This qualifies doctors, dentists, attorneys, barbers, beauticians, and even owners of small grocery stores who operate their business from their homes. ■

Example:

June Quill, an attorney, works three days a week in her city office. She works two days a week in her home office, which is used only for business. She regularly meets clients there. Her home office qualifies for a business deduction because she meets clients there in the normal course of her business [IRS Pub. 587, p. 5]. ■

Separate Structures. This exception applies to the freestanding structure apart from the taxpayer's residence if such structure is used exclusively and regularly in the taxpayer's trade or business. To qualify for the exception, it is not necessary that the taxpayer establish that the structure is his or her principal place of business or that it is a place where he or she meets patients, clients, or customers [§280A(c)(1)(C)].

Example:

A guest cottage used as a dentist's office or a separate garage converted into an artist's studio qualifies under this exception. ■

Example:

Jim Caras operates a floral shop in town. He grows the plants for his shop in a greenhouse behind his home. Because he uses the greenhouse exclusively and regularly in his business, he can deduct the expenses for its use. ■

Example:

If Jim's greenhouse was located behind the floral shop, instead of his home, the greenhouse deductions would not be governed by the stringent office-in-home rules (e.g., the exclusive and regular requirements). Instead, the easier to meet "ordinary and necessary" requirements would apply. ■

Principal Place of Business

Prior to 1997, neither the Internal Revenue Code nor congressional committee reports explained what was meant by *principal place of business* and left it to the administrative and judicial branches to define "principal place of business," which they did, much to taxpayers' chagrin, in *Commissioner v. Soliman,* [113 S.Ct. 701 (1993); IRS Notice 93-12; and Rev. Rul. 94-24].

How the Supreme Court defined principal place of business. Essentially, the Supreme Court and the IRS draconianly ruled that the principal place of business is where "client contact" occurs, as that is where the primary income-generation function is performed. This eliminated approximately 95% of the previously deducted home offices. The legislative branch corrected this inequitable result, but only effective for tax returns filed starting in 1999.

Investor Hint

This legislative correction gives small home-based businesses parity with those companies who choose to rent space and deduct the lease payments. Political pundits also claim that it recognizes advances in technology that encourage operating a home-based business, helps cut down on commuting and conserves energy, provides a financial boost to these businesses, helps create jobs, and even is pro-family. At last, tax law with a moral purpose!

Applying the principal place of business test when the taxpayer has only one "regular" business location. If a taxpayer has only one place of business, this is considered the taxpayer's "regular" place of business, a location deemed superior to a principal place of business.

Tax Tip

If this regular place of business is in the home, the taxpayer would have a deduct-ible office-in-home, assuming the exclusive and regular requirements are met.

I R S e x a m p l e :

Danny is a self-employed author who uses a home office to write. He spends 30 to 35 hours of his work time per week writing in his home office. Danny also spends another 10 to 15 hours of his work time per week at other locations conducting research, meeting with his publishers, and attending promotional events. The essence of Danny's trade or business as an author is writing. Danny's research, meetings with publishers, and attendance at promotional events, although essential, are less important and take less time than his writing. Therefore, Danny's office in the home is his principal place of business, and he can deduct expenses for the business use of the home [Rev. Rul. 94-24; IRB 1994-15,5]. ∎

Home Office Definition Expanded—Supreme Court's Opinion in Soliman *Overturned!*

Applying the principal place of business test when the taxpayer engages in business at multiple locations. To reverse the *Soliman* decision, Congress created a simple, two-step test to determine if the home office is the taxpayer's principal place of business. A home office qualifies as the taxpayer's "principal place of business" if the following apply:

1. INSIDE TEST: The home office is used by the taxpayer for the administrative or management activities of any trade or business of the taxpayer, and
2. OUTSIDE TEST: There is no other fixed location of the trade or business where the taxpayer conducts substantial administrative or management activities of the trade or business [new §280A(c)(1) flush language and effective for tax years after December 31, 1998].

Tax Tip

This liberal expansion restores the office deduction to the vast majority of the estimated 34 million business persons who work out of their home, such as

- home-based employees who telecommunicate to the main office,
- doctors who perform their duties in hospitals but need to do their billings from their home offices,
- outside salespeople who call at the customer's places of business,
- professional speakers who prepare at home but deliver the presentation at hotels and convention centers, and
- plumbers and other tradespeople who perform their duties at job sites away from the shop.

Tax Tip

Many taxpayers who have a second business conducted out of their homes will be able to deduct their traveling to and from their "home offices" to their main offices (previously considered nondeductible commuting mileage) under this expanded definition. This topic is discussed later in this chapter.

Congressional examples are extraordinarily liberal. The House Committee Report provides the following examples of the type of taxpayers who will be able to use this new expanded definition of principal place of business. The home office is the "principal place of business" if

1. the administrative or management (A/M) activities performed by the taxpayer outside the home are *not substantial*, even if some A/M activities are performed

at an outside fixed location and even if A/M like activities (e.g., billing activities) are performed by other people at other locations;

2. *substantial nonadministrative or nonmanagement activities are performed outside* the home office by the taxpayer (e.g., taxpayer meets with, or provides services to customers, clients, or patients at a fixed location of the business away from the home office, such as outside salespeople);

3. substantial administrative or management activities are *not performed anywhere* by the taxpayer, as long as the home office is used for *any* A/M activities regularly; even if

4. administrative or management activities are performed at nonpermanent locations by the taxpayer (e.g., in a car or hotel room), in addition to performing those same activities in the home office; or

5. some administrative or management activities are performed outside the home at other fixed locations by the taxpayer, as long as the outside A/M activities are not substantial (e.g., the taxpayer occasionally does minimal paperwork at another fixed location of the business) [see Chairman's Mark, Revenue Reconciliation Bill of 1997].

Investor Hint

Therefore, taxpayers who perform administrative or management activities for their trade or business at places *other than* the home office are not automatically prohibited from taking this deduction. Additionally, in cases where a taxpayer's use of a home office does not satisfy the two-part test, the taxpayer nonetheless may be able to claim a home office deduction under any other provision of §280A.

Special Rules for Home Day-Care Services

A number of unique IRS rules governing the deduction of business expenses for a day-care facility exist that are unlike any other rules applying to home-based businesses. These special rules include the following:

- The home must be used on a *regular* basis in providing day care services.
- There is *no* requirement to use the space exclusively for day care.
- The operator must meet day-care licensing requirements.
- If an area is not used exclusively for day care, the operator must reduce any expenses by the percentage of time the area is not available for business use [§280A(c)(4)].

What is a day-care facility? To deduct expenses for using part of the home to provide day-care services, the following requirements must be met:

1. The day-care operator must be in the trade or business of providing day care for children, persons 65 or older, or persons who are physically or mentally unable to care for themselves.

Caution

The regular, exclusive requirements still valid. Of course, the home office deduction is allowed only if the office is also exclusively used on a regular basis as a place of business by the taxpayer [§280A(c)(1)].

Caution

The employer convenience requirements still valid. In the case of an employee, the home office is only deductible only if such exclusive use is for the convenience of the employer. The question of whether an employee chose not to use suitable space made available by the employer for administrative activities would be relevant to determining whether the "convenience of the employer" test is satisfied [§280A(c)

2. The day-care operator must have applied for, been granted, or be exempt from having a license, certification, registration, or approval as a day-care center or as a family or group day-care home under applicable state law (if any). They do not meet this requirement if the application was rejected or their license or other authorization was revoked [§280A(c)(4)(A)&(B)].

Calculation of business use percentage for licensed day-care providers—regular vs. exclusive.

Day-care providers need only to meet the more liberal "regular use" test, not the "exclusive use" test, to claim a room in the home as business. Those day-care providers who can meet the stricter exclusive (no personal use) test will be eligible for a larger deduction. That is:

- **Formula for exclusive use—space:** If the space is used "exclusively" for day-care operations, providers may allocate expenses based either on the number of rooms or the square footage of the business portion of the home (i.e., just like deducting an office-in-home).
- **The special exclusive use rule:** Many child day-care providers use a play room or a sleeping room filled with cribs *exclusively* for their business. Publication 587 sets forth a unique rule: If the provider regularly uses part of the home *exclusively* for day care, they can deduct *all* the allocable expenses as any other user would do (i.e., no requirement to subtract personal use percentage).
- **Formula for regular use—time and space:** If the day-care provider mixes both business and personal use of the same room, the "regular use" test requires an allocation based on the *time* that the *space* was used for business. This results in a very complicated calculation, a mixture of time and space [§280A(c)(4)(C)].

Space: Only rooms "regularly used" can be included in the day-care facility usage calculation.

If a room is available throughout the business day and is regularly used for day care, the square footage of that room will be considered as used for day care for the entire business day [Rev. Rul. 92-3]. Even though day-care providers have been relieved of keeping contemporaneous time records on a room-by-room basis, they are *not* relieved of keeping records on a day-by-day basis [*S. C. Simpson*, TC Memo 1997-223] and can deduct only the portion of the dwelling unit used regularly for day care [§280A(c)(4)(A)]. They may use the area occasionally for personal reasons. However, a room used only occasionally for business does not qualify for the deduction.

Example:

IRS quote: "Instead of providers having to say, for example, that a bedroom was used three hours a day and the kitchen two hours, they can count the rooms as being used for the total day as long as they are regularly used and available for day care" (IRS spokesman Gail Ellis, AP wire).

Example:

All rooms, even the garage! "A provider who uses her master bedroom for the day-care children to take a half-hour nap in each day is using this room regularly for business. Most providers use their living rooms, kitchens, hallways, dining rooms, pantries and bathrooms regularly for day care." "The garage [detached or attached] should [also] be included . . . when calculating the business use of the home . . . by using it for storage for the [business] car, bicycles, tools, lawn maintenance items, [etc.]" ("The Unique Business of Family Child Care," by Tom Copeland, J.D., *EA Journal,* spring 1996, page 27]. ■

Tax Tip

Because of the above mentioned cases, many child care providers are starting to claim that they are using 100% of the rooms in their home for their business (*The Unique Business of Family Child Care*, by Tom Copeland, JD, *EA Journal*, Spring 1996, page 27).

Example 1:

Kate, a state-licensed day-care provider, uses a bedroom for child care throughout the business day for the children's morning and afternoon naps. Even though the bedroom is not used during every hour of the business day, the total square footage of that room is considered as day-care usage for the entire business day.

Time: Calculate "business hours."

If the use of part of the home as a day-care facility is regular, but *not* exclusive, the provider must additionally figure what part of the available *time* is actually used for business. Providers can count the number of hours that their day-care children were present in the home, *as well as the number of hours spent on business activities when the day-care children were not present* (e.g., hours spent on cleaning, lesson planning, parent interviews, bookkeeping, meal preparation, parent telephone calls, etc., but not hours spent away from the home).

Children do *not* have to be present in the room to be counted. The regular use by the provider of a basement laundry room and storage room to do business laundry and to store items for the business met the definition of regular use, without the presence of children [*Brian Uphus*, TC Memo 1994-71; *Robert B. Neilson*, 94 TC 1, Dec. 46,301].

Tax Tip

35% to 40% is typical for a provider to claim as a total business use percentage of the home ("*The Unique Business of Family Child Care*," by Tom Copeland, J.D., *EA Journal,* Spring 1996, page 27).

The "regular use" formula. *Regular* use requires that the provider calculate two fractions, set forth by the following formula, and best illustrated by an example [§280A(c)(4)(C); Rev. Rul. 92-3]. The formula is (1) the total square footage that is available throughout each business day and regularly so used divided by the total square footage of the home, multiplied by (2) the total hours in the year that the day care is operated (including preparing before and cleaning after normal operating hours) divided by the total number of hours in a year, i.e., 8,760 hours, equals (3) the percentage of time the home is used for business purposes:

$$\frac{\text{Sq. ft. used for day care}}{\text{Total sq. ft. of house}} \times \frac{\text{Hrs. used for day care}}{\text{Total hrs. in yr. (8,760)}} = \frac{\text{Business}}{\text{Percentage}}$$

Example 2:

Kate needs to multiply the total costs incurred during the year with respect to her home (e.g., $10,000 for interest, taxes, utilities, and depreciation), by the two fractions.

The square-foot formula: The total floor area of Kate's home is 1,600 square feet. Although no rooms in Kate's home are used exclusively for the day-care business, several rooms are available for day-care use throughout Kate's business day and are regularly so used as part of Kate's routinely providing day care. The total floor area of these rooms is 1,200 square feet.

The hours used formula: Kate's day-care business is regularly operated 11 hours each day (i.e., from 7:00 A.M. to 6:00 P.M.), five days a week, 250 days a year. In addition, Kate spends one-half hour before and one-half hour after regular business hours preparing for and cleaning up after the children. At any particular time during Kate's business day, she has at least one child (other than her own children) in the house being provided day-care services. The night "stand-by" hours are considered personal unless the room is used exclusively for day-care use. Therefore:

$$\frac{1,200 \text{ sq. ft.}}{1,600 \text{ sq. ft.}} \times \frac{12 \text{ hrs.} \times 250 \text{ days (3,000 hrs.)}}{8,760} = \frac{25.68\%}{\text{Bus. Percent}}$$

$10,000 \times 25.68\% = $2,568 deductible home office expenses

Combining the special exclusive use rule and the regular use rule greatly expands deduction!

Example 3:

Kate has a 1,600-square-foot home with one 200-square-foot room being used *exclusively* for day care. 1,200 square feet of the home is used *regularly* for day care, calculated as using her home 34.25% of the time for her business.

1. Calculate the business use percentage of the *exclusive* use room: 200 sq. ft. ÷ 1,600 sq. ft. = 12.5%
2. Calculate the business use percentage of the *regular* use: 1,200 sq. ft. ÷ 1,600 sq. ft. = 75% × 34.25% time usage = 25.69%
3. Add the two business use percentages together: 12.5% + 25.7% = 38.2% can be claimed as overall business use percentage [*]

[*] Enter this amount on line 7 of Form 8829, leaving lines 1-6 blank. Attach worksheet to Form 8829 showing above calculations.

> ### *Investor Hint*
>
> As the preceding illustration shows, this option can greatly increase the business use percentage!

IRS Examples

IRS Example 1:

Deborah J uses her basement to operate a day-care business for children. Her home totals 3,200 square feet. The basement is 1,600 square feet, or 50% of the total area of the home (1,600 ÷ 3,200). She uses the basement for day care an average of 12 hours a day, 5 days a week, for 50 weeks. During the other 12 hours, the family can use the basement. During the year, the basement is used for day care for a total of 3,000 hours (250 days × 12 hours). The basement can be used 8,760 hours (24 hours × 365 days) during the year. Only 34.25% (3,000 ÷ 8,760) of the expenses of her basement are business expenses. Deborah J can deduct 34.25% of any *direct* expenses for the basement. However, only 34.25% of the basement part of her *indirect* expenses are business expenses. Because the basement is 50% of the total area of her home, she can deduct 17.13% (50% of 34.25%) of her indirect expenses.

IRS Example 2:

Assume the same facts as in Example 1, except that Deborah J also has another room that is available each business day for children to take naps in. Although she did not keep a record of the number of hours the room was actually used for naps, it was used for part of each business day. Because the room was available during regular operating hours each business day and was used regularly in the business, it is considered to be used for day care throughout each business day. In figuring her expenses, 34.25% of any direct expenses of the basement and room are deductible. In addition, 34.25% of the indirect expenses of the basement and room are business expenses. Because the basement and room are 60% of the total area of her home, Deborah J can deduct 20.55% (60% of 34.25%) of her indirect expenses.

IRS MAKES ACCOUNTING FOR HOME OFFICE EXPENSES DIFFICULT

For the self-employed. The self-employed homeworker, when filing Schedule C (Form 1040), must complete Line 30 titled "Expenses for Business Use of Your Home (Attach Form 8829)."

For farmers. Farmers who file Schedule F (Form 1040) report their entire deduction for business use of the home, up to the limit discussed earlier, on line 34 of Schedule F. Write "Business Use of Home" on the dotted line beside the entry.

For employees. Employees must itemize deductions on Line 20 of Schedule A (Form 1040) to claim expenses for the business use of a home and any other employee business expenses. But statutory employees are to use Schedule C (Form 1040) to claim the expenses. The Statutory Employee box 15 on Form W-2 should be checked if the worker is a statutory employee; alternative worksheets other than Form 8829 can be used (see Pub 587 for a sample).

The reason for Form 8829. It is apparent that the IRS wants to prevent the home office deduction from being hidden under some other heading (e.g., office expenses, miscellaneous expenses, or spread throughout Schedule C as interest, taxes, and utilities). In addition, the agency wants to determine if the taxpayer is properly deducting these expenses.

Another reason for Form 8829 is that Congress believes taxpayers are abusing the office-in-home deduction and asked the IRS to analyze the potential misuse. The IRS wants to determine if the taxpayer is complying with the home office limitations and if the calculation is being done correctly.

Tax Tip

Even though an office-in-home deduction may act as a red flag for audit, the author emphasizes that the taxpayer should take *all legitimate deductions.* A red flag doesn't mean an audit is imminent. This material is designed to examine proper tax reporting, and the author emphatically believes in the philosophy of eminent jurist Learned Hand who said that "tax avoidance is a constitutional right." But also keep in mind the consequences faced by ex-Congressman Jim Traficant (D-Ohio): "tax evasion is 'Club Fed' time."

THE OFFICE-IN-HOME CALCULATION—THE FORMULA

When a portion of the taxpayer's personal home is used for business purposes, the fill-in-the-blank worksheet shown next helps determine the business deduction for the office-in-home.

	Total	Personal Percentage	Schedule A*
Casualty losses	____ ×	____ % =	____ *
Mortgage interest	____ ×	____ % =	____ *
Property taxes	____ ×	____ % =	____ *
Insurance	____		
Repairs and maintenance	____		
Janitor or maid services	____		
Utilities	____		
Depreciation (39 years)	____		
Total	____		
Multiply by business percentage	× ____ %		
Office-in-Home deduction	____ †		

*Deduct personal percentage on Schedule A, Form 1040

†Subject to §280A(c)

Calculating the allowable home office expenses. Two types of expenses, direct and indirect, are deducted on Form 8829 when the home is used for business purposes. Any other expenses, such as salaries, supplies, and business telephone expenses, are deductible elsewhere on Schedule C and should not be entered on Form 8829.

Part-year use. Only deductions after business use of the home starts are allowable. For example, if the taxpayer began using part of the home for business on July 1, and meets all the tests from that date until the end of the year, only the expenses for the last half of the calendar year are used in calculating the allowable deduction.

Direct expenses. These expenses benefit only the actual office itself, such as painting or repairs made to the specific area or room used for business. All of these expenses (100%) are entered on the appropriate expense line in column (a) of Form 8829.

Indirect expenses. These expenses are for keeping up and running the entire home. They benefit both the business and personal parts of the home, for example, interest, taxes, roof repairs, and utilities. Generally, 100% of these expenses are entered on the appropriate expense line in column (b) of Form 8829, totaled and deductible only to the extent of the business percentage.

Exception. If the business percentage of an indirect expense is more accurately determined separately, it is to be included as a direct expense. For example, if the electricity of the home office is on a separate meter, or the taxes are itemized between business personal property and home personal property, these normally indirect expenses should be considered direct expenses.

Expense Type	Description	Deductibility
Direct	Expenses only for the business part of home *Example:* Painting or repairs only in the area used for business	Deductible in full (subject to deduction limit) *Exception:* May be only partially deductible in a day-care facility
Indirect	Expenses for running entire home *Example:* Real estate taxes, utilities, and general repairs	Deductible based on the percentage of home that is used for business
Unrelated	Expenses only for the parts of home *not* used for business *Example:* Lawn care, painting room not used for business	Non-deductible

Calculation of business percentage. Previously, the business percentage was determined either by dividing the square footage of the office-in-home by the total square footage of the home (e.g., 200-square-foot office ÷ 3000-square-foot home = 6.67%) *or* by dividing the office room by the number of rooms in the house (e.g., 1 room ÷ 10 rooms = 10%) and using the percentage most advantageous to the taxpayer. No more!

Using the square-footage method because room-by-room allocation is no longer permitted. According to the instructions of Form 8829, the room-by-room method is available only if "the rooms in the house are all about the same size" (i.e., each bathroom is the same size as the living room, etc.), which is a ridiculous requirement. In a recent court case, Edward Andrews claimed a deduction based on the ratio of rooms in the house, but the court determined that the home-office expenses should more reasonably be allocated on a square-footage basis [*E. W. Andrews v. Comm.,* 60 TCM 277, TC Memo. 1990-391; CA-1 91-1 USTC ¶50,211; *A. Swain,* CA-4, 96-2 USTC ¶50,480].

Expense descriptions:

Real estate taxes. Real estate taxes are generally deductible as an indirect expense.

Deductible mortgage interest. Mortgage interest expenses are also deductible as an indirect expense. Second mortgage interest can be included in this computation. If the total mortgage debt is more than $1,000,000 or the home equity debt is more than $100,000, the deduction may be limited, as the home mortgage interest limitations [§163(h)(3)] apply before the office-in-home limitations [§280A].

Casualty losses. If there is a casualty loss on the home used in the business, treat the casualty loss as a direct expense, an indirect expense, or an unrelated expense, depending on the property affected, using the following guidelines:

1. *Direct expense.* If the loss is on the portion of the property used *only* in the business, use the entire loss to figure the business use of the home deduction.
2. *Indirect expense.* If the loss is on property used for *both* business and personal purposes, use only the business portion to figure the deduction.
3. *Unrelated expense.* If the loss is on property *not* used in the business, do not use any of the loss to figure the deduction.

Form 4684, *Casualties and Thefts,* will also need to be filed.

Insurance. The cost of insurance that covers the business part of the home can be deducted as an indirect expense.

Rent. If the homeworker rents, rather than owns, a home and meets the requirements for business use of the home, he or she can deduct part of the rent paid. To figure the deduction, multiply the rent payments by the percentage of the home used for business. The homeworker cannot deduct the fair rental value of the home.

Repairs. The cost of repairs and supplies that relate to the business, including labor (other than your own labor), is a deductible expense. For example, a furnace repair benefits the entire home. A homeworker who uses 10% of the home for business, can deduct 10% of the cost of the furnace repair. Repairs keep the home in good working order over its useful life. Examples of common repairs are patching walls and floors, painting, wallpapering, repairing roofs and gutters, and mending leaks. However, repairs are sometimes treated as a permanent improvement, which must be depreciated.

Depreciation. When the homeworker begins to use part of the home for business, depreciate that part as nonresidential real property under the modified accelerated cost recovery system (MACRS). To figure the depreciation deduction, first determine the adjusted depreciable basis of the home, which is generally its cost, plus any improvements, minus the cost of land and any casualty losses or depreciation deducted in earlier tax years. Next, calculate the depreciable basis of the business part of the home by multiplying the adjusted depreciable basis by the business percentage. This amount is nonresidential real property and under MACRS is depreciated using the straight-line method over 39 years. Only depreciation for the number of months of ownership is allowed in the year of acquisition and in the year of disposition. For example, in the first year the homeowner used the home for business, figure the first year's depreciation for the business part of the home by using the appropriate percentage from the following table.

Partial-Year Depreciation Table
Month of Tax Year

First Used for Business	Percentage To Use
1	2.461%
2	2.247
3	2.033
4	1.819
5	1.605
6	1.391
7	1.177
8	0.963
9	0.749
10	0.535
11	0.321
12	0.107

Multiply the depreciable basis of the business part of the home by the percentage from the table for the first month in the tax year that the home is used for business. In the year of disposition, reverse the table (e.g., if the property were sold in December, the individual homeworker would use 2.462%).

Example:

In May, George Miller began to use one room in his home exclusively and regularly to meet clients. This room is 8% of the square footage of his home. He bought the home in 1990 for $125,000. He determined from his property tax records that his adjusted basis in the house (exclusive of land) is $115,000. The house had a fair market value of $165,000 in May. He multiplies his adjusted basis (which is less than fair market value) by 8%. The result is $9,200, his depreciable basis for the business part of the house.

George files his return based on the calendar year. May is the fifth month of his tax year. He multiplies his depreciable basis of $9,200 by 1.605% (.01605), the percentage from the table for the fifth month. The result is $147.66, his depreciation deduction. ■

Security system. If a security system is installed that protects all the doors and windows in the home, the business part of the maintenance and monitoring expenses may be currently deducted. Additionally, a depreciation deduction may be taken for the part of the cost of the security system improvements relating to the business use of the home.

Utilities and services. The business portion of the expenses for utilities and services, such as electricity, gas, trash removal, and cleaning services, deductible as indirect expenses.

Telephone. These expenses can be deducted even if the homeworker does not qualify to deduct expenses for the business use of the home. *Deduct these charges separately on the appropriate schedule. Do not include them in the home office deduction.*

Example:

The following example illustrates the office-in-home deduction as well as the proper use of the Form 8829 and Schedule C. See Figure 11.1 and Figure 11.2 at the end of this chapter.

Jill, a real estate agent, operates an advertising agency from her 2,000-square-foot home, and makes qualified business use of a 500-square-foot home office, i.e., a 25 percent business use.

Case Study—Office-in-Home Deduction and Limitations

Gross income		$25,000
Less: Expenses for operating agency but not home office		
(e.g., supplies, wages, taxes)		– 24,000
Tentative profit (or loss)		$ 1,000
Less: Home office expenses		
Total interest and taxes	$2,000	
Total other expenses	$2,000	
Total home office expenses	$4,000	
Limit on home office expenses		– $ 2,000
Disallowed deduction	$2,000#	
Net profit (or loss) on Schedule C		($1,000)

Home office expenses	Total	Indirect (25%)
Interest and property taxes	$8,000	$2,000
Insurance, utilities, repairs	$2,000	$ 500
Depreciation (39 yrs.)	$6,000	$1,500
		$4,000

#Carried forward to next year, subject to same limitations.

A HOME-OFFICE DEDUCTION IS NOT ALLOWED TO THE EXTENT THAT IT CREATES OR INCREASES A NET LOSS OF A BUSINESS

If the gross income from the business use of the home equals or exceeds the total business expenses (including depreciation), all the business expenses, including the office-in-home expenses, can be deducted. But if the gross income from that use is less than the total business expenses, the deduction for certain expenses for the business use of a home is limited.

The ordering rule for loss disallowance. The deduction of otherwise nondeductible expenses such as insurance, utilities, and depreciation (with depreciation taken last) allocable to business is limited to the gross income from the business use of the home minus

1. the business part of expenses that can be deducted even if the home was not used for business (such as mortgage interest, real estate taxes, and casualty and theft losses) and
2. the business expenses that relate to the business activity in the home (for example, salaries or supplies), but not to the use of the home itself. The self-employed do not include here the half of the self-employment tax deducted above the line.

Carryover of unallowed expenses. Homeworkers can carry over to the next tax year deductions over the current year's limit, whether or not the dwelling unit is used as a residence during the tax year. These deductions are subject to the gross income limit from the business use of the home for the next tax year. Any unused carryover amounts are lost if the business closes.

Figuring deduction limit and carryover. Part IV of Form 8829 (lines 41 and 42) helps calculate the amount of the deduction limit and carryover. Employees and Schedule F filers must make this calculation on a worksheet.

IRS Example:

Adam meets the requirements for deducting expenses for the business use of his home. He uses 20% of his home for this business. In 2002, his gross income, business expenses, and expenses for the business use of his home are as follows:

Gross income from business	$6,000
Less: Deductible mortgage interest and real estate taxes	
(20% allowable as business part)	−3000
Balance	$3,000
Less: Business expenses other than for use of home (business phone, supplies and depreciation on office equipment)	2,000
Gross income limit	$1,000
Less: Other expenses allocable to business use of home	
1. Maintenance, insurance, and utilities (20%)	800
Limit on further deduction	$ 200
2. Depreciation (20%)	$1,600
Depreciation carryover to 2003 subject to gross income limit in 2002	$1,600

Adam can deduct all the business part of his deductible mortgage interest and real estate taxes ($3,000). He also can deduct all his business expenses other than for the use of his home ($2,000). Additionally, he can deduct all the business part of his expenses for maintenance, insurance, and utilities because the total ($800) is not more than the $1,000 gross income limit. But his deduction for depreciation for the business use of his home is limited to $200 ($1,000 minus $800) for 2002 because of the gross income limit. He can carry over the $1,400 balance and add it to his depreciation for 2003, subject to his 2003 gross income limit. ■

HOME OFFICE CREATES NO GAIN WHEN RESIDENCE IS SOLD

Exclusion of gain available on portion of home used for business! No allocation of gain is required if both the residential and nonresidential portions of the property are within the same dwelling unit. The fact that a residence is rented or is used partially for business (i.e., a home office) at the time of sale does not disqualify the gain attributable to the business use, other than depreciation recapture, from the $250,000/$500,000 exclusion. But the §121 exclusion will not apply to the gain allocable to any portion of property sold or exchanged with respect to which a taxpayer does not satisfy the use requirement if the nonresidential portion is separate from the dwelling unit [§1.121-1(e)(1)]. The final regulations provide that the term *dwelling unit* has the same meaning as in §280A(f)(1) but does not include appurtenant structures or other property [§1.121-1(e)(2)].

Example:

Kate sells her personal residence, which contains her deductible office-in-home, for a $100,000 gain. She estimates that the office occupies 10% of her home. She can exclude the entire $100,000 gain other than the depreciation recapture of $2,000. The $10,000 gain associated with the office-in-home is not taxable [§1.121-1(e)(4), Ex. 5 and 6].

	Total
Sales Price	$300,000
Original Cost	− 200,000
Less: Depreciation	− 2,000
Adjusted Basis	$198,000
Total Gain	$102,000
121 Exclusion	− 100,000
Total Gain	$ 2,000

Depreciation recapture still required on office-in-home! But §121 does not apply to the gain to the extent of any post-May 6, 1997, depreciation adjustments [§1.121-1(e)(1)]. If the depreciation for periods after May 6, 1997, attributable to the non-residential portion of the property exceeds the gain allocable to the nonresidential portion of the property, the excess will not reduce the §121 exclusion applicable to gain allocable to the residential portion of the property. The taxpayer must use the same method to

---

Investor Hint

This is a reversal of prior IRS pronouncements [see previous §1.1034-1(c)(3)(ii)] and Tax Court cases [*Poague, William W.*, DC-Va 90-2 USTC ¶50,539], which ruled if the residence was used partially for residential purposes and partially for business purposes (mixed-use property), only that part of the gain allocable to the residential portion was excludable under §121.

Tax Tip

This makes the office-in-home deduction extraordinarily attractive, i.e., a taxpayer is allowed a current tax break with no future taxable gain at time of sale! No longer does the homeowner need to convert the home office back to personal use for two-of-the-last-five years to eliminate the gain associated with the prior business use, as previously permitted by Rev. Rul. 82-26. Additionally, because taxpayers may elect to adopt these regulations retroactively, this might create a refund for taxpayers who previously reported taxable gain allocable to the business portion of the home in an amount in excess of the depreciation claimed after May 6, 1997.

---

allocate the basis and the amount realized between the business and residential portions of the property as he or she used to allocate the basis for purposes of depreciation, if applicable [§1.121-1(e)(3)].

TRANSPORTATION EXPENSES FROM HOME OFFICE— COMMUTING FROM A HOME OFFICE

A deductible home office often converts commuting mileage to business mileage!

If a taxpayer has a home office that is the principal place of business, each of that taxpayer's business trips from home is considered a deductible transportation expense, as he or she is traveling between different business locations. Because this may amount to a substantial annual tax deduction, it may pay to have an office-in-home. However, if the principal office is at another location (e.g., a real estate office located downtown), the mileage from the home to the *first* business location is a nondeductible commuting trip [Rev. Rul. 190; Rev. Rul. 55-109].

Tax Tip

Beginning in 1999, the liberalized definition of a principal place of business allowed many more taxpayers to deduct their "commuting" costs. Financially, this is a much larger deduction for most taxpayers than the office-in-home deduction.

Example:

Marianne is a real estate broker who is also a professional singer at the local jazz club. As she is the administrative manager of the brokerage firm, with a corner office, any brokerage office-in-home would not be deductible. But as she has no other administrative office for her singing business, and as she conducts substantial nonadministrative and nonmanagerial business activities at a fixed location other than at the home office, her musical home office qualifies. Therefore, if every morning she first performs work duties at her home office before going to her second job site, she will be able to deduct the mileage between her home and her downtown brokerage office. But if she has only one job, the trip from home to the real estate office is a nondeductible commuting trip. ■

A nondeductible office-in-home and the transportation deduction. May a taxpayer still call a nondeductible office-in-home a "principal place of business" and retain the transportation deduction by arguing that he or she is traveling between two places of business? The Tax Court, in one disturbing antitaxpayer case, concluded "because the automobile expenses were incurred in commuting to and from a home office which does not qualify under section 280A(c)(1), the automobile expenses are not deductible" [*A. W. Hamacher v. Comm.*, 94 TC 348, No. 21]. We don't know if *Hamacher* made the argument that a nondeductible office may still be a principal place of business. We would have! At last, so did the attorneys in the following case.

A deductible office-in-home, even in the same metropolitan area, is irrelevant for determining if mileage is commuting. In a more recent pro-taxpayer case, in which the court was clearly presented with the above argument, the court found that even though a taxpayer is not deducting (or cannot deduct) an office-in-home, this does not negate the fact that the office in the home is a regular place of business. Charles Walker did not establish that his residence was his "principal place of business" (a requirement to establish a deductible home office), but he did convince the court that his home was a "regular place of business" (a more liberal requirement). As Charlie was "going between two specific business locations," the mileage between his home and his next business location is a deductible business expense [Rev. Rul. 55-109, 1955-1 C.B. 261]. Charlie kept daily records showing that he spent approximately seven hours per week in the workshop adjacent to his residence maintaining and repairing his equipment, even though no office-in-home deduction was taken [*Charles W. Walker and Cathe R. Walker v. Comm.*, 101 T. C. 537 (1993)].

Example:

Charlie Walker was allowed a deduction from his nondeducted home office to his workplace, the forest, 90 miles one way from his home, as he regularly maintained his saws in his home shop. The IRS disagreed. ■

IRS disagreed with *Walker:* How it interpreted a temporary assignment within a metropolitan area with a regular place(s) of business. The IRS stated that there were only two situations in which a transportation deduction was allowed for expenses incurred in traveling between a residence and a temporary place of business in the same metropolitan area. These situations were

1. when the taxpayer also has a regular place of business that is not located at the taxpayer's residence, or
2. when the taxpayer's residence is his or her *principal* place of business [Rev. Rul. 94-47, 1994-29 IRB 1].

Example:

Charlie Walker (if the IRS had its way), who maintained an office/shop *away* from home, could deduct transportation expenses in going from home to a customer's location. However, if his office/shop were in his residence, the same trip would have been deductible *only* if that residence were also his deductible principal place of business. ■

Tax Tip

As of 1999, Charlie Walker had no problem deducting mileage from his principal residence to the forest as he had only *one* home office—his garage. Why? The IRS stated: "Generally, commuting is travel between your home and a work location. However, such travel is not commuting if you meet . . . the following condition(s): . . . Your home is your principal place of business under section 280A(c)(1)(A) (for purposes of deducting expenses for business use of your home) and you travel to another work location in the same trade or business, regardless of whether that location is regular or temporary and regardless of distance" (Schedule 2106 instructions, page 3). After 1999, this requirement became much easier to meet because of the liberalized office-in-home rules.

FIGURE 11.1   Sample IRS Form 8829

		OMB No. 1545-1266
Form **8829**	**Expenses for Business Use of Your Home** ► File only with Schedule C (Form 1040). Use a separate Form 8829 for each home you used for business during the year. ► See separate instructions.	**200** **66**
Department of the Treasury Internal Revenue Service (99)		

Name(s) of proprietor(s) | Your social security number
517–

Part I   Part of Your Home Used for Business

1	Area used regularly and exclusively for business, regularly for day care, or for storage of inventory or product samples (see instructions)	1	500
2	Total area of home	2	2,000
3	Divide line 1 by line 2. Enter the result as a percentage	3	25.00 %
	• For day-care facilities not used exclusively for business, also complete lines 4 - 6.		
	• All others, skip lines 4 - 6 and enter the amount from line 3 on line 7.		
4	Multiply days used for day care during year by hours used per day	4	hr
5	Total hours available for use during the year (365 days x 24 hours) (see instructions)	5	hr
6	Divide line 4 by line 5. Enter the result as a decimal amount	6	
7	Business percentage. For day-care facilities not used exclusively for business, multiply line 6 by line 3 (enter the result as a percentage). All others, enter the amount from line 3	7	25.00 %

Part II   Figure Your Allowable Deduction

8	Enter the amount from Schedule C, line 29, **plus** any net gain or (loss) derived from the business use of your home and shown on Schedule D or Form 4797. If more than one place of business, see instructions		8	1,000.

	See instrs for columns (a) and (b) before completing lines 9-20.		**(a) Direct expenses**	**(b) Indirect expenses**		
9	Casualty losses (see instructions)	9				
10	Deductible mortgage interest (see instructions)	10		6,000.		
11	Real estate taxes (see instructions)	11		2,000.		
12	Add lines 9, 10, and 11	12		8,000.		
13	Multiply line 12, column (b) by line 7			13	2,000.	
14	Add line 12, column (a) and line 13				14	2,000.
15	Subtract line 14 from line 8. If zero or less, enter -0-				15	0.
16	Excess mortgage interest (see instructions)	16				
17	Insurance	17		500.		
18	Repairs and maintenance	18				
19	Utilities	19		1,500.		
20	Other expenses (see instrs)	20				
21	Add lines 16 through 20	21		2,000.		
22	Multiply line 21, column (b) by line 7			22	500.	
23	Carryover of operating expenses from 2001 Form 8829, line 41			23		
24	Add line 21 in column (a), line 22, and line 23				24	500.
25	Allowable operating expenses. Enter the **smaller** of line 15 or line 24				25	
26	Limit on excess casualty losses and depreciation. Subtract line 25 from line 15				26	
27	Excess casualty losses (see instructions)			27		
28	Depreciation of your home from Part III below			28	6,000.	
29	Carryover of excess casualty losses and depreciation from 2001 Form 8829, line 42			29		
30	Add lines 27 through 29				30	6,000.
31	Allowable excess casualty losses and depreciation. Enter the **smaller** of line 26 or line 30				31	
32	Add lines 14, 25, and 31				32	2,000.
33	Casualty loss portion, if any, from lines 14 and 31. Carry amount to **Form 4684**, Section B				33	
34	Allowable expenses for business use of your home. Subtract line 33 from line 32. Enter here and on Schedule C, line 30. If your home was used for more than one business, see instructions				34	2,000.

Part III   Depreciation of Your Home

35	Enter the **smaller** of your home's adjusted basis or its fair market value (see instructions)	35	
36	Value of land included on line 35	36	
37	Basis of building. Subtract line 36 from line 35	37	
38	Business basis of building. Multiply line 37 by line 7	38	
39	Depreciation percentage (see instructions)	39	%
40	Depreciation allowable (see instructions). Multiply line 38 by line 39. Enter here and on line 28 above	40	6,000.

Part IV   Carryover of Unallowed Expenses to 2003

41	Operating expenses. Subtract line 25 from line 24. If less than zero, enter -0-	41	500.
42	Excess casualty losses and depreciation. Subtract line 31 from line 30. If less than zero, enter -0-	42	6,000.

BAA **For Paperwork Reduction Act Notice, see separate instructions.**   FDIA6902L 10/28/02   Form **8829** (2002)

FIGURE 11.2   ## Sample IRS Form Schedule C

SCHEDULE C (Form 1040)	**Profit or Loss from Business** (Sole Proprietorship)	OMB No. 1545-0074
Department of the Treasury Internal Revenue Service (99)	► **Partnerships, joint ventures, etc, must file Form 1065 or Form 1065-B.** ► **Attach to Form 1040 or 1041.** ► **See instructions for Schedule C (Form 1040).**	**200** **09**

Name of proprietor	Social security number (SSN) 517-

A Principal business or profession, including product or service (see instructions)

Dealer

B Enter code from instructions ► 531210

C Business name. If no separate business name, leave blank.

D Employer ID number (EIN), if any

E Business address (including suite or room no.)► _____
City, town or post office, state, and ZIP code

F Accounting method: **(1)** [X] Cash **(2)** [ ] Accrual **(3)** [ ] Other (specify) ► _____

G Did you 'materially participate' in the operation of this business during 2002? If 'No,' see instructions for limit on losses.... [X] Yes [ ] No

H If you started or acquired this business during 2002, check here .... ► [ ]

Part I   Income

1	Gross receipts or sales. **Caution.** If this income was reported to you on Form W-2 and the 'Statutory employee' box on that form was checked, see the instructions and check here........... ► [ ]	**1**	25,000.
2	Returns and allowances	**2**	
3	Subtract line 2 from line 1..	**3**	25,000.
4	Cost of goods sold (from line 42 on page 2).............................	**4**	
5	**Gross profit.** Subtract line 4 from line 3	**5**	25,000.
6	Other income, including Federal and state gasoline or fuel tax credit or refund	**6**	
7	**Gross income.** Add lines 5 and 6 .... ►	**7**	25,000.

Part II   Expenses. Enter expenses for business use of your home **only** on line 30.

8	Advertising...........	**8**		19 Pension and profit-sharing plans........	**19**	
9	Bad debts from sales or services (see instructions).....	**9**		20 Rent or lease (see instructions): a Vehicles, machinery, and equipment.....	**20a**	
				b Other business property.................	**20b**	
10	Car and truck expenses (see instructions)...........	**10**		21 Repairs and maintenance...............	**21**	
11	Commissions and fees........	**11**		22 Supplies (not included in Part III)........	**22**	
12	Depletion..................	**12**		23 Taxes and licenses....................	**23**	
13	Depreciation and section 179 expense deduction (not included in Part III) (see instructions)...........	**13**		24 Travel, meals, and entertainment: a Travel........................	**24a**	
14	Employee benefit programs (other than on line 19)........	**14**		b Meals and entertainment....		
15	Insurance (other than health)...	**15**		c Enter nondeductible amount included on line 24b (see instrs)..		
16	Interest:					
a	Mortgage (paid to banks, etc)........	**16a**		d Subtract line 24c from line 24b..........	**24d**	
b	Other.....................	**16b**		25 Utilities...........................	**25**	
17	Legal & professional services....	**17**		26 Wages (less employment credits)........	**26**	
18	Office expense.............	**18**		27 Other expenses (from line 48 on page 2)........	**27**	24,000.
28	**Total expenses** before expenses for business use of home. Add lines 8 through 27 in columns............ ►				**28**	24,000.

29	Tentative profit (loss). Subtract line 28 from line 7...................	**29**	1,000.
30	Expenses for business use of your home. Attach **Form 8829**..................	**30**	2,000.
31	**Net profit or (loss).** Subtract line 30 from line 29. ● If a profit, enter on **Form 1040, line 12,** and **also** on **Schedule SE, line 2** (statutory employees, see instructions). Estates and trusts, enter on Form 1041, line 3. ● If a loss, you **must** go to line 32.	**31**	-1,000.

32 If you have a loss, check the box that describes your investment in this activity (see instructions).

● If you checked 32a, enter the loss on **Form 1040, line 12,** and **also** on **Schedule SE, line 2** (statutory employees, see instructions). Estates and trusts, enter on Form 1041, line 3.

32a [X] All investment is at risk.

● If you checked 32b, you **must** attach **Form 6198.**

32b [ ] Some investment is not at risk.

BAA For Paperwork Reduction Act Notice, see Form 1040 instructions.   Schedule **C** (Form 1040) 2002

FDIZ0112L   08/31/02

12

The Purchase and Operation of a Passive Activity

THE PASSIVE LOSS LIMITATION (PAL) RULES

To limit the use of tax shelters by individuals, Congress has placed limitations on the ability of a taxpayer to use deductions, losses, or credits from one business or investment to offset the profits of another unrelated business or investment.

Example:

Kill the tax shelter! Brad can't deduct a $140,000 real estate limited partnership loss against his $150,000 salary, resulting in his annual tax refund being reduced by approximately $37,500! ▨

This congressional barrier is called the "Passive Loss Limitation Rules" (or PAL rules). Taxpayers must "materially participate" in a business to be eligible for most tax incentives and, as such, tax preference benefits are directed primarily to taxpayers with a substantial and *bona fide* involvement in the activities to which the preferences relate. It is this attempt at balancing the halting of investments in tax shelters while encouraging savings and investments in active businesses that led to the vast complexity of the passive loss rules. Therefore, even though Congress wants to continue giving tax preferences, it *does not* want those preferences used against unrelated income.

The §469 Passive Loss Rules—Overview

As a first giant step toward implementing a loss deduction limitation philosophy, Congress simply states that losses (and credits) from passive trade or business activities, to the extent they exceed income from all such passive activities, generally, may not be deducted against other income, such as salaries and wages or interest and dividends. The two major exceptions are (1) the exemption granted real estate professionals [§469(c)(7)] and (2) the ability of middle-income taxpayers to deduct up to $25,000 of rental losses from "actively managed" real estate [§469(a)].

Passive losses (and credits) disallowed in prior year are deductible against current passive income. Any passive activity loss not currently deductible (disallowed) is suspended and becomes deductible in a subsequent year in which the taxpayer *either* has net passive activity income *or* completely disposes of the passive activity property in a taxable manner. In addition, with exceptions, the PAL rules continue to allow losses and credits from one passive activity to be applied against income for the taxable year from another passive activity [§469(b)].

PALs are "triggered" at time of sale. If the disallowed losses are not fully utilized when taxpayers dispose of their entire interest in the activity in a fully taxable transaction, the remaining losses are allowed (i.e., "triggered") in full, even against active income. In addition, losses from earthquakes, fire, storm, and shipwreck and certain other casualty or theft losses are nonpassive deduction losses. These rules also exclude casualty and theft reimbursements from passive activity gross income and exclude capital loss carrybacks from passive activity deductions. This exception does not apply if similar losses recur regularly in the business (e.g., shoplifting losses at Nordstroms or accident losses at Hertz) [§469(g)(1); Notice 90-21].

These "simple" changes greatly influence the way an investor both purchases and operates his or her business and requires convoluted accounting of income and expenses, best demonstrated by an example. The taxpayer must divide his or her income into three separate "buckets," each of which is fully defined on the following pages and illustrated in Figure 12.1.

FIGURE 12.1 **Passive Loss Categories**

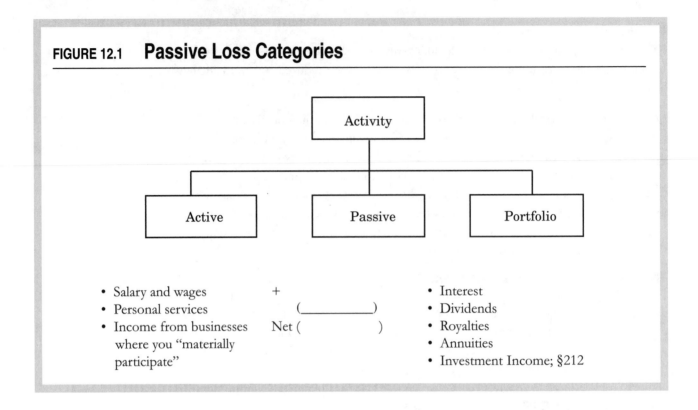

- Salary and wages
- Personal services
- Income from businesses where you "materially participate"

+

(_____)

Net (_____)

- Interest
- Dividends
- Royalties
- Annuities
- Investment Income; §212

Tax Tip

Tax Tip: For tax-planning purposes, it is *very* important to note that the PAL rules are only a "deferral-of-deductions" code section and not a "denial-of-deductions" code section. Theoretically, taxpayers will be able to use these deductions against *all* other income sometime in the future—and get their "prepaid" taxes back!

Example:

Dan is an accountant with a W-2 salary income of $40,000. He is married, has no children and claims $8,000 of itemized deductions. He invests $5,000, plus recourse notes, in a real estate *limited partnership* tax shelter at the suggestion of his real estate broker. At the end of the year, he receives a "K-1" partnership tax schedule from the real estate company reporting that a $15,000 operating loss is allocated to him. Because of the "passive-limitation rule," the total $15,000 loss is nondeductible!

	Activity	
Active	**Passive**	**Portfolio**
$40,000	$15,000	

§469 applies after all other tax treatments. All other tax limitations such as the at-risk rules and the investment interest limitations rules apply first, and thereafter the passive loss limitation rules apply [Reg. §1.469-1T(d)(1)].

BACKGROUND OF DEFINING AN ACTIVITY

Combining, or separating, multiple businesses properly; a tax disaster if taxpayer does this wrong! When applying the passive loss rules, the first, and most important, determination made by a taxpayer is defining how many different businesses (i.e., activities) the taxpayer must report to the IRS on the Passive Activity Form 8582. The taxpayer may aggregate, for passive loss purposes, two or more activities reported separately elsewhere on his or her tax return [§1.469-4(c)]. (Remember, each business must have its own set of books!) But, defining separate activities too narrowly, or too broadly, can either lead to evasion of the passive loss rules or, more tragically, make it impossible for the investor to take advantage of the relief provisions afforded them under the passive loss regulations.

Example 1:

If two businesses are part of the same passive activity (e.g., a tire shop and a lingerie store), the taxpayer may offset the loss of one business against the income of the other business. (Generally, a tire shop and a lingerie store would be considered two separate businesses and the PAL restriction rules would apply to each separately.) ▪

Example 2:

At the other extreme, if one business is deemed two passive activities (e.g., a gas station and a grocery store), potential triggering of loss occurs by selectively disposing of portions of an activity where there has been a loss of value while retaining portions that experience appreciation. However, if the businesses are separate activities (as in the tire shop and the lingerie store), the taxpayer may have to establish material participation for *each* activity to offset the loss of one against the current income of the other. ▪

Reasons for identifying each activity. It is also necessary to identify every separate activity of a taxpayer for the following purposes:

- For determining whether the activity is a rental activity
- For determining whether the taxpayer materially participates in the activity (if the activity is a trade or business)

- For determining whether the taxpayer has completely disposed of his or her entire interest in the activity (to ascertain if the triggering of loss occurs)
- For applying the transitional rules for pre enactment interests in passive activities

Entrepreneur learns, the hard way, why failure to make the "single activity" election leads to "heads, IRS wins; tails, taxpayer loses"! Sidney Shaw, of Stillwater, Oklahoma, owned, or partially owned, through four partnerships (a) real estate investment properties; (b) interests in various business activities, such as convenience stores, gas stations, car washes, and Western Sizzlin' restaurants; (c) gasoline-hauling trailers; and (d) an airplane, receiving a separate K-1 from each partnership. Shaw, or his partnerships, generally purchased and developed the property and *leased* them to Shaw's Gulf, Inc., which managed the day-to-day business operations through on-site managers. Shaw was a 44.9% shareholder, and president, of Shaw's Gulf. He did not take into account the impact of the passive loss rules by making the election to treat each separate business as a "single activity." Instead he created extensive taxable rental income for himself as a landlord while simultaneously creating large nondeductible passive losses as the tenant! Shaw's use of multiple entities in which to operate his various businesses is very common in the business community, and, as will be shown, can be disastrous.

Investor Hint

Tax law greatly impacts the type of entity smart investors must use (or avoid) after the passage of the passive loss rules!

Entrepreneur forgot to group businesses into one activity! Shaw, who participated on both sides of the rental activity (e.g., as both lessor and lessee), did not treat all of his business interests as a single business activity. To avoid the passive loss rules, he needed to materially participate (defined later) in *each* activity (e.g., 500 hours at each of his 50+ businesses[1]), an impossible task. Additionally, Shaw did not materially participate in *each* activity because each activity had a day-to-day manager! To make matters worse, the self-rented property recharacterization rule (explained later) applied to Shaw's rental activities, which resulted in the net rental income from his profitable self-rented property being treated as nonpassive (i.e., active) income and the net rental losses from his losing self-rent property being treated as passive losses [§1.469-2(f)(6)]. In other words, all his businesses that were profitable created "active" income and all his businesses that were generating losses created nondeductible losses, with no offsetting between the activities allowed! Because of Shaw's decision to treat each business entity as a separate passive activity, the IRS essentially said to Shaw: "heads, I win; tails, you lose!" [(*Sidney Shaw v. Comm.*, TC Memo 2002-35].

---

[1] To materially participate in all 50+ activities, Shaw would have to prove he worked a total of 25,000+ hours a year and there are only 8,760 hours in a year!

Tax Tip

When the entrepreneur's profitable businesses generate income that more than offsets the other business losses each year, the "single activity" reporting, as explained in the next section, will generally create the best tax result. Why? By simply treating all his separate businesses as one activity, Shaw would have totally avoided the passive loss rules after working 500 hours!

Tax Tip

Once a taxpayer has grouped or kept separate activities, the taxpayer may not regroup unless the original grouping was inappropriate or a material change has occurred [§1.469-4(d)(2)].

WHAT IS AN ACTIVITY?

Any reasonable method allowed! In spite of the importance of this definition, §469 does not define the term *activity* (e.g., determining how many different businesses the taxpayer owns). As a general rule, the legislative history suggests a definition of activity that entails dividing economic "endeavors" into fairly small units, but Congress, in its infinite wisdom, left to the Department of the Treasury the definition of the term in regulations (which it frustratingly has changed four times since the inception of the law) [see Notice 88-94, Temp. Reg. §1.469-4T; Prop. Reg. §1.469-4; and Final Reg. §1.469-4, adopted October 3, 1994].

It's a "facts-and-circumstances" test. The final regulations allow taxpayers to use a multiple-factor general facts-and-circumstances test that permits them to use any reasonable method when grouping their activities into "appropriate economic units" (non-bureaucrats more commonly call this determining their "different number of businesses"). Even though flexible, the regulations leave the investor with substantially more uncertainty when making the determination of "How many businesses do I have?" The problem is that the IRS feels some test factors are more important than other test factors although it readily admits that there *may be more than one reasonable method* for grouping a taxpayer's activities after taking into account all the relevant facts and circumstances [§1.469-4(c)].

The five most important factors. The factors given the greatest weight when determining whether activities should be grouped together or kept separate are as follows [§1.469-4(c)(2)]:

1. The similarities and differences in the respective types of businesses

Example:

A convenience food store combined with a gas station (e.g., a Circle K store) is commonly considered one business, whereas a lingerie shop selling tires (e.g., a Corset & Chrome Store) would normally be considered dissimilar. ▪

2. The extent of common control between the businesses

Example:

Billy is a partner in Video Variety, a partnership selling videotapes to grocery stores. Billy also is a partner in Madonna Movie Producers, a warehousing partnership principally supplying videotapes to Video Variety and whose largest customer is Video Variety. Both partnerships are located in the same industrial park and are under the same common control. Billy treats Video Variety's wholesale trade activity and Madonna Movie Producers' warehousing activity as one activity [§1.469-4(c)(3)(Example 2)]. ▪

3. The respective geographic locations of each business
4. The extent of common ownership between the businesses

Example:

Charlene has a significant ownership interest in a bakery and a movie theater at a shopping mall in Baltimore and in a bakery and a movie theater at a shopping mall in Philadelphia. Charlene may consider it reasonable to group these four businesses in any one of four combinations:

- *Combining the movie theaters and bakeries into* one single activity;
- *Separating the* movie theaters *into one activity and the* bakeries *into another activity;*
- *Separating the* Baltimore businesses *into one activity and the* Philadelphia businesses *into another activity; or*
- *Segregating them all into* four separate activities *[§1.469-4(c)(3) (Ex. 1)].* ▪

> ### Caution
>
> Activities not "directly owned" by the taxpayer cannot be combined. For example, the activities of a partnership (or S corporation) cannot be combined with similar activities owned by one of the partners (or shareholders) [PLR 9722007]. This is true even when the two businesses are conducted at the *same* location . . . they are *not* owned by the *same* person [*Douglas. E. Kahle,* TC Memo 1997-90].

> ### Tax Tip
>
> It is this extraordinarily liberal interpretation of business(es) that has tax planners salivating. But don't celebrate too early . . . the IRS has extraordinary powers to regroup those activities if the IRS agent feels the original grouping is inappropriate!

5. The interdependencies between the businesses, i.e., the extent to which the different businesses:
   - purchase or sell goods between themselves,
   - involve products or services that are normally provided *together,*
   - have the same customers,
   - have the same employees, or
   - are accounted for with a single set of books and records [§1.469-4(c)(2)(v)].

   See the above "Billy" example under factor 2.

The "any reasonable method" method for grouping also permitted! Remember, other factors may end up being important as the taxpayer may use "any reasonable method" to determine the number of activities. The final regulations clarify that there *may be more than one reasonable method* for grouping a taxpayer's activities after taking into account all the relevant facts and circumstances [§1.469-4(c)(2)].

Consistency rule. Once businesses are grouped together or kept separate, the taxpayer generally must be consistent in the treatment of these activities in subsequent years unless the previous determination was clearly in error (e.g., it was originally inappropriate, or there has been a material change in the facts and circumstances). Then the taxpayer must regroup the businesses and inform the IRS of the regrouping [§1.469-4(e)].

Tax Tip

Business activities reported separately throughout an individual's Form 1040 tax return, e.g., multiple K-1s and Schedule Cs, can still be combined on Form 8582, the passive loss reporting form.

If you made the bed, you must sleep in it! Here is what the Tax Court said in *Sidney Shaw* (TC Memo 2002-35): "[the taxpayer] must accept the tax consequences of his business decisions and the manner in which he chose to structure his business transactions. The Supreme Court has observed that 'while a taxpayer is free to organize his affairs as he chooses, nevertheless, once having done so, he must accept the tax consequences of his choice, whether contemplated or not and may not enjoy the benefit of some other route he might have chosen to follow but did not.' *Commissioner v. Natl. Alfalfa Dehydrating & Milling Co.* (74-1 USTC ¶9456)."

No combining of business and rental activities—unless "insubstantial." No grouping of business and rentals is allowed unless either is "insubstantial" in relation to the other. The problem is that the final regulations do not spell out *insubstantial*. The lapsed temporary regulations contained a "bright-line" 20% test (if the rental income is less than 20% of the combined business and rental income, the rental activity is "insubstantial," and vice versa). It is assumed that this test may be used to help determine if the rental may be an insubstantial part of the business or if the business may be involved in insubstantial rental activities without breaking them into two activities [§1.469-4(d)(1)].

Real property and personal property rentals. Real property rental activities and personal property rental activities may never be grouped together unless the personal property is provided in connection with the real property [§1.469-4(d)(2)].

Tax Tip

This allows most landlords to rent fully furnished apartments to tenants without dividing the business into two rental activities and maintaining two separate sets of financial records.

Grouping when taxpayers rent to their own businesses. The portion of a rental activity that involves the rental of items of property to a business activity may be "grouped" with the business activity regardless of whether one activity is insubstantial in relation to the other, *provided each owner of the business has the same proportional ownership interest in the rental activity* [§1.469-4(d)(1)(i)(C)].

When the IRS can regroup your groupings. The IRS retains broad anti abuse powers "to prevent inappropriate aggregation of traditional shelter activities with other activities." This regrouping is to prevent tax avoidance. The IRS reserves the power to regroup a taxpayer's activities if his or her businesses have been *inappropriately* combined (whatever that means) *and* a principal purpose of the taxpayer's grouping is to circumvent the PAL rules (e.g., taxpayer possesses a dirty mind) [§1.469-4(f)(1)].

Investor Hint

This seems to allow taxpayers to retain their groupings *if they honestly tried to comply* (i.e., a clean mind), even if the IRS auditor considers the groupings inappropriate (i.e., a dirty business)! One tax practitioner told the author that he must group appropriately as the IRS is convinced that tax planners already have dirty minds!

Caution

This leaves a great amount of flexibility for the IRS agent at the time of audit. I doubt the IRS agent would have come to this same conclusion, i.e., one unit, if the rental business were generating a loss that the medical doctors wanted to offset against their active medical income! That is why this determination is inherently unfair.

Example:

Four medical doctors own rental property throwing off losses that are not deductible under the passive loss rules. They form a limited partnership that purchases and operates X-ray equipment at a fairly substantial profit. The doctors make sure of its profitability, as this limited partnership primarily serves only their patients. Is the profit passive, as none of the doctors materially participates in this limited partnership? If so, the doctors have lowered their active medical income by the money flowing to the limited partnership, and this money is converted into passive business income, which is offset by the passive rental losses (normally not currently deductible). ■

This proposed regulation determines that the limited partnership and the medical practice are one "appropriate economic unit," thereby making the X-ray operations active income, with the result that there is no passive income to offset the rental losses. In addition, if the IRS determines that it appears the limited partnership was created to circumvent the passive loss rules, the 20% (or more) substantial tax understatement penalties [§6662] may be imposed [§1.469-4(f)(2)]!

Corporation and partnership groupings. Once a corporation (including a personal service and a closely held corporation) or a partnership to which §469 applies has grouped its activities, a shareholder or partner may group those activities with each other, with activities conducted directly by the shareholder or partner, and with activities conducted through other entities in accordance with these same activity rules. But a shareholder or partner may not treat activities grouped together by the entity as separate activities [§1.469-4(d)(5)(i)].

Tax Tip

Because of the last sentence, corporations and partnerships generally should create as many entities as possible. This allows the shareholder or partner the flexibility to combine activities in a manner most advantageous to the taxpayer.

Because closely held and personal service C corporations are separate taxable entities, "an activity that a taxpayer conducts through a C corporation subject to §469 may be grouped with another activity of the taxpayer, but only for purposes of determining whether the taxpayer materially or significantly participates in the other activity" [§1.469-4(d)(5)(ii)].

Special rules when activity is conducted through limited partnerships. Limited partners and certain limited entrepreneurs may not group specifically designated activities with any other activities unless they are the same type of business or meet the "facts-and-circumstances" test. For limited partners involved in (a) holding, producing, or distributing motion picture films or videotapes; (b) certain types of farming activities (commonly known as "tax shelter farm" activities); (c) leasing any §1245 personal property; (d) exploring for, or exploiting, oil and gas resources; or (e) exploring for, or exploiting, geothermal deposits, these may be combined only with activities of the *same type of business* (whether or not these other activities are also owned as limited partnership interests) if appropriate [§1.469-4(d)(3)].

Because it is required, for PAL purposes, to calculate the income and loss of *each* activity conducted by the individual, partnership, S corporation, or small C corporation, the next step involves the actual calculation of the passive loss or passive gain. This requires knowing the difference between (1) an active activity, (2) a portfolio activity, and (3) a passive activity.

WHAT IS AN ACTIVE ACTIVITY?

A business where a taxpayer materially participates is an active activity. An activity is determined to be active as long as the taxpayer materially participates in a trade or business and the business is not a rental activity [§1.469-1T(e)(1)]. The definitions of *material participation, trade or business,* and *rental activity* are discussed later.

A business where a taxpayer provides personal services is an active activity. Personal service income is generally defined for passive loss purposes as gross income that is treated as "earned income" from the fields of health, law, engineering, architecture, accounting, actuarial services, performing arts, or consulting [§911(d)(2)(A)]. Personal service income includes all amounts paid to an individual for services performed by the individual. It does not include an individual's share of partnership or S corporation income, even if a substantial portion of the income from the activity is attributable to services performed by the individual [§469(e)(3); §1.469-2T(c)(4)(i)].

WHAT IS A PORTFOLIO ACTIVITY?

Portfolio income generally consists of income from investments other than those in trades or businesses. Portfolio activities normally give rise to income and are not likely to generate losses.

Why did Congress create a portfolio activity? To permit interest and dividend income to be offset by passive losses would create the inequitable result of restricting sheltering by wage earners, while permitting sheltering by those with investment portfolio income. It is for this reason that the §469 limitation rules restrict passive losses to be offset only against passive income and not against "active" or "portfolio" income.

What is "portfolio income"? Amazingly, the term *portfolio income* is not even used in §469 but it is defined in the regulations [at §1.469-2T(c)(3)] as all gross income, other than income derived in the ordinary course of a trade or business that is attributable to the following:

1. *Interest income* on debt obligations (including amounts treated as interest relating to certain payments to partners for the use of capital).

2. *Dividend income* from regular C corporation stock (e.g., AT&T stock) and S corporation stock, as well as income (including dividends) from real estate investment trusts (REITs), regulated investment companies (RICs), real estate mortgage investment conduits (REMICs), common trust funds, controlled foreign corporations, qualified electing funds, or cooperatives.

3. *Royalty income,* including fees and other payments for the use of intangible property, but not "earned income" royalties (e.g., book and music royalties by original authors). Generally, taxpayers may not treat "mineral royalties" as derived in the ordinary course of a trade or business without obtaining a ruling.

4. *Annuity income* earned on funds set aside for future use in an activity (but not retirement annuity income).

5. *The gains (or losses) from sale of assets producing the above* interest, dividend, or royalty income.

6. *Gains (or losses) from the sale of §212 investment property,* such as unimproved raw land and vacation homes (but not the sale of active depreciable trade or business property or the sale of passive activity property) [§469(e)(1)(A)(ii)].

7. *Dealer's investment gain or income.* Normally, dealer income is considered active income. But if a dealer held property as an investment *at any time* before the income or gain is recognized, the income will be considered portfolio income. Sadly, any loss from such property remains passive or active, depending upon the level of participation of the taxpayer [§1.469-2T(c)(3)(iii)(A)].

8. Portfolio income from a passive activity is taken into account separately from other items relating to the activity. For example, interest income earned from a

business's setting aside funds for the future use of the business (e.g., interest earned on working capital funds) is portfolio income.

Example:

If a general partnership, such as a construction firm, owns a portfolio of appreciated stocks and bonds and also conducts a business activity, a part of the gain on sale of a partnership interest would be attributable to portfolio income and would, consequently, be treated as portfolio income. ■

Tax Tip

Any gross income that is excluded from the passive activity classification because it is a portfolio activity is automatically taken into account as "investment income" for purposes of computing the §163(d) investment interest limitations [§163(d)(5)(A)].

PASSIVE ACTIVITIES: ONLY TWO ACTIVITIES ARE CONSIDERED PASSIVE

Generally an activity is a passive activity for a taxable year if the activity is

1. a *"rental activity"* without regard to whether or to what extent the taxpayer participates at all in such activity (therefore, a rental activity is treated as a passive activity regardless of the level of the taxpayer's participation) and
2. a *"trade or business activity"* in which the taxpayer does not materially participate for such taxable year.

A special $25,000 relief provision for rental real estate activities may permit a moderate-income taxpayer to offset a portion of nonpassive income with losses from the rental real estate, even though this is a passive activity.

PASSIVE ACTIVITY 1: RENTAL ACTIVITIES

A rental activity is any transfer of property for compensation. With some major exceptions, an activity is a rental activity for a taxable year if

1. during the taxable year, tangible property held in connection with the activity is used by customers or held for use by customers; and
2. the gross income attributable to the conduct of the activity during the tax year represents amounts paid principally for the use of the tangible property [§469(j)(8); §1.469-1T(e)(3)].

When is a rental activity really a business? The real complexity of the passive loss rules, in light of the above definition, is in making the determination whether a particular activity is a "rental activity," a "trade or business," or an "investment." The regulations exclude from the definition of a rental activity those activities in which the importance of providing services to customers outweighs the importance of providing tangible property to customers (i.e., normally a hotel is a business, not a rental activity). It is important to note that substance controls over form, and use of a legal document stating that a relationship is a lease is irrelevant.

Six Exceptions—Activities That Are *Not* Rental Activities

If *any one* of the following six tests is met, the activity will not be treated as a rental activity even though it involves the rental of tangible property [Reg. §1.469-1T(e)(3)(ii)].

Tax Tip

The following definitions have no relief provision, as is granted to many of the other rules [§1.469-4(b)(2)].

---

1. When average tenant use is 7 days or less, it is a business. Rental of tangible property for an "average period of customer use" of seven days or less is not a rental activity.

Tax Tip

Because of this regulation, most vacation condominiums are considered a business, not a rental, which therefore makes them *ineligible* for the $25,000 relief provisions. Most tenant use of vacation homes averages less than seven days!

Average period of customer use is defined as the aggregate number of days of customer use (*not* the number of *days available for rent!*) during the taxable year divided by the actual number of periods of customer use. When rent varies during the year (e.g., a high season rate and a low season rate), a weighted average is calculated wherein the "average period of customer use" equals the *sum* of the average use of each class of property [§1.469-1(e)(3)(iii)].

Example:

Jill uses her vacation condominium two weeks a year and leaves the property in the hands of a property manager for the other 50 weeks. The property manager rents it to five different families for a total of 30 days. The average period of customer use is six days (30 days divided by five periods). Therefore, Jill does *not* have a rental—it is a trade or business—and the $25,000 real estate relief provision (discussed *in* toward the end of this chapter) is *not* available to her for that taxable year. ■

> ### Tax Tip
>
> Therefore, most hotels, motels, U-hauls, Hertz rent-a-cars, flea markets, and the like are not rental activities. They are "trade or business activities."

2. When the average tenant use is greater than seven days but not greater than 30 days and significant personal services are provided, it is a business. Rental of tangible property for an average customer use of 30 days or less is not a rental activity if significant personal services (i.e., maid service, registration service, room service, etc.) are provided by the owner (or on behalf of the owner) in connection with making the property available for customer use.

> ### Tax Tip
>
> For vacation homes, if the average tenant use is less than 30 days but maid services are provided, vacation condominiums are still considered a business, not a rental, which therefore makes them *ineligible* for the $25,000 relief provision! The result is that most vacation homes probably do not qualify for the $25,000 annual deduction [*Floyd A. Toup,* 66 TCM 370, TC Memo 1993-359].

How "significant" must the personal services be? The term *significant* means that, at a minimum, the personal services must be (based on all the facts and circumstances) provided frequently, the type and amount of labor required to perform them must be significant, and their value relative to the rent charged for the use of the property must be significant [§1.469-1T(e)(3)(iv)].

What are personal services? Personal services include only services other than "excluded services" performed by individuals, not artificial entities such as corporations and partnerships. The term *excluded services* means

- services necessary to permit the lawful use of the property,
- services performed in connection with the construction of improvements (i.e., repairs), and
- services commonly provided in connection with long-term rentals of high-grade commercial or residential real property (e.g., cleaning and maintenance of common areas, routine repairs, trash collection, elevator services, and security at entrances or perimeters) [§1.469-1T(e)(3)(iv)(B)].

3. If extraordinary personal services are provided to the tenant, it is a business.
Rental of tangible property (without regard to average period of customer use) when extraordinary personal services are provided is not a rental activity.

Tax Tip

Therefore, most rentals of 30 days or longer will generally be considered long-term rentals and generally treated as rental activities, not business activities, unless extraordinary personal services are provided (discussed next) [TAM 9343010].

Extraordinary personal services are services provided in connection with making property available for use by customers only if the services are performed by individuals and the *use of the property is incidental* to the receipt of the services. A corporation or partnership cannot perform these extraordinary services [§1.469-1T(e)(3)(v)].

Example:

Hospital boarding houses and college dormitories are not deemed rentals, as the rental activity is usually incidental to the supplying of medical or educational services. ▨

4. If the rental is incidental to the business activity, the rental also is a business.

The rental of tangible property that is simply incidental to a business activity will not be tainted as a rental activity. This "relief" provision applies only to the following *three* activities [§1.469-1T(e)(vi)(A)]:

1. *Rental property that is normally treated as an investment—a tax problem with renting out raw land.* The rental of property is treated as incidental to an investment activity if the principal purpose is to realize gain from its appreciation and the gross rental income is less than 2% of the *lesser* of the property's unadjusted basis or fair market value [§1.469-1T(e)(3)(vi)(B)].

Example:

Bill Sunpade owns unimproved land with an unadjusted basis of $200,000. The land has a fair market value of $300,000 in 2003 and a fair market value in 2004 of $325,000. Bill is holding the land principally for appreciation. The local chapter of The Future Farmers of America talks Bill into renting it the land at a nominal amount so that it can raise sheep for the annual county fair. The FFA members pay Bill $3,500 in lease payments in 2003 and $4,500 in 2004.

In 2003, the lease is not a rental activity because $3,500 is less than $4,000 (i.e., 2% of $200,000). Any related interest and taxes on the unimproved land is generally deductible on Bill's Schedule A as an investment activity.

The tax problem.

But in 2004, the FFA lease is now a passive rental activity separate from the holding of the land for appreciation because $4,500 is more than the maximum $4,000 allowable. If Bill has a large amount of interest and taxes on this unimproved "passive" property, he may find the amount in excess of the rental income as currently nondeductible and be required to carry it forward. ▨

2. *The occasional renting out of idle business property—a tax problem with renting out occasional vacant office space.* The rental of property is treated as incidental to a trade or business activity if

- the taxpayer owns an interest in the trade or business during the taxable year;
- the property was predominantly used in the trade or business during the taxable year or at least two of the five preceding taxable years; *and*
- the gross rental income is less than 2% of the *lesser* of the property's unadjusted basis or fair market value [§1.469-1T(e)(3)(vi)(C)].

Tax Tip

This "relief" provision creates the same tax problem as experienced by those renting out the previously-mentioned "raw land" relief provision, e.g., if the taxpayer has a large amount of expenses (e.g., taxes, insurance, repairs, janitorial, etc.), he or she may find the amount of prorated expenses in excess of the rental income as currently nondeductible and be required to carry it forward.

---

3. *Lodging is furnished to tenant for convenience of employer.* Providing employee (or spouse) lodging supplied for the employer's convenience (see §119) is incidental to the business of the taxpayer in which the employee performs services [§1.469-1(e)(3)(vi)(D)].

5. When the business activity is renting to customers—the "Tools-R-Us" exception.
Property customarily made available during defined business hours for nonexclusive use by various customers *is not a rental activity* [§1.469-1T(e)(3)(ii)(E)].

Example:
The payment of greens fees or renting a golf cart at a golf course and the renting of beach towels and umbrellas at the ocean are all business activities, not rental activities. ■

6. When the owner provides property to a partnership or S corporation, the rental is a business—the "cropshare leasing" disaster.
If the taxpayer owns an interest in a partnership, S corporation, or joint venture that is not conducting a rental activity, and provides property for use in the activity "in the capacity as an owner," the providing of such property will not be considered a rental activity. Answering the question of "capacity as an owner" is based on all the facts and circumstances [§1.469-1T(e)(3)(ii)(F)].

For example, if a partner contributes the use of property to a partnership, none of the partner's distributive share of partnership income will be considered as income from a rental activity [§1.469-1T(e)(3)(vii)].

A rental activity that is not a passive activity—certain vacation homes.
An activity involving the rental of a dwelling unit that is used as a residence by the taxpayer during the taxable year [within the meaning of §280A(c)(5)] is not a passive activity of the taxpayer for such year [§1.469-1T(e)(5); *Fudim v. Comm.,* TC Memo 1994-235; *Dinsmore v. Comm.,*TC Memo 1994-135].

Caution

The taxpayer makes farmland available to a tenant farmer via a "cropshare lease." The taxpayer is obligated to pay 50% of the costs incurred in the activity (without regard to whether any crops are successfully produced or marketed) and is entitled to 50% of the crops produced (or 50% of the proceeds from marketing the crops). The taxpayer is treated as providing the farmland for use in a farming activity conducted by a joint venture in the taxpayer's capacity as an owner of an interest in the joint venture. Accordingly, the taxpayer is not engaged in a rental activity, without regard to whether the taxpayer performs any services in the farming activity [Reg. §1.469-1T(e)(3)(viii) (Example 8)]. What a disaster this can be for the retired farmer living in a retirement village 1,000 miles from the farm!

PASSIVE ACTIVITY 2: TRADE OR BUSINESS ACTIVITY WHERE TAXPAYER DOES NOT MATERIALLY PARTICIPATE

The second passive activity (a rental activity being the first) is a trade or business activity in which the taxpayer does not materially participate for the taxable year.

The answers to three questions determine if a business activity is an active or passive activity. An activity is determined to be an active activity if the taxpayer is able to answer yes to the following three questions [§1.469-1T(e)(1)]:

1. Is the business not a rental activity (as previously defined)?
2. Is the activity a trade or business?
3. Did the taxpayer "materially participate"?

A *no* answer to any of these questions may relegate the property to the passive classification.

What is a "trade or business"? An activity is a trade or business activity for a taxable year if

1. the activity involves the conduct of a trade or business (i.e., a §162 business that is not a §183 hobby business or a §212 investment business);
2. it is an activity in which research or experimental expenditures deductible under §174 [or §174(a)] are treated as a trade or business; *or*
3. future regulations deem the activity as a trade or business (e.g., certain §212 investment activities deemed trade or business); *and*
4. it is not a rental activity [§1.469-1(e)(2); §1.469-4(b)(1)].

What is "material participation"? Material participation in a trade or business activity is participation on a "regular, continuous, and substantial" basis. The regulations separately define the words *participation* and *material* [§469(h)(1)].

What is "participation"? Participation is any work done by an individual *in any capacity,* management or operations, in connection with an activity in which the individual owns an interest (directly or indirectly other than through a C corporation) at the time the work is done. Thus, work done by an individual in an activity in the individual's capacity as an employee of a related or unrelated employer is counted as participation in the activity [§1.469-5(f)(1)].

- *Owner can "tack" spouse's time.* Any participation by one spouse is attributed to the other spouse, even if no joint return is filed and/or the participating spouse has no ownership interest in the activity. In effect, therefore, material participant status of both spouses is determined as though the two spouses were one individual [§1.469-5T(f)(3)].
- *When management does not count—work not customarily performed by an owner.* Management time is disregarded when determining participation if it is *not* a type "customarily performed" by owners (e.g., Magic Johnson acting as a security guard at one of his movie theaters) *and* one of the principal purposes of such work is avoiding the PAL rules [§1.469-5T(f)(2)(i)].

- *When management does not count—only counting the money.* If the total amount of the taxpayer's involvement is studying and reviewing financial statements, preparing or compiling summaries or analyses of the finances or operations of the activity for the individual's own use, and monitoring the finances or operations of the activity in a nonmanagerial capacity, this management time is ignored [§1.469-5T(f)(2)(ii)].

How do individuals prove participation? Keep good time records. The extent of an individual's participation may be established by any reasonable means. Contemporaneous daily time reports, logs, or similar documents are not required if the extent of such participation may be established by other reasonable means. Reasonable means include, but are not limited to, the identification of services performed over a period of time and the approximate number of hours spent performing such services during such period, based on appointment books, calendars, or narrative summaries [§1.469-5T(f)(4)].

Tax Tip

Remember, the burden of proof is on the taxpayer to prove he or she did (or did not) work 500 hours a year! Taxpayers will find the courts difficult to convince without good records [*Goshorn v. Comm.*, 66 TCM 1499, TC Memo 1993-578; *Toups v. Comm.*, 66 TCM 370; TC Memo 1993-359; *Sidney Shaw v. Comm.*, TC Memo 2002-35; *William C. Fowler v. Comm.*, TC Memo 2002-223]. The author guesses that the same number of taxpayers who fill in the auto log will keep this time log!

Caution—vacation home investors. The courts have consistently found that taxpayers cannot materially participate in a condominium hotel activity not located in their immediate vicinity. Because a vacation condominium usually has full-time staff, taxpayers have to prove they materially participated, other than as "investors," for at least 500 hours (discussed next). For example, Professor Scheiner was a board member, which constituted "investor participation," but failed to prove material participation [*Barry H. Scheiner*, TC Memo 1996-554; also see *J.V. Patterson v. Comm.*, TCS 2002-57]. Also, Robert Serenbetz could not deduct rental activity losses involving an out-of-state condominium partnership because he did not "materially participate"; full-time condominium staff managed the day-to-day rental operations and (his) activities of preparing tax returns, reviewing budgets, attending partner meetings, and paying bills were considered "investor activities" [*Robert Serenbetz v. Comm.*, TC Memo 1996-510; also see *Braniskis v. Comm.*, TC Memo 1999-258].

Tax Tip

One winner: In *G. Pohoski v. Comm.* [TC Memo 1998-17], the taxpayers convinced the court that they spent more time, 200 hours annually, than did their management firm in maintaining their condo, therefore meeting the 100-hour test. Key to the decision was the rejection of the IRS's contention that the time the front desk was open should count as time for the management firm!

ESTABLISHING MATERIAL PARTICIPATION

An individual is treated as participating "materially" in an activity for the taxable year if the individual's participation meets *one* of the following six tests or a seventh residual test based on all of the facts and circumstances [§1.469-5T(a)(1)-(7)].

How to "Materially Participate" (MP) Using Any of the Four "Time" Tests

1. Work 500 hours in the business. An individual participating in the activity for more than 500 hours during the taxable year is materially participating in that activity. This 500-hour test cannot be annualized in the first (short) year, thereby making it difficult, if not impossible, to use the 500-hour test if the business starts in the last three months of the year, e.g., 12 weeks × 40 hours per week = 480 hours [*Steven A. Gregg v. Comm.*, 2001-1 USTC ¶50,169 (DC Ore.)].

Tax Tip

There is no requirement that the 500 hours be spread throughout the year. Therefore it seems that the statutory language "regular and continuous" is not required.

Tax Tip

This test may be unthinkable to use when a taxpayer reports multiple businesses as separate activities on Passive Activity Loss Limitation Form 8582. As discussed at the beginning of this chapter, Sidney Shaw found it impossible to materially participate in the 50+ businesses he partially or wholly owned (50 × 500 hours = 25,000 hours per year would be required).

---

2. Do substantially all the work—the "cottage industry" relief provision. When an individual's participation in the activity for the taxable year constitutes *substantially all* (e.g., more than 70% of the total business hours for the year are performed by the owner) of the participation in such activity (including nonowner employees) for such year, the individual is materially participating in the activity.

Tax Tip

This test does allow a taxpayer to materially participate in an activity even when participating less than 100 hours a year. But it's apparent that the regulations discourage joining with other partners or employees. Therefore, this is of restricted use—to those Schedule C taxpayers or independent contractors with limited staff.

---

3. Work 100 hours and no one in the firm does more. An individual participating in the activity for more than 100 hours during the taxable year is materially participating so long as such individual's participation in the activity for the taxable year is not less than that of any other individual (including nonowner employees) for such year.

Example:

Bob and Carl are partners in a van conversion activity. The activity is conducted only on weekends because both partners hold full-time jobs during the week. Bob and Carl keep a daily log showing that Bob recorded 250 hours and Carl recorded 251 hours during the year. This example illustrates how capricious this rule is. As Carl worked one hour more than Bob, only Carl would be considered to "materially" participate. The result is that one partner is active while the other partner is passive in the same van conversion activity!

Tax problem.

If both Bob and Carl work exactly 250 hours, would both be deemed to materially participate, as "no one did more"? Is there any IRS auditor who will accept two time logs reporting exactly 250 hours? ■

Tax Tip

If, in the above example, Carl were an employee, Bob would *not* have materially participated. The employee did more work during the year than the owner.

Tax Tip

Most owners of time-share condominiums try to use this 100-hour argument to prove material participation, but without much success [*Toups v. Comm.*, 66 TCM, TC Memo 1993-359; *Barry H. Scheiner*, TC Memo 1996-554; *Robert Serenbetz*, TC Memo 1996-510].

---

4. Working 500 hours in all the multiple small businesses owned. An individual is deemed to materially participate when the activity is a "significant participation activity" (SPA) for the taxable year, *and* the individual's aggregate participation in all SPAs during such year exceeds 500 hours.

Investor Hint

This test is to be used by those taxpayers who have their fingers in many pies.

What is a "significant participation activity" (SPA)? An SPA is any trade or business in which the individual participates for more than 100 hours during the year but does not materially participate (i.e., for 500 hours) for the taxable year [§1.469-5T(c)]. In other words, activities that the individual has materially participated in during the year cannot also be an SPA in the same year [*Steven A. Gregg v. Comm.*, 2001-1 USTC ¶50,169 (DC Ore.)].

Example:

Win Erluze owns interests in three trade or business activities, X, Y, and Z. Win does not materially participate in any of these activities for the taxable year but participates in activity X for 210 hours, in activity Y for 160 hours, and in activity Z for 135 hours. Win has no other significant participation passive activities. Win's net passive income (or loss) for the taxable year from activities X, Y, and Z is as follows:

	X	Y	Z	Total
SPA gross income	$600	$700	$900	$2,200
Less: SPA deductions	− 200	−1,000	− 300	−1,500
Equals: SPA income (loss)	$400	($ 300)	$600	$ 700

As X, Y, and Z are "significant participation activities" for the taxable year (Win participated for more than 100 hours but did not materially participate, i.e., for 500 hours), and Win's aggregate participation in all "significant participation activities" during such year exceeds 500 hours (505 hours), Win is considered to be materially participating in all three activities.

How to "Materially Participate" (MP) Using Either of the Two Long-Standing (or "Look-back") Participation Rules

1. Materially participate for five of the last ten years.
An individual is treated as materially participating in an activity if that individual materially participates in it (without regard to this rule) for any five taxable years (whether or not consecutive) during the ten taxable years that immediately precede the taxable year (including taxable years before 1987). To determine whether an individual materially participated in any activity for a taxable year beginning before January 1, 1987, only the 500-hour rule (test 1 above) may be used [§1.469-5(j)].

Example:

In 1999, Robin Banks acquires stock in an S corporation engaged in a trade or business activity. For every taxable year from 1999 through 2003, Robin is treated as materially participating (without regard to the five-of-the-ten-years rule) in the activity. Robin retires from the activity at the beginning of 2004 and does not materially participate in the activity during 2004 and subsequent taxable years. Under the five-of-the-ten-year rules, however, Robin is treated as materially participating in the activity for taxable years 2004 through 2008 because he materially participated in the activity for five taxable years during the ten taxable years that immediately precede each of those years. Robin is not treated as materially participating in the activity for taxable years after 2008 under the five-of-the-ten-years rule.

2. Materially participate in any three previous years in a "personal service activity."
In the case of a personal service activity, an individual who materially participates in the activity for *any* three taxable years prior to the current taxable year is treated as materially

participating in the activity for every year thereafter. For purposes of this three-year rule, a *personal service activity* is an activity involving the performance of services in

1. the field of health, law, engineering, architecture, accounting, actuarial science, performing arts, or consulting [§1.448-1T(e)(4)], *or*
2. any other trade or business in which capital is not a material income-producing factor [§1.469-5T(a)(6); §1.469-5T(d)].

Tax Tip

This means that real estate agents, appraisers, and so on will be considered providing "personal services" but only for this three-year "look-back" rule. Although the regulations are silent about the definition of "material income-producing factor" as used previously, it would seem that the IRS auditors have a "blank check" on classifying activities as "personal service activities."

Example:

Frank Phurter, attorney at law, had an interest in a real estate firm prior to completing his law degree. If he worked as a broker for three years before starting his legal practice, all future income paid to him by his real estate partners is "tainted" as trade or business income in which he materially participated. ■

The Last Way Taxpayers May Prove Material Participation Is by the "Facts-and-Circumstances" Test

A taxpayer who does not satisfy *any* of the previous six tests may try to convince the IRS that he or she is materially participating (or not materially participating if he or she wants the income to be determined passive) based on all the facts and circumstances. In this case the taxpayer *must* prove that he or she participated during the taxable year in the activity on a "regular, continuous, and substantial" basis.

Hopefully, future IRS regulations will provide more details concerning the criteria needed to satisfy this seventh test. To date, however, the IRS has established only that the following three areas of participation will *not* be classified as material participation under the facts-and-circumstances test [§1.469-5T(b)(2)]:

1. *Paying self-employment tax is irrelevant.* This test does *not* care if the taxpayer has to pay FICA or self-employment tax or satisfies any other participation standards established by Internal Revenue Code sections other than the PAL rules. Therefore, the taxpayer may have to pay self-employment tax and still not be considered materially participating. One of the exceptions to this rule is granted to retired or disabled farmers if they were materially participating before their retirement or disability (or are a surviving spouse of an individual who was materially participating) [§1.469-5T(h)(2)].
2. *Management time may not count either.* The performance of management services will not be taken into account unless, for the taxable year, no other person who per-

forms services in connection with the management of the activity receives "earned income" such as wages, salaries, professional fees, and other compensation [described in §911(d)(2)(A)] *and* no other manager's hours exceed (by hours) those of the taxpayer for the year.

3. *The taxpayer must work at least 100 hours annually.* The facts-and-circumstances test will not apply unless the taxpayer participates at least 100 hours in the activity during the tax year [§1.469-5T(b)(2)(iii)].

A special material participation rule for partners and S corporation shareholders.

For a holder of an interest in a passthrough entity, the general rule is that each item of gross income and deduction allocated to a taxpayer shall be determined, in any case in which participation is relevant, by reference to the participation of the taxpayer in the activity that generated that item. Such participation is determined for the taxable year of the passthrough entity (and not the taxable year of the taxpayer) [§1.469-2T(e)(1)].

Even a limited partner *may* be able to materially participate.

Generally, a limited partner is not considered as materially participating in any activity in which he or she is a limited partner. The regulations similarly adopt this rule but also provide four exceptions. The general rule does not apply if the limited partner would otherwise be treated as materially participating for the taxable year

1. by participating *more than 500 hours,*
2. having participated for *five of the last ten years,*
3. having participated for *any three years in a personal service activity, or*
4. if the limited partner *is also a general partner* at all times during the partnership's tax year that ends with or within the partner's tax year [§469(h)(2); §1.469-5T(e)(2); §1.469-5T(e)(3)(ii)].

LLC members are not limited partnerships. The court, in *Steven A. Gregg v. Comm.* [2001-1 USTC ¶50,169 (DC Ore.)], felt that the limited liability statutes create a new business entity that is materially distinguishable from a limited partnership, for no other reason than that a limited partnership must, by definition, have at least one general partner; limited partners in a limited partnership cannot, by definition, participate in the management; and LLC members retain limited liability regardless of their level of participation in the management of the LLC. The court concluded, "the limited partnership test is not applicable to all LLC members, because LLCs are designed to permit active involvement by LLC members in the management of the business." Therefore, the higher standard of material participation test for limited partners did not apply to *Gregg* and Gregg was allowed to use all seven material participation tests in his defense.

RECHARACTERIZATION OF PASSIVE INCOME IN CERTAIN SITUATIONS

According to the regulations, but not mentioned specifically in the Code itself, taxpayers are required to reclassify passive income to "active" income or "portfolio" income in certain situations.

Why do we have these recharacterization rules? Congress is concerned that taxpayers will purchase passive income generators (commonly known as "investing in a PIG"), thereby offsetting their nondeductible passive activity losses (commonly known as "holding a PAL").

Example:

Win Erluze owns interests in one trade or business activity, X, and one piece of real estate, Y. Win does not materially participate in business X and does not actively participate in real estate Y. Win has no other passive activities. Win's net passive income (or loss) for the taxable year from activities X and Y is as follows:

	Business X	**Real Estate Y**	**Total**
Passive activity gross income	$2,200	$1,500	$3,700
Less: Passive activity deductions	– 1,500	–2,200	–3,700
Net passive income (or loss)	$ 700	($ 700)	$ 0

Win could, under the regular passive loss rules, offset PIG X against PAL Y.

	Activity		
	Active	**Passive**	**Portfolio**
Passive activity X		$700	
Less: Passive activity Y		–700	
Equals: Net passive loss		0	

It is this offsetting that, in certain situations, the IRS wants to stop. This is achieved, as is discussed below, via the recharacterization rules.

Where did the recharacterization rules come from? Congress gave the Department of the Treasury sweeping authority to prescribe regulations "requiring net income or gain from a limited partnership *or other passive activity* to be treated as 'not from a passive activity.'" Even though Treasury personnel state that the recharacterization rules are required "to maintain the integrity of §469," most tax practitioners look at these recharacterization rules as giving the IRS the right to say in audit, "Taxpayer—heads I win, tails you lose!" [§469(l)(3)].

The recharacterization rules applicable to passive activities during their operational years may be divided into two major categories: (1) rules preventing the conversion of active business income into passive activity gross income, and (2) rules preventing the conversion of portfolio income into passive activity gross income [§1.469-2T(f)].

> ### Investor Hint
>
> In these cases, the taxpayer is involved in a new type of activity that is passive but whose income may be treated as active. This is the Department of the Treasury's attempt to eliminate these types of activities from becoming a PIG.

What is the theory of the recharacterization rules? The regulations provide that an amount of gross income generally equal to the "net income" is excluded from passive activity gross income. The result of these recharacterization rules is that the taxpayer will have a passive activity with no net income or loss as well as an amount of income that has been recharacterized as "active" or "portfolio" income.

How to apply the recharacterization rules. Generally, each of the recharacterization rules treats as either "active" or "portfolio" an amount of gross income (which otherwise would be treated as passive activity gross income) equal to the net income from the activity to which the rule applies. This recharacterization of passive income is required, regardless of whether the income is classified as passive income under the general passive activity rules [§1.469-2T(f)].

Example (continued):

Referring to the previous Win Erluze example, if the recharacterization rules apply to business property X, Win would be required to reduce the business's actual passive activity gross income of $2,200 by the business's net income of $700.

	Business X	**Real Estate Y**	**Total**
Passive activity gross income	$1,500	$1,500	$3,000
Less: Passive activity deductions	– 1,500	–2,200	–3,700
Net passive income (or loss)	$None	($ 700)	($ 700)

Win, under the recharacterization rules, would now have $700 of taxable active income that came from a passive activity and $700 of nondeductible passive loss! (This isn't fair!)

	Activity		
	Active	**Passive**	**Portfolio**
Active/Passive income	$ 700	$3,000	
Less: Passive deductions		– 3,700	
Equals: Active income/passive loss	$ 700*	($ 700)†	

* Recharacterized passive income that is currently taxable.

† Nondeductible passive activity loss.

Recharacterizing Passive Gross Income to "Active" Income

There are five situations in which some or all of the taxpayer's gross income from a passive activity must be recharacterized as "active" income. They are:

1. Certain rental property developed by the taxpayer, rented less than 12 months, and sold for a gain may have to be recharacterized.

A portion of a taxpayer's (e.g., a developer of commercial real estate) gross rental activity income for the tax year shall be recharacterized as active income if three tests are met:

- *Gain:* The gain (but not a loss) for the sale (exchange or other disposition) is included in the taxpayer's income for the taxable year;
- *Twelve months:* The use of the property in an activity involving its rental started less than 12 months before the date of its disposition; and
- *Participation and increased value:* The taxpayer materially participates or significantly participates for the tax year in the activity in which the performance of services enhances the value (e.g., construction, renovation, lease-up expenses, and development) of the property (or any other item of property if its basis is determined by reference to the basis of the property whose value is enhanced by the performance of services) [§1.469-2(f)(5)(i)].

> ### Tax Tip
>
> This recharacterization rule requires that many developers who rent out developed property hold the property for 12 months or more before sale.

2. The self-rental rule: a taxpayer renting property to the taxpayer's own business will have to recharacterize income.

Gross rental income equal to net rental income (including any income from a sale) is recharacterized as active income if the property is rented to a trade or business activity in which the taxpayer materially participates for the taxable year (without regard to the limited partner rules) as long as the property is not property rented incidental to a development activity [§1.469-2(f)(6); §1.469-2(f)(9)(iii)].

Rental to C corporations. This recharacterization rule is not limited to rental arrangements with passthrough entities such as partnerships and S corporations. The Tax Court has required rental income from a C corporation to be recharacterized as nonpassive (active) if the taxpayer receiving the income materially participated in the C corporation's trade or business [*Chester and Faye Sidell,* (CA-1) 2000-2 USTC ¶50,751; *Thomas Krukowski v. Comm.,* (CA-7) 2002-1 USTC ¶50,219].

Example:

Wanda Dance, a senior partner in a ten-partner law firm, owns, with only two other lawyer-partners, the commercial building housing the law firm. The three-lawyer partnership leases the building to the law firm under a "net lease" arrangement at an arm's-length, fair rental value of $48,000 per year. If the rental expenses, including depreciation, are $60,000 per year, Wanda's passive activity computation would be as follows:

> ### Caution
>
> The self-rental rule negatively affects more taxpayers than any other recharacterization rule. It is intended to deter taxpayers from attempting to generate passive rental income and active business rental deductions by establishing rental arrangements between their own businesses. It does that and more [see *A. B. Fransen, Jr.,* (CA-5) 99-2 USTC ¶50,882; *Michael and Jane Connor v. Comm.,* (CA-7), 2000-2 USTC ¶50,560; *Chester and Faye Sidell,* (CA-1) 2000-2 USTC ¶50,751; *Sidney Shaw v. Comm.,* TC Memo 2002-35; *Thomas Krukowski v. Comm.,* (CA-7) 2002-1 USTC ¶50,219].

	Activity		
	<u>Active</u>	<u>Passive</u>	<u>Portfolio</u>
Passive income		$16,000	
Less: Passive deductions		−20,000	
Equals: Net passive loss		($4,000)*	

* A nondeductible net lease,

But if the partners' annual gross income and expenses are reversed, thereby generating a net passive income, the recharacterization rules require that Wanda reduce the passive activity gain to zero. Wanda's passive activity income before the recharacterization rules would be

	Activity		
	<u>Active</u>	<u>Passive</u>	<u>Portfolio</u>
Passive income		$20,000	
Less: Passive deductions		−16,000	
Equals: Net passive profit		+$4,000*	

* a passive income generator!

The recharacterization rules force Wanda, now that the rental is profitable, to reduce the passive activity income by the amount of the $4,000 PIG. (This isn't fair! Now Wanda has $4,000 more *active* income and $4,000 less PIG.)

	Activity		
	<u>Active</u>	<u>Passive</u>	<u>Portfolio</u>
Passive income	$4,000	$16,000	
Less: Passive deductions		−16,000	
Equals: Active income/passive loss	4,000*	$ 0†	

* Recharacterized passive income that is currently taxable.

† Nondeductible passive activity loss.

Special effective date. This recharacterization rule does not apply to rental income from *written* binding contracts entered into before February 19, 1988 [§1.469-11(c)(1)(ii)].

3. Significant participation passive activity net income will have to be recharacterized.

A special rule applies when a taxpayer satisfies the significant participation standards (the 100-hour but not materially participating rule—see definition previously discussed) but is still unable to satisfy the requirements of material participation in *all* these activities (e.g., the 500-hour material participation rule) [§1.469-2T(f)(2)].

Caution

Generally, lease renewals are not considered part of the original binding contract [*Thomas Krukowski v. Comm.*, (CA-7) 2002-1 USTC ¶50,219]. In addition, any subsequent change to the lease voids this prior written binding contract transition rule [*Michael and Jane Connor vs. Comm.*, (CA-7) 2002-2 USTC ¶50,560].

Tax Tip

Income in excess of losses from significant participation activities cannot be used to offset other passive losses.

4. Qualified working interest in gas and oil. If a taxpayer used the qualified working interest exception to take any active losses with respect to an oil and gas property, gross income from that property will be active income to the extent of the net income from it for such taxable year. Thus, even if the taxpayer converts his or her qualified working interest into an interest in a limited liability entity, gross income will be recharacterized as active income [§1.469-2(c)(6)(i)].

5. The renting of dealer property—a problem if the property is sold during the year. Any rental income during the taxable year from property that is held primarily for sale to customers in the ordinary course of a trade or business [i.e., a dealer or developer as defined at §1221(1)] at the time it is sold (in a transaction in which gain or loss is recognized) will be deemed incidental to such sale. Therefore, the year a rental held primarily for sale to customers is sold or exchanged, the income is deemed active, not passive, rental income [§1.469-1T(e)(3)(viii)(Ex. 7)].

Example:

Chuck Ells, a developer, finds himself in the unenviable position of having to rent out some buildings before being able to sell them. The fact that a developer, contractor, or builder rents a building for 11 months before selling it does not alter the treatment of the building rental as incidental to the building sale and is therefore not a passive rental activity. ▪

But what about renting it out the year before? This rental will probably *not* be considered incidental. Under this provision, the taxpayer is deemed involved in two activities, building rentals and building sales.

Example:

In 2003, Ben Dover acquires vacant land for the purpose of constructing a shopping mall. Before commencing construction, Ben leases the land under a one-year lease to an automobile dealership, which uses the land to park cars held in its inventory. The taxpayer commences construction of the shopping mall in 2004.

Ben acquired the land for the principal purpose of constructing the shopping mall, not realizing gain from the appreciation of the property. The rental of the property in 2003 is *not* treated as incidental to an investment activity [see (1) above]. Also, the land has not been used in any taxable year in any of Ben's trade or businesses. Therefore, the rental of the property in 2003 is not treated as incidental to a trade or business activity [see (2) above.] The result is that the rental of the land in 2003 is a rental activity [§1.469-1T(e)(3)(viii)(Ex. 7)]. ▪

But be careful about the special rule (covered later in this chapter) that recharacterizes gross income from the rental of nondepreciable property to portfolio income [§1.469-2T(f)(3)].

Recharacterizing Passive Gross Income to "Portfolio" Income

There are three situations in which some or all of the taxpayer's gross income from a passive activity must be recharacterized as "portfolio" income. They are described here.

1. Rental from nondepreciable property must be recharacterized—the "raw land" exception.

If less than 30% of the "unadjusted basis" (i.e., do not subtract depreciation) of the property used, or held for use, by customers in a rental activity during the taxable year is subject to depreciation, an amount of the activity's gross income equal to the net passive income for the activity is treated as portfolio income. This rule comes from a suggestion in the Conference Report that "ground rents that produce income without significant expenses" are similar to portfolio income [H. Rep. 99-841, 99th Cong., 2d Sess. (Sept 18, 1986), at (II-147); §1.469-2T(f)(3)].

Example:

Pam Permie is a limited partner in a partnership. In prior years, the partnership acquired vacant land for $300,000, estimating the property now to be worth $500,000. Vacant land is considered a §212 investment, a "portfolio" activity. To change the property to a passive activity (and thereby creating a $200,000 PIG), the partnership constructs improvements on the land at a minimal cost of $100,000 and leases the land and improvements to a tenant. The partnership then sells the land and improvements for $600,000, realizing a gain on the disposition.

Applying the recharacterization rule to this example. The unadjusted basis of the improvements ($100,000) equals only 25% of the unadjusted basis of all property ($400,000) used in the rental activity. Therefore, the $200,000 net passive income must be recharacterized as "portfolio" income.

2. Passive equity-financed lending activity.

Some or all passive income is recharacterized as portfolio income if an activity is an equity-finance activity involving certain types of lending institutions [§1.469-2T(f)(4)].

3. Intangible property leased by a passthrough entity.

With certain limited exceptions, net royalty income will be recharacterized as portfolio income if a taxpayer acquires an interest in a certain passthrough entity (e.g., partnership, S corporation, estate, or trust) after it has either created an item of intangible property, performed substantial services, or incurred substantial costs. In other words, activities generating nonportfolio royalty income in cases of taxpayers investing in the activity after the royalty-producing property was developed must recharacterize the net royalty income as portfolio income. There is a "safe harbor" rule on what is deemed substantial services or costs [§1.469-2T(f)(7)].

Recharacterizing Self-Charges—Limited to Interest, No Other Items

The problem that needed to be solved–self-charged interest can create excessive passive losses.

In certain lending transactions, a taxpayer may have interest income that is characterized as portfolio income (i.e., taxable) under §469(e)(1) and interest expense that is characterized as a passive activity deduction (i.e., potentially not deductible) under §1.163-8T. The legislative history of §469 indicates that this result is inappropriate because the items of interest income and expense are essentially "self-charged" and thus lack economic significance. The IRS addressed, by final regulation, this unfair result for lending transactions between a passthrough entity and its owners [§1.469-7].

Example:

Problem with self-charged interest rules. Sharon, Vern, and Lynn are equal partners in the Santana Road Shopping Center Partnership. Sharon lends the partnership $200,000 at 10% to pay for a new roof. That year, Sharon receives a Form 1099-INT showing (taxable) interest income of $20,000 and a Form 1065 K-1 showing an ordinary (potential nondeductible passive) loss of $35,000. The interest income is properly reported on Sharon's Schedule B. Since Sharon's AGI exceeds $150,000, except for the self-charged interest rules, the passive activity rules would suspend the losses for Sharon on a loan that she essentially loaned to herself!

	Active	Activity Passive	Portfolio
Passive loss/Portfolio income		$15,000	
Less: Passive interest deduction		–20,000	$20,000†
Net passive loss and portfolio income		($35,000)*	

* Nondeductible passive activity loss.

† Portfolio income that is currently taxable.

Investor Hint

Without the self-charged exception, the interest income would remain portfolio income, which is nonpassive income, that cannot be offset by PAL deductions. Congress specifically stated this is not fair, ordering the IRS to create a relief provision.

The self-charged interest provisions. The IRS developed the self-charged rules to address the above-mentioned unfair result, but the rules apply only to items of interest income and interest expense that are recognized in the same taxable year. The rules:

- Allow the taxpayer to recharacterize self-charged interest income as passive rather than portfolio, thereby allowing the interest income to be offset by the taxpayer's related interest expense of the passive activity. Interest includes guaranteed payments for the use of capital [§1.469-2(e)(2)(ii)].
- Create an "applicable percentage" formula to determine the amount of the owner's self-charged interest income and passed-through interest expense that may be treated as passive items when loans are made to a passthrough entity by its owners.

- Apply to owner/entity loans when the owner owns any direct or indirect (loan held through one or more passthrough entities) interest, without regard to percentage of ownership[1] and without regard to amount, in the passthrough entity, including identically owned passthrough entities.
- Apply to loans between passthrough entities if each owner of the borrowing entity has the same proportionate ownership interest in the lending entity [§1.469-7].

The following formula calculates the applicable percentage.

$$RI \quad = \quad SI \quad \times \quad \frac{PE}{\text{Greater of: SI or E}}$$

RI = Owner's self-charged interest *income*
SI = Owner's self-charged interest *income to be recharacterized as passive*
PE = Owner's passed-through share of entity's passive interest *expense* from all owner loans
E = Owner's passed-through share of entity's interest *expense* (passive or otherwise) from all owner loans.

The owner's self-charged interest income from the loan to the entity is multiplied by the owner's passed-through share of the entity's passive interest expense deductions from all owner loans (including loans by other owners) and divided by the greater of (1) that owner's passed-through share of interest expense deductions from all owner loans used for passive activities or otherwise or (2) that owner's self-charged interest income.

Example (continued):

Sharon is eligible to recharacterize as portfolio income her proportionate one-third share of the interest income, i.e., $6,667.

	Active	Passive	Portfolio
		Activity	
Passive loss/Portfolio net income		– $15,000	$20,000[†]
Self-charged interest		+ 6,667	– 6,667
Less: Passive interest deduction		– $20,000	
Net passive loss and portfolio income		($28,333)[*]	$13,333[†]

* Nondeductible passive activity loss.
† Portfolio income that is currently taxable.

Example:

The "share" requirement. Marcie and Joe are 50% partners in Diamond Imaging, a passive activity. Marcie lends the partnership $10,000 at 10%, receiving at year-end $1,000 of interest income. Joe lends the partnership $20,000 at 10%, receiving at year-end $2,000 of interest income. Therefore, Marcie loans "less than her share," while Joe loans "more than his share." As shown on their respective Schedule K-1s, Marcie and Joe are each allocated $1,500 of Diamond Imaging's interest expense for the year.

---

[1] Prior IRS regulations provided that a taxpayer must have at least a 10% indirect interest in a passthrough entity to qualify for self-charged treatment. The regulations no longer contain the qualifying indirect interest rule.

Marcie will treat 100% ($1,000) of her interest income as passive activity income. The $1,000 represents her interest income ($1,000) multiplied by Joe's passed-through share of passive interest expense from all owner loans ($1,500) divided by the greater of (a) her passed-through share of Diamond Imaging's interest expense from all owner loans used for passive activities or otherwise ($1,500) or (b) her self-charged interest income ($1,000).

Joe will treat 75% ($1,500) of his interest income as passive activity income. The $1,500 represents his interest income ($2,000) multiplied by his passed-through share of Diamond Imaging's passive interest expense from all owner loans ($1,500) divided by the greater of (a) his passed-through share of Diamond Imaging's interest expense from all owner loans used for passive activities or otherwise ($1,500) or (b) his self-charged interest income ($2,000) [§1.469-7(h) Ex. 2]. ◼

Tax Tip

The owner's share of the interest expense paid by the passthrough entity should be disclosed by the entity on the "Supplemental Information" line of the owner's K-1.

Electing out of the self-charged interest rules. Investors may elect not to use the self-charged relief provisions. This election is made by the passthrough entity by attaching a written declaration to its return (or amended return) that an election-out is being made under §1.469-7(g). The election may be revoked only with IRS consent and applies to the current and all subsequent years [§1.469-7(g)].

Tax Tip

This may be advisable when the taxpayer has adequate passive income (a PIG) but needs portfolio income to deduct investment interest expense or to increase a net operating loss (NOL) by deducting more nonbusiness deductions (which are limited to nonbusiness income).

Some provisions are restrictive and not pro-taxpayer! The IRS has refused to extend the self-charged interest rules to noninterest items, to transactions in different tax years or to transactions with quasi-passthrough entities such as trusts, estates, and mutual funds:

1. *Self-charged management fees:* The regulations do not extend the self-charged treatment to other transactions involving rental real estate. Thus, for example, self-charged management fees do not enjoy the same offset resulting from the self-charged interest rules [*David H. and Suzanne Hillman v. Comm.*, (4th Cir.), 2001-1 USTC ¶50,354].

Caution

There seems to be no basis for applying the self-charged recharacterization rules to transactions other than loans.

2. *Taxable year:* The final regulations adopt the rule of the proposed regulations that the self-charged rules apply only to self-charged items recognized in the same taxable year. The suggestion to treat passive interest income when ultimately recognized was rejected by the IRS.

3. *Trusts, estates, and REMICs:* The final regulations do not extend self-charged interest rules to transactions between taxpayers and their trusts, estates, REMICs, and housing cooperatives.

Effective date. These regulations are applicable for taxable years beginning after December 31, 1986. However, for taxable years beginning before June 4, 1991, a taxpayer who owns an interest in a passthrough entity is not required to apply these provisions and may use any reasonable method to offset items of interest income and interest expense from lending transactions between the passthrough entity and its owners or between certain passthrough entities. Items from nonlending transactions cannot be offset under the self-charged rules.

Tax Tip

To the preparer: If the taxpayer receives a Form 1099-INT and a Form 1065 K-1 from the same partnership, consider using the self-charged interest rules.

THE $25,000 RELIEF PROVISION FOR RENTAL REAL ESTATE

Under the general PAL rules, net losses from rental activities do not reduce taxable income unless the taxpayer has positive net income from other passive activities.

The rule. Under this relief provision for rental real estate, moderate-income individuals (but not corporations) may use up to $25,000 of excess losses (and deduction-equivalent credits) from all rental real estate activities against active, portfolio, and other nonpassive income if the individual actively participates (spouse's services also count) in the management of the property. This relief applies only if the individual does not have sufficient passive income for the year, after considering all other passive deductions and credits, to fully offset the losses and credits from such rental real estate activities.

Example:

Marcie is a real estate agent with a 2004 commission income of $40,000. She is married with no children and has itemized deductions of $8,000. She purchases a certified historic apartment house for $5,000, assumes an underlying mortgage, and rehabilitates the property. At the end of the year she receives a rental income schedule from her accountant reporting a $15,000 rental loss and $500 of rehabilitation tax credit. The $25,000 relief provision allows Marcie to offset her salary and commission income with the real estate losses and credits if she actively participates in the management of the apartment house. ■

It is a $25,000-per-taxpayer relief. A single $25,000 amount each tax year applies on an aggregate basis to deductions and credits. It is not a $25,000 relief provision for each rental owned.

$25,000 for single taxpayers. Each single taxpayer is eligible for this $25,000 relief provision each tax year.

$25,000 for married couples. This relief is a per-tax-return provision. Therefore, husband and wife on a joint return receive only a $25,000 relief.

$12,500 for married couples filing separate returns. If married individuals file separate tax returns *and* live separately *for the entire year,* this relief provision reduces to $12,500 for each [§469(i)(5)(B)].

Zero for married couples filing separate returns and living together at any time during the year. If married individuals filing separately live together *at any time* during the taxable year, the amount of the $25,000 relief reduces to *zero* [§469(i)(5)(B)].

Investor Hint

This is weird tax planning by Congress. What a strange law—penalizing married couples getting divorced but allowing single couples living together $50,000 of relief!

Estates can also use the $25,000 deduction. The estate of a deceased taxpayer also qualifies for the $25,000 exception for the first two tax years following the death of the taxpayer if the decedent was actively participating in the rental real estate activity in the year of the death.

$25,000 for each partner. This provision is a $25,000-per-partner relief and not a per-partnership relief as long as the partner is an individual taxpayer.

Four Basic Requirements To Use the $25,000 Relief Provision

Certain rules must be followed before this $25,000 relief provision is available to an individual. The rules, in synopsis form (followed by a full explanation of each), are as follows:

1. It can only be *rental real estate.*
2. *The taxpayer must have at least 10% ownership.*
3. *The taxpayer must actively participate* in the management.
4. The taxpayer must be an *individual* (not a corporation).

The relief is available only to rental real estate. The $25,000 exception to the limitation rule is available only to rental real estate and not to any other rental activity or other passive activity. Rental real estate is where payment is primarily for the use of real property. Apartment houses, commercial rental properties, and similar properties are defined as passive rental real estate.

Tax problem with "net lease" property. Most net lease arrangements are considered rental real estate but can use the $25,000 relief provision only if the landlord also "actively manages" the net lease property—a task normally performed by the tenant.

Caution

There is a phase-out of the relief provision! As mentioned previously, these losses generally apply only to middle-income taxpayers and are limited to $25,000 annually. But even this relief amount is phased out, in a 2:1 ratio, as the taxpayer's adjusted gross income (without regard to net passive losses, IRA contributions, and taxable Social Security benefits) increases from $100,000 to $150,000. A taxpayer forfeits $1 of the $25,000 relief for each $2 of modified adjusted gross in-come (AGI) over $100,000. Therefore, a taxpayer earning $125,000 of modified AGI is permitted to deduct only half, or $12,500, of the loss created by the rental real estate. For low-income housing credits and rehabilitation credits, the $25,000 allowance (in deduction-equivalent credits) is reduced by one-half of the taxpayer's AGI in excess of $200,000 [§469(i)(3)].

This relief provision does not apply to active real estate (such as a vacation home in a rental pool). Passive real estate activities that are not treated as rental activities under this provision (e.g., hotel, motel, or a vacation home rental pool) may not use the $25,000 relief provision. Therefore, this relief provision is not available simply because the taxpayer owns real estate. For example, a hotel is treated neither as a rental real estate undertaking nor as consisting of two activities, only one of which is a rental real estate undertaking (*J. V. Patterson v. Comm.,* TCS 2002-57).

The 10% ownership rule. A taxpayer must (in conjunction with such taxpayer's spouse, even in the absence of a joint return) own 10% or more (by value) of *all* interests in the real estate activity for the entire year.

If the activity owns multiple buildings, does the taxpayer have to own at least 10% of each separate building? Separate buildings are treated as separate rental real estate activities if the degree of integration of the business and other relevant factors do not require treating them as parts of a larger activity (e.g., an integrated shopping center).

What about condominiums and cooperatives? A cooperative apartment in an apartment building, owned by a taxpayer unrelated to those owning the other apartments in the building, generally will qualify as a separate activity, despite the fact that the ownership of the building may be shared with owners of other apartments in the building, and despite the sharing with owners of other apartments of such services as management and maintenance of common areas.

What about time-shares? By contrast, ownership of an undivided interest in a building (e.g., owning a two-week interest in a ski condominium) or of an area too small to be rented as a separate unit (or that is not rented as a separate unit) does not qualify as a separate activity.

Tax Tip

For vacation home investors: Therefore, most time-share arrangements do not qualify for the $25,000 relief provision [*Toups v. Comm.,* 66 TCM 370; *Fudim v. Comm.,* TC Memo 1994-235].

Active participation in the rental management is required. In the case of an individual taxpayer owning an interest in a rental real estate activity and meeting the 10% ownership requirement, *up to $25,000 of relief may be available, but only if the landlord actively participates in the activity.* Therefore, what is meant by "active participation"? To start, it is important to ascertain the following:

The difference between "active participation" and "material participation." The active-participation standard is designed to be less stringent that the material-participation requirement. Material participation requires the taxpayer to be involved in the operations of the real estate "in a regular, continuous, and substantial manner." Active participation requires only that the taxpayer be involved "in a significant and bona fide sense."

So what is "active participation"? The determination of whether a taxpayer satisfies the "active participation" criteria of management of real estate is made by looking at all the facts and circumstances. Active participation occurs when a taxpayer participates in the making of management decisions or arranging for others to provide services (such as repairs) "in a significant and bona fide sense." Management decisions that are relevant in this context include

1. approving new tenants,
2. deciding on rental terms,
3. approving capital or repair expenditures, and
4. other similar decisions.

Property managers may be used. Hiring a property manager will still allow the taxpayer to meet the "active participation" rule so long as the taxpayer "shares" in the management decision. But there is a warning to heed when using property managers. Services provided by an agent are not attributed to the principal, and a merely formal and nominal participation in management, in the absence of a genuine exercise of independent discretion and judgment, is insufficient.

Example:

Tyson, who owns and rents out an apartment that formerly was his primary residence or that he uses as a part-time vacation home, may be treated as actively participating even if he hires a rental agent and others provide services such as repairs. So long as Tyson participates in a "significant and bona fide sense," a lack of participation in operations does not lead to the denial of relief. ■

Tax Tip

This should allow many rental vacation homes, other than vacation homes in rental pools and rented for seven days or less, to use the $25,000 relief provision.

Real estate owned in a limited partnership cannot use the $25,000 relief provision as, by state statute, a limited partner cannot participate in management at all!

Low-income housing. In the case of low-income housing and rehabilitation credits, the active participation requirements need not be satisfied and are exempt from the restrictive limited-partnership tests.

Net lease property, other than in the year of negotiation and the year of termination, probably cannot use the $25,000 relief provision. In most cases, the landlord will not be able to meet the active participation requirement.

Only individuals can use the $25,000 relief provision. No relief is provided to taxpayers other than individuals (e.g., a regular C corporation subject to the passive loss provisions).

Estates. If a taxpayer actively participated in a rental real estate activity in the taxable year in which he or she died, his or her estate is deemed to have actively participated for the two years following the death. This treatment applies to the taxpayer's estate during the two taxable years of the estate following death to facilitate the administration of the estate without requiring the executor or fiduciary to reach decisions about the appropriate disposition of the rental real property within a short period following the taxpayer's death [§469(i)(4)].

Trusts. A trust is not intended to qualify for the allowance of up to $25,000. As a result, individuals cannot circumvent the $25,000 ceiling or multiply the number of $25,000 allowances simply by transferring various rental real properties to one or more trusts.

CONCLUSION

Even though the passive activity rules were designed to curb the abuses from tax shelters, the IRS's sweeping regulations deeply impact virtually any loss reported on an individual's income tax return. They also greatly influence the way an investor both purchases and operates his or her business. For example, a time bomb exists when investors do not properly combine, or separate, multiple businesses. Renting property to the investor's own business triggers the draconian "recharacterization" rule, putting the taxpayer into a "heads IRS wins, tails, taxpayer loses" position. Understanding the self-charged interest rules and the $25,000 provision for rental real estate provides taxpayer relief from the passive loss limitation rules. This chapter reveals how to avoid the seldom understood tax traps sprinkled throughout the PAL rules and regulations.

Chapter

13

Applying the Passive Loss Rules to Real Estate Professionals

REAL ESTATE PROFESSIONALS ARE EXEMPT FROM PASSIVE LOSS RULES!

One of the most unfair tax provisions contained in the passive loss rules

is the general rule that all real estate rental activities must be treated

passively, no matter what the owner's level of personal participation

[§469(c)(2)].

Example (prior to relief provision):

Marilyn, a full-time real estate agent making $160,000 in commissions a year, purchased an apartment complex in 1991 throwing off a $40,000 loss. From 1991 through 1993, none of this $40,000 loss was deductible. (The $25,000 relief provision was not available to Marilyn as she makes more than $150,000 in modified income.) She is carrying forward $120,000 of rental losses deductible against future income or deductible when the property is sold. ■

Real Estate Professionals Can Deduct Real Estate Losses Against Ordinary Income

The relief provision. Properly, Congress has made one exception to the general rule that all rental activities must be treated passively [Revenue Reconciliation Act of 1993]. Starting January 1, 1994, a taxpayer's rental real estate activities (RREAs) in which he or she materially participates are not subject to limitation under the passive loss rule *if* the taxpayer meets eligibility requirements relating to real property trades or businesses in which the taxpayer performs services. This means that those state investors who qualify are now permitted to deduct their rental real estate losses from their current commissions, wages, interest, and dividends [§469(c)(7)]!

WHAT PROPERTY, WHAT INVESTORS, AND HOW DO THEY QUALIFY?

The general rule. The only RREAs that qualify for this exceptional relief provision are real property rentals in which the *qualified taxpayer* materially participates in the management and operation of the RREA.

> ### Caution
>
> Danilo DeGuzman failed in his attempt to include time he spent helping his wife, Dr. Daisy DeGuzman, manage her medical clinic [*Danilo DeGuzman v. Comm.*, (DC N.J.), 2001-2 USTC ¶50,560].

> ### Tax Tip
>
> In other words, if real estate investors are not materially participating in their real estate rentals, there is no sense spending time calculating the complicated eligibility requirements!

The courts have concluded that a taxpayer cannot include time operating or managing real property used in an active trade or business in order to meet the 750-hour requirement.

Spending Enough Time as a Landlord?

Material participation. An individual is treated as participating "materially" for the taxable year if the individual's participation meets *one* of the seven enumerated material participation tests previously discussed in Chapter 12 [Reg. §1.469-5T(a)(1)-(7)]. The three most common ways real estate investors may meet this "material participation" test are by

1. managing and operating the rental real estate activity for more than 500 hours during the year,

2. doing substantially all the work required to manage and operate the rental real estate during the year (probably more than 70% of the total business hours are performed by the landlord), or

3. working more than 100 hours during the year with no one (including nonowner employees and independent property managers) participating more than the landlord [Reg. §1.469-5T(a)(1)-(3)].

Tax Tip

How will real estate investors be required to prove participation? The IRS encourages them to keep good time records based on appointment books, calendars, or narrative summaries [§1.469-5T(f)(4)]. Apparently, landlords will carry these rental time logs along with their auto logs! Many taxpayers have been found by the courts to have insufficient records [*Osama A. Mowafi v. Comm.*, TC Memo 2001-111; *Sidney Shaw v. Comm.*, TC Memo 2002-35].

Tax Tip

"Participation" is an individual doing any work *in any capacity*, management or operations, unless (1) the total amount of the taxpayer's involvement is studying and reviewing financial statements or monitoring the finances or operations in a nonmanagerial capacity (e.g., acting as or being a limited partner), or (2) the work is management not "customarily performed" by owners *and* one of the principal purposes of such work is avoiding the passive loss rules [§1.469-5(f)(1)]. Sylvester Monroe, Jr. (TCS 2002-79), failed to convince the court that his time "on call" or "available" to his tenants qualified as good time when calculating either the 50% or 750-hour test (nice try, though)!

Tax Tip

For the material participation test only (not the 50% test and 750-hour test discussed below), an owner can "tack" a spouse's time for calculating the tests mentioned above (e.g., an owner/investor performing 51 hours could add a spouse's time of 50 hours to exceed the 100-hour requirement!) [Reg. §1.469-5T(f)(3)].

Aggregation of Rental Real Estate

Each rental is a separate activity, unless all rentals are combined. Each interest of the taxpayer in rental real estate is to be considered as a separate activity, but a taxpayer may elect to treat all interests in real estate, including real estate held through passthrough entities, as one activity [§469(c)(7)(A)].

Tax Tip

The aggregation option permits the investor to meet the material participation test after *cumulatively* materially participating (e.g., working 100 hours or 500 hours) *in all the real estate rentals*. Without the aggregation option, the investor would be required to materially participate (i.e., spend 100 hours or 500 hours) in each activity, probably an impossible task for investors owning more than four rentals! Because Sidney Shaw (TC Memo 2002-35) failed to attach to his tax return an election to treat his multiple interests in rental real estate as a single rental real estate activity, he failed to met the 750-hour requirement *for each rental*, and therefore was not a real estate professional. If he had made the election, he would have qualified! (Also see *William C. Fowler v. Comm.*, TC Memo 2002-223).

Tax Tip

When would investors *not* want to aggregate their rental real estate? When the rental real estate is throwing off passive income, and they purposely want to flunk this test! The rental real estate passive profit is then usable against other passive losses, such as other rentals in which they are not materially participating or vacation homes in rental pools in which they cannot materially participate.

The election must be properly made. The election to treat all interests in rental real estate as a single rental real estate activity is binding for all future years unless there is a material change in a taxpayer's facts and circumstances. The taxpayer makes the election by filing a statement with his or her original income tax return. This statement must contain a declaration that the taxpayer is a qualifying taxpayer for the taxable year and is making the election pursuant to section 469(c)(7)(A) [§1.469-9(g)]. The IRS has granted numerous extensions when the taxpayer intended to elect single rental real estate activity treatment, but failed to include the required statement with the taxpayer's return, when the IRS determined the taxpayer had acted reasonably and in good faith (LTR 200303058; LTR 200245025).

Wording for single rental real estate activity election. "In accordance with §1.146-9(g)(3), the taxpayer hereby states that he (or she) is a qualifying real estate professional under IRC §469(c)(7), and elects under IRC Sec. 469(c)(7)(A) to treat all interests in real estate as a single rental real estate activity."

Real estate owned by passthrough entities. If a taxpayer owns a 50% or greater interest in the capital, income, gain, loss, deduction, or credit of a pass-through entity at any time during a taxable year, each interest in rental real estate held by the pass-through entity will be treated as a separate interest in rental real estate, regardless of the pass-through entity's grouping of activities. However, the taxpayer may elect to treat it as a single rental real estate activity [Prop. Reg. §1.469-9(g)].

THE TWO MAJOR REQUIREMENTS

How an Individual Satisfies the Two-Step Eligibility Requirements

1. The 50% test. More than 50% of the individual's personal services during the tax year must be performed in real property trades or businesses (defined below) in which the individual materially participates (defined previously), and

2. The 750-hour test. The individual must perform more than 750 hours of service in those same trades or businesses [§469(c)(7)(B)].

Restriction for employees. When this eligibility test is applied, the personal services of an employee are not counted unless the employee is also at least a 5% owner (i.e., owns more than 5% of the outstanding stock or more than 5% of the total combined voting power) [§469(c)(7)(D)(ii)].

Eligible corporations. A closely held C corporation satisfies the eligibility test if, during the tax year, more than 50% of the gross receipts of the corporation are derived from real property trades or businesses in which the corporation materially participates [§469(c)(7)(D)(i)].

Tax Tip

This relief provision does not apply to estates, trusts, or limited partnerships owning real estate rentals. It only grants relief to individuals and closely held corporations.

Calculating The 50%/750 Hours Test

As mentioned previously, more than 50% of the individual's time must be performed in the real estate trades or businesses in which the individual materially participates and an individual must perform more than 750 hours of service in the same real estate businesses.

Caution

Judy Bailey (TCM 2001-296) failed the 50% test, as she spent 876 hours practicing law and only 828 hours managing her rentals. William C. Fowler (TC Memo 2002-223) failed the 50% test, even though he spent 1,555 hours managing his three rentals and spent only 664 hours managing his heating and air-conditioning business because he didn't make the "single rental real estate activity" election and didn't spend more than 664 hours managing any rental separately!

Spouse's hours. In the case of joint returns, each spouse's personal services are taken into account *separately* when calculating the 50% test and the 750-hour test. But when determining "material participation," the participation of the spouse of the taxpayer is taken into account.

Example:

A husband and wife filing a joint return meet the eligibility requirements of the provision if during the taxable year *one* spouse performs at least half of his or her business services in a real estate trade or business in which either spouse materially participates. The couple does not fail the eligibility requirements if less than half of their business services, taken together, are performed in real estate trades or businesses in which either of them materially participates, provided that more than half of one spouse's business services qualify.

Tax Tip

"Stay-home" spouses may now want to become active real estate agents. If they spend at least 750 hours cumulatively in selling and managing their family rentals, this converts the family rentals to *active* rentals!

Example (Marilyn continued):

Remember Marilyn, the full-time real estate agent making $160,000 in commissions a year, who purchased an apartment complex, throwing off a $40,000 loss? Assume she worked 1,000 hours in the brokerage business and only an additional 100 hours managing the real estate rental. The 50% test calculation is 550 hours (1,100 hours × 50%) and the 750-hour calculation is 1,100 hours, which is more than the minimum required and more than the 50% minimum required hours (550 hours). Therefore, starting in 1994, *all* the $40,000 loss is currently deductible against her commission income! ■

Tax Tip

This seems to be a fairly liberal relief provision for those taxpayers involved in the real estate profession who own rental real estate! The flowchart in Figure 13.1 titled "Rental Real Estate Activity Determination for Individuals Worksheet" makes this calculation very easy.

The Real Estate Businesses That Can Be Combined!

Real property trade or business means any real property development, redevelopment, construction, reconstruction, acquisition, conversion, rental, operation, management, leasing, or brokerage trade or business [§469(c)(7)(C)].

FIGURE 13.1   **Rental Real Estate Activity Determination for Individuals Worksheet**

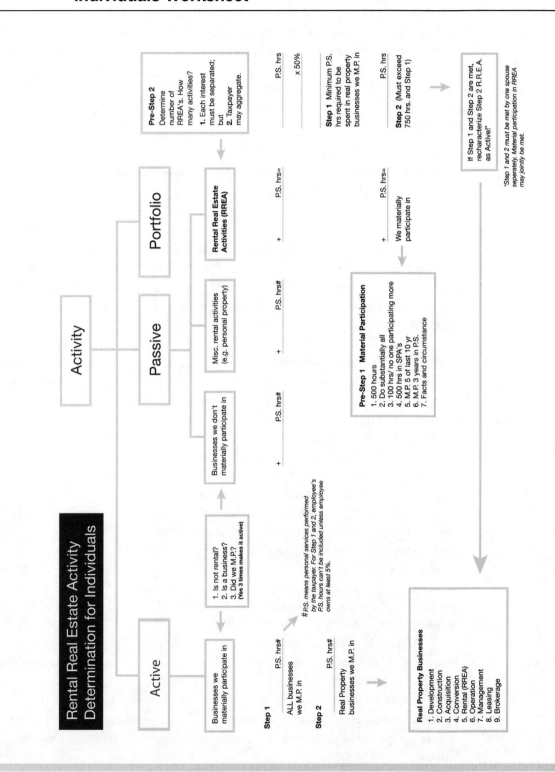

Tax Tip

According to the new passive loss relief provision, the "blessed" businesses generally include most (1) real estate builders and contractors, (2) owners of rentals, (3) property managers, and (4) participants in the real estate brokerage business—if they meet the 50% participation and the 750-hour requirements.

Tax Tip

Any hourly combination in these four "blessed" businesses is permitted; a taxpayer, for example, who spends 100 hours managing his or her rentals and 651 hours selling real estate exceeds the 750-hour minimum!

What is included in "brokerage trade or business"? There is much discussion about the definition of *brokerage trade or business*. Do only brokers qualify, not agents or salespersons? (The *Kiplinger Letter* of February 11, 1994 asserts that the new relief provision applies only to real estate brokers and not agents and salespersons!) What about appraisers, real estate mortgage brokers and auctioneers?

Neither the law nor the IRS tells us. Neither the Internal Revenue Code section 469(c)(7)(C) nor the associated Conference Committee Report discusses the width or breadth of brokerage, and therefore neither specifically mentions real estate agents (i.e., brokers and salespersons) or those in the real estate financing business (i.e., real estate mortgage bankers and brokers). Nor do they mention real estate appraisers, although under most state laws appraising is included in the definition of brokerage. Many state real estate licensing acts also specifically exempt or require auctioneers to be licensed as real estate brokers. Therefore, we are left only with prior case law or state law for the definition of real estate "brokerage trade or business."

Real estate brokerages typically encompass brokers, agents, and salespersons [*Robert C. Kersey,* 66 TCM 1863]; therefore, all should qualify. People involved in brokerage firms are generally "involved in the sale, leasing, acquisition, and development of industrial and commercial real estate" [*Alfred Rice,* 38 TCM 990] and may even specialize "in sales, property management, mortgage financing, appraisals, and insurance primarily on a commission or fee basis" [*Norman A. Grant,* CA-4 *aff'g* 64-2 USTC 9586, 333 F2d 603] or simply "appraisal" [*Charles W. Yeager,* 18 TCM 192].

Brokerage businesses hire salespersons [*FB Tippins, Jr.,* 24 TCM 521], and both salespersons and brokers may be involved in the same real estate brokerage business [*Floyd Wright,* 49 TCM 906].

Another place to find the definition of real estate brokerage is state law; all 50 states have real estate brokerage licensing acts, and generally states require that real estate salespeople and brokers be licensed under the same statutory provisions [*J. G. Mendoza,* 22 TCM 528].

> ### Tax Tip
>
> It is hoped that future IRS rules will clarify this confusion. Regulation §1.469-4(h) has been reserved for these rules.

So What Can Be Done with the Rental Losses Previously Suspended?

As we can now fully deduct the current rental losses against our other current *active* income, can we also "trigger" the prior rental losses we have not deducted? Not easily!

Sadly, these suspended losses do not immediately convert to active losses. They maintain their passive status and may not be immediately deductible. The suspended nondeducted losses from an earlier year are treated as losses from a *former passive activity* [see §469(f)]. These previously suspended losses, however, unlike passive activity losses generally, *are* allowed against income realized from the activity after it ceases to be a passive activity. Thus, such suspended losses are limited to the income from that specific activity but are not allowed to offset other income. Of course, the matching-of-income burden of proof is on the taxpayer.

> ### Tax Tip
>
> When the taxpayer disposes of his or her entire interest in the activity in a fully taxable transaction with an unrelated party, any remaining suspended losses allocable to the activity are allowed in full.

Example (continued):

Marilyn, in the above example, is carrying forward $120,000 of rental losses that were suspended from 1991 through 1993. These carry-forward losses are not immediately triggered but are deductible either against future income from this new real estate rental activity or deductible when sold. ■

Can we combine rental and business enterprises to get around these rules? In spite of the new rental real estate activity relief provision, no grouping of businesses and rentals is allowed unless either is "insubstantial" in relation to the other. The problem is that the proposed regulations do not spell out "insubstantial." The lapsed temporary regulations contained two "bright-line" insubstantial tests: (1) the 2% test (i.e., if the gross rental income is less than 2% of the smaller of the property's unadjusted basis or fair market value, the rental activity is insubstantial) and (2) the 20% test (i.e., if the rental income is less than 20% of the combined business and rental income, the rental activity is insubstantial). It is assumed that these tests may be used to help determine if the rental is an "insubstantial" part of the business . . . or if the business may be involved in "insubstantial" rental activities without breaking them into two activities [§1.469-4(d)].

> **Tax Tip**
>
> If the grouping of rental activities with the other real property businesses is permitted by the IRS, a large tax loophole for most real estate investors exists. But such aggressive tax planning is questionable!

Example (continued):

If Marilyn, in the previous example, can combine her two real property businesses (e.g., brokerage and RREA) into one activity, her $120,000 carry-forward rental losses can offset her $120,000 current brokerage income! This will bring her taxable income to zero for 1994! We seriously doubt that future IRS regulations will allow this type of activity grouping! ■

Stupid tax planning. What happens if the rental is sold for a large profit and the minimal annual losses were previously treated as an "active" rental loss? Rental properties treated as "active" rental losses in the year of the sale will create "active" gain at time of sale, with the result that this gain can only offset the carryover loss from that specific activity and is not available to offset any other passive losses.

> **Tax Tip**
>
> *Any related gain on sale shall not be considered passive (it stays active) unless the property was used in a passive activity for either (1) 20% of the period owned or (2) the entire 24 months prior to the date of the signing of the offer-to-purchase agreement [§1.469-2T(c)(2)(iii)].*

Example:

Sandy purchases a large residential rental property with a large down payment. It throws off only a $4,000 per year rental loss. If she meets the 50% and 750-hour tests each year, after ten years she will have deducted $40,000 of "active rental losses." If she sells the property for a $1,000,000 profit, her gain is considered an active gain, unless she treated it as passive for 24 months prior to the signing of the offer-to-sell! Therefore, it is not available to be used against her other "limited partnership" passive losses. ■

Effective date. The provision is effective for taxable years beginning after December 31, 1993.

CONCLUSION

Real estate agents, contractors and developers who own rental real estate should be overjoyed over the return of the tax benefits previously enjoyed by everyone before 1987! But Congress exacted a price: To use this relief provision requires a time log and a few extra hours with a tax preparer!

14

The Disposition of Passive Activities

The theory. Congress felt that only when a taxpayer disposes of the *entire* interest in a passive activity can the actual economic gain or loss on the investment be determined with total accuracy. Upon a taxable disposition, net appreciation or depreciation with respect to the activity can be finally ascertained. Prior to a disposition of the taxpayer's interest, it is difficult to determine whether there has actually been gain or loss with respect to the activity (e.g., allowable deductions may exceed actual economic costs or may be exceeded by untaxed appreciation).

Passive losses become deductible . . . eventually. Under the passive loss rules, upon a fully taxable, arm's-length disposition (i.e., taxable dispositions of the entire interest in the activity), any overall loss from the activity realized by the taxpayer is recognized (i.e., "triggered") and allowed against income (even against active or portfolio income) [§469(g)(1)].

Transfers other than by "taxable dispositions of the entire interest in the activity" are covered by special rules (discussed later), such as transfer by reason of death, transfer by gift, installment sales, activity ceasing to be passive, corporation changes from closely held (per §469) to nonclosely held, and nontaxable transfers.

TAXABLE DISPOSITIONS OF ENTIRE INTEREST IN ACTIVITY

The type of disposition that triggers full recognition of any loss from a passive activity is a fully taxable disposition of the taxpayer's entire interest in the activity. What does this definition entail?

Fully taxable disposition. A fully taxable disposition generally includes a sale of the property to a third party at arm's length and thus, presumably, for a price equal to its fair market value.

Abandonment. An abandonment constitutes a fully taxable disposition [if it gives rise to a deduction under §165(a)].

Worthlessness of security. Worthlessness is also a disposition [to the extent that §165(g) applies to a worthless security].

Entire interest. Originally, the taxpayer was required to dispose of the "entire interest" in the activity in order to trigger the recognition of loss. If less than the entire interest was sold, then the ultimate economic gain or loss computation in the activity remained unresolved [§469(g)(1)].

Example:

Charlene has a significant ownership interest in a bakery and a movie theater at a shopping mall in Baltimore and in a bakery and a movie theater at a shopping mall in Philadelphia. Even though Charlene may consider it reasonable to group these four businesses into any one of four combinations, the last option, four separate activities, generally will be the best of the following options if losses are expected from all four businesses:

1. Combining the movie theaters and bakeries into one single activity
2. Separating the movie theaters into one activity and the bakeries into another activity
3. Separating the Baltimore businesses into one activity and the Philadelphia businesses into another activity
4. Segregating them all into four separate activities *[§1.469-4(c)(3) (Example 1)]* ▪

> **Caution**
>
> Tax credits (e.g., low-income housing and rehab credits) may be lost upon sale. Since the purpose of the disposition rule is to allow only "real" economic losses of the taxpayer to be deducted, credits (which are not related to the measurement of such loss) are not allowed at disposition. Therefore, credits are allowed only when sufficient passive income is generated.

Tax Tip
_____

Most taxpayers, therefore, try to create as many small activities as possible.

Exception: Triggering of carryforward loss: A disposition of "substantially all" of an activity will trigger carryforward losses so long as the taxpayer can establish with reasonable certainty the previous carryforward losses of that specific segment of the activity and the segment's current year's gross income and expenses [§1.469-4(g)].

Proprietorship. A disposition of the taxpayer's entire interest involves a disposition of the taxpayer's interest in all entities that are engaged in the activity. To the extent that they are held in a proprietorship form, all assets used or created in the activity must be disposed.

Partnerships (general or limited) or S corporations. If a general partnership or S corporation conducts two separate activities, a fully taxable disposition by the entity of all the assets used or created in one activity constitutes a disposition of the partner's or shareholder's entire interest in the activity.

Grantor trust. Similarly, if a grantor trust conducts two separate activities and sells all the assets used or created in one activity, the grantor is considered to be disposing of his entire interest in that activity.

Records required. If losses are to be allowed in full upon disposition, the taxpayer is required to have adequate records of the suspended losses allocable to that activity that includes in income the gain (if any) allocable to the entire interest in the activity.

WHERE DOES THE GAIN (OR LOSS) GO?

Gain first offsets that activity's carryforward losses. Gain recognized on a transfer of an interest in a passive activity generally is treated as passive, and is *first* offset by the *suspended losses from that specific activity.* This accomplishes the purpose of recognizing net income or loss with respect to the activity when it can be finally determined [§469(g)(1)].

Example:

Full recognition of suspended losses. Terry sold an apartment house, which has an adjusted basis of $100,000, for $180,000. In addition, Terry has suspended losses associated with that specific apartment house of $60,000. The total gain, $80,000, and the taxable gain, $20,000, are calculated as follows:

Net sale price	$ 180,000
Less: adjusted basis	−100,000
Equals: Total gain	80,000
Less: Suspended losses	− 60,000
Equals: Total Gain	$ 20,000

The remaining ordering rules for any enduring (and "triggered") losses. If suspended losses exceed the gain recognized, the excess is allowed to offset income in the following order:

1. Net passive activity income or gains (if any)
2. Nonpassive income or gains (e.g., active and/or portfolio losses)

Example:

Partial recognition of suspended losses. Terry sold an apartment house with an adjusted basis of $100,000 for $150,000. In addition, Terry has suspended losses associated with that specific apartment house of $60,000. The total gain, $50,000, and the *deductible loss,* $10,000, are calculated as follows:

Net sale price	$ 150,000
Less: adjusted basis	−100,000
Equals: Total gain	50,000
Less: Suspended losses	− 60,000
Equals: Deductible loss	($ 10,000)

The $10,000 deductible loss can now be used against the taxpayer's other passive income. If any of the loss then remains, it may be used against ordinary income and portfolio income.

Loss from disposition. The loss on sale would simply be an additional deduction of the activity, added to the previously suspended losses, and the above rules would continue to be followed.

IS THE GAIN TREATED AS ACTIVE, PASSIVE, OR PORTFOLIO?

The year of sale determines whether the gain is active, passive or portfolio. Any gain recognized upon the sale, exchange, or other disposition (a "disposition") of property used in an activity, or of an interest in an activity held through a partnership or S corporation, is treated as follows:

1. The gain is treated as gross income from the activity for the taxable year or years in which it is recognized.
2. If the activity is passive in the year of disposition, the gain is treated as passive activity gross income for the taxable year in which it is recognized.
3. If the activity is not passive in the year of disposition, the gain is treated as nonpassive [§1.469-2T(c)(2)].

Example:

A. J. owns an interest in a trade or business activity in which he has never materially participated. In 2003, A. J. sells equipment that is used exclusively in the activity and realizes a gain on the sale. The gain is passive activity gross income. ▮

Example:

B. J. owns an interest in a trade or business activity in which she materially participates during 2003. In 2003 B. J. sells a building used in the activity in an installment sale and realizes a gain on the sale. B. J. does not materially participate in the activity for 2004 or any subsequent year. As the year of the sale determines the character of the gain, none of B. J.'s gain from the sale (including gain taken into account after 2003) is passive activity gross income. ■

What happens when one asset that is being used for two purposes simultaneously is sold? In cases where a material portion of the property that was used at any time before the disposition in any activity in which the remainder of the property was not used, the material portion shall be treated as a separate interest in property. The amount realized from the disposition and the adjusted basis of the property must be allocated among the separate interests in a reasonable manner.

Example:

Sam sells a ten-floor office building for a $500,000 total gain. Sam owned the building for three years preceding the sale and at all times during that period used seven floors of the building in a trade or business activity and three floors in a rental activity. The fair market value per square foot is substantially the same throughout the building, and Sam did not maintain a separate adjusted basis for any part of the building. The seven floors used in the trade or business activity and the three floors used in the rental activity are treated as separate interests in property. The amount realized and the adjusted basis of the building must be allocated between the separate interests in a reasonable manner.

Under these circumstances, an allocation based on the square footage of the parts of the building used in each activity would be reasonable. Therefore 70% ($350,000) of the total gain is active income and 30% ($150,000) is passive income. ■

DISPOSITION OF INTEREST IN PASSTHROUGH ENTITIES

Allocation among activities. If an interest in a partnership or S corporation (i.e., a passthrough entity) is sold or disposed of, a ratable portion of any gain or loss from the disposition is treated as gain or loss from the disposition of an interest in *each* trade or business, rental, or investment activity in which the passthrough entity owns an interest on the applicable valuation date (this date is generally either the sale date or the beginning of the tax year).

Example:

Allocation of gain (or loss) when selling a partnership interest. Abe owns a one-half interest in BobJoe, a calendar year partnership. In 2003, Abe sells 50% of his interest and the gain is determined as follows:

Sales price:	$ 50,000
Less: Adjusted basis	– 30,000
Equals: Gain	20,000

BobJoe is engaged in one business and one rental in addition to owning marketable securities that are portfolio assets. A ratable portion of Abe's $20,000 gain is allocated to each appreciated activity in which BobJoe owns an interest on the applicable valuation date. The marketable securities are treated as owned by BobJoe as a single investment activity. ■

Gain. The ratable portion of any gain from the disposition of an interest in a passthrough entity that is allocable to each activity is

$$\text{Total gain} \times \frac{\text{Net loss from a specific activity on valuation date}}{\text{Sum of all activities net loss on valuation date}}$$

Loss. The ratable portion of any loss from the disposition of an interest in a passthrough entity that is allocable to an activity is

$$\text{Total loss} \times \frac{\text{Net loss from a specific activity on valuation date}}{\text{Sum of all activities net loss on valuation date}}$$

Optional allocation rule. If the gain or loss recognized on the disposition of an interest in a passthrough entity cannot be allocated, the gain or loss is allocated among the activities in proportion to the respective fair market values of the passthrough entity's interests in the activities at the applicable valuation date, and the gain or loss allocated to each activity is treated as gain or loss from the disposition of an interest in the activity.

Gain allocated to certain passive activities may be deemed not from a passive activity. Recharacterization rules on substantially appreciated property sales exist for passthrough entity sales [§1.469-2T(e)(3)(iii)].

HOW THE RECHARACTERIZATION RULES APPLY TO SALES

Recharacterization of passive income when selling passive property. The last three recharacterization rules to be discussed relate to the sale of passive property by the taxpayer. As mentioned previously in Chapter 12, the basic rule for determining if property sold is passive or not passive is, "How is the property being used in the year of the sale?" The IRS is greatly concerned that taxpayers will use this rule to artificially create a PIG (passive income generator) by converting property to be sold for a gain into a passive activity immediately before sale. To prevent potential taxpayer abuse at time of sale, the regulations establish three major exceptions: (1) the "12-month rule," (2) the "20%/24-month rule," and (3) income from a dealer's investment property [§1.469-2T(f); §1.469-1T(f)].

> ### *Investor Hint*
>
> Under the recharacterization rules, the "net income" from a sale is characterized as active or portfolio income, thereby eliminating much-needed "passive income" that could be offset by carryforward passive losses.

The "12-month rule"—treatment of gain (or loss) when selling. If there is a sale within 12 months of conversion, a monthly allocation is required unless the gain is either (1) considered *de minimis* (i.e., under $10,000) or (2) subject to the next rule for "substantially appreciated property."

The "20%/24-month rule"—sale of substantially appreciated property formerly used in a nonpassive activity. Generally, if the fair market value of an interest in any property exceeds 120% of that property's adjusted basis (i.e., after subtracting accumulated depreciation) at the time of sale, it is deemed substantially appreciated. Therefore, any related gain shall not be considered passive (it's either active or portfolio) unless the property was used in a passive activity for either (1) 20% of the period owned *or* (2) the entire 24 months prior to the date of the signing of the offer-to-purchase agreement [§1.469-2(c)(2)(iii)].

Example:

On January 1, 1991, Scott purchases and moves his law firm into a new building. He materially participates in the law firm until March 31, 2001. On April 1, 2002, Scott leases the building to his former partners. On December 31, 2003, Scott sells the building. Assuming Scott's lease of the building to his old partners constitutes a rental activity under the passive loss rules, the building is used in a passive activity for 21 months (April 1, 2002, through December 31, 2003).

Thus, the building was not used in a passive activity for the entire 24-month period ending on the date of the sale. In addition, the 21-month period during which the building was used in a passive activity is less than 20% of Scott's entire holding period of the property (13 years, or 156 months).

Therefore, the gain from the sale is treated as not being from a passive activity (nor would it be portfolio income, as the property was not held as an investment for more than 50% of its holding period as an investment). The result is that the gain must be recharacterized as an "active" gain [§1.469-2(c)(2)(iii)(D); §1.469-2T(c)(2)(iii)(A)].

The 20%/24 Month Test

1. Was the asset used in the activity the entire 24 months?

	Yes	X* No

* Rents to partnership	April 1, 2002
Sells to partnership	December 31, 2003
Total time used	21 months
	or

2. Was the asset used in the passive activity for 20% of the holding period?

	Yes	X* No

* Date acquired	January 1, 1991
Date sold	December 31, 2003
Total time owned	156 months × .20 = 31 months

| Total time used | 21 months |

> **Caution**
>
> The end of the 24-month period terminates on the day the offer-to-purchase-and-sell agreement is executed, *not* on the day of closing. Therefore, the seller cannot simply defer closing for 24 months!

> ### Tax Tip
>
> In essence, this creates another "holding period" for taxpayers. Therefore, in many cases, taxpayers must hold passive property for a minimum of 24 months to convert active or portfolio gain to passive gain.

Income from a dealer's investment property—another recharacterization rule. Normally, dealer income is considered active income. But if the dealer held the property as an investment *at any time* before the income or gain is recognized, the income will be considered portfolio income. Sadly, any loss from such property remains passive or active depending on the taxpayer's level of participation [§1.469-2T(c)(3)(iii)(A)].

> ### Tax Tip
>
> Dealers should *never* call property "investment" property!

Example:

Robin originally purchases 20 acres of land to be held for appreciation. He later subdivides the property for a $200,000 profit. Because of this recharacterization rule, this normally active income must be recharacterized as portfolio income. Paradoxically, if Robin sold the property for a $200,000 loss, the loss would be considered active or passive, depending on whether Robin "materially participated" in the subdivision activity. ■

WHAT ABOUT TRANSFERS OTHER THAN ARM'S-LENGTH SALES?

As previously discussed, under the passive loss rules, only upon a fully taxable, arm's-length disposition (i.e., taxable disposition of an entire interest in an activity) is any overall loss from the activity realized by the taxpayer recognized (triggered) and allowed against income (even against active or portfolio income) [§469(g)(1)].

Suspended losses are not triggered when disposition is not arm's length. Where the taxpayer transfers an interest in a passive activity but the form of ownership merely changes, *suspended losses generally are not allowed* under the theory that the gain or loss realized with respect to the activity has not been finally determined. Of course, any losses created by the transfer could potentially be deductible by other passive income.

Transfers not considered "taxable dispositions of the entire interest in the activity" are covered by special rules. Examples include the following:

1. Transfers to related parties
2. Transfer by reason of death [§469(g)(2)]
3. Transfer by gift [§469(j)(6)]

4. Installment sales [§469(e)(3)]
5. Activity ceases to be passive [§469(f)(1)]
6. Corporate changes from closely held [per §469] to not closely held [§469(f)(2)]
7. Nontaxable transfers

The rules are discussed in the following sections.

RELATED-PARTY TRANSACTIONS

Losses are not triggered. As transfers between related parties (e.g., transactions between a partner and the partnership, a shareholder and the corporation, or a mother and a daughter) are not "arm's-length," any carryforward loss is *not* triggered. The investor is *not* treated as having disposed of his or her entire interest in a passive activity if it is sold to a related party [within the meaning of §267(b) or §707(b)(1)].

Keep the loss. Suspended losses are not triggered, remain with the investor, and may be utilized to offset passive activity income.

When do we get the loss? If the entire interest is later sold by the related party to an *unrelated* party in a fully taxable transaction, then any suspended losses remaining may be deducted.

> **Caution**
>
> The penalty is too high. In most cases, do not sell passive property with carryover losses to a relative. Why?

TRANSFER BY REASON OF DEATH

Congress says, "You can take it with you!" A transfer of an investor's interest in an activity by reason of death causes suspended losses to be allowed (to the decedent) only to the extent they exceed the amount, if any, by which the basis of the interest in the activity is increased at death under §1014. *Suspended losses are eliminated to the extent of the amount of the basis increase.* The losses allowed are generally reported on the final return of the deceased taxpayer [§469(g)(2)].

> **Caution**
>
> This penalty is usually too high. In most cases, do not die holding passive property with carryover losses. Why?

Example:

Transfer by death causes suspended losses to be lost. Dad dies with passive property having an adjusted basis of $40,000, suspended losses of $10,000, and a fair market value at the date of death of $75,000. The basis increase is $35,000 (fair market value at date of death or alternative value), and therefore none of the $10,000 suspended losses is deductible by either Dad or his children. The total of adjusted basis ($40,000) and the suspended losses ($10,000) did not exceed the fair market value of the property ($75,000). ■

> **Tax Tip**
>
> The result is that Dad has reported $10,000 more in income during his lifetime than what economically occurred. If Dad had sold the property prior to his death, he would have had a $10,000 deduction (the suspended losses) in the year of disposition and, a $35,000 gain, and the children would have inherited property (cash, notes, etc.) with a fair market value of $75,000, net of tax paid on the $25,000 net gain.

Alternative tax planning. It might be recommended, though, that taxpayers die holding passive property with suspended losses when the property's appreciation exceeds the suspended losses.

Example:

Transfer by death sufficient for a partial recognition of suspended losses. Dad dies with passive property having an adjusted basis of $40,000, suspended losses of $10,000, and a fair market value at the date of death of $45,000. As the basis increase under §1014 is only $5,000 ($45,000 − $40,000), the suspended losses allowed are limited to $5,000 ($10,000 suspended loss at time of death minus $5,000 increase in basis). The $5,000 loss now available to Dad is reported on his last income tax return. ▓

Tax Tip

In this case, Dad should not normally own appreciated passive property with suspended losses at time of death. This may not be true when the adjusted basis exceeds the fair market value of the activity. Compare the "loss" property in the following example with the "gain" property in the previous example.

Example:

Transfer by death creates a complete recognition of a passive activity loss. Dad dies with passive property having an adjusted basis of $40,000, $10,000 of suspended losses, and a $35,000 fair market value at date of death. The basis decrease for the children is $5,000 to $35,000 (fair market value at date of death). The tax result: All $10,000 of the suspended losses is deducted on the final return; none of the losses are lost. ▓

Tax Tip

This yields a much more favorable tax result than dying with appreciated passive property. Therefore, proper estate and income tax planning "in contemplation of death" now requires analyzing the type of property, active versus passive, that the taxpayer owns, the taxpayer's suspended losses, and the adjusted basis and fair market value of passive activity property.

TRANSFER BY GIFT

A gift of all or part of the taxpayer's interest in a passive activity does not trigger suspended losses. However, §469 allows suspended losses to be added to the basis of the property immediately before the gift [§469(j)(6)].

Example:

Dad gifts passive property having an adjusted basis of $40,000, suspended losses of $10,000, and a fair market value at the date of the gift of $100,000. Dad cannot deduct the suspended losses in the year of the disposition. Instead, the suspended losses transfer with the property.

In this example, the basis to a child when property is transferred by gift is the carryover basis, $40,000, plus the suspended losses immediately before the gift, $10,000, for a new adjusted basis to the child of $50,000. If this is business property, the child's new depreciable basis is $50,000. ■

> ### Caution
>
> The penalty with this transfer is the conversion of a potentially current deduction to a long-term deduction. Why?

> ### Tax Tip
>
> If Dad sells the property, he triggers the loss, which is a current deduction. He then can gift the cash to his child, and let the child purchase other commercial property for $40,000, which would have a 39-year life. A much smarter tax solution!

INSTALLMENT SALES

An installment sale of the taxpayer's entire interest in an activity in a fully taxable transaction triggers the allowance of suspended losses. However, the losses are only allowed in each year of the installment obligation in the ratio that the gain recognized in each year bears to the total gain on the sale [§469(g)(3)].

Installment gains will continue to be reported by using the gross profit percentage and then offset by a proportional amount of carryforward losses.

Installment reporting of passive losses. The new provision requires that the taxpayer report passive losses (if any) on the installment basis when the property is sold at a loss or at a gain less than the carryforward losses. This creates deferral of recognition of loss and is a radical change for those (passive) properties sold for a loss after adding back the carryforward losses. Under the normal installment sales rules [§453], the total losses for business and investment properties are fully deductible in the year of the sale and cannot be reported on the installment plan over the life of the contract.

> ### Caution
>
> The penalty on a sale of passive property with a carryover loss is that the loss must be spread over the contract period, and if it was sold for cash, the loss would be immediaely and entirely deductible in the year of the sale! Why?

> ### Tax Tip
>
> This new change will probably require sophisticated investors to sell passive property for cash only.

Pre-1987 installment sales with gain reported after 1986. Taxpayers who sold or exchanged an interest in a passive activity in a pre-1987 tax year and who recognize gain during a post-1986 tax year under the installment method of accounting may treat this as income from a passive activity. However, the taxpayer must be able to prove that the activity would have been treated as a passive activity if the PAL rules had applied for the year of disposition and all succeeding tax years.

ACTIVITY CEASES TO BE PASSIVE

Sometimes the passive loss rules may cease to apply to a taxpayer even though a disposition does not occur.

Example:

Jim, an attorney, owns Northwest Travel Agency, which is managed by a full-time manager. It has been producing a $20,000 loss for each of its last five years that Jim has *not* been materially participating. Jim quits the legal profession to spend full time in the travel agency. What happens to the $100,000 of previously nondeducted carryforward passive losses? ▨

Material participation. An individual who previously was passive in relation to a trade or business activity that generates net losses may begin materially participating in the activity [§469(f)(1)].

So what happens with the previous passive losses? When a taxpayer's participation in an activity is material in any year after a year (or years) during which he or she is not a material participant, previously suspended losses remain suspended and continue to be treated as passive activity losses. These previously suspended losses, however, unlike passive activity losses generally, are allowed against income from the activity realized after it ceases to be a passive activity with respect to the taxpayer. Of course, the matching-of-income burden of proof is on the taxpayer.

The $25,000 relief provision. A similar rule applies to active participation. A change in the nature of the taxpayer's involvement does not trigger the allowance of deductions carried over from prior taxable years. If a taxpayer begins to actively participate in an activity in which, in prior years, he or she did not actively participate, the rule allowing up to $25,000 of losses (or credits) from rental real estate activities against nonpassive income does not apply to losses from the activity carried over from such prior years.

CORPORATION CHANGES TO NOT CLOSELY HELD

A similar situation arises when a corporation (such as a closely held corporation or personal service corporation) subject to the passive loss rule ceases to be subject to the passive loss rule because it ceases to meet the definition of an entity subject to the rule [§469(f)(2)]. But suspended passive activity losses from C corporation years can be carried over to years of S corporation [*St. Charles Investment Co. v. Comm.,* (CA-10), 2000-2 USTC ¶50,840].

> ### *Tax Tip*
>
> If a closely held corporation makes a public offering of its stock and thereafter ceases to meet the stock ownership criteria for being closely held, it is no longer subject to the passive loss rule.

NONTAXABLE TRANSFERS

Nonrecognition transactions. An exchange of the taxpayer's interest in an activity in a nonrecognition transaction, such as an exchange governed by §351 (tax-free transfers into a corporation), §721 (tax-free transfers into a partnership), and §1031 (tax-free exchange of property held for productive use or for investment), in which no gain or loss is recognized, *does not trigger suspended losses.*

To the extent the taxpayer does recognize gain on the transaction (e.g., boot in an otherwise tax-free exchange), the gain could be treated as passive activity income against which passive losses may be deducted.

So what happens to the suspended losses? The taxpayer keeps the suspended losses (they do not transfer with the property), and the suspended losses become "frozen" *and, in most cases, deductible in the year of the disposition of the received property!*

A second major penalty. Such suspended losses may not be applied against income from the property that is attributable to a different activity from the one that the taxpayer exchanged. There is no special rule permitting suspended losses from the prior interest to be offset by income from the new activity unless it, too, is a passive activity.

> **Caution**
>
> The penalty with transferring tax-free (such as by means of a like-kind exchange) is that the investor's carry-forward loss becomes frozen in limbo—maybe never to be seen again. Why?

Example:

Contributing passive property for partnership interest. Donna exchanged a duplex for a limited partnership interest, using a §721 nonrecognition transaction. The suspended losses from the duplex would never be deductible until the limited partnership interest is sold. Two separate activities exist, a rental real estate activity and a limited partnership activity. If Donna had continued to own the duplex and the duplex had future taxable income, the suspended losses would have become deductible prior to the time of disposition. ■

Example:

Exchanging for like passive property. Donna exchanges, via a §1031 tax-free exchange, a duplex for an apartment house. The suspended losses from the duplex are deductible against future taxable income of the apartment house. The same activity exists. ■

Example:

Exchanging for like, but active, property—a terrible penalty! Donna exchanges, via a §1031 tax-free exchange, an apartment house for a hotel. The suspended losses from the apartment house would not be deductible since a "passive" for an "active" activity exchange occurred. *This is a real tax penalty!* Therefore, unless Donna can show that income against which suspended losses are offset is clearly from the passive activity (which she exchanged for a different form of ownership), no such offset is permitted. If Donna cannot clearly prove like-kind activity or passive activity, the suspended losses are not deductible. ■

If a passive activity conducted by a general partnership is contributed to an S corporation, followed by the dissolution of the partnership, subsequent income from the activity may be offset by suspended losses from the activity of a shareholder who was formerly a passive general partner. When the taxpayer disposes of his or her entire interest in the property received in the tax-free exchange, then the remaining suspended losses, if any, are allowed in full.

15

Cancellation of Debt, Bankruptcy, and Repossessions

Cancellation of debt by lenders, investor bankruptcy, and repossession of collateral often cause taxable income to the borrower! How can this be averted? The problems in this chapter will be avoided if the investor pays cash for all investments. Real estate, though, is primarily purchased with a combination of equity financing (money from the investor) and outside financing (money from banks, savings associations, or insurance companies). The higher the ratio of debt is to equity (commonly called *leverage*), the higher the repayment of debt and chance of financial stress.

Leverage may cause both financial and tax problems for the investor when (not if) future problems occur, such as low occupancy, inflation, or changes in the tax rules. The interest and principal reimbursement may eventually be more than the investor can pay back.

When the investor realizes that a problem exists in paying back the debt, this usually causes additional tax problems with the Internal Revenue Service—the focus of this chapter.

Settlement of a mortgage debt at a discount may create cancellation of debt income for the borrower. On the other hand, if the lending institution is not willing to settle the debt voluntarily, foreclosure generally occurs and the borrower has, essentially, a taxable sale. Even a voluntary transfer to avoid foreclosure is considered a taxable sale. When property is financed by the seller, called a *purchase-money mortgage,* special benefits exist. Bankruptcy and insolvency provisions soften the income tax created.

Investor Hint

It is impossible to cover all the tax ramifications of troubled financing in one chapter. On the other hand, it is derelict not to alert the reader to the tax concerns. If any of the following options are contemplated by the investor, the decision should be planned with a competent tax attorney and tax preparer.

Borrowing starts out nontaxable. Often investors borrow a substantial portion of the funds when purchasing real estate. It also is common to refinance real estate to enable the investor to "pull out the equity." These economic benefits received by the investor are not taxable, as there is a future obligation to repay the debt, even when the mortgage is in excess of the basis [*Woodsam v. Comm.,* 198 F2d 357 (2nd Cir. 1952)].

Example:

Cathy bought her home for $80,000 *cash* in 1988. The home is now worth $130,000, and she takes out a refinanced loan of $110,000. Even though she has immediate use of $30,000 more in cash than her original investment, no gain is realized at the time of the loan as she must repay the entire amount in the future. ■

The loan is part of the sales price. If later this debt obligation is partially or totally eliminated (most commonly by a sale), the borrower *then* enjoys an economic benefit related to the earlier receipt of the money. The borrower is not being required to repay all the cash received, which, in theory, increases the taxpayer's net worth. When property is sold, the sales price is the cash, other property received, *and the amount of the unpaid liability,* even if the liability debt is a nonrecourse mortgage involving no personal risk [§1001(b); §1.1001-2(a); *Crane v. Comm.,* 47-1 USTC ¶9217, 331 U.S. 1; *Estate of Franklin v. Comm.,* 544 F2d 1045 (9th Cir. 1976)]. See Chapter 1 for additional discussion.

Example (continued):

If Cathy later sells the property for $130,000 (payable with $20,000 in cash and assumption of the $110,000 mortgage), her sales price includes both the cash and the assumed mortgage. Thus, Cathy's gain is $50,000 ($130,000 sale price less her original $80,000 purchase price), even though she only will receive $20,000 in cash.

A mortgage placed on property after purchase does not increase the owner's basis [*Woodsam v. Comm.*, 198 F2d 357 (2nd Cir. 1952)]. A mortgage is not a taxable event.

Investor Hint

The effect of this rule is that in spite of the earlier financial enrichment, the gain (or loss) is postponed from the time the mortgage is taken out to the time when the property is sold or exchanged.

A settlement of a loan at a discount may create income. This can occur either as a gain at time of sale *or* as cancellation of debt (COD) income [§1001(b); §61(a)(12)].

When is a loan cancellation a sale? When it is in connection with the surrender of the property. When property is deeded to a secured lender in satisfaction of the debt, this is considered, in whole or in part, a taxable sale (as discussed later in this chapter).

Example:

Sale. Cathy buys her home for $80,000 *cash* in 1988. When the home is worth $130,000, she takes out a refinanced loan of $110,000. The property subsequently reduces in value to $85,000 and she talks the lending institution into accepting a "deed-in-lieu-of-foreclosure" (i.e., the bank forgives the $110,000 current mortgage if Cathy voluntarily deeds the property to the bank). In this case, Cathy has a taxable sale that *may* be accompanied by cancellation of debt income, even though she has no assets to pay the taxes associated with this "sale"!

When is a loan cancellation COD income? To many investors' surprise, any reduction in the principal amount of the debt at the time of, or prior to, sale or exchange may result in "cancellation-of-indebtedness income" [§61(a)(12)].

Example:

Prudent financial planning with a nasty tax result. Cancellation-of-debt income is most common when the investor wishes to prepay a mortgage *at a discount* (i.e., for less than the principal balance of the mortgage). Most investors erroneously think this is simply a reduction in the original purchase price. In many cases the investor "realizes" COD income, whether the mortgage is recourse or nonrecourse and whether it is partially or fully prepaid [Rev. Rul. 82-202, 1982-2 CB 35]!

Some COD income dodges tax. Whether this "realized" income converts to "taxable" income depends on a number of factors. Some COD income escapes taxation by exclusions, enumerated next.

CANCELLATION OF DEBT (COD)

General rule: Cancellation of debt (COD) creates income. An investor's gross income, for tax purposes, includes income from discharge of indebtedness, or cancellation of debt (COD), in addition to the more common sources of income, such as salaries and commissions [§61(a)(12)].

Taxable ordinary income. Cancellation of indebtedness income is taxable ordinary income and results when any of the borrower's debt is reduced (by compromise, negotiation, or otherwise) for less than the full amount due. COD income most commonly emanates when restructuring or settling a loan [*U.S. v. Kirby Lumber Co.,* 284 U.S. 1 (1931)].

COD income creates a tax problem for the solvent borrower. As discussed previously, the solvent borrower generally is subject to an immediate tax from the income created by the cancellation of debt. The problem is that this reduction in mortgage debt does not produce the immediate cash flow necessary to pay the tax associated with this "phantom" income.

Example:

Reduction in debt. Instead of transferring the property to the Last Chance Savings & Loan, Cathy talks the lending institution into reducing the $110,000 refinanced debt to the fair market value of $85,000, with the promise that Cathy will restart making her monthly payments. In this scenario, Cathy has received a $25,000 economic benefit and still has possession of the property. Therefore, she has a $25,000 COD income tax problem. ■

Forgiveness of nonrecourse debt also creates COD income—not reduction in purchase price. The lender's reduction of the principal amount of an undersecured nonrecourse loan (i.e., the borrower is not personally liable on the note and the lender looks to the property for security) results in COD income, not a purchase price reduction. The fair market value of the property is irrelevant when determining COD income or purchase price reduction [Rev. Rul. 91-31, IRB 1991-20].

In a 1934 case involving nonrecourse financing, the court decided that subsequent reduction in the debt *would* be a purchase price reduction and therefore not create an immediate income. Presently, the courts and the IRS disagree on this point [*Fulton Gold Corp. v. Comm.,* 31 BTA 519 (1934)].

Example:

In 2003, wealthy Fran purchases an office building from Kukla for $1,000,000, borrowing the entire amount from Pioneer Federal S&L with a nonrecourse note (i.e., Fran has no personal liability with respect to the note) secured by the office building. In 2004, when the property's fair market value is $800,000 and the outstanding principal on the note is still $1,000,000, Pioneer agrees to reduce the note to $800,000. The $200,000 is taxable as COD income to Fran in 2004 (not a reduction in the purchase price) unless she is bankrupt or insolvent. ▉

Exception to the COD income rule—a relief provision. If the cancellation of debt (in whole or in part) occurs (1) in bankruptcy, (2) to an insolvent borrower, or (3) with qualified farm debt, this normally taxable income becomes *not* taxable [§108(a)(1)].

Investor Hint

Many financially troubled transactions combine both sales *and* cancellation of debt. If the cancellation of a loan is part of the sales price and not a stand-alone cancellation of debt, it may *not* be excluded by this relief provision and is therefore taxable! This "short sale" is fully illustrated later in this chapter.

Excluding COD in a bankruptcy case. Income from the discharge of debt incurred by a taxpayer in bankruptcy is excluded from income altogether, provided the bankruptcy case is not dismissed prior to debt discharge. However, to the extent available, a certain amount of a borrower's future tax benefits (called *tax attributes* and discussed later) will be reduced. This exclusion from income is allowed, though, regardless of whether the amount of such income exceeds the borrower's future tax benefits (tax attributes) available for reduction [§108(a)(1)(A); §108(b)].

What is bankruptcy? Bankruptcy is the status of a person on whose behalf a petition has been filed and proceedings are in progress in a federal bankruptcy court.

Tax Tip

Income from debt discharge *before* the filing of a bankruptcy petition does not quali-fy for this exclusion (and may not be entitled to either the insolvency or qualified farm-indebtedness exclusion). Thus, for tax-planning purposes, it is important for a borrower who will be involved in a bankruptcy to have the debt discharged through the bankruptcy court and not by voluntary action of the taxpayer.

Excluding COD when the taxpayer is insolvent. Gross income also does not include COD income when the borrower is insolvent. However, the amount excluded cannot exceed the amount by which the borrower is insolvent. Certain of the borrower's future tax benefits (i.e., tax attributes) must be reduced by the amount of income excluded under this insolvency exception. If the borrower remains insolvent after the discharge, all income from the discharge is permanently excluded, regardless of whether the amount of such income exceeds the amount of future tax benefits (i.e., tax attributes) available for reduction [§108(a)(1)(B); §108(a)(3); §108(b)].

What is insolvency? Being insolvent means the investor's liabilities exceed the fair market value (FMV) of his or her assets determined immediately before the discharge (i.e., FMV assets less liabilities equals a negative number). Nonrecourse debt is included in this calculation only when it is involved in the debt discharge transaction itself, and in such cases only the amount discharged is counted [§108(d)(3); Rev. Rul. 92-53, 1992-27 IRB].

Excluding COD when discharging qualified farm debt.

Cancellation of certain farm debt may also be excluded from COD income even if the farmer remains solvent! Debt is qualified farm debt if the taxpayer is directly operating a farm business and at least 50% of the farmer's gross receipts for the three tax years preceding the year of debt cancellation were from the farming business. Again, the penalty is the reduction of certain future tax benefits, and the exclusion cannot exceed the tax benefits [§108(g)(3); §1017(b)(2)].

Reduction of certain future tax benefits (tax attributes).

The price (or curse) for excluding COD from current gross taxable income under any of the above three exclusions is that the borrower loses certain future tax benefits, such as net operating loss carryover and future depreciation deductions [§108(b)]. However, prior to decreasing these future tax benefits, the borrower *may* elect to reduce the basis of his or her *depreciable* property. This reduction is done at the beginning of the tax year *following* the tax year of the debt discharge.

Election to reduce basis of depreciable property. The borrower may elect (on Form 982, which must be attached to the taxpayer's timely filed income tax return relating to the year of the discharge) to apply any of the COD income *first* to reducing the basis of depreciable property (but not below zero) *before* reducing any other future tax benefits. Depreciable property means any property subject to depreciation, but only if the basis reduction reduces future potential depreciation [§108(b)(5)].

Example:

Why electing to first reduce depreciable basis might be good tax planning. This election allows the borrower to reduce the depreciable basis (for commercial real property, an expense spread over the next 39 years) and preserve a net operating loss (potentially currently deductible). ▨

The exclusion of COD as a result of bankruptcy or insolvency requires a corresponding reduction of future tax benefits [§108(b)].

In the absence of an election to first reduce depreciable basis, future tax benefits (tax attributes) of the borrower shall be reduced to the extent of debt discharge income (or its equivalent) in the following order:

1. *Net operating losses:* Reduce NOL dollar for dollar.
2. *General business credit:* Reduce at a 33.3% rate for each dollar of COD excluded.
3. *Alternative minimum tax credits:* Reduce the minimum tax credits as of the beginning of the tax year *immediately* after the tax year of the discharge.

4. *Capital losses:* Reduce dollar for dollar.

5. *Basis reduction:* Reduce, dollar for dollar, the basis of both depreciable and *nondepreciable* property. But this basis cannot be reduced below total liabilities immediately after the discharge [§108(b)(2)(D)].

6. *Passive activity losses (and credits):* Reduce the passive activity losses and credit carryovers from the tax year of the discharge.

7. *Foreign tax credit carryovers:* Reduce at a 33.3% rate for each dollar of COD excluded.

Tax Tip

If the taxpayer makes the previously mentioned election to first reduce depreciated basis, then basis can be reduced below total liabilities all the way to zero [§108(b)(5)]. See the next example, which shows when an election is not smart.

Tax Tip

The previously-mentioned election to first reduce depreciable basis may cause tax benefits to be pointlessly eliminated when the total liabilities remaining after the COD are high in relationship to the property's basis.

Example:

How electing to first reduce depreciable basis might be bad tax planning. Mary is discharged of $350,000 of debt, which she excludes because she is insolvent even after the COD. Immediately after the cancellation, her debts are $650,000 and the fair market value of her assets is $600,000 with a basis of $400,000 ($300,000 depreciable and $100,000 nondepreciable). Mary's tax benefits are a net operating loss (NOL) of $50,000 and the $400,000 property basis.

If Mary does not reduce her depreciable basis first, she must initially eliminate her NOL. However, her total after-discharge liabilities ($650,000) exceed her total after-discharge basis ($400,000), with the result that none of her basis need be reduced, even though $350,000 of COD is excluded [§1017(b)(2)].

If Mary elected to reduce her depreciable basis first, she would have lost the entire $300,000 adjusted basis of her depreciable basis and would still be required to reduce her $50,000 NOL [§1017(b)(2)]! ■

The price of fun—basis reduction requires recapture (an increased amount of taxable gain) when the property is sold in the future. If the basis of a property is reduced and the property is later sold (or otherwise disposed of) at a gain, the part of the gain created by the COD basis reduction is taxable as ordinary income, not capital gain. This is Congress's way of giving the taxpayer a current benefit at the time of the COD but ensuring recapture of that added benefit when the taxpayer later sells the property (preferably for cash, as this could result in 100% of the sales price being taxable as ordinary income)[§1017(d)].

Other common income exclusions when there is a cancellation of debt. *COD income is excluded if the payment of the liability would be deductible* [§108(e)(2)].

Example:

Cameron incurs $1,000 of deductible interest expense but talks his lender down to $600. Even though there has been a $400 cancellation of debt, Cameron may exclude the COD income because the payment for interest is a deductible expense. In addition, there is no reduction of any future tax benefits or tax attributes.

Other exclusions from COD income include (1) a lender's canceling a loan in exchange for a capital contribution to a corporation and (2) a borrower corporation's transferring stock to a creditor [§108(e)(6); §108(e)(8), (10)]. ▪

A wonderful relief for installment sales—a purchase price adjustment [§108(e)(5)]. If property is sold on the installment plan and the seller subsequently reduces the installment debt amount, the reduction to the buyer of this owner-financed debt (called a *purchase-money mortgage*) is a reduction of the purchase price, not COD income. This exception applies only if the buyer is neither bankrupt nor insolvent [§108(e)(5)(C),(B)].

Example:

Jeanette purchased her home from Shannon for $100,000 with Shannon "carrying the paper" in the amount of $85,000. After two years, the property value slipped to $80,000, with Jeanette still owing $84,000. Shannon reduced the balance due to $80,000. This normally taxable $4,000 cancellation of debt is actually a nontaxable $4,000 reduction of the $100,000 purchase price. ▪

Requirements to use the purchase price reduction. To use this purchase-price-reduction exception, the lender must also be the seller, and the debt reduction must occur between the original buyer and the original seller of the property. It does not apply if (1) the purchase money debt has been transferred by the seller to a third party, (2) the buyer has transferred the property to a third party (but see PLR 9037003 that allowed a reduction of purchase price to a subsequent buyer on the original seller's reduction of debt), or (3) the debt is reduced because of factors not involving direct agreements between the buyer and seller, such as the running of the statute of limitations on the enforcement of the debt.

Example:

Jeanette bought Shannon's home for $100,000, borrowing $85,000 from the Last Chance Savings & Loan. When the home's value dropped to $80,000, Cathy talked the lending institution into reducing the $84,000 remaining debt to the fair market value of $80,000, with the promise that Cathy would continue making her monthly payments. In this scenario, Cathy has received $4,000 of taxable COD income. It is *not* a purchase price reduction, as the money came from a third-party lender, not the original seller! ▪

Miscellaneous tax treatments of solvent borrowers. Some other COD income items that are excluded are described below.

> **Caution**
>
> This relief is *not* available to buyers borrowing money from banks, savings associations, and mortgage companies unless these lending institutions are also the sellers—not a common situation except when you are buying from the Resolution Trust Corporation! Why?

The debt forgiveness is a gift. When the forgiveness or reduction of the loan is really a gift from the lender to the borrower, no COD income exists. But it is not a gift simply because the debt is reduced voluntarily by the lender. It must be coupled with an intent to "donate" with "detached generosity," a requirement almost impossible to meet in the financial community. Normally, the discharge of a mortgage for an amount less than the principal balance due is taxable as income to the borrower because the lender does not act with disinterested generosity but is motivated by sound economic reasons of ridding itself of problem or low-interest mortgages [*William DiLaura,* 53 TCM 1077, TC Memo 1987-291].

The debt is acquired by a related party. Can we get around this rule by having one of our relatives, or one of our corporate or partnership businesses, buy the loan at a discount? No. An outstanding loan acquired from an unrelated lender by a person *related to the borrower* is treated as if the borrower had acquired the debt. If the debt is acquired below face value, COD income exists.

DISCHARGE OF REAL PROPERTY BUSINESS DEBT

As mentioned previously, the discharge of indebtedness generally gives rise to "phantom" income to the third-party debtor-taxpayer who is not bankrupt, solvent, or a farmer. The newest exception to this general rule applies to certain real property business debt. The amount elected to be excluded cannot exceed the aggregate adjusted basis of the taxpayer's depreciable real property immediately before the debt discharge. Any amount excluded is treated as a reduction in the property's basis, which is similar to the §108(e)(5) purchase price adjustment allowed the buyer on owner-financed debt [§108(a)(1)(D); §108(c)].

Investor Hint

Prior to 1987, the Code contained an elective exception for the discharge of qualified business debt [§108(c) was repealed by the Tax Reform Act of 1986]. This same §108(c) relief provision is back, in a more restrictive form, starting in 1993. This is recognition by Congress that the value of real property has declined, often below the underlying debt it secures.

New Exclusion for Debt Discharge Income

Debt relief on real property may not create COD income. Starting in 1993, Congress granted taxpayers, other than C corporations, the option of excluding from income the discharge of qualified real property business indebtedness. The price to pay is that the amount so excluded is treated as a reduction in the basis of that property (therefore, the future depreciation will be lower and the gain on sale will be larger) and the reduction cannot exceed the basis of certain depreciable real property of the taxpayer.

Example:

Robert purchases a $1,000,000 office building financed by a $900,000 nonrecourse loan from the Last Chance S&L and $100,000 of his own cash. Afterward, the value plummets to $700,000 and Robert goes to his friendly loan officer and says "You can have this pig back." The loan officer, as an alternative, offers to reduce his loan from $900,000 to $700,000 if he continues to make the agreed monthly payments. Robert accepts. Under prior law Robert would have had $200,000 of "phantom" taxable income from discharge of debt as he is not bankrupt, insolvent, or a farmer. This new law allows an alternative—Robert simply reduces his depreciable basis by $200,000. ■

Required Qualifications

Qualified real property business indebtedness (QRPBI) is debt that meets the following three requirements:

1. The debt is incurred or assumed in connection with real property used in a trade or business (but qualified farm debt cannot be QRPBI).

Tax Tip

This is more restrictive than in the past; the old rules allowed *all* qualified business debt forgiveness to be excluded, not just real property business debt.

---

2. The debt is secured by that real property.

Tax Tip

This rule can be a real tax "sucker-punch" for the unwary businessperson! Secured debt is defined as a security instrument (such as a mortgage, deed of trust, or land contract), and
  (a) the qualified property is specific security for the payment of the debt;
  (b) in the event of default, the property could be subject to the satisfaction of the debt; and
  (c) it is recorded [§1.163-10T(o)(1)].

Tax Tip

It is very common for business debt (e.g., revolving credit line) to not be recorded, which means the investor's debt does not qualify for this relief provision . . . because of a sneaky technicality! Also, general liens on all business property would not qualify as no specific property is identified.

3. The taxpayer makes a proper election.

The election must be made on Form 982. Regulations provide that Form 982 must be attached to the return as originally filed for the year in which the discharge occurred. However, a taxpayer who can show reasonable cause can file the election with an amended return. The revised form includes a new check box to make the election (box 1d) and a line (line 4) to indicate the amount to be applied against depreciable basis [IRS Ann. 94-11, 1994-3 IRB and Temp. Reg 1.108(c)-1T].

Post-1992 Debt Must Be "Acquisition" Debt

Real property business indebtedness does not include indebtedness incurred or assumed on or after January 1, 1993, unless it qualifies under one of two options.

Tax Tip

This is a grandfather clause that allows the investor to be exempt from the "tracing" rules for debt created prior to 1993.

---

1. Certain refinanced debt. QRPBI includes debt incurred to refinance qualified real property business debt incurred or assumed before that date (but only to the extent the amount of debt does not exceed the amount of debt being refinanced).

Tax Tip

The refinanced debt in excess of the debt just prior to refinancing is not qualified debt unless it is qualified acquisition debt.

Investor Hint

Does this mean that as the debt is paid off, the "qualified" real property debt slowly becomes zero? Future regulations will tell!

---

2. Qualified acquisition indebtedness. QRPBI includes qualified acquisition indebtedness. Qualified acquisition debt is debt incurred to acquire, construct, or substantially improve real property that is secured by such debt, *and* debt resulting from the refinancing of qualified acquisition debt to the extent the amount of such debt does not exceed the amount being refinanced.

> ### Tax Tip
>
> When is an improvement "substantial"? Until future regulations specifically define *substantial* in this context, uncertainty exists. Definition of the word *substantial* as used in other IRC sections ranges from 15% to 35% or more of the fair market value. On a $500,000 property, this would require an improvement to cost $75,000 to $175,000 before the debt would be qualified! Would this mean if the business borrows $50,000 for real property improvements that the business debt would not qualify? It would seem so.

Limitations on Exclusion from Income

Must take into account taxpayers' basis, outstanding debt, and fair market value.

The amount of income excluded because of the discharge of any QRPBI cannot exceed the taxpayer's basis in the property. In addition, it cannot exceed the excess of

1. the outstanding principal amount of such debt (immediately before the discharge) over
2. the fair market value (immediately before the discharge) of the business real property that is security for the debt.

> ### Tax Tip
>
> For this purpose, the fair market value of the property is reduced by the outstanding principal amount of any other QRPBI secured by the property immediately before the discharge.

Example:

Dan owns a building worth $150,000 and used in his business that is subject to a first mortgage securing a $110,000 debt of Dan's and a second mortgage securing a $90,000 debt of Dan's. Dan is neither bankrupt nor insolvent, and neither debt is qualified farm indebtedness. Dan agrees with his second mortgagee to reduce the second mortgage debt to $30,000, resulting in discharge of indebtedness income in the amount of $60,000. Under §108(c), assuming that Dan has sufficient basis in business real property to absorb the reduction, Dan can elect to exclude $50,000 of that discharge from gross income. This is because the principal amount of the discharged debt immediately before the discharge (i.e., $90,000) exceeds the fair market value of the property securing it (i.e., $150,000 of free and clear value less $110,000 of other qualified business real property debt, or $40,000) by $50,000. The remaining $10,000 of discharge is included in gross income. ■

Additional overall limitation. The amount excluded may not exceed the aggregate adjusted bases (determined as of the first day of the next taxable year or, if earlier, the date of disposition) of depreciable real property held by the taxpayer immediately before the discharge, determined after any reduction for insolvent or bankrupt taxpayers or solvent farmers. Depreciable real property acquired in contemplation of the discharge is treated as not held by the taxpayer immediately before the discharge [§108(c)(2)(B)].

Reduction in Basis

The amount of debt discharge excluded is applied (using the rules of §1017) to reduce the basis of business real property held by the taxpayer at the beginning of the taxable year following the taxable year in which the discharge occurs.

Tax Tip

There is no specific requirement that the basis to be reduced must be the property securing the debt.

Calculating Recapture as Ordinary Income

The recapture amount may disappear into the future. On a later sale of the property, the basis of which was reduced by this reduction-in-basis provision, the amount of the basis reduction that is recaptured as ordinary income is reduced over the time the taxpayer continues to hold the property, as the taxpayer forgoes depreciation deductions due to the basis reduction.

The exclusion is not limited to the basis of the particular real property secured by the discharged debt; rather, the aggregate adjusted bases of all depreciable real property (determined as of the first day of the next taxable year or, if earlier, the date of disposition) is available.

Partnerships and Partners

The election to use the exclusion is made at the partner level. However, the determination of whether the debt is qualified real property debt is made at the partnership level [§108(d)(6)].

S Corporations and S Shareholders

All elections are at entity level. In applying this provision to income from the discharge of indebtedness of an S corporation, the election is made by the S corporation, and the exclusion and basis reduction are both made at the S-corporation level. The shareholders' basis in their stock is not adjusted by the amount of debt discharge income that is excluded at the corporate level [§108(d)(7)].

Effective date. The provision is effective with regard to discharges of indebtedness occurring after December 31, 1992, in tax years ending after that date.

> ### Tax Tip
>
> As a result of these rules, if an amount is excluded from the income of an S corporation under this provision, the income flowing through to the shareholders will be reduced (compared to what the shareholders' income would have been without the exclusion). Where the reduced basis in the corporation's depreciable property later results in additional income (or a smaller loss) to the corporation because of reduced depreciation or additional gain (or smaller loss) on disposition of the property, the additional income (or smaller loss) will flow through to the shareholders at that time and will then result in a larger increase (or smaller reduction) in the shareholders' basis than if this provision had not previously applied. Thus, the provision simply defers income to the shareholders.

TAX RESULTS WHEN BORROWER LOSES PROPERTY BY FORECLOSURE, DEED IN LIEU OF FORECLOSURE, OR ABANDONMENT

As mentioned in this chapter's introduction, when an investor surrenders property to a lender in exchange for debt forgiveness, phantom income from the transaction may be created, either as "income from the discharge of debt" or as "income from the sale of property" or a combination of both.

Methods of Surrender of Property by Borrower to Lender

Property commonly is surrendered by a borrower to a lender by the following methods:

1. Foreclosure
2. Deed in lieu of foreclosure
3. Repossession
4. Abandonment

Foreclosure—A Forced Surrender of Property by the Borrower to the Lender

Definition. When a borrower fails to pay a mortgage on time, the lender generally starts legal proceedings to sell the property securing that debt. This involuntary sale normally causes adverse tax ramifications to the borrower.

Debt relief causes transfer of property to be a sale—and sale creates a gain (or loss). A foreclosure, even though the investor has no choice, is a sale for tax purposes (it is not a gift from the borrower back to the lender!) [*G. Hammel v. Helvering,* SCt, (*rev'g* CA-6), 41-1 USTC ¶9169, 311 U.S. 504, 61, S. Ct 368].

Review on calculating gain. As with any sale, the gain or loss is calculated by subtracting the taxpayer's adjusted basis from the "amount realized" (as discussed in Chapter 1).

FIGURE 15.1   **Cancellation of Debt Formula**

$_____
Recourse debt

$\underline{\text{\$ Ordinary income (A)(B)}}$ Step 2
Income from discharge of debt

$_____ (C)
Sales proceeds

$\underline{\text{\$ Capital gain or loss}}$ Step 1
Gain (or loss) from foreclosure

$_____
Adjusted basis

(A) COD income can be offset if bankrupt or insolvent (§108)
(B) Taxable only in the year lender releases liability
(C) Sales price at sheriff's sale or fair market value

Personal liability (recourse debt) versus nonpersonal liability (nonrecourse debt). Strangely, the amount realized, which is usually the debt forgiven in these situations, may be different, depending on whether the taxpayer is personally liable on the mortgage (i.e., a recourse mortgage) or not personally liable on the mortgage (i.e., a nonrecourse mortgage) [*J. G. Abramson,* CA-2, 42-1 USTC ¶9200, 124 F2d 416].

A foreclosure when the borrower is personally liable (a recourse mortgage) requires a two-step calculation. Generally the deemed "sales price" when a recourse mortgage is turned back to the lender is the actual debt relief as a result of the foreclosure. But this sales price cannot include any COD income. Therefore, a foreclosure involving a recourse debt must be bifurcated or divided into two parts: (1) gain (or loss) created by foreclosure and (2) income from the discharge of indebtedness [§1.1001-2(a)(2), and (c) (Example 8); Rev. Rul. 90-16, 1990-1 CB 12; *Bressi v. Comm.,* TC Memo 1991-651, 62 TCM 1668].

The income on the surrender of secured property in exchange for the discharge of recourse debt is calculated as follows:

Step 1. Gain or loss from foreclosure. The sales price (or fair market value when there is no sale) of property surrendered less the property's adjusted basis is the gain or loss from the disposition of property (generally capital gain or loss).

Step 2. COD income. The excess of the amount of the debt discharge over the property's fair market value, if any, is income from the discharge of indebtedness (ordinary income). This is the only amount that may be sheltered by bankruptcy and insolvency relief provisions. Of course, there is no COD income if the borrower remains liable for the deficiency [§1.1001-2(a)(2); Rev. Rul. 90-16, 1990-1 CB 12].

The formula when surrendering secured property in exchange for the discharge of recourse debt is shown in Figure 15.1 above.

Example:

Recourse debt. Sharon purchased property for $85,000 with an $80,000 30-year mortgage (recourse debt). After eight years, she has accumulated depreciation of $35,000 (using a 15-year life), leaving her an adjusted basis of $50,000, but she has paid down the mortgage to only $75,000. Life is tough and Sharon stops making payments. The lending institution forecloses, the property is sold at a sheriff's sale for $60,000, and *the lending institution forgives the remaining amount due* as it determines there "tain't no blood left in that turnip." Even though Sharon is broke, the IRS doesn't care—she has both capital gain and ordinary income.

<u>$75,000</u>
Recourse debt

<u>$15,000 Ordinary income (A)(B)</u>   Step 2
Income from discharge of debt

<u>$60,000</u>   (C)
Sales proceeds

<u>$10,000 Capital gain or loss</u>   Step 1
Gain (or loss) from foreclosure

<u>$50,000</u>
Adjusted basis

(A) COD income can be offset if bankrupt or insolvent (§108)
(B) Taxable only in the year lender releases liability
(C) Sales price at sheriff's sale or fair market value

Tax Tip

Only the COD income can be offset if Sharon is bankrupt or insolvent. She still is taxed on the $10,000 capital gain.

A foreclosure when the borrower is not personally liable (a nonrecourse mortgage) requires only a one-step approach. In a nonrecourse debt, the lending institution looks only to the property for recovery of the mortgage and cannot additionally look to the borrower's other assets. In effect, the investor never owes more than the fair market value of the asset securing the loan! Therefore, the sales price is the entire nonrecourse debt, even if the fair market value is less than the amount of the loan. The result is that there will never be COD income in a nonrecourse debt [§1.1001-2(b); *Comm., v. John F. Tufts,* SCt, 83-1 USTC ¶9328, 461 U.S. 300 (1983)].

The gain on the surrender of secured property in exchange for the discharge of nonrecourse indebtedness is calculated as follows:

Step 1: Gain or loss from foreclosure (the one and only step). Subtract the adjusted basis from the mortgage relief. Foreclosure results in income to the borrower when the mortgage forgiven exceeds the borrower's adjusted basis in the secured property [§1.1001-2(c)(7); §7701(g)].

Example:

Nonrecourse debt. Sharon purchases property for $200,000 with a $200,000, 30-year mortgage (nonrecourse debt). After eight years she has accumulated depreciation of $35,000 (using 15-year life), leaving her an adjusted basis of $165,000, but she has paid down the mortgage to only $190,000. Life is tough and Sharon stops making payments. The lending institution forecloses and the property is sold at a sheriff's sale for $150,000 (which is irrelevant as Sharon is not personally responsible for any deficiency judgment).

The formula when surrendering secured property in exchange for the discharge of nonrecourse debt is as follows:

$N/A Recourse debt		
	$ N/A Income from discharge of debt	Step 2
$190,000 Sales proceeds are nonrecourse debt		
	$10,000 Capital gain or loss Gain (or loss) from foreclosure	Step 1
$165,000 Adjusted basis		

Investor Hint

The calculation is the same even if the property is voluntarily transferred by a deed in lieu of foreclosure, discussed later in this chapter [§1.1001-2(c)(7)].

Character of the gain or loss in a foreclosure. Foreclosure gain or loss is governed by the normal gain or loss rules; that is, a capital asset creates a capital gain or loss, business assets create capital gain and ordinary loss, and dealer realty creates ordinary gain and loss. Tragically, foreclosure on a personal residence may create a taxable gain or a nondeductible loss! The $250,000/$500,000 MFJ exclusion rule is available (see Chapter 3 for the general rules).

Year to report the gain or income. Gain or loss on foreclosure is generally reportable in the year the foreclosure sale and debt discharge takes place unless state law allows the borrower a right-of-redemption period (e.g., one-year right of redemption). Then the gain is reported after the right-of-redemption period lapses [*William A. Belcher, Jr. v. Comm.,* 24 TCM 1; TC Memo 1965-1; *Derby Realty Corp. v. Comm.,* 35 BTA 335 (1937)].

> ### Tax Tip
>
> If the investor needs the loss, or can use the gain in a specific tax year, this loss can be deferred or accelerated by voluntarily quitclaiming his or her right of redemption to the lender [*Atmore Realty Co.,* BTA Memo, Dec. 12,517-A, April 30, 1942].

Deed in Lieu of Foreclosure—A Voluntary Transfer of Property to the Lending Institution

Definition. In a deed in lieu of foreclosure, a borrower voluntarily delivers the property deed to the lender before the lender starts foreclosing on the property (normally to avoid the embarrassment and/or the legal fees involved in a foreclosure).

It is a taxable sale. A voluntary transfer by a deed in lieu of foreclosure is a sale for tax purposes [§1.1001-2(a)(4)(iii); Rev. Rul. 78-164, 1978-1 CB 264; Rev. Rul. 90-16, 1990-1 CB 12].

Recourse debt. Similar to a foreclosure, a deed in lieu of foreclosure involving a recourse debt must also be bifurcated, or divided into two parts: (1) gain (or loss) created by the transfer and (2) income from the discharge of indebtedness [§1.1001-2(a)(2); Rev. Rul. 90-16, 1990-1 CB 12].

The two-step approach formula. The income on the surrender of secured property in exchange for the discharge of recourse indebtedness is the same as is used in a foreclosure (previously discussed).

> ### Tax Tip
>
> When the investor is insolvent (or bankrupt), keep the capital gain on sale (step 1) low and the COD income (step 2) high. COD income may end up being excluded from income. The gain on sale will never enjoy this exclusion.

How? This may be done by obtaining a credible *low* fair market value appraisal of the surrendered property.

Example:

Recourse debt. As in the prior example, Sharon finds herself owing $75,000 on a property worth $60,000 that has an adjusted basis of $50,000. Instead of Sharon's going through foreclosure proceedings, she agrees to voluntarily transfer the property by a deed in lieu of foreclosure.

__$75,000__
Recourse debt

__$15,000 Ordinary income (A)(B)__ Step 2
Income from discharge of debt

__$60,000__ (C)
Fair market value

__$10,000 Capital gain or loss__ Step 1
Gain (or loss) from foreclosure

__$50,000__
Adjusted basis

(A) COD income can be offset if bankrupt or insolvent (§108)

(B) Taxable only in the year lender releases liability

(C) Sales price at sheriff's sale or fair market value

Tax Tip

If the fair market value is low enough, this can create a deductible capital "loss," with the accompanying increase of COD income being completely excluded by the bankrupt or insolvent investor!

Nonrecourse debt. As discussed previously, the rules generally are the same as for foreclosures, that is, the transaction is treated as a sale.

There is no ordinary COD income until the liability is released. What happens if the lending institution exercises its right to recover, via a deficiency judgment, for the unrecovered portion (e.g., Sharon's $15,000 in the previous example)? In this situation the lender does *not* release the owner from liability and decides to collect the deficiency. This results in the borrower's not having COD income unless, and until, the debt is discharged.

Losses are possible. If the adjusted basis of the property exceeds the amount realized at time of transfer, there is a loss [Rev. Rul. 73-36, 1973-1 CB 372; *E. Harris,* 34 TCM 597, TC Memo, 1975-125].

Example:

A loss on foreclosure. Linda purchased property for $135,000 with an $80,000, 30-year mortgage (recourse debt). After eight years she has accumulated depreciation of $35,000 (15-year life), leaving her an adjusted basis of $100,000, but she has paid down the mortgage to only $75,000. Linda stops making payments, the lending institution forecloses, the property is sold at a sheriff's sale for $60,000, and *the lending institution forgives the remaining amount due.*

<u> $75,000 </u>
Recourse debt

                         <u>$15,000 Ordinary income </u>   Step 2
                         Income from discharge of debt

<u> $60,000 </u> (A)
Sales proceeds

                              <u>$40,000 loss </u>   Step 1
                         Gain (or loss) from foreclosure

<u> $100,000 </u>
Adjusted basis

(A) COD income can be offset if bankrupt or insolvent (§108)

Repossession

Repossession is the act of taking back property from a buyer who has failed to make payments when due.

Is it a forced taking? If repossession amounts to an involuntary transfer of the property by the secured creditor, which is most often the case, the tax consequences to the borrower are the same as those outlined in the "foreclosure" section.

Or is it a voluntary transfer? If, on the other hand, repossession amounts to a voluntary surrender of property by a borrower to the secured creditor, the tax consequences parallel those for the deed in lieu of foreclosure.

Abandonment—A Voluntary Surrender of Property by the Borrower

Abandonment occurs when an investor voluntarily surrenders possession of real estate without vesting this interest in any other person. Is an abandonment treated like a sale or exchange? Early case law indicated that certain abandonments were not sales and might result in an ordinary loss [W. *W. Hoffman,* CA-2, 41-1 ¶9280, 117 F2d 987].

An abandonment is treated like a sale. Recent Tax Court cases find that a sale occurs when property is abandoned and that a capital loss, rather than an ordinary loss, results for the borrower [E. *L. Freeland,* 74 TX 970, CCH Dec. 37127; *M. L. Middleton,* 77 TC 310, CCH Dec. 38,124, *aff'd* CA-11, 693 F2d 124, 82-2 USTC ¶9713; *L. J. Arkin,* 76 TC 1048, CCH Dec. 38,017; *J. W. Yarbo,* CA-5, 84-2 USTC ¶9691, *aff'g* 45 TCM 170, CCH Dec. 39513(M), TC Memo 1982-675].

Example:

A taxpayer abandoned a residence when the fair market value of the residence was substantially less than the amount of the first and second mortgages encumbering the house. The IRS states that an abandonment is like a voluntary sale (per §1001). The IRS also suggested (but did not rule) that the §1034 rollover provision may be available [PLR 9120010]. ■

Other courts have ruled that abandonment does not create a taxable loss, as there has been no sale or exchange because the taxpayer has not committed to the foreclosure action.

Short Pay or Short Sales—How Are They Taxed?

One California phenomenon in the residential mortgage market is dubbed a "short pay" or a "short sale." Typically, the lender agrees to the sale of mortgaged property by the debtor for an amount less than the outstanding nonrecourse debt. In addition, the debtor usually is required to pay some cash to the lender.

The problem. If the loan being extinguished is nonrecourse, is the sales price the loan (reduced by the cash the debtor pays to the lender) or is it the amount that the new buyer actually pays for the property?

Investor Hint

It seems the debtor is merely selling the property on the lender's behalf (the lender must agree to the sale) and that the amount realized by the debtor is the amount of the debt pursuant to §1.1001-2(a)(1), as would be the case if the lender took back the property.

Example:

Basis	$130,000
Outstanding loan	105,000
Sales price	85,000

Does the transaction result only in loss on sale as follows?

Basis	$130,000
Debt	– 103,000
Loss on sale	$27,000*

Or, does the transaction unfairly result in cancellation of debt (COD) income and loss on sale as follows?

Basis	$130,000
Sales price	– 85,000
Loss on sale*	$45,000*
Debt	$105,000
Sales price	– 85,000
COD income	$20,000†

* Loss would not be deductible if this were the debtor's personal residence.
† Yet the same taxpayer would have $20,000 of "phantom" income. Under the first scenario, there is no "phantom" income.

Tax Tip
_____

The IRS has unofficially told this author that it will respond to the above scenario soon! Make sure you check with your tax practitioner for current status.

REPOSSESSION OF SELLER-FINANCED PROPERTY

When the seller forecloses on property sold to another on the installment plan, what are the tax results for the seller? Nothing, you say, as the seller is just getting back what he or she originally owned? Wrong!

A gain is recognized when property is reacquired. Even though the foreclosure has the seller (lender) in effect reacquiring property he or she previously owned, the seller now has all the payments previously made by the ex-buyer *and* the entire property back! Therefore, the government has devised a system that basically converts all the previous payments into taxable gain, limited only by the original gain itself. This can be very troublesome, as usually there is no cash to pay this "phantom" gain. As a matter of fact, the repossessor/seller normally has to pay repossession expenses to his or her attorney—and then, in addition, owes taxes to the IRS [§1038].

Requirements of the repossession rules. *Section 1038 is mandatory.* Therefore, if a seller forecloses on an installment contract, the gain must be calculated as described in this section [§1.1038-1(a)(1)].

What is the purpose of the reacquisition? The reason for the reacquisition must be to secure the rights of the seller under the purchase-money mortgage and not simply to reacquire the property for income or appreciation purposes. The note and the mortgage must give the seller the right to take title to, or possession of, the property. The note may be recourse or nonrecourse [§1.1038-1(a)(3); §1.1038-1(a)(2)(ii)].

Default is not necessary—but the reacquisition must be based on a default (or default is imminent) under the original sales contract. In other words, §1038 is not available if the seller simply repurchases the property [§1.1038-1(a)(3)(i)].

The manner of reacquisition is generally immaterial (e.g., voluntary, involuntary, sheriff's sale, strict foreclosure, abanadonment, etc.) [§1.1038-(1)(a)(3)(II)].

The property can be repossessed from anyone. The person from whom the property is repossessed need not be the original purchaser as long as the debt can be traced back to the original sale and is secured by the property, but the repossessor *probably* has to be the original seller [§1.1038-1(a)(4); §1038(a)].

Determining the amount of gain on foreclosure. The gain upon reacquisition of property is equal to the cash and fair market value of other property (other than the purchaser's, i.e., buyer's, obligations) received by the seller (i.e., lender) prior to the acquisition, less the gain previously reported [§1.1038-1(b)(1)(i)].

Limitation on reacquisition gain. The gain reported cannot exceed the total gain less the gain previously reported and any reacquisition costs paid by the seller because of the foreclosure [§1.1038-1(c)(1)]. What does this mean?

Formula for calculating gain on repossession

Gain from foreclosure (before limitation)

1. Cash received prior to reacquisition	$	
2. Less: Gain previously reported	−	(A)
3. Equals: Gain before limitation	=	

(A)	×	÷
Total prior cash received	× Gain	÷ Contract price
		(Gross profit ratio)

Limit on gain from foreclosure

4. Sales price	$	
Less:		
5. Basis at time of sale	+	
6. Gain previously reported (line 2)	+	
7. Reacquisition costs	+	
8. What seller paid to reacquire	+	
9. Subtotal	−	
10. Equals: Limit on gain	=	
11. **Gain resulting from acquisition**		*

*[smaller of (3) or (10)]

What is included in "cash received prior to reacquisition"? The amount of the cash received prior to reacquisition includes all payments and other property transferred by the buyer to the seller *and* all payments made for the seller's benefit (including underlying mortgage payments), unless the debt was placed on the property after the sale [§1.1038-1(b)(2)(i)].

Payments by buyer to seller at reacquisition. "Cash received prior to acquisition" also includes any payments made by the buyer at the time of repossession to settle the contract. Of course, any interest payments received are taxed as interest, not principal payments [§1.1038-1(b)(2)(ii)].

What is "sales price"? Sales price is the gross sales price reduced by the selling commissions, legal fees, and other expenses incident to the sale [§1.1038-1(c)(3)].

What are "reacquisition costs"? These are amounts paid by the seller to reacquire the property, including court costs, attorney fees, auctioneer costs, title costs, advertising, and recording fees [§1.1038-1(c)(4)(i)].

What is included in "what seller paid to reacquire"? The assumption of (or subject to) indebtedness that is not an indebtedness of the buyer to the seller shall be considered an amount paid by the seller in connection with the reacquisition. For example, if the buyer placed another mortgage on the property after purchase, which the seller now is subject to, this new mortgage (be it a first, second, or otherwise) is considered "what seller paid to reacquire" [§1.1038-1(c)(4)(ii)].

Example:

Shirley purchases real property for $20,000 and sells it to Paula for $100,000. Under the contract, Paula pays $10,000 down and gives a $90,000 installment note, with a properly stated interest rate, to be paid at $10,000 a year over the next nine years. Shirley properly reports the gain on the installment method. After making two installment payments, Paula defaults and Shirley accepts a voluntary reconveyance of the property in complete satisfaction of the indebtedness. Shirley pays $5,000 in connection with the reacquisition of the property. The gain Shirley must report on reacquisition is shown below [§1.1038-1(h), (Example 1)].

Gain from foreclosure (before limitation)

1. Cash received prior to reacquisition		$30,000
2. Less: Gain previously reported	−	24,000 (A)
3. Equals: Gain before limitation	=	$ 6,000

(A)	$10,000 + $20,000	×	$80,000	÷	$100,000
	Total prior cash received	×	Gain	÷	Contract price
					(Gross profit ratio)

Limit on gain from foreclosure

4. Sales price				$100,000
Less:				
5. Basis at time of sale	+	$20,000		
6. Gain previously reported (line 2)	+	24,000		
7. Reacquisition costs	+	5,000		
8. What seller paid to reacquire	+			
9. Subtotal			−	49,000
10. Equals: Limit on gain			=	51,000
11. Gain resulting from acquisition				$ 6,000*

*[smaller of (3) or (10)]

Basis of reacquired property. The basis of the reacquired property is the adjusted basis of the seller in all indebtedness of the purchaser on the date of reacquisition, increased by the amount of the reacquisition gain recognized by the seller and by the amount paid by the seller in connection with the reacquisition. A formula makes it easy to compute the basis for the previous example [§1.1038-1(g)(1)].

Basis of reacquired property

12. Remaining debt to be received	+ $70,000	
13. Debt adjustment	−$56,000(B)	
14. Adjusted basis of debt		+ $14,000
15. Plus: Gain on reacquisition (line 11)		+ $6,000
16. Plus: Seller's reacquisition costs (line 7)		+ $5,000
17. Equals: New basis		= $25,000

(A) $\dfrac{\$100,000 - \$30,000 = \$70,000}{\text{Remaining debt to be received}} \times \dfrac{\$80,000}{\text{Gain}} \div \dfrac{\$100,000}{\substack{\text{Contract price} \\ \text{(Gross profit ratio)}}}$

No bad debt deduction. No bad debt deduction is allowed on reacquisition, and if the seller deducted a bad debt deduction in a year prior to the reacquisition, this bad debt deduction must be included in income in the year of reacquisition [§1.1038-1(f)(1); §1.1038-1(f)(2)(i)].

Repossession of personal residence—sell it within one year. If a homeowner is forced to repossess a principal residence that was previously sold on an installment contract and he or she had excluded all or part of the gain because of the $250,000/ $500,000 MFJ exclusion rule, this repossession gain method is not applicable, *provided* that the property is resold within one year from the date of reacquisition. The reacquisition is disregarded and the subsequent resale of the home is treated as a sale occurring on the date of the original sale of the home. If the home is not sold within one year, these repossession rules apply, even to the sale of a personal residence [§1.1038-2(a)(2); §1038(a)].

Character of the gain. If the gain on the original sale was reported on the installment method, the reacquisition gain maintains its character (e.g., if the property was a capital asset, the reacquisition gain would be a capital gain; if the property was a §1231 business asset, the gain would be a §1231 gain) [§1.1038-1(d); §1.453-9(a)].

Holding period of reacquired property. Because the reacquisition of the property acts as a revocation of the original sale of the property, the holding period of the property after its reacquisition includes the period the seller held the property before the original sale. Therefore, the holding period does not include the period between the original sale date and the reacquisition date [§1.1038-1(g)(3)].

CONCLUSION

Settlement of a mortgage debt at a discount may create cancellation of debt, which is ordinary income, for the borrower. On the other hand, foreclosure generally creates a taxable sale. A deed in lieu of foreclosure is also considered a taxable sale. Bankruptcy and insolvency provisions soften the income tax created. When property is financed by the seller, known as a *purchase-money mortgage,* the reduction is simply a reduction of the purchase price and not a taxable event.

Index